D0219429

The English Police

The English Police

Police

A Political and Social History
Second Edition

CLIVE EMSLEY

An imprint of **Pearson Education**

Harlow, England · London · New York · Reading, Massachusetts · San Francisco
Toronto · Don Mills, Ontario · Sydney · Tokyo · Singapore · Hong Kong · Seoul
Taipei · Cape Town · Madrid · Mexico City · Amsterdam · Munich · Paris · Milan

Pearson Education Limited
Edinburgh Gate, Harlow,
Essex CM20 2JE, England

and Associated Companies throughout the world.

Visit us on the World Wide Web at:
www.pearsoned.co.uk

First edition © Clive Emsley 1991
Second edition © Addison Wesley Longman Limited 1996

All rights reserved; no part of the publication may be
reproduced, stored in a retrieval system, or transmitted
in any form or by any means, electronic, mechanical,
photocopying, recording, or otherwise, without either the
prior written permission of the Publishers or a licence
permitting restricted copying issued by the Copyright Licensing Agency Ltd.,
90 Tottenham Court Road, London W1T 4LP

First edition published by Harvester Wheatsheaf, 1991
This edition published 1996

ISBN 0 582 25768 9

British Library Cataloguing-in-Publication Data
A catalogue record for this book is
available from the British Library

Library of Congress Cataloging-in-Publication Data
Emsley, Clive.
The English police : a political and social history / Clive
Emsley. — 2nd ed.
p.   cm.
Includes bibliographical references and index.
ISBN 0–582–25768–9 (pbk.)
1. Police—England—History.   I. Title.
HV8196.A2E47   1996
363.2'0942—dc20   96–21225
                                       CIP

10   9   8   7
06   05   04

Set by 35 in 10/12pt Baskerville
Printed in Malaysia, PP

For Jenny

Contents

List of Tables

Abbreviations Used in the Notes

CJH	*Criminal Justice History*
CUP	Cambridge University Press
EHR	*English Historical Review*
HJ	*Historical Journal*
HO	Home Office (Papers in Public Record Office)
MEPO	Metropolitan Police (Papers in Public Record Office)
OUP	Oxford University Press
PA	Police Archive
PP	*Parliamentary Papers*
RO	Record Office
TRHS	*Transactions of the Royal Historical Society*
UCL	University College London

Preface and Acknowledgements

Today in England the police are permanently under the spotlight. Over the last few years it must have been difficult to get into some police stations thanks to journalists with tape-recorders and television film crews preparing the latest investigation into contemporary policing; and as I write this there are a whole series of official investigations into complaints against different police forces as well as inquiries into the activities of both the highest ranking police woman in the country and an Assistant Commissioner of the Metropolitan Police. Yet our knowledge of police history and how the institution and the job developed, especially in the first half of the twentieth century, remains thin. I hope that this book will go some way towards filling the gaps, or at least pointing to those areas where more research is needed.

There is always a problem with writing about institutions in that the text can finish as a celebration of a steady progress to the present. I trust that this book does not do that; I also hope that it does not appear to set out to do the opposite. That may read as an argument for fence-sitting, or a genuflection towards the demands for 'balance' in discussing controversial subjects. It is not meant to; 'balance' in this context often means that criticism must be muted. Historians should weigh their arguments and analyse their evidence carefully, but decisions have to be made and conclusions drawn, and these may not always be palatable if they run counter to long-cherished beliefs.

In studying police and policing over the last decade or so I have benefited from the advice of, and from discussions with, many friends and colleagues. In particular I would like to thank Bob Storch, Barbara Weinberger, David Englander, René Levy and the members of the seminar on the police at the CSEDIP in Paris. Ian Bridgeman and Mark Clapson helped me enormously in cataloguing police archives, entering personnel files on to a computer database, and sharing their own knowledge of different aspects of policing. Louis Knafla and Richard Bessel kindly read much of the manuscript and commented helpfully. The errors, of course, are mine.

Thanks are also due to the ESRC, which funded my investigation of police archives and the construction of a database of police personnel. The general conclusions drawn from the latter appear in the first part of Chapter Nine; a more detailed and extended analysis will be forthcoming.

No historian can work without the assistance of librarians and archivists. I owe a debt of gratitude to many, and also to the serving police officers in the Police History Society who smoothed my way into seeing several police 'archives' (the term has to be used in a very wide sense) and who are busy encouraging their colleagues that such archives need careful preservation and proper organisation.

Finally, my thanks to my wife for putting up with my disappearances to distant archives, to conferences, or simply into my study when it would be so much more helpful if I did something constructive around the house – hence the dedication.

Preface to the Second Edition

Interest in, and contemporary debates about, the police and their role in society appear as alive now as they were when I embarked on the first version of this book. While some sections of society are extremely critical of an institution which they perceive as oppressive, the notion that the English policeman is somehow 'different', more approachable, less oppressive than many – perhaps most – others remains. As my redrafting drew to a close, accusations of corruption and 'fitting up' by officers at Stoke Newington were brought to a conclusion – though whether or not the conclusion was satisfactory depended on personal perception – and, in the wake of horrendous physical assaults on beat officers, chief constables and the tabloid press called for C.S. gas or Pepper sprays to incapacitate assailants.

I have taken the advantage of this paperback edition to incorporate some of the work published on English policing over the last five years, and also to bring the story into the mid-1990s. The structure and the basic arguments, however, remain unaltered. Once again my thanks are due to all of those who helped me with the first edition, and to those cited in the notes whose work stimulated me then, and since. Once again, and for the same reasons as before, my thanks to my wife – whatever the changes, the dedication remains the same.

Bedford, January 1996

Introduction

The subjects of this book are the police of England and Wales, by which I mean the bureaucratic and hierarchical bodies employed by the state to maintain order and to prevent and detect crime. This may appear a common-sense definition and, partly for this reason, most of those who have written histories of the English and Welsh police have never felt the need for definitions. However, other individuals and organisations are involved with what is broadly understood by 'policing': gamekeepers and security guards are obvious examples; and there can be movement between such private police and what might be termed the state police. Well into the twentieth century, private individuals and organisations were able to pay for additional men in county or borough police forces; the police of the railway companies were incorporated into a national British Transport Police after the Second World War. It has always been possible for individuals to move from private police into the state police; on retirement from the latter some individuals have moved in the opposite direction. My subjects then are the state police of England and Wales; I stress England and Wales since Scotland has a separate and distinct legal system, and while today the Scottish police may look similar to their neighbours and may exchange officers, particularly at a senior level, the origins and development of the police in Scotland merit a separate study.

My use of the term 'state police', even to differentiate from private police, may already have caused some to wince since the English and Welsh police forces like to boast of their separate identities and both they, and many others, insist that even at the close of the twentieth century, while there is a 'police service' there is no 'national police force' in the country, and that the different police forces are answerable not to any politician or political institution, but only to the law. Such arguments are also implicit in the traditional police histories. However, especially since the 1970s such notions have been challenged in political debate as well as by more critical historians and sociologists. Many of the critics have tended

1

to describe the police as an instrument created by and for the capitalist state as a means of imposing and maintaining class hegemony. These issues will recur in what follows; and while no-one can be neutral in such a controversy, my use of the words 'state police' is simply to differentiate the policeman or woman who is paid by central and local government. The word 'state' is used here in a very broad sense to cover both national, county and municipal authority. It was the state in this broad sense that defined the modern bureaucratic policeman and his tasks in laws and by-laws, and it was the state in this sense that acted as his employer.

In the same way that the definition of the police as a body has been unproblematic for many traditional police historians, so too have been the tasks of the police. The police have been portrayed by such historians as the rational solution to obvious problems of rising crime and increasing disorder. The implicit argument is that they were created, and were steadily developed and improved, to protect the law-abiding citizen from the criminal and disorderly element which preys upon society. But this presupposes a consensual society in which the state and the police are identified with the public, and in which the law, from which the police claim their authority, is neutral and unproblematic.[1] A belief in the centrality of class conflict to the economic, political and social development of England since the mid-eighteenth century is not a prerequisite for recognising that there are problems in such assumptions about the tasks of the police. The policing of political demonstrations and of industrial disputes are the most obvious examples of potentially contentious policing tasks; furthermore, here, it can be argued, 'the breadth and vagueness of the law . . . actually encourages the use of police discretion not to enforce the law'.[2] In the past the law has also limited voting rights which are now taken for granted, it has prohibited various forms of leisure activity among the working class, notably street betting, and it has restricted the opening of shops on Sunday which, during the Victorian period, was often the most convenient day for much of the working class to shop. In these instances, and others, it has fallen to the police to enforce the law. They may have done so with reluctance and discretion, but to the policed the action did not appear as the neutral upholding of an impartial law. In essence, in enforcing these laws the police were enforcing a dominant ideology.

1. See, *inter alia*, Cyril D. Robinson, 'Ideology as history: a look at the way some English police historians look at the police', *Police Studies* II (1979), 35–49.
2. Barbara Weinberger, *Keeping the Peace? Policing Strikes in Britain, 1906–1926* (Oxford: Berg, 1991), pp. 1–2.

The legislation regarding Sunday trading and street betting draws attention to the wide variety of tasks undertaken by the police in England and Wales, and how their role has gradually converged with the original meaning of the word 'police'. The Greek *politeia* meant all matters affecting the survival and well-being of the state (*polis*). The word and the idea were developed by the Romans (the Latin *politia* can be translated as the state), largely disappeared with their Empire, but were resurrected in the medieval universities to justify the authority of a prince over his territories. By the early eighteenth century in continental Europe *la police* and *die Politzey* were being used in the sense of the internal administration, welfare, protection, and surveillance of a territory. The word 'police' was not popular in England as it smacked of absolutism, and in particular of Bourbon spies and of the military *maréchaussée* which patrolled the main roads of eighteenth-century France. But the word was increasingly used towards the end of the eighteenth century, and while the principle duty of the new police when they were first established in London in 1829 was declared to be the prevention of crime, as the nineteenth century wore on, English policemen found themselves carrying out a variety of tasks which fitted with the older definitions: they regulated traffic, ensured that pavements were unimpeded, kept a watchful eye for unsafe buildings and burning chimneys, adminstered first aid at accidents and drove ambulances, administered aspects of the Poor Law, looked for missing persons, licensed street sellers and cabs, and supervised the prevention of disease among farm animals. Such tasks rarely figure prominently in police histories or police memoirs, and some of these tasks have subsequently been yielded to specialist agencies; yet the fact remains that since their creation the police have become more and more responsible for the smooth running of a variety of different aspects of society and not simply for the prevention and detection of crime and the maintenance of public order. Defining the state police by their tasks of preventing and detecting crime and maintaining public order therefore conceals at least as much as it explains about police tasks, unless the word 'order' is taken in a very wide sense. Problems such as this have led one student of the police to define them by the tools which they employ to perform their tasks, and thus 'Police are institutions or individuals given the general right to use coercive force by the state within the state's domestic territory'.[3]
The idea of defining the police by their potential for the use of

3. Karl B. Klockars, *The Idea of Police* (Beverley Hills: Sage, 1985), p. 12.

force would have found little sympathy among the traditional historians of the English police. Until the 1970s police history in England was largely informed by a Whig view which saw history in relatively simple terms of progress and presupposed the emergence of a broad consensus in politics and society from the Victorian period. Such history was often written by former civil servants or former policemen: its most lively exponent was Charles Reith, but it is also to be found more subtly in the work of T.A. Critchley, David Ascoli, and even in Sir Leon Radzinowicz's comprehensive *History of English Criminal Law*.[4] They accepted the arguments of the police reformers of the nineteenth century first, that the old parochial system of policing was, at best, inefficient, and second, that England at the close of the eighteenth and beginning of the nineteenth century was faced with a serious increase in crime and disorder. The police, in such an interpretation, were the obvious answer to the problem: they checked crime and disorder and thus played a considerable part in the emergence of England's consensual society. An alternative view, from the opposite end of the political spectrum, has always been available. This also maintains that the police are best understood as the obvious answer to a problem; but rather than an increase in crime and disorder, the advocates of the alternative view identify the problem as being the growth of an industrial society and the need of the ruling class to maintain its position and to discipline the new industrial working class. The appearance of consensus within Victorian society in this interpretation similarly owes much to the new policeman, and to his truncheon. The first academic historian to develop arguments along these lines, in a series of important articles published during the 1970s, was Robert Storch;[5] though it must be emphasised that Storch's arguments were far more subtle than this brief survey will allow, and also far more restrained than many of those who cite, and profess to draw on, his work.

4. Charles Reith, *The Police Idea* (Oxford: OUP, 1938); idem, *British Police and the Democratic Ideal* (Oxford: OUP, 1943); idem, *A Short History of the Police* (Oxford: OUP, 1948); idem, *The Blind Eye of History* (London: Faber, 1952); T.A. Critchley, *A History of Police in England and Wales* revised edn (London: Constable, 1978); David Ascoli, *The Queen's Peace: The Origins and Development of the Metropolitan Police 1829– 1979* (London: Hamish Hamilton, 1979); Sir Leon Radzinowicz, *A History of English Criminal Law* (London: Stevens, 1948–86).

5. Robert D. Storch, ' "The plague of blue locusts": police reform and popular resistance in Northern England 1840–1857', *International Review of Social History* XX (1975), 61–90; idem, 'The policeman as domestic missionary: urban discipline and popular culture in Northern England, 1850–1880', *Journal of Social History* IX (1976), 481–509.

Both the traditional and the revisionist views of police history portray the development of the police in terms of rational solutions to genuine problems.[6] In the traditional view it is great, far-sighted men who recognise the solutions; in the radical alternative the solutions tend to be class needs, and police reformers and politicians act as spokesmen for their class. At times 'great men' were important – certainly Sir Robert Peel's role was crucial in the creation of the Metropolitan Police; class perspectives were also important – men of property in England appear to have developed a new threshold for order maintenance in the late eighteenth and early nineteenth centuries and sought improved policing to achieve this. But politics and history can be extremely messy. As will be argued below, the problems which brought about the creation of the police were not clear-cut; and neither were the solutions. It often seems a popular assumption that ideas go into the legislative process at one end and come out virtually unchanged, except for being converted into laws, at the other. In fact there were considerable changes between the hopes and plans of the reformers and the legislation which eventually emerged establishing the police forces of England and Wales. Such changes reflected new ideas being fed into the legislative process as well as serious criticism which forced the politicians drafting, and then guiding, the bills to trim and compromise. There was also always the problem of finance, with the Treasury acting as a check on over-enthusiastic ministers, and local ratepayers performing the same function in the provinces. Finally, once the first of the new police forces was established, the police themselves became an important and significant influence on their own development; this influence grew as the police surrounded themselves with a professional mystique and began to be accepted as the experts on questions of crime and order.

This book is an attempt to write a history of the police which is critical of the traditional Whig view, but is equally sceptical of the notion that the police can best be understood as an instrument of class power. The police have always enforced a dominant ideology; they have the power of coercion, but they have generally preferred to act by consent. It might be argued that the claims of the police to protect the ordinary, law-abiding citizen whatever his wealth or social status are a form of deception, given that so much property and so much power are in the hands of a few, and that the law is

6. For a valuable, critical introduction to orthodox and revisionist histories of the police, see Robert Reiner, *The Politics of the Police* 2nd edn (Hemel Hempstead: Harvester Wheatsheaf, 1992), ch. 1.

very much concerned with the protection of property and the maintenance of the *status quo*. Alternatively, without accepting the Whig consensual view of English politics and society but recognising where power lay within that society, it seems more realistic to conceive of the law and the police as multi-faceted institutions used by English people of all classes to oppose, to co-operate with, and to gain concessions from, each other.

The book also seeks to put the development of the English police into the broad framework of English history since the late eighteenth century. While overt comparison is largely confined to the concluding chapter, an underlying theme of the book is that the English police developed their particular characteristics primarily because of the cultural and political environment in which they spent their formative years.

The first eight chapters constitute a broad chronological sweep of the history of the police to the present. Two subsequent chapters, drawing on some of the little-used archival sources which remain in the hands of the English police forces, focus on the questions of who the policemen were, what their job entailed, and the kind of trade culture which they evolved. The conclusion explores the question of to what extent the Bobbies of the English constabularies were different from their counterparts elsewhere in the world.

There is a popular old saying about letting facts speak for themselves, but a book which is nothing but facts is a chronicle and a history requires its author to put some interpretation on the facts by constructing a narrative and an argument. Of course historians should attempt to draw conclusions from their evidence rather than deploying their evidence to prove an interpretation previously determined, but they cannot divorce themselves from their personal attitude towards society. What follows then cannot but draw on my own woolly liberalism, a liberalism which lacks the confidence and certainty of the old Whig historians. I began this introduction by referring to the 'state police' of England and Wales, and stressing that 'state' was being taken in a very broad sense. Nevertheless, the underlying argument of this book is that at least since the middle of the nineteenth century there has been a growing centralisation of the police in England. This centralisation has not been the result of any conspiracy or the 'needs' of any particular economic order; rather it has been a process evolving from three different kinds of pressure and incident. First, at times it has seemed natural to governments and their advisors to introduce legislation for rationalising the police in the interests of what has been seen as economy and efficiency; the tendency of this legislation has been to reduce differences between forces, to limit the authority of the police committees of local government, and to bring the police into closer contact with central government. Second, closer contact with central government has also been established in periods of national emergency, such as world war or widespread strike activity; while the emergency measures have been labelled 'temporary', precedents have been set and a complete return to the *status quo ante* has never been fully achieved. Finally, as the police became acknowledged as the professionals in handling crime and public order, so there developed a tendency on the part of ministers and professional civil servants to communicate directly with the experts and to by-pass the amateur local police committees; this has been particularly marked when and where the local police committees, albeit with claims to democratic legitimacy, have been considered politically partial or suspect by those at the centre of power. The growth of professional pride and expertise similarly has led senior police officers to discuss policy with each other, thus pushing their local police committees further to the margins; at the same time many local police committees connived at their own decline by deciding, partly no doubt because of other demands on individuals' time, to leave policing to the experts. All of these developments have been facilitated first, by a general perception of central authority in England – what some would term 'the state' – as essentially benign, and second, by the fact that over the last two centuries, and in contrast to the other major powers in Europe, the constitutional structure in England has been stable, has rarely faced serious internal challenges to its legitimacy, and has never been forced to reconstitute itself as a result of defeat in war.

CHAPTER ONE

Policing Before the Police

Early institutions of law enforcement

Traditional histories of the police in England and Wales have argued along lines similar to the police reformers of the nineteenth century, namely that the system before 1800 had been in steady decline for perhaps as much as half a millenium. T.A. Critchley, one of the more astute of the historians of the English police, for example, begins his account with Saxon tythingmen and the first appearance of the word 'constable' under the Normans, but he then maintains that the emergence of the office of justice of the peace degraded the constable's office to the extent that over a period of 500 years it 'was gradually going downhill'.[1] David Ascoli, the historian of the Metropolitan Police, argues similarly and adds: 'the decline of the constable in Elizabethan times from a man of authority to a figure of fun is perfectly illustrated by Shakespeare'.[2] Indeed, Shakespeare is commonly quoted as revealing the comic and ignorant nature of the law enforcement agents before the new police; I will return to his reliability as an analyst of Elizabethan administration, but first it will help to look, very briefly, at the origins of the agents who have received so much criticism: constables, watchmen and, to a lesser extent, justices of the peace.

'Constable' was a Norman term.[3] By the middle of the thirteenth century the name covered a variety of functionaries of whom the most significant, at least for the future, were the high constables of

---

1. T.A. Critchley, *A History of Police in England and Wales* revised edn (London: Constable, 1978), pp. 15–16.
2. David Ascoli, *The Queen's Peace: The Origins and Development of the Metropolitan Police 1829–1979* (London: Hamish Hamilton, 1979), p. 21.
3. The etymology of the term is discussed in W.L. Melville Lee, *A History of Police in England* (London: Methuen, 1901), p. 55.

the hundreds and the petty constables of the manors, tythings or vills. The petty, later commonly known as the parish, constable had acquired two distinct characteristics. The first of these went back to the Saxon tradition of collective responsibility when families were grouped in tens, or tythings, and made responsible for the good behaviour of each other. The medieval constable, a man appointed from within his community and charged with carrying out the duties of the office for probably no more than one year, increasingly became the executive agent of the manor or parish for which he was appointed and it was his task to make regular reports, or 'presentments', to the local court leet about felons, miscreants and nuisances. But the medieval constable also acquired royal authority and was responsible for maintaining the King's peace in his district. Watchmen were local agents of law enforcement who had long been recruited by, and from among, urban dwellers. A succession of royal writs during the thirteenth century made the appointment of watches obligatory and these were cemented by legislation of 1285: the Statute of Winchester ordered boroughs to provide watches of a dozen men, while the smaller towns had to find between four and six watchmen depending upon their population; a separate act, *Statuta civitatis*, divided the City of London into 24 wards each of which was required to have a watch of six men supervised by an alderman, while a 'marching watch' was to patrol the whole city. Justices of the peace were royal officials from the outset; they originated from the knights commissioned by Richard I in 1195 to keep the peace and received full legislative recognition during the fourteenth century, principally by an Act of 1361 (34 Edw. III cap. 1). The justices were the social superiors of the constables; they were often lords of the manor and therefore they, or their stewards, presided at the courts leet to which the petty constables brought their presentments. The constable thus could appear to be the justice's man; and this is one reason why Critchley sees the constable's authority degraded by that of the justice.

Perhaps the constable's authority was undermined by the emergence of the justice of the peace, but it will not do to quote passages from Shakespeare as illustrations of this. Both Dogberry, the headborough in *Much Ado About Nothing*, and Elbow, the simple constable from *Measure for Measure*, talk in malapropisms, but this is a comic fault allegedly found also in twentieth-century English policemen,[4] and none of the critics of Shakespeare's constables

4. See below, p. 234.

think of condemning twentieth-century policemen as comic and degraded characters for this reason. Literary evidence is something which needs to be handled with infinitely more care than the historians of the police have generally applied in their references to Tudor constables. Furthermore, a brief, broad survey of constables as portrayed by a variety of Elizabethan and Jacobean dramatists has shown that whereas there were other comic characters of the Dogberry variety, there were also some who were not comic and who demonstrated courage and efficiency in organising the hue and cry and in making arrests.[5] Oliver Cromwell, in explaining to a parliamentary committee how he understood his office of Lord Protector, declared:

> so far as I can, I am ready to serve you not as a King, but as a Constable . . . for truly I have, as before God, often thought that I could not tell what my business was, nor what I was in the place I stood in, save comparing myself to a good Constable set to keep the peace of the parish.

As J.A. Sharpe has pointed out, it is unlikely that Cromwell was suggesting himself as either Dogberry or Elbow.[6] Shakespeare's characters are best left for what they are, literary creations, rather than being taken for any serious representation of Tudor constables. However, the Tudor and Stuart constables were not without their contemporary critics. Prominent among the latter was the Kent justice and legal scholar William Lambarde, who complained of their ignorance and lack of diligence and who published a prototype handbook for them, *The Duties of Constables, Borsholders, Tythingmen, and such other low and lay ministers of the peace.* Quarter sessions and assize courts often heard charges against constables for negligence in letting offenders escape or for not using their powers to apprehend vagrants. At the summer assizes for Sussex held in 1613 the Grand Jury lamented: 'Our constables in most parts are honest men but of meane estate, and fewe of them knowe what belongeth to there office.'[7] The courts were also prepared to use their powers to ensure that only fit and proper men were appointed constable. In Kent, in 1598, some two dozen men from the

5. A.M.P., 'The Old-Time Constable as Portrayed by the Dramatists', *Police Journal* II (1929), 656–73.

6. J.A. Sharpe, 'Policing the parish in early modern England', in *Police and Policing*, Past and Present Colloquium, 1983, p. 19. The quote from Cromwell is taken from W.C. Abbott (ed.), *The Writings and Speeches of Oliver Cromwell* 4 vols (Cambridge: Mass., 1937–47), iv, p. 407.

7. J.S. Cockburn (ed.), *Calendar of Assize Records: Sussex Indictments, James I* (London: HMSO, 1975), no. 279.

Hundred of Cranbrook were indicted at the assizes for contempt because they had elected William Sheafe to serve as constable, 'although they knew him to be an infirm man incapable of discharging the office'.[8] The problems highlighted by the courts show that there were corrupt, idle, ignorant and poor constables during the Tudor and Stuart periods, so some of the criticisms are justified. But this is only a part of the picture.[9] The parish constables were chosen in a variety of ways depending on local custom. Most served for one year, but some for two, with the appointments overlapping so as to give some continuity. Constables often had experience in other local government or community roles: they may well have served as overseers of the poor, surveyors of the highways, or church-wardens. They were not poor men but were most commonly drawn from the higher strata of village and small town society. They may well have been illiterate, but this was more the result of the general literacy rate of society than the particular ignorance of the men serving as constables. They may well have been in trouble with the law themselves, but probably as a result of a general affray or the infringement of economic regulations; the application of modern standards of decorum and behaviour is anachronistic in the study of early modern society.

Some constables were less than diligent in the apprehension of offenders; while others, when called upon, went to considerable lengths and arrested both members of their own community as well as outsiders. The constables were local men and they were fully aware that, after their brief term of office, they would have to continue living in the community which they had policed, consequently they might try a variety of expedients to solve a dispute or settle an offence before recourse to the courts. In 1636, for example, John King, an Essex villager, stole eight hens. He was quickly apprehended by Thomas Burrowes, the local constable. King begged not to be prosecuted, stressing that it was his first offence; after a long talk with the victim of the theft, Burrowes resolved to release King as the lesser of two evils.[10] Similarly, constables could be involved in

8. Idem (ed.), *Calendar of Assize Records: Kent Indictments, Elizabeth I* (London: HMSO, 1979), no. 2617.

9. The following is based on Joan Kent, *The English Village Constable 1580–1642: A Social and Administrative Study* (Oxford: Clarendon Press, 1986); and see also Cynthia B. Herrup, *The Common Peace: Participation and the Criminal Law in Seventeenth-Century England* (Cambridge: CUP, 1987), and J.A. Sharpe, *Crime in Seventeenth-Century England: A County Study* (Cambridge: CUP, 1983).

10. Keith Wrightson, 'Two concepts of order: justices, constables and jurymen in seventeenth-century England', in John Brewer and John Styles (eds), *An Ungovernable People: The English and their Law in the Seventeenth and Eighteenth Centuries* (London: Hutchinson, 1980), pp. 31–2.

community action directed at individuals who had offended against locally accepted forms of behaviour; they might be the organisers of a *charivari* against, for example, a couple living together out of wedlock. Such cases highlight the alternative views of order in early modern society. On the one hand there was the view of the community which stressed the avoidance of conflict and conformity with local custom; this was much more flexible than statute law. On the other hand there was the jurist's view of order which sought uniformity based on statute law. This was the view which probably underlay the criticisms of local constables by men like William Lambarde when they demanded greater diligence on the part of the peace officers. Lambarde himself was a Puritan with a high sense of morality and he was inclined to measure a constable's diligence by his number of presentments and prosecutions.

The major socio-economic and political changes of the Tudor and Stuart periods also had an impact on parish constables. It appears that, as greater divisions developed between tenant farmers and landless labourers, many of the former were attracted to the office of constable as a way of controlling and better supervising the latter. This was especially the case where the wealthier farmers and villagers were inspired by Puritan concerns about the control and the reform of the ungodly. At the same time the growth of the central government and its attempts to exert its authority in the provinces generated a growth in county administration and an increase in the administrative and judicial duties of the constable; in addition to maintaining the king's peace the constable was expected to enforce legislation on church attendance, keeping the Sabbath, drunkenness, swearing, and vagrancy, as well as on taxation and military recruitment. Given the increasing burdens it is no small wonder that some men may have become reluctant to serve, especially when, in the aftermath of the Glorious Revolution of 1688, central government largely withdrew from the supervision of local government. In 1714 Daniel Defoe could describe the office of constable as one of 'insupportable hardship; it takes up so much of a man's time that his own affairs are frequently totally neglected, too often to his ruin'.[11] It may be that the office of constable went into gradual decline from the late seventeenth century: the question awaits an historian. However, work on law enforcement in the metropolis in particular has suggested that matters were improving

11. Quoted in S. and B. Webb, *English Local Government: The Parish and the County* (London: Longmans Green, 1906), p. 62.

substantially towards the end of the eighteenth century. By 1800, constables of the metropolitan parishes may often have been substitutes, but they were more numerous, better supervised, better informed, and increasingly used to making criminal charges and acting as prosecutors.[12]

In his guide for the early Stuart justice of the peace Michael Dalton urged his readers to ensure that night watches were kept in the towns from sunset to sunrise. The watchmen were authorised to arrest 'persons suspect . . . night-walkers, be they strangers, or others that bee of evill fame and behaviour'. Constables were to make presentments to the justices about any laxity on the part of the watch.[13] Like the constables, the pre-police watchmen have been derided by historians. Those historians fond of citing Shakespeare conveniently ignore the fact that it is Dogberry and Verges's comic watchmen who arrest Don John's evil henchmen, and that Friar Lawrence warns Romeo:

> Either be gone before the watch be set,
> Or by the break of day disguis'd from hence.

By the early seventeenth century, in London at least, the householder's obligation to serve watch and ward had largely been replaced by the payment of an assessment which enabled the hiring of substitutes. Yet in times of emergency it appears that principals did turn out and act with courage and some effectiveness.[14]

The suppression of serious rioting created major problems for the local authorities of Tudor and Stuart England; watchmen, constables, and men sworn in as special constables for the emergency might cope, but, often of necessity, magistrates also relied on 'good words' to pacify crowds. If 'good words' and the local forces of order failed, then the magistrate could call on military support. The Trained Bands were county militias run by the local gentry; they were scarcely trained and sometimes unreliable, but little else existed in the Elizabethan and early Stuart periods. During the Interregnum, for the first time, there were well-disciplined, professionally led soldiers who could be, and were, called upon to suppress

12. J.M. Beattie, *Crime and the Courts in England 1660–1800* (Oxford: OUP, 1986), p. 71; Elaine A. Reynolds, 'The night watch and police reform in metropolitan London, 1720–1830', Ph.D., Cornell University, 1991, pp. 261–70.

13. Michael Dalton, *The Countrey Justice, Containing the Practices of the Justices of the Peace out of their Sessions* (London, 1619), pp. 127, 266.

14. K.J. Lindley, 'Riot prevention and control in early Stuart London', *TRHS* 5th series XXXIII (1983), 109–26, at p. 119; Max Beloff, *Public Order and Popular Disturbances 1660–1714* (Oxford: OUP, 1938), pp. 131–2.

rioting. The use of troops in this way was disliked and resented; it became linked in the popular recollection with Cromwell's short-lived experiment to keep order and to get local government working efficiently by deploying major-generals as administrators across the country. The memory of the 'tyranny' of the major-generals ensured that the idea of a standing army remained unpopular in late Stuart and Hanoverian England. Nevertheless, with the Restoration came the beginnings of a small regular army which could be, and regularly was, made available to magistrates during riots, or when riots threatened. Policing duties appear to have been unpopular with the soldiers, both officers and men; and the use of troops in policing actions continued to be a vexed constitutional issue.[15]

In general the justices of the peace have received a much more favourable press than the parish constables and watchmen. The justices were appointed by the Crown from among the gentry of a county. It was patronage or personal wealth and influence which generally ensured that a man's name was put before the Lord Chancellor for insertion in the commission of the peace for a particular county. If the man then wished to act as a justice he was required to swear an oath before the clerk of the peace and pay the appropriate fee. While the office of justice had been created, initially, as an experiment in the maintenance of order, by the late sixteenth century the justices of the peace had become central, not only to the maintenance of law and order, but also for the entire system of local government in the county. The county courts of quarter sessions, presided over by the bench of magistrates, heard cases of felony and misdemeanour; they also discussed the upkeep of roads and county buildings, appointed local officials and decided upon county rates. Petty sessions developed as an institution in many counties during the seventeenth century with justices acting in pairs to carry out an increasing variety of judicial and administrative tasks. As with the constables it is clear that some justices upheld a community view of order, while others, like Lambarde,

15. For the unreliability of provincial Trained Bands see Buchanan Sharp, *In Contempt of All Authority: Rural Artisans and Riot in the West of England 1580–1660* (Berkeley and Los Angeles: University of California Press, 1980), pp. 118–23; but see also Lindley, 'Riot prevention', 122–4. For the use of Cromwell's troops against rioters see J.S. Morrill and J.D. Walter, 'Order and disorder in the English revolution', in A.J. Fletcher and John Stevenson (eds), *Order and Disorder in Early Modern England* (Cambridge: CUP, 1985), pp. 146–7. For the major-generals see Ivan Roots, 'Swordsmen and decimators – Cromwell's major-generals', in R.H. Parry (ed.), *The English Civil War and after, 1642–1658* (London: Macmillan, 1970). For the use of the army as police during the eighteenth century see Tony Hayter, *The Army and the Crowd in Mid-Georgian England* (London: Macmillan, 1978).

took the stricter, jurist's, line. The justice's workload largely depended upon his personal inclination; he was not required to attend quarter sessions or to act in petty sessions, and Lambarde himself, for all his exhortations to others, did not act frequently in his judicial capacity.[16] For every dedicated justice committed to working for his community and the Crown and prepared also to act as a detective when confronted with a serious crime,[17] there were probably several more who were lax and doubtless some who were inept – but, at the risk of labouring a point, it is not common for Shakespeare's Shallow and Silence to be described as typical of the Tudor and Stuart justice.

Georgian anxieties

There were growing concerns in eighteenth-century England over crime and disorder. For the traditional police historians these growing concerns reflected a growing reality. Melville Lee believed that 'there is no exaggeration in saying that, at the dawn of the nineteenth century, England was passing through an epoch of criminality darker than at any other in her annals'. Reith wrote of 'the golden age of gangsterdom in England' and the 'increasing menace of disorder'. For Ascoli, Georgian London was 'a more dissolute [and] disorderly place' than at any other time in its history, with crime its 'principal industry'.[18] But it is extremely difficult to measure any increase in the levels of crime and disorder even in a society which keeps statistics, and eighteenth-century England kept none. There is some agreement among the historians of crime in eighteenth-century England, based on the study of indictments and other court records, that larceny probably was increasing; the statistics which the government began to collect from 1805 also show an increase

16. Louis A. Knafla, ' "Sins of all sorts swarmeth": criminal litigation in an English county in the early seventeenth century', in E.W. Ives and A. Manchester (eds), *Law, Litigants and the Legal Profession* (London: Royal Historical Society, 1983), pp. 50–76, at pp. 50–1.

17. For an example of a sixteenth-century justice acting as a detective see William B. Robison, 'Murder at Crowhurst: a case study in early Tudor law enforcement', *CJH* 9 (1988), 31–62; for an eighteenth-century example see John Styles, 'An eighteenth-century magistrate as detective: Samuel Lister of Little Horton', *Bradford Antiquary* 47 (1982), 98–117.

18. Melville Lee, *A History of Police*, p. 203; Charles Reith, *The Police Idea* (Oxford: OUP, 1938), p. v; idem, *British Police and the Democratic Ideal* (Oxford: OUP, 1943), p. 3; Ascoli, *The Queen's Peace*, p. 27.

continuing until the middle of the nineteenth century.[19] There were riots throughout the Georgian period, particularly when bad harvests meant high prices and bread shortages, and in wartime when military recruiters came looking for men. The Gordon Riots of 1780 when, for several days, London seemed at the mercy of a mob, were the most frightening and the most serious of the eighteenth-century disorders and they burned themselves into the recollections of Englishmen until well into the nineteenth century. The fears thus generated were aggravated by the lurid tales reported in the English press of the crowd violence during the French Revolution. These tales coincided both with the growth of an indigenous popular radical movement, which gloried in its affinity with French Jacobins and *sans-culottes*, and with internal unrest brought about by serious food shortages and the demands and disruptions of a war qualitatively and quantitatively greater than its predecessors. The appearance of popular radicalism and the popular disorder in turn coincided with, and fostered, a growing intolerance of plebeian crowd action and turbulence. In the early 1790s Pitt's government urged local magistrates to act against English Jacobins and began building small cavalry barracks in turbulent industrial districts and on the fringe of London. During the food riots at the turn of the century the government criticised local magistrates who showed any sympathy for the crowds' notions of a 'moral economy'. At the same time there were increasing demands for curbs on boisterous and brutal plebeian sports and pastimes.[20] It seems that, from about the middle of the eighteenth century, what had been accepted, more or less, as social phenomena – a degree of social disorder and a degree of crime – began increasingly to be perceived as a serious threat to the social order and a growing problem which required a solution. More and more, crime and disorder were regarded as things which should not exist in civilised society as it was beginning to be conceived by the articulate, and by the country's rulers. Whether or not the incidence of crime and disorder was actually increasing is of far less importance than the

19. Clive Emsley, *Crime and Society in England 1750–1900* 2nd edn (London: Longman, 1996), ch. 2, has a general survey of the current debate on eighteenth- and nineteenth-century crime statistics.

20. See, *inter alia*, Clive Emsley, 'The military and popular disorder in England, 1790–1801', *Journal of the Society for Army Historical Research* LXI (1983); idem, 'Repression, "terror" and the rule of law in England during the French Revolution', *EHR* C (1985); E.P. Thompson, 'The moral economy of the English crowd in the eighteenth century', *Past and Present* 50 (1971); R.W. Malcolmson, *Popular Recreations in English Society 1700–1850* (Cambridge: CUP, 1973).

contemporary belief that it was increasing, and the growing demands that a new threshold of order and decorum be established. The main focus of concern over increasing crime and disorder was London. Eighteenth-century London was an enormous and expanding city. At its heart was the square mile of the City of London proper, a booming centre of finance and commerce presided over by a Lord Mayor and Corporation proud and jealous of their privileges and independence. The population of the square mile itself declined during the century as more and more space was taken over by business property. But from the City, and from the adjacent City of Westminster, the population spilled over into the counties of Middlesex, Surrey and, to a lesser extent, Kent. In 1700 the metropolis as a whole had some 670,000 inhabitants; the numbers increased very gradually to the middle of the century, and then soared so that by 1800 about one million people lived in London, more than one Englishman in ten. The burgeoning sprawl of London was viewed with a mixture of fascination and horror. The city was unquestionably prosperous and its ever-increasing physical size and population were seen as much demonstrations of this prosperity as was its growth as a financial and commercial centre. But the size, the squalor, and the maze of streets, courts and alleyways, also alarmed many contemporaries when they contemplated questions of crime and disorder. In 1751 Henry Fielding, the novelist and principal magistrate in Bow Street, wrote:

> Whoever indeed considers the Cities of *London* and *Westminster*, with the late vast Addition of their Suburbs; the great Irregularity of their Buildings, the immense Number of Lanes, Alleys, Courts and Bye-places; must think, that, had they been intended for the very Purposes of Concealment, they could scarce have been better contrived. Upon such a View, the whole appears a vast Wood or Forest, in which a Thief may harbour with as great Security, as wild Beasts do in the Desarts of *Africa* or *Arabia*. For by *wandering* from one Part to another, and often shifting his quarters, he may almost avoid the Possibility of being discovered.[21]

Some 30 years later William Blizzard recalled his service with the Honorable Artillery Company in suppressing the Gordon Riots; he and his comrades penetrated the lodging-house districts of Chick Lane, Field Lane, and Black-boy Alley: 'The buildings in these parts constitute a sort of distinct town, or district, calculated for the

21. Henry Fielding, *An Enquiry into the Causes of the Late Increase of Robbers* 2nd edn (London, 1757), p. 116.

reception of the darkest and most dangerous enemies to society.'[22] In the following decade the stipendiary magistrate Patrick Colquhoun estimated that there were about 115,000 people living in London wholly or partly on the proceeds of criminal activity: 'London is not only the grand magazine of the British Empire, but also the general receptacle for the idle and depraved of almost every Country, and certainly from every quarter of the dominions of the Crown.'[23]

The problems of administering justice and of pursuing offenders in the burgeoning metropolis led to the appearance of two kinds of individual much criticised by contemporaries and subsequent historians – the trading justice and the thief-taker. Any county magistrate who acted in one of the urban parishes during the late seventeenth or eighteenth centuries soon found that, if he took his judicial tasks seriously, he was having to spend more and more time on them; at the same time he was having to deal with more and more cases of a serious nature. In consequence, the gentleman justice in these districts began to give way to the trading justice, a man who, probably because he lacked sufficient estate, opted to profit from the fees paid for performing judicial tasks. Again there is a literary example which can be wheeled out to demonstrate the corruption of these justices – Justice Thrasher from Henry Fielding's *Amelia*. Other individuals, encouraged by the system of statutory rewards offered for bringing certain kinds of offender to justice, took advantage of the reluctance of the part-time parish constable to spend much time away from his trade in the pursuit of offenders, and established themselves as professional thief-takers. The most notorious of the thief-takers was Jonathan Wild who, while successfully recovering the property of many victims of theft, also became a major receiver and controller of criminal gangs, occasionally offering up a sacrifice to the gallows. Wild himself was executed in 1725, and while no subsequent thief-taker achieved a similar notoriety, the scandals continued, most notably with the exposure of Stephen McDaniel in 1754.[24]

However, while there were corrupt trading justices and corrupt and dangerous thief-takers, it was out of this system that one of the most significant developments in the policing of eighteenth-

22. William Blizzard, *Desultory Reflections on Police* (London, 1785), p. 30.

23. Patrick Colquhoun, *A Treatise on the Police of the Metropolis* 3rd edn (London, 1796), pp. vii–xi.

24. For Wild see Gerald Howson, *Thief-Taker General: The Rise and Fall of Jonathan Wild* (London: Hutchinson, 1970).

century London emerged. From the late 1730s, under an ambitious trading justice, Sir Thomas De Veil, the Bow Street magistrates' office became a centre for the administration of justice in Westminster. In 1749, some three years after De Veil's death, Henry Fielding moved into the office as principal justice for the city. Henry Fielding and, following his death, his half-brother Sir John, dispensed justice daily from the office. They both took fees, but their fees were low, and they also received government pensions for their judicial duties. To assist in the detection and apprehension of offenders they employed a group of professional thief-takers, the Bow Street Runners. The conclusion that not all trading justices and thief-takers were corrupt, and that the Fieldings and the Runners were not as dependable, honest and far-sighted as commonly portrayed in police histories, might smack of fence-sitting, but is probably closest to the eighteenth-century reality. Trading justices were providing a service which people wanted and some were dedicated and worked hard. The Bow Street thief-takers were an improvement on many of their contemporaries and a degree of professionalism did develop among them; yet Henry Fielding did not move against the notorious McDaniel when given the opportunity, and his Runners were never entirely above suspicion.[25]

Concern about crime and disorder prompted improvements in the different watches deployed in the metropolis. Beginning in 1705 a series of acts were passed on behalf of the City of London enabling reorganisation and improvements in the City Watch, though parsimony on the part of ratepayers appears to have kept the force below its official strength. During the 1770s Thomas Gates, the City Marshal, appears to have organised his men effectively against some criminal gangs, and in the following decade a small, regular patrol was organised for the City's streets. This patrol was given a uniform in 1791 and gradually increased in numbers: in 1824 it consisted of 24 men divided equally into day and night patrols.[26] Similar developments were to be found outside the City walls. In 1735 two Westminster parishes, St James, Piccadilly and St George, Hanover Square, combined to obtain an Act of Parliament

25. For a balanced assessment of the trading justices in Kentish London and the thief-takers see, respectively, Norma Landau, *The Justices of the Peace 1679–1760* (Berkeley and Los Angeles: University of California Press, 1984), ch. 6, and Ruth Paley, 'Thief-takers in London in the age of the McDaniel gang, c. 1745–1754', in Douglas Hay and Francis Snyder (eds), *Policing and Prosecution in Britain 1750–1850* (Oxford: Clarendon Press, 1989).

26. Donald Rumbelow, *I Spy Blue: The Police and Crime in the City of London from Elizabeth I to Victoria* (London: Macmillan, 1971), chs 4 and 5.

to improve their night watches. The new legislation authorised a local rate by which householders could pay for regular watchmen. In the next year five more Westminster parishes followed suit, and in the following half-century 35 parishes and liberties obtained similar acts generally establishing an improved system for most of London. First and foremost, this legislation appears to have been driven by the anxiety that property crime was rising.[27] For similar reasons, from Bow Street the Fieldings experimented with patrols for the main roads; and by the 1790s an armed patrol of about 70 men, based at Bow Street, was watching the main roads into the centre of London from evening until midnight. By 1828 this patrol had been developed in several directions and consisted of a Horse Patrol (54 men and 6 officers), a Dismounted Patrol (89 men and 12 officers), the Night Foot Patrol (82 men and 18 officers), and the Day Foot Patrol (24 men and 3 officers).[28] All of these men continued to profit from what might be termed an entrepreneurial system of policing: they could still claim statutory rewards for bringing certain offenders to justice. In the autumn of 1816 there was a scandal reminiscent of the McDaniel affair when six policemen, including a well-respected member of the Bow Street Foot Patrol and a member of the City Patrol, were prosecuted for involvement in crimes so as to claim rewards.[29] The entrepreneurial system was criticised at the time and by subsequent historians as offering opportunities and temptation to police officers; yet examples from the history of the new police, as will be shown below, should warn against any assumption that the disbanding of the entrepreneurial police ended opportunities for profiting from conspiracy, perjury and subornation.

Following the Gordon Riots a few individuals suggested that some kind of co-ordinated police system was needed for London. Yet it appears to have been fears about rising crime which, five years later, in 1785, prompted the government of the Younger Pitt to propose the establishment of a centrally controlled police for the entire metropolis. The London and Westminster Police Bill was designed to establish nine police divisions in London: each division

27. Reynolds, 'The night watch', ch. 2, pp. 17–18, for the distribution of night watch acts and a map showing the area covered by them.
28. David Philips, ' "A new engine of power and authority": the institutionalization of law-enforcement in England 1780–1830', in V.A.C. Gatrell, Bruce Lenman and Geoffrey Parker (eds), *Crime and the Law: The Social History of Crime in Western Europe since 1500* (London: Europa, 1980), p. 181.
29. Sir Leon Radzinowicz, *A History of English Criminal Law* 5 vols (London: Stevens, 1948–86), ii, pp. 333–7, 343–5.

was to have a force of mounted and foot constables; divisional chief constables were to be responsible to a head constable who, in turn, was to be answerable to three commissioners appointed by the government. The Bill was poorly presented and abysmally managed in Parliament. It provoked ferocious hostility from the City of London which was not prepared to see its independence taken away by the proposal; it awoke the anxieties of those who continued to equate the idea of police with things French, and therefore inimical to English liberty. The bill was withdrawn, though a revised version was prepared and passed for the policing of Dublin.[30] Seven years later, and just as the concern over the spread of French revolutionary principles was beginning to take hold, Pitt's government introduced a more limited measure for London with the Middlesex Justices' Bill. This was a proposal to create seven 'police offices' akin to that in Bow Street, each to be staffed by three stipendiary magistrates and six constables. The City of London was excluded from the new justices' jurisdictions and the main criticism of the bill as it went through Parliament was that it created more patronage for the king's ministers. On the third reading it was also suggested that the new authority which the bill gave to constables and watchmen over 'ill-disposed and suspected Persons, and reputed Thieves' constituted a threat to English liberty, but this was insufficient to stop the bill's passage.[31] In 1798, on the inspiration of one of the new stipendiary magistrates, Patrick Colquhoun, a private police force was set up by a group of West India merchants to protect their goods from theft while on ships in the Thames and on the wharfs and docks; in 1800 the organisation was taken over by the government and became the Thames River Police. As in the other police offices there were three salaried magistrates to supervise the new office at Wapping, but the staff of constables was much larger: by 1827 there were seven land constables and 64 river constables. When it was considered necessary both these men, and the various other constables and patrols established in the metropolis, could be summoned to assist with crowd control.[32]

Developments in the last decade of the eighteenth and first quarter of the nineteenth centuries took place against a background of increasing debate about the state of the police in the metropolis, with the word 'police' increasingly being used to describe the system

30. Ibid., pp. 165–8; Stanley H. Palmer, *Police and Protest in England and Ireland 1780–1850* (Cambridge: CUP, 1988), pp. 89–92.
31. *Parliamentary History* XXIX, 1033–6, 1182, 1466–76.
32. Palmer, *Police and Protest*, pp. 144–5.

for maintaining public order, for preventing theft, and for detecting and apprehending offenders. Colquhoun's *A Treatise on the Police of the Metropolis*, first published in 1796, was a key contribution to this debate: the *Monthly Review* considered that the public were 'VERY MUCH indebted' to Colquhoun for the book, though Colquhoun's role as an architect of the new police, like that of the Fieldings, has probably been greatly overstressed in the traditional histories.[33] Indicative of the growing concern and debate was the fact that four parliamentary select committees were appointed to investigate 'the police of the metropolis' between 1812 and 1828. The first of these followed the brutal mass killings of two families in east London in December 1811, an incident which sent nervous ripples through the whole country. But the concerns continued to be tempered by the fear of what a professional police system looked like: the French Revolution had swept away the old *lieutenant général de police* in Paris, but Napoleon had replaced him with what appeared to be the more sinister police of Joseph Fouché. While Parliament appointed its select committee on the heels of the Ratcliffe Highway murders, the Earl of Dudley could write:

> ... these things make people cry out against the laxity of our police. The fact, however, I am inclined to suspect is that it is next to impossible to prevent outrages of this sort from happening in those parts of the town that are inhabited exclusively by the lowest and most profligate wretches in the nation, except by entrusting the magistrates [stipendiary] with powers vastly too extensive to be prudently vested in such hands. They have an admirable police at Paris, but they pay for it dear enough. I had rather half a dozen people's throats should be cut in Ratcliffe Highway every three or four years than be subject to domiciliary visits, spies, and all the rest of Fouché's contrivances.[34]

The report of the select committee of 1812 resulted in the Nightly Watch Regulation Bill which proposed minimum standards for the parish watches of metropolitan Middlesex. The selection and appointment of the watchmen was to remain in parochial hands, but the stipendiary magistrates were to have overall supervision, including the power of dismissal. The strong opposition of the parishes, concerned at losing control of their watchmen, led to the bill being

---

33. *Monthly Review* 20 (1796), 408–15; there was a second review in ibid., 32 (1800), 349. For a reappraisal of the role of Colquhoun and Fielding see Ruth Paley, '"An imperfect, inadequate and wretched system"? Policing London before Peel', *CJH* X (1989), 95–130, at 96–8.

34. Quoted in Philips, '"A new engine"', p. 174.

dropped; but it is worth emphasising here that the succession of private acts which had begun in Westminster in 1735 had not been left untouched. Throughout the eighteenth and early nineteenth centuries many parishes had revised their parliamentary acts and rethought their regulations, imposing strict requirements on those wishing to be considered as recruits, establishing inspectors and supervisors, and rotating beats to prevent corruption.[35]

The parliamentary select committee which Peel appointed to investigate the policing of the metropolis when he became Home Secretary in 1822 concluded that a large, centralised police force would be inconsistent with the traditions of English liberty. Six years later, after a succession of legal reforms, Peel convinced the Commons that, because the statistics of crime were continuing to rise, there should be a new select committee. This committee gave Peel the recommendation that he had sought and enabled him to introduce the legislation for the creation of the Metropolitan Police. Consummate politician that he was, Peel skilfully guided the bill through Parliament, and he cautiously avoided any confrontation with the City of London by excluding the square mile from the jurisdiction of his new force. In September 1829 the first constables of the Metropolitan Police began patrolling their beats.

35. Paley, ' "An imperfect, inadequate and wretched system" ', 112–13; Reynolds, 'The night watch', passim.

CHAPTER TWO

The Coming of the Police

The Metropolitan Police of London

The traditional historians of the police have tended to see a logical progression from the Fieldings and the developments in Bow Street, through the Middlesex Justices' Act and the work of Colquhoun, to the appearance of the Metropolitan Police in 1829. Yet the force which was created in 1829 bore little resemblance to what had gone before in London, and little resemblance to the proposals made by Sir John Fielding in his General Preventative Plan of 1772 or by Colquhoun in his *Treatise*. Essentially, the Fieldings and Colquhoun envisaged police reforms centred on the emerging stipendiary magistrate system; the new police were actually established in parallel to this system and, contrary to the received opinion of the traditional histories, they were, initially at least, probably less efficient than several of the old night watches.[1]

When Peel became Home Secretary in Lord Liverpool's government in 1822 there were already Tories contemplating the need for some kind of police reform. In the early summer of 1820, for example, the Duke of Wellington, concerned about radical demonstrations, had urged that the government 'ought, without the loss of a moment's time, to adopt measures to form either a police in London or military corps, which should be of a different description

---

1. Ruth Paley, ' "An imperfect, inadequate and wretched system"? Policing London before Peel', *CJH* X (1989), 95–130, at pp. 115–16, makes the point that Metropolitan Police beats were measured in miles, while those of the old watches were rarely longer than 500 or 600 yards, and that there were, perhaps, only half as many police constables on the ground as watchmen. For Fielding's General Preventative Plan see John Styles, 'Sir John Fielding and the problem of criminal investigation in eighteenth-century England', *TRHS* 5th series, 33 (1983), 127–49.

from the regular military force, or both'.[2] Peel himself told Parliament in June 1822 that the country needed 'a vigorous system of police', but of course, not one based on the French model: 'God forbid that he should mean to countenance a system of espionage.'[3] Though his initial attempt at getting a select committee to recommend the creation of a police force failed, throughout the middle years of the 1820s, as he pushed through his legislation for rationalising the criminal law, Peel never failed to urge the Commons that an effective, preventive police was important to underpin these reforms. It is possible that some of Peel's legal reforms themselves increased the crime statistics in London, notably the greater liberality in the payment of expenses to both prosecutors and witnesses, and the better regulation of the Old Bailey courts which meant that people did not have to lose time and money away from their trade while waiting for a case to come up.[4] Yet this did not prevent Peel from making much of the apparent increase in crime in the metropolis when, in April 1829, he introduced his Metropolis Police Improvement Bill; taking the seven-year periods 1811–18 and 1821–8, he had figures to show a population increase of 19 per cent in London and Middlesex, but an increase in crime of 55 per cent.[5] These figures, the demand for a new threshold of order, the lurking fears of crowd action and radical agitation, the growing belief that some sort of police reform was necessary, astute political management, and the sidestepping of confrontation with the City of London by omitting it from the proposed jurisdiction of the new force, all combined to help the bill's passage. The controversial Catholic Emancipation Bill may also have diverted some of the potential parliamentary and public hostility.

The prevention of crime was stressed as the first duty of the new Metropolitan Police constables, and the whole system of beat patrols – largely what the parochial watchmen had been doing, often successfully, for a century or more – was ostensibly designed with this in mind. But the uniform, the discipline, and the organisation of the new force suggest that Peel had imported into London many of the policing practices developed in Ireland to deal with civil disorder. Peel had been intimately connected with the development

2. *Despatches, Correspondence, and Memoranda of Field Marshal Arthur Duke of Wellington (New Series) 1819–1832*, edited by his son, 8 vols (London, 1867–80), i, pp. 127–9, and see also ii, pp. 173–7.
3. *Parliamentary Debates*, VII, 803.
4. *PP* 1828 (533) VI, *Police of the Metropolis*, pp. 48, 50, 57, 66, 83.
5. *Parliamentary Debates*, XXI, 871.

of the Irish Constabulary during his period as Chief Secretary for Ireland between 1812 and 1818. He maintained his connection with, and interest in, this force; in 1829, when he was busy establishing the London Metropolitan Police, he was also in frequent contact with the Chief Secretary for Ireland about the reform of the Irish Constabulary.[6] The policing conducted from Bow Street and the other police offices had been directed by magistrates with a loose supervision by the Home Office. In 1828 the number of constables working from these offices was just over 300, with the largest component being the River Police. Peel's new parallel police system was ten times larger and with a much more rigid and hierarchical structure. His two new police commissioners, Colonel Charles Rowan and Richard Mayne, a barrister, were sworn in as magistrates, but they did not act as such from their new office in Scotland Yard. Recognising the English antipathy to a standing army quartered at home, efforts were made to ensure that the new police did not look like soldiers: they were given top hats, uniforms of blue, swallow-tail coats with the minimum of decoration, in contrast to the short scarlet tunics with coloured facings and piping of the British infantry; the constable's weaponry was limited to a wooden truncheon, though cutlasses were available for emergencies and for patrolling dangerous beats, and inspectors and above could carry pocket pistols. Much of the early criticism of the new force focused on its military character: the *Weekly Dispatch* protested about 'these military protectors of our civil liberties' and labelled them 'a gendarmerie'; the *Monthly Magazine* complained similarly, and wrote off Colonel Rowan as 'a Horseguard dependent' and 'a military retainer of the Duke [of Wellington]'.[7] Given the hierarchical structure of the force, the uniforms, the rigid discipline, and the way that, from very early on, the men were deployed as riot squads in both London and the rest of the country, there was some justification in these protests.

But Londoners' protests were not confined simply to the military nature of the new police. Local government in London was expected to pay for the police out of the rates, in the same way that it had paid for the old watch. However, each watch had been directly under the control of the local authority for which it worked;

6. Stanley H. Palmer, *Police and Protest in England and Ireland 1780–1850* (Cambridge: CUP, 1988), p. 294.

7. *Weekly Dispatch*, 27 Sept. 1829, and see also 6 Sept., 4 Oct. and 1 Nov. 1829; Anon, 'The state of the Empire: police, press, popery and foreign relations', *Monthly Magazine*, new series, 8 (Oct. 1829), 361–9, at 362–3.

the commissioners of the Metropolitan Police alone gave orders to the superintendents in charge of the police divisions, and the commissioners themselves were answerable only to the Home Secretary. Moreover, the overall cost of the police was much greater than that of the watch. Admittedly some parishes had no watch, or a very poor watch before 1829, when the overall annual cost had amounted to £137,000; but the yearly expense of the Metropolitan Police between 1830 and 1832 was £207,000, and the extra money was actually funding less policemen than watchmen.[8] Parishes petitioned for a degree of control over the new police, and withheld money from the government and even lowered the valuation of house rentals to frustrate the new system. The government ignored the petitions, but given the large sums of money that were not forthcoming from the metropolitan parishes – £70,000 by the end of 1832 – it introduced legislation in 1833 by which a quarter of all police expenses up to £60,000 were to be met out of the Consolidated Fund. As a result of this Act (3 & 4 Will. IV cap. 89) the rate assessment for policing in 1834 was only some £14,000 above that of 1828.[9] Even so, many parishes were not satisfied. In March 1843 the Vestry of Marylebone appointed a committee under the chairmanship of the local MP, Henry Tufnell, to compare the new police with the old watch. The committee reported that under the old system the Vestry had been served by a parochial watch of 256 men at an average annual cost, between 1818 and 1828, of £9,566. The division of the Metropolitan Police responsible for Marylebone consisted of only 211 men, and even after the financial reform of 1833 the Vestry was still required to find, on average, £20,000 a year for the police.[10]

There was bound to be a degree of friction between two parallel systems of policing. Historians such as Ascoli and Reith have portrayed it in Manichaean terms with Rowan, Mayne and the

---

8. Paley, ' "An imperfect, inadequate and wretched system"?', 115, notes: 'Since the boundaries of a police division did not correlate to those of the parishes it is difficult to make an exact comparison. But it is perhaps worth pointing out that in 1828, some 1,700 watchmen were employed in the City of Westminster and other urban parishes. Even if all the parishes employed a double shift system (which they did not), this meant that well over 800 men were on patrol at any hour of the night. In 1829 they were replaced by some 900 police constables – only a quarter of whom were on patrol at any one time.' The increase in the Metropolitan Police over the next year, and the concentration of men on night duty, meant that by the end of 1830 there were 2,000 men patrolling the entire Metropolitan Police district at night.

9. Palmer, *Police and Protest*, p. 308 and note 95.

10. *PP* 1843 (248) XLII, *Report of a Committee of the Marylebone Vestry on the Expenses of the Police borne by that Parish*, pp. 2–3.

Metropolitan Police as the forces of light, ranged particularly against Sir Frederick Roe, the Chief Magistrate of Bow Street, 'a deliberately provocative appointment' made in 1832 by Lord Melbourne, the Whig Home Secretary.[11] Roe was a key figure in the criticism directed against the police over the manner in which they confronted the crowd during the Coldbath Fields disorder of May 1833, and he pushed hard for an enquiry and for disciplinary action following the alleged rape, while held in police cells, of Ruth Morris by Inspector Wolvendon. But whether this amounts to the venomous personal vendetta described by Ascoli and Reith is a moot point. At least part of the problem stemmed from the confusion over the powers of the commissioners of the Metropolitan Police, and particularly over their position *vis-à-vis* the chief magistrate of Bow Street, none of which was clearly explained in the 1829 Act.[12] The two police systems were performing separate, but overlapping, functions, and there is no reason why they could not have developed side by side – one concentrating on detection, the other on prevention.

Much of the discussion by parliamentary committees during the 1830s focused on the need to sort out the different tasks of the parallel organisations. Roe explained to the select committee which investigated the police of the metropolis in 1834 that the Metropolitan Police was best suited to 'watching, prevention, preservation of the peace, maintenance of good order in the town, and everything connected with out-door and street-duty', but that another force was needed to deal with more complicated cases and crimes. The same point was made by other police magistrates. 'I do not think,' declared Henry Moreton Dyer of the Marlborough Street Office, 'that patrolling the street by the police constables during the day can prevent the congregation of bad characters in public-houses and such places of resort.'[13] Samuel March Phillips, the Under Secretary of State at the Home Office and another of Ascoli's villains, believed that the constables in the police offices were 'more

---

11. David Ascoli, *The Queen's Peace: The Origins and Development of the Metropolitan Police 1829–1979* (London: Hamish Hamilton, 1979), p. 102; Charles Reith, *British Police and the Democratic Ideal* (Oxford: OUP, 1943), ch. 18.

12. Reith, *British Police and the Democratic Ideal*, p. 40. Ascoli maintains that the Bow Street Police establishment under Roe was 'technically illegal under the terms of the 1829 Act' (*The Queen's Peace*, p. 102), which is not something that ever appears to have been argued at the time, and says little for the way that Peel – one of Ascoli's heroes – left the situation in that year.

13. *PP* 1834 (600) XVI, *Select Committee on the Police of the Metropolis*, qq. 1545, 1970, and see also the comments of John Hardwick, a magistrate of Lambeth Street, q. 2222.

expert in tracing out and detecting crime, than the common Metropolitan Police officer'.[14] Senior police officers themselves recognised that men patrolling in uniform would rarely catch thieves and accordingly deployed some of their men in plain clothes;[15] while vacancies for constables in the offices of the stipendiary magistrates during the 1830s were commonly filled by men from the Metropolitan Police – the fact that the pay of the former, being based on fees, was substantially higher than the fixed wage of the latter was an obvious attraction.[16] On the other hand, this payment by fees was recognised as leading to abuses among constables of the old system. John Hardwick, the senior stipendiary at the Lambeth Street Police Office, maintained that his own constables now left the supervision of suspicious characters and the apprehension of thieves to the Metropolitan Police and 'content[ed] themselves simply with the execution of the orders of the magistrates and summonses in assault, etc.'; in other words, they only performed the tasks which provided fees.[17]

In 1833 three parliamentary select committees published reports on the Metropolitan Police. Two of these enquiries were brought about by actions of the Metropolitan Police which had caused concern. The first investigated the affair of William Popay, a police sergeant who had exceeded his instructions by infiltrating the National Political Union and playing the role of *provocateur*.[18] The second reported on the Coldbath Fields disorder in which the police had baton-charged a demonstration by the National Political Union; a police constable was killed during the ensuing mêlée, but, as a result of their perception of the circumstances of the police charge, the coroner's jury which sat on the unfortunate Constable Culley brought in a verdict of 'justifiable homicide'.[19] Both of these enquiries largely exonerated the police. The third select committee report of 1833 was a brief interim paper from a committee which reported in detail on the workings of the new system in 1834.[20] The 1834 report contained, in its minutes of evidence, continuing parochial criticisms of police costs and their lack of local accountability,

14. *PP* 1837 (451) XII, *Metropolis Police Offices*, q. 83.
15. *PP* 1833 (627) XIII, *Report from the Select Committee on the Petition of Frederick Young and Others*, qq. 1127, 1759 and 1845.
16. *PP* 1834 (600) XVI, . . . *Police of the Metropolis*, qq. 2156, 2165 and 2446–8; *PP* 1837 (451) XII, *Metropolis Police Offices*, qq. 235–6.
17. *PP* 1837 (451) XII, *Metropolis Police Offices*, q. 603.
18. *PP* 1833 (627) XIII, . . . *Petition of Frederick Young*.
19. *PP* 1833 (718) XIII, *Select Committee on the Coldbath Fields Meeting*.
20. *PP* 1833 (675) XIII, *Select Committee on the Metropolitan Police*.

but overall it was a warm endorsement of the Metropolitan Police. The select committee believed that the new force was inhibiting crime but was not a restraint on English liberty. It praised the commissioners for the ways in which they handled their men and dealt with complaints from the public. It recommended that the Bow Street Horse Patrol and the constables of the old police offices be incorporated into the new police.[21] The Horse Patrol was amalgamated with the new police in 1836, but it was not until 1839, and only then after another select committee, meeting over two sessions of Parliament, had investigated the interrelationship between the parallel police systems,[22] that the old police offices were transformed into police courts, with their stipendiary magistrates becoming responsible for judicial tasks only, and their constables and the remaining Bow Street patrols being offered the opportunity of transferring into the Metropolitan Police.

Much of the discussion in the select committee of 1837–8 focused on whether or not the square mile of the City of London should come under the jurisdiction of the Metropolitan Police commissioners. The City authorities no longer presented a common front; some welcomed the idea of amalgamation, but others, some of whom gave evidence to the committee, were keen to preserve their independence. While the arguments of the latter often tended to be appeals to tradition rather than to logic, they were able to point to the police clauses of the recent Municipal Corporations Act as a precedent for their continuing independence.[23] The select committee concluded that incorporation was the best option and the Metropolitan Police Bill announced by the Whig government in February 1839 proposed not only the end of the old system of police offices, of Bow Street Patrols and independent River Police, but also the abolition of the separate police jurisdiction of the City. As had happened in earlier years, the City reacted to preserve its independence; on this occasion, however, after discussion with Lord John Russell, the Home Secretary, the City authorities introduced their own private bill into Parliament to create a separate police force for the square mile modelled on the Metropolitan Police, with a commissioner answerable to the City authorities. The bill had a stormy passage, not the least of which was brought about by the ambitions of Daniel Whittle Harvey, the independent MP for

21. *PP* 1834 (600) XVI, *Select Committee on the Police of the Metropolis.*
22. *PP* 1837 (451) XII, *Metropolis Police Offices*; *PP* 1837–38 (578) XV, *Metropolis Police Offices.*
23. See, *inter alia*, *PP* 1837 (451) XII, *Metropolis Police Offices*, qq. 1266–71.

Southwark, who hoped to become the first Commissioner of the City of London Police and, at the same time, to maintain his seat in Parliament. Harvey had strong support for his police candidature among the City fathers, but his independence and his controversial career had provided him with few friends among either Tories or Whigs in Parliament. The question took on constitutional overtones: could a chief of police serve as an MP? Both Whigs and Tories supported an amendment to the City Police Bill disqualifying the commissioner from holding a seat in Parliament. Peel, as leader of the opposition, explained that the Metropolitan Police commissioners were similarly disqualified, and he warned the Commons of the possible dangers that could occur if a commissioner of police was to confront the Home Secretary in parliamentary debate. The amendment was carried, as were some three dozen others establishing considerable uniformity with the Metropolitan Police; but the bill was passed allowing for the creation of an independent police force for the City right in the middle of the jurisdiction of the Metropolitan Police.[24]

While the City fought to maintain its independence with a private bill, the public bill, which abolished the last vestiges of the old metropolitan system and extended the jurisdiction of the Metropolitan Police from a radius of about 10 miles from Charing Cross to about 15, had a much easier passage through Parliament. A decade after its creation, the Metropolitan Police was increasingly being perceived by London's property owners as an effective preventive force; equally, many 'respectable inhabitants' were no doubt delighted by the fact that, within days of the creation of the Metropolitan Police, squads of them were seen to be deployed in clearing the street of 'scenes of drunkenness, riot and debauchery'.[25] Outside of London the new police became an element in the debates on policing as men read or heard reports of the experiment. Also during the 1830s, Metropolitan policemen began to appear in the provinces at the request of local authorities; sometimes they were called in to form the cadre of a local police, occasionally they supervised race meetings, but the largest numbers were deployed as riot squads and were used to suppress first Anti-Poor Law disturbances and later Chartists.[26]

24. Donald Rumbelow, *I Spy Blue: The Police and Crime in the City of London from Elizabeth I to Victoria* (London: Macmillan, 1971), pp. 125–33.
25. *The Times*, 14 Oct. 1829.
26. F.C. Mather, *Public Order in the Age of the Chartists* (Manchester: University Press, 1959), p. 105.

Provincial police reform

It was not only in London that Peel considered police reform to be necessary. Disorder in Lancashire in 1826 led him to contemplate some new kind of permanent force: 'Three hundred men, acting in concert, well armed, and determined to resist to the utmost any attack upon property would do much good in such places as Burnley or Blackburn.'[27] But it was one thing to establish a police force in London, and something very different and more difficult to attempt to establish a national organisation of this sort given the independence which had been allowed to develop in English local government particularly over the previous 150 years. Peel's comment in 1829 that he would like to see a similar organisation to the Metropolitan Police established in Manchester, in preference to the quartering of troops in the area in time of trouble, brought an angry retort from the Tory *Manchester Herald*: the town's police were perfectly adequate, declared the paper, except in the most exceptional circumstances. The outcry was such that Peel felt it necessary to qualify his statement in a letter to the borough reeves and constables; what he had meant, he explained, was that if the Metropolitan Police was a success, then he would like to see other towns and cities applying to Parliament for legislation to establish similar organisations.[28]

But hostility to the idea of a police controlled from Westminster, something which did appear to resemble a French-style gendarmerie, did not mean that people in the English provinces were not also growing concerned about crime and disorder, nor that they were unfavourable to some improvements in policing practice. Sir John Fielding's General Preventative Plan was circulated to the magistrates of England and Wales between September 1772 and September 1773. It proposed making his Bow Street Police Office the centre of a national system for the collation and circulation of information about crimes and known fugitives and offenders. The Plan was received enthusiastically and, once implemented, was regarded as a success. However, when Fielding suggested reorganising the policing of counties in 1775 by making high constables responsible for the pursuit of offenders in addition to their existing tasks of supervising the petty constables, the response was unfavourable: the proposal would have meant a major reorganisation of local

27. C.S. Parker, *Sir Robert Peel: from his Private Papers*, 3 vols (London: John Murray, 1891), i, p. 405.
28. Charles De Motte, 'The dark side of town: crime in Manchester and Salford 1815–1875', Ph.D., University of Kansas, 1977, p. 53.

government and of the way in which these functionaries, often men of some social standing, were selected.[29]

The aftermath of the American War of Independence witnessed an increase in the numbers of local, private subscription societies organised for the prosecution of offenders. The Associations for the Prosecution of Felons were made up of local worthies, usually gentlemen, farmers and tradesmen. They paid a small subscription to finance the prosecution of any individual who committed a criminal act against them or their property; sometimes they might also finance a prosecution for a less well-to-do neighbour. Like the men who gave limited approval to Sir John Fielding's ideas, the members of these associations do not appear to have been dissatisfied with the prevailing system of law enforcement, but they wanted it to function better and to deal with more offenders – symptomatic, perhaps, of a belief that there were more offenders to apprehend and prosecute.[30] During the years of war against revolutionary and Napoleonic France the provinces witnessed major food riots in 1795–6 and 1799–1801, the Luddite industrial disorders in 1811–12, and sporadic rioting over the government's recruitment policies and practices. At the same time many people with property feared insurrection of some sort by English Jacobins sympathetic to ideas espoused by the French revolutionaries. There were calls for the appointment of stipendiary magistrates in the provinces, particularly in the burgeoning manufacturing districts where it could be difficult to find gentlemen prepared to act as justices; and rotation offices were established in Manchester (in 1795) and Birmingham (in 1799) at which local county magistrates took it in turns to administer justice on a regular basis. The wide use of both regular and auxiliary troops for policing the country during the war years, and the small cavalry barracks built as a police measure in the industrial districts early in the 1790s, may also have contributed to a slight breaking down of the hostility to the idea of uniformed policemen. Peace with France did not bring plenty and passivity to the provinces; there was renewed food rioting, as well as agricultural, industrial, and political disorder, and an apparent increase in crime. Perception of the latter was less likely to have been gleaned from consulting the statistics now collected by government than from reading colourful reports in the press now devoid of exciting

29. Styles, 'Sir John Fielding and the problem of criminal investigation', passim.
30. David Philips, 'Good men to associate and bad men to conspire: associations for the prosecution of felons in England, 1760–1860', in Douglas Hay and Francis Snyder (eds), *Policing and Prosecution in Britain 1750–1850* (Oxford: Clarendon Press, 1989), pp. 113–70.

war news, and from noting the increased numbers of accused being brought before the local assizes or quarter sessions.

By the early 1820s at least men were discussing the need for new, more professional systems of policing in rural England. In September 1821, for example, John Hopkins Warden, an auctioneer and constable of the borough of Bedford, was outlining the problem, and the remedy, for a local magistrate. Crime in Bedfordshire, he declared, was the work of organised gangs; it needed a professional response rather than the part-time parish constable,

> who is perhaps new to his office every year [and] cannot be aware of their manuvres, in short he has other objects in view, his Business of all things must be attended and knowing that his term of office will soon expire he cannot *he does not* give it the attention his office and the county require.

Community pressure also militated against a part-time constable fulfilling the office satisfactorily since, if he was diligent,

> he becomes an object of attack, he is call'd Busy, Meddlesome, and a troublesome man, the lower classes in life attack him with every approbrious name in the *Society they move*, and every Endeavour is made by them to Injure him in his profession, thus fearing the Injury likely to be sustained he becomes passive, winks at crime, and passes by a depredation not wishing to observe it.[31]

Warden proposed that one or two professional policemen should be based in the county town and should act as a clearing-house for information for both the county's part-time parish constables and magistrates and the stipendiary magistrates in the London police offices. These policemen should also be available 'free of expense' to any place or parish in the county and should keep a journal, for inspection by the magistrates, of all the occurrences to which they were called. The following year he developed his plan further; there were now to be three professional officers based in separate towns in Bedfordshire, and he hoped that these could become part of a national network.[32] The plan was not adopted by the Bedfordshire Quarter Sessions, but another county, Cheshire, established a police system with similarities to Warden's plan by Act of Parliament in 1829.

31. Beds. RO QSR 1821/711, Warden to ?, 11 Sept. 1821. There were gangs in early nineteenth-century Bedfordshire but not, it seems, of the kind described by Warden: Clive Emsley, *Crime and Society in England 1750–1900* 2nd edn (London: Longman, 1996), pp. 108–10.
32. Robert D. Storch, 'Policing rural southern England before the police: opinion and practice, 1830–1856', in Hay and Snyder (eds), *Policing and Prosecution*, p. 217.

People in Cheshire towards the end of the 1820s were concerned by the 'wide spreading and awfully increasing dissemination of crime'.[33] The Cheshire Police Act of 1829 (10 Geo. IV cap. 97) authorised the appointment of professional high constables in the different hundreds of the county with salaries related to the size of population. It was expected that they would forge links with the efficient urban police who were thought already to exist in towns like Altringham, Macclesfield and Stockport, as well as in Liverpool and Manchester, 'and from the knowledge officers had of the persons and habits of thieves who had resided in their own districts, the information they could furnish would materially tend to promote the detection and apprehension of offenders who were in the habit of making excursions for the sole purpose of committing felonies in [Cheshire]'. Trafford Trafford, the chairman of the quarter sessions responsible for these optimistic remarks, also urged against annual appointments and against the appointment of men involved in other business as the part-time constables who were to assist the new, professional high constables: 'for annual officers commenced their labours without any knowledge of the duties they had to perform, and as soon as they became acquainted with those duties, they were obliged to vacate their situations, and were succeeded by others as ignorant as themselves'.[34] There was criticism that the act increased the powers and patronage of the magistracy but the Cheshire Bench itself was well pleased with the new system. In April 1830 Trafford expressed his satisfaction:

> that in those districts in which the Constabulary Act has been carried fully into operation, crime is greatly diminished; and, on the other hand, where the provisions of that act have been partially adopted, crime has increased . . . and I would also add, that in several townships where the constables have been appointed, the constable's rate has been diminished, while protection has been afforded to the farmer, the shopkeeper, and every other class of society.

The local press could also write favourably of the new system, comparing the efficiency of individual high constables with the old-style 'country dogberry'.[35]

33. *Chester Chronicle*, 13 Mar. 1829; see also ibid., 29 May 1829, for concern about the prevalence of burglary, and *PP* 1839 (169) XIX, *First Report of the Commissioners Appointed to Enquire as to the Best Means of Establishing a Constabulary Force in the Counties of England and Wales*, p. 111.
34. *Chester Chronicle*, 17 July 1829.
35. Ibid., 23 Apr. 1830, and see also 23 Oct. 1829, 15 Jan. and 22 Oct. 1830. R.W. James, *To the Best of our Skill and Knowledge: A Short History of the Cheshire Constabulary 1857–1957* (Chester: Chief Constable of Cheshire, 1957), pp. 23, 25.

It is important to recognise that both Warden's proposal for Bedfordshire and the structure of the new Cheshire Constabulary took very different forms to the new Metropolitan Police. They were attempts to develop the old system of part-time parish and town constables with a supervisory force of paid professionals. These professionals were not a uniformed, disciplined body organised in a military-style hierarchy; they could be deployed in a body to police crowds, as were the Cheshire high constables with a reinforcement of part-time specials at the Knutsford Races in 1830,[36] but their prime function was dealing with crime.

The pre-police 'police' of urban provincial districts, with which Trafford wanted his Cheshire constables to link, were organisations which had developed out of the traditional constables and watchmen. Some towns had appointed street commissioners under private Acts of Parliament; these commissioners, in turn, established day and/or night patrols. The Lighting and Watching Act of 1833 (3 & 4 Will. IV cap. 90) provided local authorities with an enabling framework to create, or to improve, daytime patrols and night watches. As the ardent nineteenth-century police reformers like Edwin Chadwick and subsequent traditional police historians have maintained, there was laxity and a reluctance to act among some of the parochial police, and some of the watchmen were drunkards or too old and lame for their tasks. But there were many contemporaries who believed that the developments in the existing system of watches and parochial constables were helping to control crime and disorder, and such historical research as has been done into these police systems suggests that they should not be dismissed out of hand as corrupt, lax and inefficient. In 1830, shortly after the appointment of a new city watch, the Recorder of Exeter commented on 'a great improvement in the quiet and order of our streets since the establishment of a night police'.[37] The serjeants-at-mace in the growing industrial borough of Wigan were increased in number from two to four in 1832, and they appear to have been reasonably competent in apprehending offenders of different kinds.[38] Like many other towns, Newcastle-upon-Tyne was policed by a mixture of constables, town serjeants and night watchmen. In

36. *Chester Chronicle*, 22 Oct. 1830.
37. Roger Swift, 'Urban policing in early Victorian England, 1835–56: a reappraisal', *History* 73 (1988), 211–37, at pp. 215–16.
38. Philip Charles Barrett, 'Crime and punishment in a Lancashire industrial town: law and social change in the borough of Wigan, 1800–1850', M.Phil., Liverpool Polytechnic, 1980, pp. 122–8.

1829 Mayor George Shadforth summoned the serjeants and constables to a meeting and gave them strict instructions on how they were to carry out their duties and improve their efficiency; laxity and the hint of corruption were not tolerated under Shadforth.[39] In Liverpool there were constables appointed by the corporation, a night watch responsible to the Commissioners of Lamps, Watch and Scavengers, and a dock police directed by the Dock Committee; there could be friction over jurisdiction between the three forces at all levels, but there were also attempts to develop and improve the forces by recruiting senior officers from the Metropolitan Police. In 1835 the corporation was contemplating a private parliamentary bill to establish a new and improved system; the plans were cut short by the Municipal Corporations Act of that year, but it is worth noting that the Municipal Corporations Commissioners considered Liverpool to be well policed.[40] None of this is to suggest that the English boroughs were well policed by modern standards in the early 1830s, but the situation was probably not as bad as has been commonly supposed.

The Municipal Corporations Act applied to 178 boroughs in England and Wales. It established a uniform electorate for the municipalities, enfranchising all male rate-payers who were residents of three years' standing; it also created a degree of uniformity among the tasks and organisation of the town councils chosen by this rate-payer electorate. Among these tasks was the appointment of a watch committee which, in turn, was to appoint and to supervise a town police force. Some of the new watch committees responded to the Act as a few local authorities had behaved before its passage: they sought the advice of, and occasionally made senior appointments from, the Metropolitan Police. But this was by no means always the case; moreover, the men who made up the rank and file were often the watchmen, serjeants and beadles of the old town police now put into a semblance of uniform and called by the new name of 'policemen'.[41]

The Whigs who introduced the Municipal Corporations Act had already shown an interest in police reform. When Grey's government

39. H.A. Mitchell, *A Report of the Proceedings in the Mayor's Chamber, Newcastle-upon-Tyne, during the Mayoralty of George Shadforth Esq. 1829–30* (Newcastle, n.d.), pp. 11, 16.

40. W.R. Cockcroft, 'The rise and growth of the Liverpool police force', M.A., University College, Bangor, 1969, follows the traditional line but contains a wealth of detail; C. Anne Bryson, 'Riot and its control in Liverpool, 1815–1860', M.Phil., The Open University, 1990, ch. 2.

41. Emsley, *Crime and Society*, p. 226; Swift, 'Urban Policing', 217–18.

took office in 1830 ministers found themselves having to deal with the agrarian disturbances of 'Captain Swing', followed by the Reform Bill riots in Bristol, Derby and Nottingham. In March 1832 Lord Melbourne, the Home Secretary, informed Grey that he had issued instructions for a bill to be prepared for establishing a system of police across the whole country. Melbourne's bill proposed a national network of stipendiary magistrates with powers similar to those running the London Police Offices; these were to appoint and supervise professional constables paid for out of a local police rate. The new police districts were to be formed in towns, both corporate and also non-corporate with a population in excess of 10,000; in addition there was the provision for forming such police in unions of towns or in rural districts where the government felt them to be necessary. The political turbulence surrounding the passage of the Great Reform Act pushed the bill into the background; and after this, the subsidence of popular disorder, together with the complexity of handling the immunities of corporate towns and the difficulties inherent in getting agreement over local rates, combined to see the bill dropped.[42] Nevertheless, its existence remains significant for illustrating how the opinion of central government was shifting towards perceiving a need for a better police provision across the country; and if country gentlemen were not all in agreement, the discussions and developments of the 1820s, which were to gather pace in the 1830s, were indicative of a similar, possibly more gradual, shift among most of the rulers of provincial England.

In 1836, with Melbourne now Prime Minister, the Whig Home Secretary, Lord John Russell, agreed to a proposal from Edwin Chadwick for the appointment of a Royal Commission to enquire into the best means of establishing a rural constabulary. Chadwick, an incorrigible advocate of Utilitarian reform, had already achieved a considerable reputation as the driving force behind the Poor Law report and reform of 1834; police reform for Chadwick was part and parcel of his plan for the well-regulated state. The printed report of the constabulary commissioners was presented early in 1839. It was largely the work of Chadwick, but his hopes for a centralised police were rejected early on in the deliberations by his fellow commissioners, Colonel Rowan of the Metropolitan Police and the country gentleman, Charles Shaw Lefevre. Rowan and

---

42. David Philips and Robert D. Storch, 'Whigs and coppers: the Grey ministry's National Police Scheme, 1832', *Historical Research* 67 (1994), 75–90.

Lefevre later rejected his proposal to make the rural constabulary responsible to the boards of guardians appointed under the New Poor Law; any new police in the counties, as far as Rowan, Lefevre, Russell, and other members of the government were concerned, was going to be under the control of the county magistrates.[43]

Traditional police historians have described the Royal Commission on the Rural Constabulary as 'enterprising' and 'far-seeing' and have accepted its report as demonstrating 'the prostrate condition of English police under the parochial system'.[44] The report contained a wealth of anecdotal material about the poor quality of policing: twenty pages, for example, were devoted to describing the 'honourable' failure of the experiment in Cheshire which, according to the Royal Commission, had not lived up to the hopes of 1829.[45] But Chadwick carefully selected the material for inclusion in the report. This may have been missed by some historians, but the *Justice of the Peace* detected his hand throughout for 'the same magnifying of petty evils, the same unqualified condemnation of existing things, the same absolute persuasion of the perfect efficacy of his nostrums and his alone'. While not unsympathetic to a degree of police reform, the journal considered that much of the evidence quoted was 'gossiping twaddle'.[46] Chadwick did have a predilection for colourful thieves' tales which proved his point, but more seriously he studiously ignored much of the detailed evidence of the other experiments being tried throughout the country. The investigations made for the report show that in addition to the old parish constables and watchmen there were a variety of forces paid for by a local rate levied under the 1833 Lighting and Watching Act; there were forces recruited and paid by private subscription, sometimes attached to associations for the prosecution of felons; there were forces linked directly with the New Poor Law machinery. If the printed report describes a 'prostrate condition', the commissioners' unprinted evidence suggests a growing opinion among country gentlemen that there was a need for changes and

43. Anthony Brundage, 'Ministers, magistrates and reformers: the genesis of the Rural Constabulary Act of 1839', *Parliamentary History* 5 (1986), 55–64.

44. Quotations from T.A. Critchley, *A History of Police in England and Wales* 2nd edn (London: Constable, 1978), pp. 69, 75; and W.L. Melville Lee, *A History of Police in England* (London: Methuen, 1901), p. 291.

45. *PP* 1839 (169) XIX, *First Report of the Commissioners*, pp. 110–29. The Cheshire Bench did not agree and two proposals for the implementation of the Rural Constabulary Act in the county were rejected by large majorities. *PP* 1852–53 (603) XXXVI, *First Report of the Select Committee on Police*, q. 2276.

46. *Justice of the Peace* III (1839), 13 Apr., pp. 206–7, and 20 Apr., p. 221.

improvements, and growing activity on their part to make such changes and improvements. No doubt the example of the Metropolitan Police had influenced some of the county gentry and in some instances they turned to that force for the leaders of their experimental forces. But the country gentlemen did not perceive policing solely in terms of the metropolitan model.[47]

The Whig government of Lord Melbourne was already considering some reform of the system of policing in the counties before the Royal Commission began its deliberations. The completion of the Commission's report was hurried, with government urging, so that a bill could be introduced early in 1839. The speedy passage of the bill itself is indicative of the fact that few now questioned the need for improvements in the policing of the provinces. Support for the bill was spread across the political spectrum with opposition largely concentrated on the extremes of the Tory right and the Radical left – members of the Chartist Convention meeting in London perceived the legislation as directed specifically against their aspirations, and spoke of 'one of the most barefaced attempts which ever had been attempted to be perpetrated against a nation's rights', 'the first step to a despotism', and recalled 'the vagabond conduct' of the Metropolitan Police in Coldbath Fields.[48] The contentious recommendations of the Commission, which smacked of centralisation, were omitted from the bill, notably the suggestion that the Treasury should pay one-quarter of the cost of any forces established under the legislation, and the proposal that the Metropolitan Police might be responsible for appointing and training new county policemen.[49] The debates in county quarter sessions, on whether or not to create a rural constabulary under the legislation, similarly did not often dispute the need for some change and improvement in the existing system. They focused generally on the cost of a professional constabulary and on definitions of local control. Local attitudes for and against the creation of a rural constabulary cut across party lines; often the position taken by the most influential county gentleman was the most significant in deciding one way or another. It seems that those counties which had experienced serious disturbances against the New Poor Law were those

47. Storch, 'Policing rural southern England', passim.
48. W. Watts Miller, 'Party politics, class interest and reform of the police, 1829–56', unpublished paper, Department of Sociology, Bristol University, 1978, quoted in Storch, 'Policing rural southern England', 213 n. 5. The furious comments of delegates at the Chartist Convention in London on 18 Mar. 1839 are to be found in several newspapers, e.g. *The Northern Star*, 23 Mar. 1839.
49. Brundage, 'Ministers, magistrates and reformers', passim.

most sympathetic to adopting the Act; while estimates of the potential expense were the most powerful disincentive.[50]

The Rural Constabulary Act of 1839, and the amending Act of 1840, left the decision to establish a rural police and the control of that police in the hands of the county magistrates. But other legislation introduced in 1839 took control of their police out of the hands of the local authorities of three large industrial cities: Birmingham, Bolton and Manchester. The Whig government decided on this radical step partly because of the fear of Chartist disorder, but also because of problems within local government. In Bolton there was hesitancy and uncertainty on the part of the new town council and only a tiny police force had been recruited. In Manchester the situation was more serious, for here local government was deadlocked as the new town council squabbled with the still powerful vestiges of the old authorities. Manchester had become an incorporated borough in October 1838, and its first borough council was elected in December of that year. Among the earliest acts of the new council was the creation of a police force of 295 constables and 48 officers. The old Police Commissioners, established in 1792, linked with the parochial and manorial authorities to oppose the new force; they refused to hand over their arms and their lock-ups, and they continued to pay their day constables and night watchmen. The borough magistrates imposed fines; the old authorities refused to pay them. Warrants of distress were issued for the fines; the old authorities instituted legal proceedings against the magistrates who had signed the warrants. The situation was aggravated still further when, allegedly in an attempt to meet the threat of potential disorder from Chartists and agitation over the corn laws, the old Police Commissioners established a new patrol of 50 policemen.[51]

In Birmingham disputes over the new charter of incorporation prevented the new town council from raising the necessary finances for a police force, but central government was also concerned over Chartism in the city. Some of the town council had Chartist sympathies and Birmingham had become the meeting place for the national Chartist Convention in July 1839. There was serious rioting in the middle of that month which was aggravated by the decision

50. Storch, 'Policing rural southern England', 236–52; and for separate county studies see Clive Emsley, 'The Bedfordshire police, 1840–1856: a case study in the working of the Rural Constabulary Act', *Midland History* 7 (1982), 73–92, at 74; David Foster, 'Police reform and public opinion in rural Yorkshire', *Journal of Local Studies* 2 (1982), 1–8, at 6–7.

51. Arthur Redford, *The History of Local Government in Manchester: Volume II, Borough and City* (London: Longman, 1940), pp. 42–4.

of local magistrates to deploy Metropolitan Police sent up to help maintain order.[52] The proposal that a police force be established in the city under a commissioner appointed by the central government came from Peel, now leader of the parliamentary opposition, who used Irish examples as a precedent. The proposal reawoke the concerns about 'the French system of police' and prompted furious protests from Birmingham's MPs and the town council, which condemned it 'as an insidious and alarming step towards that system of centralisation which is so alien from the habits of the people of this country and from the ancient usages of the Constitution'.[53] But Peel's suggestion was warmly received by the Whig government. The Birmingham bill drew most of the fire; the similar bills for Bolton and Manchester were carried along in its wake. In spite of the threat which this legislation posed to local authority, each of the three Acts received large majorities in sparsely attended Houses. Crime was not an issue in the debates; local authority was, but always in the background was the spectre of Chartist disorder.[54]

The development of new police systems in late eighteenth- and early nineteenth-century England grew out of a heightened concern about crime and disorder. Opinion formers and the ruling elite perceived a new problem: it was initially centred largely in London, but as the Gordon Riots, the French Revolution, the disruption and dislocation of war, and the statistics of rising crime aggravated the concerns, so the problem was seen as spreading to the provinces. The moving force behind the major change in policing – the creation of London's Metropolitan Police – was the determination and astute political management of Robert Peel as Home Secretary. In some instances, such as the formation of the Cheshire Constabulary, it was the fear of crime which was the principal spur to improvement and change; in others, such as the legislation for Birmingham in 1839, it was the fear of disorder. But it is not possible to pin-point a particular incident or a particular individual as the prime cause for each national, let alone each local, development. Police reform, like so much other reform, was a slow process involving experiment, debate and compromise; debates over, and experiments with, a variety of different models were to continue throughout the 1840s and early 1850s.

52. Mather, *Public Order*, pp. 13, 107; for a detailed, and partisan, description of the problems of the new town council see J.T. Bunce, *History of the Corporation of Birmingham*, 3 vols (Birmingham, 1878–1902), i, pp. 185–95.
53. Quoted in Bunce, *History*, i, p. 203.
54. Palmer, *Police and Protest*, pp. 416–20.

CHAPTER THREE

A Police for Victorian England

A continuing variety of models

As the 1840s dawned there was no single model of policing dominant in England. The Metropolitan Police continued to have a significant influence. This influence grew when, while the other capitals of Europe were rocked by the revolutions of 1848, London saw Chartism contained with relatively little disorder and violence; and when, in 1851, tens of thousands of visitors poured into London to visit the Great Exhibition and were supervised by the new police, without disorder and without serious crime being committed.[1] Provincial forces often looked to the Metropolitan Police for advice and for senior officers, but the London model was not suited to everyone: as the Earl of Chichester explained to the East Sussex Bench in October 1850, even Colonel Rowan, who had emphasised the importance of prevention to the Metropolitan constables when they began to walk their beats in 1829, considered that 'a rural police was rather to prevent crime by detecting offenders than to prevent it by their actual presence in every village'.[2]

Most of the boroughs had implemented the policing requirements of the Municipal Corporations Act by the end of the 1830s, but as late as 1856 there were at least six, and possibly as many as 23, recalcitrants.[3] Even where men were recruited from the Metropolitan Police, the tasks of the new municipal constables included

1. According to the author of 'The police system of London', *Edinburgh Review* XCVI (1852), 1–33, at p. 21, the police at the Great Exhibition prevented crime to such an extent that there were only eight instances of picking pockets and only ten of pilfering; moreover, all of the stolen property was recovered.

2. *The Times*, 15 Oct. 1850, p. 5.

3. Jenifer Hart, 'Reform of the borough police, 1835–1856', *EHR* LXX (1955), 411–27, at p. 416.

many of those previously undertaken by functionaries of the old unreformed boroughs and had little to do with the prevention of crime. When, for example, in 1841 Robert Chalk left London to become Superintendent of the York City Force, he found that he was also required to serve as Inspector of Nuisances, a position which involved attending meetings of the local Board of Health and implementing public health regulations, inspecting some 300 lodging houses, and supervising the city's scavengers and the sale of manure.[4] Town councils and their watch committees considered the police to be their servants who could be used at their discretion, and not simply for the prevention of crime. The town councils' dependence on the ratepayers who elected them ensured the optimum use of policemen and not necessarily for tasks wholly related to the preservation of law and order; while the strength and the wages of the police were maintained as far as possible at an assessment of what the electors would countenance in their rate bills.

Twenty-four counties had implemented the rural constabulary legislation by the end of 1841; eleven did so over the next fifteen years. Of the total, however, nine counties only implemented the Act for a part of their jurisdiction. There was no common pattern to implementation after the initial debates: in Westmorland the Act was adopted piecemeal, with the quarter sessions introducing it in one part of the county in 1844, and spreading it gradually across the whole by successive rulings in 1846, 1849 and 1852; in Surrey, by contrast, it was the brutal murder of a clergyman when he surprised a group of burglars in his house which panicked the quarter sessions into creating a constabulary under the Act in 1850.[5] Again expertise was recruited from the Metropolitan Police, but Gloucestershire and Staffordshire looked to the Irish police for their senior officers, and Northamptonshire recruited Henry Goddard, a former Bow Street Runner.[6] In both Essex and Shropshire the magistrates chose officers with both Royal Navy and Coastguard service to command their new constabulary. The Essex choice, Captain J.B.B. McHardy, was ultimately regarded as a very successful one, although an early suggestion by McHardy that his men might be given

    4. Roger Swift, *Police Reform in Early Victorian York, 1835–1856* (University of York, Borthwick Paper No. 73, 1988), p. 11.
    5. David Foster, *The Rural Constabulary Act 1839: National Legislation and the Problems of Enforcement* (London: Bedford Square Press/NCVO, 1982), p. 19; *The Times*, 3 Dec. 1850, p. 5.
    6. Bryan Gerrard, 'The Gloucestershire police in the nineteenth century', M. Litt., University of Bristol, 1977, pp. 61–2; David Philips, *Crime and Authority in Victorian England* (London: Croom Helm, 1977), p. 65; Henry Goddard, *Memoirs of a Bow Street Runner* (London: Museum Press, 1956).

commissions to capture smugglers and seize contraband alongside the Coastguard gave rise to concerns on the Bench that this would be giving central government some authority over local police which it might seek to extend. The Shropshire choice seems to have been less fortunate, and the report of the quarter sessions police committee after the first year of the force suggested that the magistrates on the committee had a much better idea of what the force should be doing than their chief constable.[7]

County magistrates were not elected and were not therefore restrained by ratepayer pressure like the town councils; but this did not prevent ratepayers from making their feelings known by petitions to the quarter sessions. During the 1840s rural ratepayers complained in much the same way as their London counterparts in the preceding decade. In January 1842 the Quarter Sessions of County Durham received petitions from 172 of the 240 townships in the county for the removal of the police. 'The signatures were entirely landowners and rated inhabitants – upwards of 6,400 in number. Their genuineness and the respectability of the parties were vouched by the overseers and churchwardens of the different townships, and in many instances the memorials included all the ratepayers in the parishes.' The petitioners insisted that the old constables, 'properly instructed and remunerated for their services', were quite sufficient for the rural districts of the county; if the burgeoning colliery districts in the county needed something else, then they alone should have to pay for it. The magistrates disagreed and, in the belief that the new police provided the best means for them to preserve the peace, they voted to keep the constabulary by 16 votes to 4.[8] In November 1842 two-thirds of the parishes in the largely agricultural county of Bedfordshire petitioned for the removal of the police which was condemned as 'EXPENSIVE; if not INEFFICIENT'. The petitions were presented 'in accordance with the expressed wish of the Magistrates to ascertain the opinions of the Rate Payers of the several parishes in the County relating to the Rural Police Establishment'. Several of the magistrates were sympathetic to the ratepayers' protest, but a majority wanted to continue with the experiment.[9] The Nottinghamshire Quarter

7. Maureen Scollan, *Sworn to Serve: Police in Essex 1840–1990* (Chichester: Phillimore, 1993), p. 16; Douglas J. Elliott, *Policing Shropshire 1836–1967* (Studley, Warwickshire: Brewin Books, 1984), p. 28.

8. *The Times*, 8 Jan. 1842, p. 6.

9. Beds. RO QEV 3 contains these petitions, many of which used the same printed form. See also Clive Emsley, 'The Bedfordshire police 1840–1856: a case study in the working of the Rural Constabulary Act', *Midland History* 7 (1982), 73–92, at 86–7.

Sessions reduced their police from 42 to 33 in January 1842; however, Chartist activity in particular meant that by the end of the year the county Bench had felt the need to increase the police to as many as 88, and the magistrates held firm against the resulting flood of angry ratepayer petitions presented over the next three years. 'We are decidedly of opinion', declared the petitioners of Blidworth, 'that the system is without efficiency, disapproved of by the people generally, and very expensive to us as rate payers. And although we are prepared cheerfully to assist and give countenance to any measures calculated to suppress crime, we cannot but express our hope that the Rural police may be discontinued.'[10] In Lancashire there was ratepayer protest backed by a large number of county magistrates. In March 1842 the county bench voted 81 to 55 in favour of abolishing the new county force; the legislation required a three-quarters majority for abolition, but the compromise solution eventually agreed by the magistrates resulted in a reduction in the force from 502 men to 355. Within a few weeks of this decision Lancashire was confronted with a new wave of Chartist disorder and, more seriously, the Plug Plot riots; Captain John Woodford, the Chief Constable, lamented that he now had insufficient men to cope with the emergency.[11] In Staffordshire, where the Plug Plot disorders were also serious, a constabulary existed in only part of the county; the scale of the riots led to the withdrawal of ratepayers' petitions for the abolition of the force and a decision to extend it to the whole county.[12] But ratepayers in general seem to have been less worried by threats to order than by threats to their pocket; after all, serious disorder could always be suppressed by use of the army and/or by squads of Metropolitan Police.

Ratepayers might protest that the rural constabulary was a 'sysem . . . quite inimical to their feelings as Englishmen',[13] but this is not to say that they, and the 22 counties which did not establish county forces under the legislation of 1839–40, did not seek improvements in the more traditional system of policing. Indeed, the complaint was often that protection had decreased under the new police, or would decrease if the new system was introduced. The corporation of the Borough of Bedford rejected the proposal that their town be policed by the new county force since the Watch Committee estim-

10. Notts. RO QAC 2/6, Petition from Blidworth Parish, n.d.
11. Bob Dobson, *Policing Lancashire 1839–1989* (Nelson, Lancs: Landy Publishing, 1989), p. 26; Foster, *Rural Constabulary Act*, pp. 26–7.
12. Philips, *Crime and Authority in Victorian England*, pp. 57–8.
13. Notts. RO QAC 2/6, Petition from Edingley Parish, 10 May 1843.

ated that nine-tenths of crime in the town occurred after dark and that they were therefore better served by the existing night watch.[14] The town of Luton, some 20 miles south of Bedford, had been policed by one day constable and two night watchmen directed by the Inspectors of Lighting and Watching established under the 1833 Act. In August 1844, after four years under the new constabulary, the old Inspectors petitioned the Quarter Sessions that there were now less police in their town than before, and these were insufficient for 'the protection of the vast property contained in the Warehouses and other buildings in the Town . . . more especially as regards the duties of the night watch when such property must necessarily be left in a great measure totally unprotected from Fire and Robbery'. This may have been special pleading on the part of town worthies who wanted some of their old authority restored; a counter petition was prepared praising the new police and pointing out that, even if the new force did cost more, there was 'the additional advantage of knowing that in cases of emergency the whole of the force of the County might be brought to our assistance at a few hours notice'.[15] But in other small towns in the country policing was still conducted under the 1833 legislation: the people of Horncastle in Lincolnshire appear to have been content that their two constables were sufficient to deal with their few 'lawless and immoral' inhabitants; the small force established similarly in Cottenham, Cambridgeshire, seems to have been equally satisfactory in dealing with the local problems which came mainly from drunks and vagrants.[16]

In Kent a proposal to establish a rural constabulary in 1840 was defeated at quarter sessions by a majority of only three. However, over the next decade the Kent justices set about improving the old system of policing with stricter regulations regarding those liable to serve as parish constables and proposals for professional police superintendents to direct and supervise them. Between 1841 and 1852 five measures, all originating in Kent, were brought before Parliament to this end.[17] Parliament adopted some of Kent's ideas

14. Emsley, 'Bedfordshire police', 76.
15. Beds. RO QEV 3, Petition from the 10 Inspectors of Lighting and Watching, Luton, 25 Aug. 1844; Petition from 43 Luton Property owners, n.d. (1844).
16. B.J. Davey, *Lawless and Immoral: Policing a Country Town 1838–1856* (Leicester: University Press, 1983); Robert D. Storch, 'Policing rural southern England before the police: opinion and practice, 1830–1856', in Douglas Hay and Francis Snyder (eds), *Policing and Prosecution in Britain 1750–1850* (Oxford: Clarendon Press, 1989), p. 257.
17. Carolyn Steedman, *Policing the Victorian Community: The Formation of English Provincial Police Forces, 1856–1880* (London: Routledge and Kegan Paul, 1984), pp. 18–19.

when passing acts establishing and developing superintending constables in 1842 and 1850.

The Parish Constables Act of 1842 (5 & 6 Vict. cap. 109) required magistrates to draw up lists of those who could be sworn in as parish constables; they were to be ratepayers, fit and of good character, between the ages of 25 and 55. Substitutes now had to be approved by the magistrates; and there was provision for the payment of constables out of the poor rate if the local vestry provided the authorisation. The Act further directed that the parish constables were to be supervised by new superintending constables appointed by the quarter sessions and paid out of the county rates. This was the system favoured by many of the ratepayers who petitioned for the removal of the new county constabularies in the 1840s; the parishioners of Maplebeck in Nottinghamshire, for example, felt the system established by the 1842 Act 'would be more efficient for the protection of persons and property likewise the preservation of the public peace than the Rural Police Force, and at a very considerable less expense'.[18] It was also argued that it was preferable to have, as parish constables, 'men who had an interest at stake and property to protect' rather than policemen who 'appeared to be employed in looking up crime'. One Bedfordshire justice was in favour of keeping the county's chief constable as a superintendent, but he believed that the new police 'must feel that it was an indolent life, wandering about in search of cases of drunkenness, which they seemed to think a great catch, when it was difficult to determine whether a man was drunk or not; then interference was sometimes indiscreet, and a spark was engendered into a flame'.[19] Kent justices were so pleased with the workings of the superintending constables system that a motion to the quarter sessions to introduce a rural constabulary in 1849 was rejected by 30 votes. The following year the Superintending Constables Act (13 & 14 Vict. cap. 20) authorised quarter sessions to appoint these officers for each of the petty sessional divisions of their county.

Each of the models had its problems. Many of the borough forces were simply too small to cope with a serious riot: one alarmed citizen, considering 'the tranquillity of the town [to be] a national and not a local matter', thought that if the Home Office would not take responsibility for these forces, then it should at least insist on a ratio of one policeman for every 800 inhabitants.[20] The county

18. Notts. RO QAC 2/6, Petition from Maplebeck Parish, May 1843.
19. *Bedford Mercury*, 22 Oct. 1842.
20. *Justice of the Peace* XVI (1852), 23 Oct., 673, 683.

constabularies were criticised for their expense; there were complaints that the men went out of their way to find offences, and that the old system provided a better protection since a parish constable was at least resident in his parish. The superintending constables, many of whom were recruited from the London or the new county forces, had considerable difficulties in smartening up the part-time parish constables; they were professionals, yet those whom they supervised were not, and had no intention of becoming such. There were also problems of jurisdiction: the superintending constables were appointed by quarter sessions and paid out of the county rate, but they were responsible to petty sessions. Of course some magistrates who sat at petty sessions also sat at quarter sessions, but this did not necessarily mean that they would act together or assist each other, and sometimes there were magistrates who, while active in their immediate locality, did not bother to attend county meetings and did not perceive of issues in the context of the county. In the summer of 1853 when, on the directions of one local Kent magistrate, the superintendent of Tonbridge applied to his neighbour at Ashford for aid because of a riot, a second Kent magistrate at Ashford refused to let his superintendent cross the divisional boundary.[21] However, by the 1850s, whatever the problems with particular models, the idea of some degree of professional policing had received a wide acceptance among the ruling elite; and the professional policemen, whether constables of London, county or borough forces, men appointed under the 1833 legislation, or superintending constables, were all making their presence felt particularly with reference to the imposition of order.[22]

The mid-1850s witnessed the passage of legislation which decided, once and for all, against developing and seeking to improve the traditional system of parochial police. The driving force behind the initial moves for reform was Lord Palmerston, who became Home Secretary in December 1852. Palmerston had already enjoyed a long career in government, though his main concern had been foreign affairs. Earlier in 1852 he had been the leading signatory to a memorial proposing the amalgamation of the police of Romsey borough, close to his country seat of Broadlands, with the Hampshire Constabulary, which suggests some interest in police reform.[23] Within a few weeks of his appointment as Home Secretary he received a letter from Lord Fortescue which appears to have fired this interest

21. Steedman, *Policing the Victorian Community*, p. 20.
22. Storch, 'Policing rural southern England', pp. 256–9.
23. *PP* 1852–53 (603) XXXVI, *First Report of the Select Committee on Police*, q. 504.

still further. Fortescue, a major Devonshire landowner and a former lord lieutenant of Ireland, was concerned about rural crime and the large numbers of 'sturdy beggars' that infested his county in the summer; he believed that present social conditions had 'outgrown the rude machinery framed by our ancestors for the enforcement of the law' and suggested that something akin to the Royal Irish Constabulary be established in England. Palmerston forwarded the letter to Horatio Waddington, his Permanent Under Secretary, who responded that the remedy lay in the hands of local magistrates who could, if they so wished, implement the Rural Constabulary Act.[24] Palmerston, however, considered that additional action was needed. In April 1853, on a motion introduced by E.R. Rice, the Whig MP for Dover, and Joseph Hume, a Radical reformer and member for Montrose who was also a magistrate for Westminster, Middlesex and Norfolk, a new parliamentary select committee was appointed 'to consider the Expediency of adopting a more Uniform System of Police'.

The select committee of 1853 heard evidence from supporters of the superintending constable system and advocates of the county police. The former were drawn from Cheshire, Herefordshire and Lincolnshire. Curiously, perhaps deliberately, no-one from Kent was called to comment on the superintending constables, and while the system undoubtedly had serious flaws, it is difficult not to accept that the cards were stacked against it. E.R. Rice chaired the committee, and his constituency was situated in Kent; he had been High Sheriff of the county in 1830 and still held the office of Deputy Lieutenant; but Rice was a man in favour of the new constabulary system.

Evidence was heard from a former superintending constable in Kent, who was also a veteran of the government-controlled Manchester Police and the Essex Constabulary, and was now the Head Constable of Norwich; he spoke most unfavourably of the system in Kent. The Metropolitan Police superintendent responsible for the parishes of Kentish London explained that his district was better policed than rural Kent; and a Poor Law inspector compared the control of vagrants in Kent most unfavourably with the situation in Essex where there was a model constabulary.[25] The Essex Constabu-

---

24. HO 45.4609, Fortescue to Palmerston, 17 Jan. 1853.
25. *PP* 1852–53 (603) XXXVI, *First Report of the Select Committee on Police*, qq. 1945–65; *PP* 1852–53 (715) XXXVI, *Second Report of the Select Committee on Police*, qq. 2810–17, 3559–79.

lary, and its Chief Constable, Captain J.B.B. McHardy, figured prominently and favourably in the select committee's minutes of evidence. Five of the eight witnesses who had experience of working as some kind of constable during the 1840s and 1850s had served in the Essex force; one of them, David Smith, a superintending constable in Oxfordshire, insisted that six constables from the Essex force would be the equivalent of the 70 parish constables now under his supervision.[26] The committee heard Edwin Chadwick comment favourably on McHardy and the way he organised his force.[27] McHardy himself appeared three times before the committee; he claimed to have experimented 'fairly' with the superintending constable system and found it wanting, and he handed over a considerable amount of written material on the workings of his force and his general recommendations for improvements in provincial policing.[28]

Much of the discussion in the committee focused on the value of professional county constabularies in the suppression of vagrancy; here the committee was following the line developed by Chadwick in the Report of the Constabulary Commission in 1839, that crime was often perpetrated by itinerants who preferred an idle life of vagrancy and theft to one of useful toil. Chadwick had been convinced that a properly organised constabulary force would solve the problem; the select committee were similarly convinced and believed that the new constabularies had contributed to a decline in vagrancy as well as 'to the maintenance of order, and the improved habits of the population'.[29] The committee declared the experiments with superintending constables to be a failure and recommended the creation of a uniform system based on the rural constabularies throughout the country. It suggested that part of the cost of the police might be met by the government without interfering with the continuance of local management of the county forces; but it also made plain its belief that the county was the correct unit for all provincial police organisation:

26. *PP* 1852–53 (715) XXXVI, *Second Report of the Select Committee on Police*, q. 3672. The other former members of the Essex Constabulary who gave evidence were John Dunne, the Chief Constable of Norwich, Thomas Redin, the governor of the county gaol at Carlisle, John Hamilton, a superintending constable in Buckinghamshire, and William Oakley, the governor of Somerset county gaol. The other witnesses who had experience of life as a constable were Alfred Hughes, the Chief Constable of Bath, formerly of the Metropolitan Police and a superintending constable in Surrey, Richard Healy, who had been Chief Constable of the Hundred of Aveland, Lincs, for some 24 years, and Robert Brown, a superintending constable in Cumberland.
27. Ibid., qq. 3645, 3652.   28. Ibid., Appendix No. 1, pp. 128–57.
29. Ibid., p. iii.

the smaller boroughs should be consolidated with districts or counties for Police purposes, and ... the Police in the larger boroughs should be under a similar system of management and control to that of the adjoining district or county, and (where practicable) under the same superintendence, by which arrangement a considerable saving would be effected in the general expenditure.[30]

The select committee's second report containing its recommendations was published in July 1853; five months later industrial disorders in the north-west focused on another policing task, that of suppressing riots, and added weight to the committee's criticism of the weakness of the forces in the smaller boroughs. When the newly elected Mayor of Blackburn made law and order one of his priorities and promised to increase the borough police force to 30 men, with an additional thirteen firemen who could be called on in an emergency, The Times was scathing. Blackburn, it pointed out, had a population of some 46,500, and following the recent riots by cotton operatives the mayor had requested a company of infantry

that is to say for 80 soldiers. Before invoking such assistance he should have tried what 80 constables would do. Let him raise his police force, as so magnanimously projected, from thirty men to a hundred, and then it will be time to ask for bayonets in aid of staves. As for the '13 firemen,' they, like all men impressed from one service to another, will be of comparatively little use, not to mention that in 'emergencies' their hands might possibly be needed in their own department. Everybody knows, and every magistrate ought well to consider, that the real power of a police force is commensurate with the number of its *regular* members.[31]

As newpapers reported, and their readers wrote letters commenting upon, the riots and the state of the police in Blackburn and Wigan, Palmerston prepared his bill for police reform along the lines recommended by the select committee. The plan was for a much more centralised system: the smallest boroughs were to be amalgamated with the counties; the smallest counties were to be amalgamated with their neighbours; chief constables were to be brought into much closer contact with the Home Office; yet the select committee's proposal for the government to pay a proportion of the costs of the police was ignored. The bill brought protest from the counties, but above all it was opposed by the boroughs; in

30. Ibid., p. iv.
31. *The Times*, 7 Dec. 1853, p. 8; for the riots in Blackburn, and also in Wigan, and the following correspondence, see ibid., 31 Oct., p. 8; 1 Nov., p. 5; 2 Nov., p. 12; 21 Nov., p. 12; 9 Dec., p. 5; 13 Dec., p. 5.

both February and June 1854 Palmerston received large deputations from the boroughs who banded together to fight the bill. Substantial alterations were made, but these were insufficient to soothe the opposition. At the end of June Palmerston was compelled to admit defeat and to withdraw the proposed reform.[32] The following summer, with Palmerston now elevated to Prime Minister, Parliament debated another private member's proposal from Kent to improve and develop the parish constable system. Lord John Russell condemned it as 'a retrograde step . . . whatever powers might be granted to the parochial constable under this measure, the fact remains, that they would be locally disconnected, and, in all probability, would be engaged in trade'. Nevertheless, the bill found supporters among MPs from those counties like Lincolnshire and Berkshire where the superintending constables system remained in force; and it was only withdrawn after its proposer, William Deedes, had had lengthy discussions with the new Home Secretary, Sir George Grey, on a new government bill.[33]

Grey's bill for police reform was introduced into Parliament on 5 February 1856; its declared object was 'to provide an efficient police force, both for counties and boroughs, as is possible under the existing system of local mangement'.[34] Grey's bill faced nothing comparable to the furious opposition of two years before. This was partly because existing local authority was now to be left intact, but also because Grey was prepared to make concessions when fears were expressed about threats to local control. The government was now also prepared to contribute to the costs of policing: those forces deemed to be efficient by the new Inspectors of Constabulary established under the legislation were to receive one-quarter of their expenses for clothing and pay out of the Consolidated Fund. There were, in addition, external forces which probably contributed to the bill's passage: the Crimean War had meant the withdrawal of troops from Britain and a consequent diminution in the potential military aid available to local government when confronted by riot; moreover, the virtual end of transportation in 1853, which meant that offenders would have to be absorbed into the home community rather than forgotten in the Antipodes, together with the

32. Stanley H. Palmer, *Police and Protest in England and Ireland 1780–1850* (Cambridge: CUP, 1988), pp. 504–7.
33. *Hansard*, CXXXVIII, 17 May 1855, cols 702–14; quotation at col. 713. Ibid., CXL, 5 Feb. 1856, col. 230.
34. *Hansard*, CXL, 5 Feb. 1856, col. 230; and for the passage of the bill see Palmer, *Police and Protest*, pp. 510–16.

imminent return of Tommy Atkins, brutalised by campaigning in the Crimea, were other pressing reasons for having policemen available. In addition to all of these factors the broad scale of support which the bill received from across the political spectrum suggests that England's elite were by now fully supportive of the idea of uniformed, bureaucratic police organisations based on the traditional local government units of county and borough.

The County and Borough Police Act (19 and 20 Vict. cap. 69) made the formation of police forces obligatory on local government at county and borough level. It provided for the creation of three Inspectors of Constabulary who, between them, were to make annual inspections of each force in the country; only if the Inspector presented a certificate of efficiency was a force to receive the Treasury grant. Clauses in Grey's original bill which gave the Home Office the authority to direct the police in the performance of their duties and to require reports from chief constables whenever the Home Secretary desired, were dropped. In their place it was required that each chief constable send an annual report of the state of crime in his jurisdiction. Perhaps it was inevitable that the new system of inspection and certification would foster similarities between the different forces; but the Act left local police forces where local authorities wanted them, firmly under local control.

The unarmed, non-military policeman?

Though she escaped the revolutions which engulfed other European states in 1830 and 1848, England was, nevertheless, wracked with internal disorder during the 1830s and the 'Hungry Forties'. Constables of the Metropolitan Police, even though their first duty was said to be the prevention of crime, invariably found themselves drafted into the provinces to deal with large-scale disorder. Such deployment led to a remonstrance being drafted by the parish vestry of St Leonard's, Shoreditch, in October 1839 'against the use of the Metropolitan Police Force in the country, leaving the Metropolitan parishes less protected than heretofore, and interfering with the police of the provincial towns, and the old constitutional plan of quelling riots by magistrates reading the Riot Act, using the local civil force, and if not sufficient, to call to their aid the military'.[35]

35. Quoted in F.C. Mather, *Public Order in the Age of the Chartists* (Manchester: University Press, 1959), p. 107.

But such considerations, and such protests, did not deter the Home Office from sending squads from London to deal with riots against the New Poor Law, the threat of Chartist disorder, and the uprising of Rebecca and her children in South Wales. In case of actual riot the Metropolitan Police squads were generally ordered against a crowd before soldiers, but they were also often deployed alongside the military and worked closely with them. George Martin, the Superintendent of G Division of the Metropolitan Police, gave the 1853 select committee details of his postings to Huddersfield and Dewsbury during election disorders in 1837, to Birmingham in 1839, and to South Wales in 1843. On each occasion, he explained, the police had worked alongside the military; in South Wales small groups of soldiers and police – the latter in civilian clothes – were quartered together in small, suspect or endangered communities.[36]

Superintendent Martin believed that policemen were far preferable to soldiers when dealing with riots. In words similar to those used by Chadwick in the Royal Commission's Report of 1839, he explained to the committee that a policeman 'could handle a truncheon with one hand, whereas a soldier's musket is as much as he can manage, and lends him no assistance . . . if a soldier is called upon to act he is obliged to charge or fire, and by doing so he stands a great chance of killing the parties, and cannot apprehend them very well'.[37] But Martin also considered that it was important to have local policemen dealing with riots, rather than men brought in from outside. A major problem in the confrontation in the Birmingham Bull Ring in July 1839 was that the Metropolitan Police had not been in the town for an hour before they went into action. A local force would have known likely troublemakers and consequently, Martin maintained, 'a great many men who threw brickbats at my men, would not have done so if they had known they would be likely to be recognised'.[38] Perhaps Martin had rather too sanguine

---

36. *PP* 1852–53 (715) XXXVI, *Second Report of the Select Committee on Police*, qq. 3727–93; see also David J.V. Jones, *Rebecca's Children: A Study of Rural Society, Crime and Protest* (Oxford: Clarendon Press, 1989), pp. 236, 242, 360.

37. *PP* 1852–53 (715) XXXVI, *Second Report of the Select Committee on Police*, qq. 3766–8. In 1839 Chadwick wrote: 'Of the military force, it may be observed that the private soldier has both hands occupied with a musket, with which his efficient action is by the infliction of death by firing or stabbing. The constable or policeman, whose weapon is a truncheon, or, on desperate occasions the cutlass, has one hand at liberty to seize and hold his prisoner, whilst with the other he represses by force.' *PP* 1839 (169) XIX, *First Report of the Commissioners Appointed to Enquire as to the Best Means of Establishing a Constabulary Force in the Counties of England and Wales*, p. 83.

38. *PP* 1852–53 (715) XXXVI, *Second Report of the Select Committee on Police*, qq. 3781–2.

a view of who policemen would be able to recognise in this sort of situation; nevertheless by the end of the 1840s the government was becoming increasingly reluctant to dispatch Metropolitan Police riot squads to the provinces where there were no local professional constabulary. In January 1850 the magistrates in Lincoln feared that a mass meeting called to protest about high rents and the behaviour of county landowners would result in disorder; they requested 'at least 20 Metropolitan Police' to assist their special constables. The Home Office refused to help, believing 'it would lead to numerous similar applications, which it would be impossible to comply with, without great inconvenience to the public service'.[39] Five years later Palmerston responded curtly to a similar request from Berkshire; if the county Bench was not prepared to establish their own police force, then 'they must abide by the Consequences of their choice'.[40]

The fear of revolution in England declined at least from the end of the 1840s, but the advent of Louis Napoleon Bonaparte first as President of the French Second Republic, then as Emperor, reawoke concerns about French aspirations of military glory and hegemony in Europe. Thus while the government was less and less inclined to authorise squads of the Metropolitan Police to be dispatched into the provinces, there were those who saw the need for a police system to be established throughout the country as a potential auxiliary force in case of invasion. In March 1852 the Earl of Ellenborough told the House of Lords that 'one reason why he wished for the establishment of a uniform system of police throughout the country was in order that there might be a uniformity of protection when those who would have to defend us from the enemy were withdrawn'.[41] Later that year Earl Grey was critical of the proposed new Militia Bill on the grounds that it was simply a resurrection of the system used during the Napoleonic Wars; the money would be better spent, he insisted, on establishing 'a general constabulary armed and trained on the Irish model' which would provide increased security in the event of war as well as being useful in time of peace.[42] Chief constables of the county constabularies thought along similar lines. One of the papers which Captain McHardy presented to the

39. HO 45.3133.
40. HO 45.6236, Palmerston to Hopkins, 5 Jan. 1855; and see Mather, *Public Order*, p. 109.
41. *Hansard*, CXIX, 18 Mar. 1852, col. 1227.
42. Ibid., CXXII, 15 June 1852, cols 748–9.

select committee of 1853 was a 'Scheme for an Efficient Constabulary and Defensive Force throughout England and Wales'. McHardy's national police, in keeping with his earlier proposal to the Essex magistrates for their county force, was designed to assist the coastguards in the prevention of smuggling. But by now, with a dozen years of police experience behind him, he had developed his ideas further:

> A well-trained constabulary of one constable to a population of 1,000 would afford an efficient and respectable defensive force of 14,000 men (exclusive of the Metropolitan Police), which, in cases of emergency, could be augmented and armed, as may appear most desirable; and by the Government directing at its pleasure . . . the police to enrol and train, at the respective petty sessional divisional stations, such numbers for the militia as it may deem expedient, not exceeding a limited number to the population, as by enrolling five men out of every 1,000, a force of 70,000 would be raised making, with the standing constabulary of 14,000, a total of 84,000, which would be more than double the number authorised by the present Militia Act . . . the expense would be considerably less than any other system; and the men so enrolled would, from being brought in contact with the constabulary, render it more efficient, and afford a source from which to complete or augment the constabulary or standing army . . .[43]

Captain W.C. Harris, the Chief Constable of Hampshire, had similar ideas. A former light infantry officer himself, he believed that his constables were 'peculiarly adapted to act as light troops'; and training his men in the use of arms 'would not only tend to the preservation of the peace of the country, but it would form a great element of national defence'. He did not consider that the arming of his men would have a detrimental effect on relations with the public, though he felt that the arms should only be issued 'on the occasion of a threatened invasion, or when some serious disturbance of the public peace has taken place, or is apprehended, when an Order in Council might be given'.[44]

There were already instances of policemen going about their duties armed. Inspectors of the Metropolitan Police from the beginning were permitted to carry pocket pistols. Some of those in South Wales during the Rebecca troubles carried firearms. But edged

43. *PP* 1852–53 (715) XXXVI, *Second Report of the Select Committee on Police*, Appendix No. 7, p. 154.

44. *PP* 1852–53 (603) XXXVI, *First Report of the Select Committee on Police*, qq. 166, 217.

weapons were more common than firearms. Exercise with swords was usual in the training and drilling of both the Metropolitan Police and the rural constabularies. Police constables patrolling beats in areas reputed to be particularly dangerous, such as an urban rookery or a lonely rural district, were issued with cutlasses; and cutlasses were also issued when the police had to deal with a serious disorder. The select committee of 1853 did not recommend any link between the police and the army or militia or any training in the use of weaponry, but this did not prevent chief constables and some local police committees from continuing to press the measures.[45] A vice-chairman of the Cheshire Bench had told the 1853 select committee that his principal objection to the Rural Police Act of 1839 was that the men were uniformed, yet by December 1859 the chairman of the Cheshire Police Committee was contemplating a significant degree of militarisation by wondering whether there 'would be any objection raised by the Home Office to the Police force of this Co. being instructed in the use of the Rifle, and if not, whether the Rifles could be supplied to the men from the Police Rate'. The Chief Constables of Cumberland and Westmorland and of Kent made similar enquiries. In August 1860 McHardy, now a rear admiral, sent the Home Office a plan 'for rendering the National Constabulary numerically efficient, and a powerful auxiliary defensive Artillery, Rocket and Rifle Corps, capable of being at least doubled, in 24 hours, by enrolling and training one Volunteer for each member of the Constabulary'; the plan included the provision of breach-loading rifles for the police and artillery pieces for police stations.[46]

The restraining influence in all of this was the Home Office. In 1844 the quarter sessions in East Suffolk authorised their chief constable to write to the Home Office requesting that his men be supplied with firearms 'in consequence of the very disturbed state of this division'; agrarian outrages in the county had already left one constable dead and a farmer shot and wounded, and there were 'Incendiary Fires occurring almost every night'. The Home Office refused the request; and the quarter sessions could only authorise

---

45. Clive Emsley, ' "The thump of wood on a swede turnip": police violence in nineteenth-century England', *CJH* 6 (1985), 125–49. For the use of firearms during the Rebecca disorders see Jones, *Rebecca's Children*, pp. 216, 285. For sword exercise as drill see *PP* 1852–53 (603) XXXVI, *First Report of the Select Committee on Police*, q. 168; *PP* 1852–53 (715) XXXVI, *Second Report of the Select Committee on Police*, q. 2869.

46. *PP* 1852–52 (603) XXXVI, *First Report of the Select Committee on Police*, q. 2276; HO 45.6811, passim.

the police to patrol with cutlasses.[47] The requests and proposals of 1859 and 1860 were received in Whitehall with increasing exasperation. The initial letter from Chester was endorsed by Horatio Waddington: 'this question is one of the most serious nature and seems to be well worthy of *Cabinet* deliberation. It has been frequently suggested to organise the Metropolitan Police *militairement*, and always repudiated. It seems to me highly unconstitutional.' The Chief Constable of Kent's plan, received a month later, was endorsed more tersely by Sir George Cornewall Lewis: 'This gentleman has very grand ideas. I wish these constables would think more of their staves and less of rifles. Same answer I suppose as to Chester.'[48]

A new level of efficiency?

The argument of traditional police history is that the new police, based on the metropolitan model, were a marked improvement on their parochial predecessors. Of course, if the old police had all been like Dogberry and Elbow, and if the new police had all been the paragons intended by Chadwick, then there would be no problem; but such was not the case.

Long before the creation of the Metropolitan Police, good night watchmen had got to know their beats and the people who lived on them; they were observant and, on occasions, it was their watchfulness which led to the arrest of offenders.[49] The new police extended this system to urban parishes where it had not been known before and they introduced a measure of uniformity, but whether they thus deterred burglars and street robbers it is impossible to say. There were those who expressed doubts. At a town council meeting in Birmingham in September 1842, for example, a councillor protested that: 'What the town wanted was an effective thief-taking police, and not merely what could be considered little better than lads parading up and down the streets. The present force could not prevent robberies taking place.'[50] This was probably unfair,

47. HO 45.7487, Chief Constable of East Suffolk to Sir George Grey, 7 Oct. 1863.
48. HO 45.6811.
49. Clive Emsley, *Crime and Society in England, 1750–1900* 2nd edn (London: Longman, 1996), pp. 219–20. Michael Weaver suggests that, while the pre-police watchmen in Birmingham received criticism, they were probably not as bad as many reformers maintained: Michael Weaver, 'The new science of policing: crime and the Birmingham Police Force, 1839–1842', *Albion* 26 (1994), 289–308, at 292.
50. Quoted in Weaver, 'New science of policing', 302.

and prompted not a little by the fact that the Birmingham force was not yet under local control. Nevertheless, it remains true that the prevention of crime cannot be measured; and, as Edwin Corbet told the 1853 select committee, 'you cannot apprehend a man that is going to commit a burglary'.[51] However, the new police were able to set about establishing a new level of order and decorum on the streets, partly because of their numbers, but also because this was a relatively simple task, though often unpopular with the working classes who passed much of their leisure time in the street. The advent of the new police in a district invariably resulted in an increase in arrests for petty offences and misdemeanours: street traders were ordered to move along, as were groups of loitering youths, prostitutes and vagrants; street games and street gambling were stopped; drunks were dragged to the police cells to sleep off their inebriation; fighting drunks were dragged with more force. Traffic was better controlled; carters, cab and omnibus drivers were forbidden from loitering; 'furious' driving, drunk driving, and driving horse-drawn vehicles without reins were all subject to police action. Yet again, during the 1830s and 1840s it was not just the members of the new constabularies who were doing this: so too were those police established under the 1833 Lighting and Watching Act; and Sir Robert Sheffield, a Lincolnshire magistrate giving evidence to the 1853 select committee, insisted that the superintending constables in his county were equally effective.[52]

The new police were much more useful in the suppression of riot and serious disorder than the old parochial constables and the special constables sworn in for an emergency. They were also less likely than soldiers to cause loss of life in such incidents. Yet the scale of deaths in riots suppressed by the army in the eighteenth and early nineteenth centuries should not be overemphasised: the massacre of St George's Fields in 1768, the Gordon Riots of 1780, and the Peterloo massacre of 1819 made an impact, at least in part, because of both the rarity of such incidents and the loss of life. Army officers were well aware of the impact of musket fire or of a cavalry charge on crowds and such actions were not, as Chadwick and others suggested, the only resort of soldiers engaged on riot duty, but always the very last.[53] Probably the mortality rate among rioters did decline with the regular deployment of policemen against

51. *PP* 1852–53 (603) XXXVI, *First Report of the Select Committee on Police*, q. 2277.
52. Ibid., qq. 593, 610.
53. Tony Hayter, *The Army and the Crowd in Mid-Georgian England* (London: Macmillan, 1978), Part III, passim.

them. Sometimes it was the sheer courage of the policemen which saved rioters: in a confrontation with rioting colliers in Wigan during October 1853 a police sergeant in charge of a squad of ten men from the Lancashire Constabulary 'steadily refused to use firearms, but said his men should stand at the gates as long as they could hold them'.[54] But police tactics were not always efficient or effective, and sometimes the innocent were hurt by what can only be described as fighting-mad policemen. Such was the case with the Cold Bath Fields riot in London in 1833, even though the only fatality here was a police constable; the select committee investigating the incident congratulated the police on handling the situation, but went on to note that 'excitement and irritation' had prompted some constables to an 'undue exercise of power'.[55] On at least two occasions during the Chartist turbulence of 1848 Metropolitan Police constables appear to have lost control and inflicted savage beatings on both Chartist demonstrators and anyone else who, innocently, got in the way. In much the same way that a coroner's jury brought in a verdict of 'justifiable homicide' on the unfortunate PC Culley after the Cold Bath Fields trouble in 1833, so, in 1848, another coroner's jury refused to accept direction and found that a Chartist weaver had died, not as a result of a fever, but because of blows inflicted by the police.[56] Complaints about police brutality in dealing with crowds were to recur throughout the century.[57]

There was collusion with offenders as well as corruption among the old police, some of which was the result of the payment of rewards. Yet the problems were not eradicated simply by the creation of the new constabularies. Metropolitan PC Charles King was sentenced to fourteen years' transportation in 1855 for robberies committed with a gang of pickpockets; there appears to have been insufficient evidence to proceed against PC Jesse 'Juicy Lips' Jeapes, but he was dismissed after fifteen years' service.[58] The parliamentary select committee on public prosecutors which met in 1855 heard evidence of policemen overclaiming on their expenses and,

54. *The Times*, 2 Nov. 1853, p. 12. The guns were not in the hands of the police but the colliery owner and officials; the crowd eventually withdrew when one of the latter fired a shot.
55. PP 1833 (718) XIII, *Select Committe on Cold Bath Fields Meeting*, p. 3.
56. David Goodway, *London Chartism, 1838–1848* (Cambridge: CUP, 1982), pp. 83–4, 120–4.
57. See, *inter alia*, Emsley, 'The thump of wood on a swede turnip', 126–9, 141–2; Phillip Thurmond Smith, *Policing Victorian London: Political Policing, Public Order, and the London Metropolitan Police* (Westport, Conn.: Greenwood Press, 1985), pp. 136–7; and see below, pp. 66–9.
58. HO 45.6099.

more seriously, colluding with, and receiving money from, attornies for pursuing vexatious prosecutions. The Chief Constable of Staffordshire reported having dismissed men for this offence, and believed that he had put a stop to it. But John Hughes Preston, a solicitor employed by the government to examine the expense of criminal prosecutions on the Oxford Circuit, had no doubt that it still continued, and he lamented having found fairly generally in his experience 'on the part of attorneys, justices' clerks, and the police, a desire to augment, to the greatest possible extent, the costs of criminal prosecution'.[59]

The constables of the new police may not have been too old and lame for their tasks as the traditional histories commonly portray the pre-police night watch, yet their attraction to drink was a major discipline problem. In 1834 Rowan and Mayne admitted that four out of the five men they had dismissed from the Metropolitan Police were guilty of drinking offences, and every other force appears to have had the same problem.[60]

The shift from an old style of policing to a new one was far more gradual than much traditional police history has allowed; and many of the faults and problems attributed to the old system were to be found with the new. Yet by the 1850s the new English 'Bobby' was already acquiring an affectionate image in the perception of many of the respectable and propertied classes. 'It is evident', declared *Punch* in the year of the Great Exhibition,

> that the police are beginning to take that place in the affections of the people – we don't mean the cooks and housemaids only, but the people at large – that the soldiers and sailors used to occupy. In the old war-time there was a sort of enthusiasm for the 'blue jackets,' the defenders of the country; but in these happier days of peace, the blue coats – the defenders of order – are becoming the national favourites.
>
> Veterans, whose boast it used to be to have distinguished themselves at the lines of Torres Vedras, find their glories eclipsed by those whose pride it is to have been present and to have performed good service at the lines of omnibuses and cabs going to and from the Crystal Palace. The taking of a foreign fort seems to sink into insignificance before the taking of a refractory cabman's number . . .
>
> Military engineering has been nothing to the engineering difficulties

59. *PP* 1854–55 (481) XII, *Select Committee on Public Prosecutors*, qq. 1144–68, 1218, 1294–5, 1319–24; quotation at q. 1144.
60. *PP* 1834 (600) XVI, *Select Committee on the Police of the Metropolis*, qq. 107–8; and see also, *inter alia*, Philips, *Crime and Authority*, p. 68; Swift, *Police Reform in Early Victorian York*, pp. 23–4.

that have been surmounted by our police force in effecting the passage of the crossings, and carrying elderly ladies with their stores and baggage from one side of the way to the other. Every one has been charmed during the Great Exhibition by the mode in which this truly civil power has been rendered effective; and if England expected, she has not been disappointed in the expectation, that every policeman should be every day on duty.[61]

The Times, without the satirical slant of *Punch*, hailed the new policeman as the representative of 'that unseen mysterious agency', the English law. '[T]he sworn professional policeman, attired as such, and acting in a known and recognised capacity, . . . exerts the strength of a dozen rioters, and paralyses the opposition by the power which is felt to be at his back.'[62] A writer in the *Quarterly Review* stressed the difference between the policeman on his beat, as a representative of the law, and the policeman off-duty, once again a human being:

> Amid the bustle of Piccadilly or the roar of Oxford Street, P.C.X. 59 stalks along, an institution rather than a man. We seem to have no more hold of his personality than we could possibly get hold of his coat buttoned up to the throttling-point. Go, however, to the section-house . . . and there you no longer see policemen, but men . . . They are positively laughing with each other![63]

These commentators were largely constructing their image around the Metropolitan Police constable, which prompted some feeling in the provinces. Superintendent Jaggard of the Cambridge Borough Police noted that the Metropolitan force was 'held up as an example' and believed that its members 'think we know nothing of the Law or duty'. He let his anger and annoyance show when the senior officers of London's M Division appeared to ignore his letters and preferred the word of 'a Thief's Advocate' to one of his sergeants armed with a magistrate's warrant: 'it would be done different even in Cambridge'.[64] There remained considerable differences in organisation and appearance between the Metropolitan Police and its provincial cousins: in Lancashire and Staffordshire, for example, the men wore uniforms of rifleman green, and in some of the boroughs the 'uniform' could be a mixture of patterns;

61. *Punch*, July–Dec. 1851, p. 173.   62. *The Times*, 7 Dec. 1853, p. 8.

63. A. Wynter, 'The police and the thieves', *Quarterly Review* XCIX (1856), 160–200, at p. 171.

64. Cambs. PA Cambridge Borough, Police Letter Book 1849–52, Jaggard to Bret, Det. Officer, Bow Lane, City, 1 Sept. 1852; see also to J. Easden, Clerk to the Justices, Cambridge, 20 July 1852.

and patrolling a London street, however 'rough' the neighbourhood, was different from trudging to conference points over muddy, country tracks. Yet it was the Metropolitan model which best suited the Victorian view of both policemen and social development. Within 25 years of his first manifestation, the English 'Bobby' was becoming, in the perception of the propertied and respectable classes of Victorian society, a pillar of the constitutional and legal structure of that society. Victorian Englishmen of the 1850s looked smugly upon their continental neighbours who were emerging from the trauma of the Year of Revolutions and still trying to catch up with Britain's buoyant new industrial economy. In the 1850s Victorian society was successful and stable; it was just entering on that period described aptly as 'the age of equipoise'.[65] The new police appeared to have played a significant, and peculiarly English, role in the recent development of that society, suppressing disorder with, it seemed, the minimum of violence, and successfully guarding its celebration of the gospel of work and progress at the Crystal Palace. Part of the success of Victorian society was rubbing off on its new guardians.

65. W.L. Burn, *The Age of Equipoise. A Study of the Mid-Victorian Generation* (London: Allen and Unwin, 1964).

CHAPTER FOUR

Policing in Victorian England

Domestic missionary and general factotum

The new police had originated in fears of crime and disorder, and in a general desire among the rulers of England to establish and maintain a new level of order within society. Different incidents in different towns and counties were the occasion of different experiments in policing. The first experience that many provincial districts had of the new, uniformed police was the arrival and deployment of a Metropolitan Police riot squad in the 1830s or 1840s. The Victorian middle class liked to think of their society as civilised and stable, yet there were plenty of 'riotous Victorians'[1] in the second half of the nineteenth century and from 1850 the police were generally recognised as the first line of defence when a problem of public order arose. The use of the police in this role commonly prompted accusations of their brutality, militarisation, and partiality.

Colonel Rowan had retired in 1850 and, after an unhappy period in which Captain William Hay was appointed as a second commissioner, Sir Richard Mayne assumed sole command of the Metropolitan Police in 1855. Mayne grew increasingly autocratic and drew considerable criticism from the press. He opposed Lord Robert Grosvenor's bill to put increased restrictions on Sunday trading in 1855: he feared that the enforcement of such legislation would provoke widespread confrontations between the police and the people. In the event it was demonstrations against the bill as it was being discussed in Parliament which brought serious rioting to the

---

1. I borrow the term from Donald Richter, *Riotous Victorians* (Athens, Ohio: Ohio University Press, 1981), though I suspect that he overstresses the good-humoured nature of many of the rioters.

streets of London in the summer of 1855. Police brutality in suppressing the disorder was widely reported by the newspapers, and the subsequent Royal Commission made a veiled criticism of Mayne with its suggestion that a high-ranking officer should have been directing the police on the spot.[2] Eleven years later demonstrations and disorder in Hyde Park in favour of parliamentary reform brought further adverse comment about Mayne's control of the situation and the brutal behaviour of some of his men. Prominent among the critics was the satirical weekly *Fun* which printed 'AN UNRE-PORTED CASE' involving one Richard Mayne who was charged with 'assaulting the Public while in the execution of its duty'. Mayne was described as 'the leader of an organised gang of ruffians, who for some time have annoyed all respectable people by "playing at soldiers" on various occasions in public places. The miscreants wear helmets, and commit other absurdities'.[3] In 1868 200 of Mayne's men deployed in Bromley, Kent, were accused of partiality towards the Tories during the general election. A 78-year-old man, William Walter, was trampled to death in a police baton charge. Magistrates refused to listen to complaints against the police in the ensuing prosecution of twenty local inhabitants for assaulting the police. The coroner who enquired into Walter's death reacted similarly, declaring that 'the police are a body of men whose duty it is to keep the peace and when soldiers or police were brought into a town, they came to keep the peace and not to break it'. The superintendent in charge of the police during the incident admitted that his men 'might, perhaps, have been provoked to behave a little roughly', but he added that 'they had not come down here to be laughed at and he did not want to be told his duty'. A petition to the Home Office from local inhabitants for an investigation into the events surrounding Walter's death appears to have fallen on deaf ears.[4]

Mayne died in office at the end of 1868, and close on two decades of relative peace from serious crowd disorder in London lulled his successor, Colonel Edmund Henderson, into a false sense of security. The trouble which developed from a mass meeting of the unemployed in Trafalgar Square in Febrary 1886 reawoke fears of

2. Brian Harrison, 'The Sunday trading riots', *HJ* VIII (1965), 219–45; Phillip Thurmond Smith, *Policing Victorian London: Political Policing, Public Order and the London Metropolitan Police* (Westport, Conn.: Greenwood Press, 1985), ch. 6.

3. *Fun*, 4 Aug. 1866, p. 208, and see also pp. 207 and 209. For a general survey of the police handling of the reform riots of 1866–67 see Smith, *Policing Victorian London*, ch. 8.

4. Carolyn Conley, *The Unwritten Law: Criminal Justice in Victorian Kent* (New York: OUP, 1991), pp. 38–41.

mob violence; the clumsy preparations of the police prompted Henderson to resign and led to his replacement by a strict military disciplinarian, Sir Charles Warren. Warren set out to reorganise and drill his new command on military lines; he systematically revised *Field Exercise and Evolutions of Infantry* into the *Drill Instruction – Metropolitan Police.*[5] It is indicative of the concern felt in the Home Office about the residuum, about socialist meetings and demonstrations by the unemployed, that the new commissioner was allowed to continue along his chosen path; Warren, however, always felt that he should be less constrained by Home Office officials and that his relationship with the Home Secretary and his civil servants should be more like that of the military commander of an overseas expedition with the War Office. On 13 November 1887 – subsequently labelled 'Bloody Sunday' – Warren's blue-coated infantry, backed by two squadrons of Life Guards and two companies of Foot Guards, were hurled against the mass meeting called by the Metropolitan Radical Federation in Trafalgar Square. The assault was hailed by much of the press and by most of the respectable classes as a triumph over the dangerous classes, but Warren's initial prohibition of meetings in Trafalgar Square became the subject of much complex legal debate, while his militarisation of the Metropolitan Police began to raise increasing disquiet. In November 1888 he published an article in *Murray's Magazine*, in which he objected to 'hostile criticism' of the Metropolitan Police and particularly the suggestion that the force was being militarised. Foolishly, Warren then went on to criticise politicians:

> It is to be deplored that successive Governments have not had the courage to make a stand against the more noisy section of the people representing a small minority, and have given way before tumultuous proceedings which have exercised a terrorism over peaceful and law-abiding citizens, and it is still more to be regretted that ex-Ministers, while in opposition, have not hesitated to embarrass those in power by smiling on the insurgent mob.

The article had not been approved by the Home Secretary, and the outcry was such that Warren resigned on 1 December.[6]

5. Brian Lewis, 'The Home Office, the Metropolitan Police and civil disorder, 1886–1893', M.Phil., University of Leeds, 1975, pp. 65–7.
6. Sir Charles Warren, 'The police of the metropolis', *Murray's Magazine* IV (1888), 577–94, quotation at 578. For the events of 1886–87 see Victor Bailey, 'The Metropolitan Police, the Home Office and the threat of outcast London', in Victor Bailey (ed.), *Policing and Punishment in Nineteenth-Century Britain* (London: Croom Helm, 1981).

In the provinces the deployment of police to deal with disorder brought similar accusations to those levelled at the Metropolitan Police. Since the county constabularies were generally much larger than most of the urban forces it was their constables who were often called out to handle riots, though there was some initial doubt in the Home Office as to the legality of requesting and deploying police from one force in the jurisdiction of another;[7] and some magistrates were worried about reducing the general level of police protection within their jurisdiction in order to handle a temporary problem in one particular area, especially when the latter was not normally under their supervision.[8] In February 1862 the Lincolnshire County force was deployed during election disorders in the city of Lincoln; in some quarters the 'rurals' were accused of brutality towards 'respectable tradesmen, women, and even children', and their withdrawal from the city was the cue for a ferocious attack to be launched on the house of the mayor which was only quietened by the arrival of troops.[9] Election troubles in Nottingham in November 1885 saw the deployment of men from the Nottinghamshire and Derbyshire County forces and the Birmingham City Police to assist the borough constables; the ferocity of the police was such that the Nottingham Watch Committee mounted an enquiry chaired by the Recorder of Lincoln. The Watch Committee eventually concluded that 'the police disobeyed instructions as to the use of truncheons and behaved intemperately'; the crumb of comfort that they could claim was that it had been 'Derbyshire and Birmingham officers, together with a few Nottingham men, [who] drew their staves and used them most improperly'. But many respectable people in Nottingham were unhappy with the findings.[10] At an early stage in the North Lancashire cotton strike

7. HO 45.6640, correspondence relating to a request from the magistrates at Guildford to have members of the Surrey Constabulary in their town to assist the borough force in handling the expected trouble on Guy Fawkes Day 1858. There was similar correspondence in the following year as to whether it was legal for police to be sent to Birmingham to assist the Carnarvonshire Constabulary in policing visitors taking advantage of excursion trains: see HO 45.6808.

8. HO 45.6750, correspondence relating to the use of men from the Worcestershire Constabulary in a colliers' strike in Dudley in April 1859; HO 45.7326, correspondence relating to the suppression of a riot in Birkenhead in October 1862 by the borough police assisted by men from the Cheshire Constabulary and supported by a reserve of infantrymen – the magistrates of Birkenhead had requested help from the Liverpool Police which had 1,000 men, but the Liverpool magistrates were reluctant to reduce the number of men available in their city.

9. HO 45.7319.

10. *The Times*, 15 Jan. 1886, p. 6, and 16 Jan., p. 9; see also 9 Dec. 1885, p. 5, 15 Dec., p. 5, 17 Dec., p. 5, and 13 Jan. 1886, p. 5.

of 1878 the police were condemned for brutality, though it seems probable that they were only giving as good as they got.[11] Questions were raised in Parliament about the partiality of the Cumberland Police and their general preparedness for trouble when an Orangemen's parade on Cleator Moor erupted into violence in July 1884.[12] Three years later a political meeting in Norwich involving Lord Salisbury brought more parliamentary questions about police brutality and partiality. '[T]hese charges of misconduct against the police were becoming monotonous', lamented R. Cunninghame Graham, the member for Lanark, North West, and he requested the Home Secretary to set up an enquiry. The Home Secretary's response was the same as that of his predecessor in 1884: the police were agents of local government and were not under Home Office jurisdiction.[13] Partiality was raised again in Parliament when the Durham County police were deployed to protect bailiffs involved in evictions during a strike at Silksworth colliery in February 1891; while a truncheon charge by a squad of 50 men prompted a pastiche of Tennyson's 'Charge of the Light Brigade' in the *Sunderland Daily Echo*:

> Flash'd all their batons bare,
> Flash'd as they turned in air,
> Thumping at back-skulls there,
> Mauling away because
>   Someone had blunder'd
> Pounding at ev'ry head,
> Quiet folks' blood was shed;
> Women and children
> Reeled from the blows that sped,
>   Moaning and sunder'd
> Then they marched back again
>   Gallant half hundred![14]

There is some debate over whether or not English society was growing less riotous during the Victorian period; the traditional police historians have tended to argue that this was, indeed, the case and that the police played a significant role in reducing the

11. J.E. King, ' "We could eat the police!" Popular violence in the North Lancashire cotton strike of 1878', *Victorian Studies* 28 (1985), 439–71.
12. *Hansard*, CCXCI, 14 July 1884, cols 896–7; 15 July, cols 1118–26; 17 July, cols 1410–13; ibid., CCXCII, 12 Aug. 1884, col. 613.
13. Ibid., CCCXVIII, 4 Aug. 1887, cols 1139–40; ibid., CCCXIX, 16 Aug., cols 675–6.
14. *Sunderland Daily Echo*, 28 Feb. 1891; for the parliamentary arguments see, *inter alia*, *Hansard*, CLI, 5 Mar. 1891, cols 237–9 and 269–97, and 16 Mar., cols 1073–5.

incidence of riot.[15] But theirs is a view first, which tends often to ignore the rationality behind a riotous demonstration, perceiving it solely as a problem of law and order, and second and more seriously, which tends to ignore that it often takes two sides to ensure that a demonstration becomes a riot. Disorder in the Victorian years could create the occasional brief moral panic, as in the case of the Trafalgar Square troubles of 1886 and 1887. But home secretaries were prepared to leave the maintenance of order in the hands of local government and local police forces, partly because of the strong traditions of local government in the country, but also because after 1850 the general social order of Victorian England did not seem under threat.

Deployment against rioters, whether or not it is possible to maintain that there was an overall decrease in riotous behaviour, was a relatively rare occurrence for Victorian policemen. The new Metropolitan Police constables had been informed in 1829 that their principal task was 'the prevention of crime'; and this was reiterated in the instructions given to men joining the provincial forces.[16] Moral panics, such as that generated by the fear of 'garotting' in the mid-1850s and early 1860s and by Jack the Ripper in 1888, blips in the crime statistics, sometimes caused by a new way of categorising offences, or a spate of unsolved crimes played on and magnified out of proportion by the press, could all lead to criticism of the police.[17] They could also lead to angry ratepayers demanding more, and better, police protection for their money. Towards the end of 1868, spurred on by a motion discussed in the Marylebone Vestry, a group of London vestries demanded to know the whereabouts of the 2,000 extra policemen promised following an increase in the police rate. 'Each vestry', explained the *East London Observer*, 'is prepared to aver that its particular locality is the worst guarded in

15. See, *inter alia*, T.A. Critchley, *A History of Police in England and Wales* rev. edn (London: Constable, 1978), p. 163.

16. The *New Police Instructions* were printed in *The Times*, 25 Sept. 1829; for similar instructions to provincial constables see, *inter alia*, Gloucs. RO Q.Y2.1.1, Chief Constable's General Order Book, 1840; Staffs. RO C.PC Box VI, *Rules and Regulations for the Government and Guidance of the Staffordshire Constabulary*, 1859, p. 3.

17. Jennifer Davis, 'The London garotting panic of 1862: a moral panic and the creation of a criminal class in mid-Victorian England', in V.A.C. Gatrell, Bruce Lenman and Geoffrey Parker (eds), *Crime and the Law: The Social History of Crime in Western Europe since 1500* (London: Europa, 1980); R. Sindall, *Street Violence in the Nineteenth Century: Media Panic or Real Danger* (Leicester: University Press, 1990); for criticism of the Metropolitan Police because of an apparent increase in crime caused by new categorisation see Clive Emsley, *Crime and Society in England 1750–1900* 2nd edn (London: Longman, 1996), pp. 27–8.

the metropolis – the plain fact being that, except in the favoured parts of the West-end, where are stored the silver forks and spoons . . . the popular joke about the invisibility of a policeman is a dull and sober reality.'[18] A meeting of delegates from the vestries met in Marylebone in January 1869 and petitioned the Home Secretary, lamenting that there had never been a parliamentary enquiry into the efficiency of the Metropolitan Police and urging a degree of local control over the force.[19] Almost 30 years later delegates from the South London vestries gathered in St George's Vestry Hall 'to call attention to the lack of police protection . . . the recent desperate assaults in Blackfriars Road, the frequent watch-snatching and highway robberies, the pilfering from shops, and the numerous burglaries'.[20] Nor was this invisibility on the part of the police simply a metropolitan problem; in March 1877, for example, the superintendent of M Division of the Devon Constabulary noted in his Order Book: 'I have frequent complaints when at Bideford that the Ratepayers see no Policeman at Abbotsham . . . I cannot see any reason why Abbotsham could not be visited at least once a week.'[21] Yet outside of these periodic concerns and panics the overall trend in the crime statistics after 1850 was downward. This trend was recognised by contemporaries. The police probably contributed to it, and they certainly claimed some of the credit for it. There were even a few who looked forward to a time when the criminal classes would be virtually eliminated. 'Given the power,' declared the Chief Constable of Chester in 1873, 'I really see no great difficulty, if not in stamping out professional criminals, at least in reducing their numbers very materially.'[22]

What the new police were especially good at was apprehending those who committed petty street offences; perhaps also their presence on the streets reduced the incidence of street robbery. They were less successful at preventing burglary, an offence which significantly increased in the judicial statistics in the second half of the nineteenth century, unlike other forms of property crime. Detective policemen began to appear in popular literature from the 1850s, notably with Inspector Bucket in Dickens's *Bleak House* and the courageous master of disguise Jack Hawkshaw in Tom Taylor's

18. *East London Observer*, 5 Dec. 1868.   19. *The Times*, 14 Jan. 1869, p. 12.
20. *Justice of the Peace* LXI (1897), 23 Oct., 681.
21. Devon and Cornwall PA Devon Constabulary, M Division Order Book, 1865–1910, 15 Mar. 1877.
22. UCL, Chadwick MSS 16, Folder 'POLICE Memoranda etc (1870s)'; for the pattern of crime see V.A.C. Gatrell, 'The decline of theft and violence in Victorian and Edwardian England', in Gatrell, Lenman and Parker (eds), *Crime and the Law*.

melodrama *The Ticket-of-Leave Man*; but detection, in the eyes of the police themselves, took second place to prevention. Concern about policemen patrolling in plain clothes still existed, and, in the traditional interpretation of police history, never more forcefully than in the mind of Sir Richard Mayne. Gathorne Hardy, Home Secretary in the Derby–Disraeli administration of 1866 to 1868, found Mayne's views on detectives 'quite inapplicable to the time and the circumstances'. Hardy's pressing problem was the terrorist threat from the Fenians and at 'a very secret interview' he experienced 'a sample of Mayne's police in plain clothes. We wondered at seeing a crowd, but found it was drawn by the constables meant to protect us walking up and down the street, and recognised for what they were by wearing the pattern police boots which rogues and roughs knew so well.'[23] However, Mayne was rather more sympathetic to detective policing than Hardy's picture, and that of the traditional historians, allows. It was, after all, Mayne who, in June 1842, persuaded the then Home Secretary, Sir James Graham, to authorise the appointment of two inspectors and six sergeants for detective work.[24] What appears to have been decisive in checking the growth of detectives within the Metropolitan Police were Home Office concerns about public reactions and the feared difficulties of supervising and controlling detectives. The scares about convicts released on tickets of leave in the mid-1860s acted as a boost to the idea of detective police and in 1868 a departmental committee was appointed to investigate policing. The committee, urged on by Mayne, recommended an increase in the detective force.[25] Mayne's death deprived him of seeing the recommendation carried into effect; it also spared him having to witness the scandal which, within a decade, rocked the newly expanded Detective Department. In 1877 three out of the four chief inspectors in the department were found guilty, at the Old Bailey, of corruption. The case underlined all the concerns about detectives, particularly the fears that low-paid, unsupervised men, working in close proximity, even if ostensibly in opposition, to criminals, could easily be corrupted. The Home Secretary, R.A. Cross appointed a confidential departmental commission to enquire into 'the state, discipline and organisation'

23. A.E. Gathorne Hardy (ed.), *Gathorne Hardy, First Earl of Cranbrook: A Memoir*, 2 vols (London: Longmans, Green and Co., 1910), i, p. 219; for the constraints on detectives under Rowan and Mayne see Smith, *Policing Victorian London*, pp. 70–2.
    24. Smith, *Policing Victorian London*, pp. 62–3.
    25. Stefan Petrow, 'The rise of the detective in London, 1869–1914', *CJH* 14(1993), 91–108, at p. 93.

of the Metropolitan Police Detective Branch. The commission's report resulted in a new reorganisation carried out under a 29-year-old former army officer and barrister, Howard Vincent, who was appointed Director of Criminal Investigation in March 1878. Vincent had no police experience, but he had brought himself to the notice of the commission, and of Cross, by presenting a succinct report, based on personal observation, of the detective system in Paris. Vincent's appointment did not see an end to anxieties about detective policing. In December 1880, when a chemist, Thomas Titley, was prosecuted for supplying abortifacients to a plain-clothes police sergeant and a 'female searcher' posing as, respectively, the seducer and the mother of an unmarried, pregnant young woman, *The Times* warned: 'There is more here than the detection of crime.' The judge, hearing the case against Titley, 'deeply regretted the course which had been followed by the police', while the jury, finding him guilty, recommended mercy 'on the ground of the provocation and indictment given him by the police'. The police officers involved in the case were subsequently prosecuted as accomplices. They were acquitted, but questions were asked in Parliament, and the Home Secretary assured the Commons that his department would have to be informed should the police ever contemplate such action in future.[26] Overall, however, Vincent's five-year tenure led to some improvement in the image of the Metropolitan Police detectives, not the least in as much as their annual tally of arrests increased from 13,128 to 18,344. Their numbers also increased from 216 men to 294, but James Monro, who succeeded Vincent in June 1884, complained that Birmingham, Dublin, Glasgow, Liverpool and Manchester all had proportionately more detectives than the Metropolitan Police.[27] In general, detective policing was not regarded as a priority among the chief constables, and training for the tasks, when there was any, remained rudimentary.

While the suppression of serious disorder and rioting was a rare requirement, and while the prevention of crime could not be

26. *The Times*, 14 and 17 Dec. 1880; *Hansard*, CCLVII, 11 Jan. 1881, cols 441–4, and 18 Jan. 1881, cols 941–2. See also the general discussion in Angus McLaren, *A Prescription for Murder: The Victorian Serial Killings of Dr. Thomas Neill Cream* (University of Chicago Press, 1993), pp. 107–10.

27. Petrow, 'Rise of the detective', 95–6; and *idem*, *Policing Morals: The Metropolitan Police and the Home Office, 1870–1914* (Oxford: Clarendon Press, 1994), pp. 57–61. For the early development of detective police in Birmingham see Michael Weaver, 'The new science of policing: crime and the Birmingham Police Force, 1839–1842', *Albion* 26 (1994), 289–308, at 303–6.

measured, the police were able to demonstrate their utility by the enforcement of new levels of order and decorum on the streets. This was very much 'order' along the lines of those demands made by jurists like William Lambarde for centuries, and it could run counter to the view taken by some local communities. Most obviously it ran counter to the street culture of many working-class communities. Crowded and cramped living conditions meant that such communities often sought their pleasure in the street; they might buy their food from street traders whose carts and barrows congested narrow roadways; their public houses could be boisterous and the back rooms could be used for betting; and when the 1853 Betting Houses Act sought to drive betting from the pubs, then the working class moved some, but by no means all, of their gambling to the streets.[28] Irish communities brought many of their peasant traditions with them to English cities, such as the keeping of pigs with the family, and the faction fight. The poorer sections of the working class, who eked out a living with casual labour, were often equated with the criminal classes during the 1850s and 1860s; they were portrayed by journalists and other commentators as exotic tribes, not greatly dissimilar from Black Africans and Red Indians, who were also in need of civilisation.[29]

The police constable was the 'domestic missionary' charged with bringing civilisation and decorum; he was armed with a battery of legislation to achieve this end. It had been possible to seize goods exposed for sale on Sunday, to move on street traders and to apprehend disturbers of the public peace long before the creation of the new police; but the police brought the potential for a new efficiency and greater strictness to such enforcement. However, the police were well aware of the problems that their civilising role might cause and both the first commissioners of the Metropolitan Police, and their senior officers, were rather more cautious in the way that they directed their constables to enforce the law than many middle-class reformers hoped or expected. They recognised that working-class life depended on street traders and on Sunday trading, that their men were thinly spread across London, and that rigorous enforcement of the laws could create more problems than it solved. Drunken and disorderly behaviour was similarly perceived primarily as a nuisance. Nevertheless, the establishments which sold drink were regarded as major breeding grounds of crime – as well

28. Mark Clapson, *'A bit of a flutter': popular gambling in English society, 1823–1961* (Manchester: University Press, 1992), pp. 23–4.
29. Emsley, *Crime and Society*, pp. 68–80.

as centres for prostitution and gaming. The 1834 Beer Act (4 & 5 Wm. IV cap. 85), the Wine and Beerhouse Act of 1869 (32 & 33 Vict. cap. 27) and the Licencing Act of 1872 (35 & 36 Vict. cap. 94) authorised increased police supervision of public drinking places and this legislation was enforced with more vigour. Such enforcement could, and did, lead to serious and continuing friction between the police and the poorer sections of the working class, notably in the industrial towns of the north where senior police officers had less independence than the London commissioners.[30]

Partly as a result of their interference in working-class community leisure, police constables were violently assaulted when on their beats throughout the century. Across the country, in some rough working-class districts the constables regularly patrolled at night armed with cutlasses. In London at least, decisions were taken at senior level to contain, rather than to confront, certain rough areas: the police never had sufficient manpower to suppress disorder entirely, establish and maintain a new level of 'respectability' within places such as the notorious Jennings Buildings in Kensington, and they permitted fights and other law-breaking activities there that they would have acted against elsewhere. Individual policemen on their beats probably often employed discretion as the better part of valour. Timothy Cavanagh, for example, who joined the Metropolitan Police in 1855, recalled allowing a fight to continue in a *cul de sac* and slum peopled by poor Irish; he had been warned that one of his predecessors had been murdered when venturing into the street. The violence meted out to policemen appears to have tempted some to get their retaliation in first, or at least with sufficient force to ensure that their assailant was incapable of striking another blow: in Birmingham in March 1875, for example, there was disquiet in the press about the 'questionable conduct' of some constables and the situation exploded into the Navigation Street riot when the police attempted to arrest a suspected burglar in a poor working-class district.[31]

30. Stephen Inwood, 'Policing London's morals: the Metropolitan Police and popular culture, 1829–1850', *The London Journal* 15 (1990), 129–46; Robert D. Storch, 'The policeman as domestic missionary: urban discipline and popular culture in Northern England, 1850–1880', *Journal of Social History* 9 (1976), 481–509; *idem*, ' "The plague of blue locusts": police reform and popular resistance in Northern England, 1840–1857', *International Review of Social History* 20 (1975), 61–90. For the relationship between watch committees and their senior police officers, see below, pp. 89–91.

31. See in general Clive Emsley, ' "The thump of wood on a swede turnip": police violence in nineteenth-century England', *CJH* 6 (1985), 125–49; and in particular Jennifer Davis, 'Jennings' Buildings and the royal borough: the construction of the

The imposition of a new level of order was also central to the behaviour of the rural constabularies. Captain George Davies RN became Chief Constable of Cambridgeshire when that county established a police force at the end of 1851. Six years later, when the neighbouring county of Huntingdonshire was required to establish a force under the County and Borough Police Act, Davies assumed command of the two constabularies. In June 1857 he issued a General Memorandum to the Huntingdonshire force outlining its tasks; the Memorandum is worth quoting at length to underline the emphasis which an experienced rural police chief gave to order, and suspect groups – 'gypsies' and 'tramps' – and his general lack of reference to crime as such:

> The immediate attention of the Constabulary is to be directed to the conducting and time keeping of public houses and Beer shops according to Law but as a preliminary every house which has not already, is to be called at and informed that such Law will be enforced and no proceedings taken where such caution has not been given neither shall I in any *first* instance sanction proceedings being taken for less time than half an hours default, but thereafter cases of obstinate perseverance and resistance are to be brought to my notice, in like manner furious driving. The encampments of Gypsies and others driving without reins, stoppage and obstructions by carts, wagons etc at Public Houses in the absence of drivers within are to be put down . . .
>
> Obstructions and profanations of the Sabbath are to be attended to as far as the Law admits and with judicious management may be put a stop to . . .
>
> In this first year I wish to have no *display* whatever of Police Force at the various village feasts or meetings beyond the presence of the located P.C. (and the Superintendent himself when convenient) and no interference on his part not imperatively called for such appearance before the people are used to it being rather calculated to induce disturbance than otherwise, but thereafter improved order will be expected from such attendance as may be directed and any extension of the restricted time of holdings prevented . . .
>
> Travelling hawkers are to be looked after their licences demanded

under-class in mid-Victorian England', in David Held and Gareth Stedman Jones (eds), *Metropolis London: Histories and Representation since 1800* (London: Routledge, 1989), p. 26; Timothy Cavanagh, *Scotland Yard Past and Present: Experiences of Thirty-Seven Years* (London, 1893), pp. 24–7; S.J. Stevenson, 'The "criminal classes" in the mid-Victorian city: a study of policy conducted with special reference to those made subject to the provision of 34 & 35 Vict. c. 112 (1871) in Birmingham and East London in the early years of registration and supervision', D.Phil., Oxford University, 1983, pp. 195–210.

and in the absence of any, proceedings to be taken. The itinerant 'Tape and Bobbin' and such like parties should be accompanied throughout villages and the support of the inhabitants solicited to discountenance these spies and advanced couriers of the Thieves to follow. But above all the interminable war is to be made on all 'Tramps' of every description with which this county appears to be infested to an extraordinary extent, and now that every county has its Police according to the conduct of the Constabularies towards them will they more or less determine their beats hereafter.[32]

The new level of decorum and order on the streets meant police action against prostitutes. Prostitution as such was not a crime, but the police again found themselves under pressure from moral reformers to take action, and again they had a battery of legislation in Vagrancy laws, Improvement, and Licencing Acts which they could use. The three Contagious Diseases Acts, in force during the period from 1864 to 1886,[33] were aimed at regulating prostitution in eighteen naval and garrison towns by authorising Metropolitan Police contingents seconded to those towns to use plain clothes squads to check on prostitutes and have them examined for venereal disease by official doctors. While some officers in the Metropolitan Police, along with the moral reformers, thoroughly approved of the Acts and hoped to see them developed into something resembling a European *police des moeurs*, once again there was police resistance to the more extreme proposals of the reformers and a policy of compromise appears more commonly to have been followed on many London streets.[34] Nevertheless, action against suspected prostitutes, particularly enforcement of the C.D. Acts, was another source of conflict between the police and the working class. The police could easily make mistakes: the women they apprehended and subjected to an humiliating examination by an official doctor were not necessarily prostitutes but simply working-class women who were walking in a place or at a time which aroused a constable's suspicions. Even after the abolition of the C.D. Acts

32. Cambs. PA Huntingdonshire Constabulary, Chief Constable's Memos, 1857–99, General Memo No. 2, 28 June 1857.
33. The Acts were 27 & 28 Vict. cap. 85 (1864), 29 Vict. cap. 35 (1866), and 32 & 33 Vict. cap. 96 (1869). The first two Acts were of temporary duration; the third was suspended in 1883, but not repealed until 1886. For a discussion of the acts see Paul McHugh, *Prostitution and Victorian Social Reform* (London: Croom Helm, 1980); Judith R. Walkowitz, *Prostitution and Victorian Society: Women, Class, and the State* (Cambridge: CUP, 1980); see also Robert D. Storch, 'Police control of street prostitution in Victorian London: a study in the context of police action', in David H. Bayley (ed.), *Police and Society* (Beverley Hills, Cal.: Sage, 1977).
34. Inwood, 'Policing London's morals', 139–40; Petrow, *Policing Morals*, Part III.

working-class women could be under threat from zealous policemen, or policemen acting under pressure from crusading local authorities or moral vigilance groups. In July 1887 questions were asked in Parliament following the arrest, on a charge of soliciting, of a young and respectable dressmaker recently arrived from Stockton; there were also allegations of the police demanding money from prostitutes to let them solicit unhindered in certain districts.[35]

Provincial police forces also deployed the law in a variety of ways against prostitutes, and occasionally there was scandal over the manner in which they labelled innocent young women as such.[36] During the university terms Cambridge had a problem akin to that of garrison towns and seaports, namely a large number of unattached young men. Superintendent William Jaggard explained to Henry Mayhew that, although his men had only counted 121 known prostitutes at the beginning of October 1850, the numbers would increase 'now the university men are coming up . . . in full term the Nos vary from 150 to 200'. The Cambridge prostitutes were of a higher class than most of those in the garrison towns and seaports; according to Jaggard, 'they are most of the middle class of girls, and all walk the streets at times generally well dressed'. The university authorities took some of the responsibility for controlling these prostitutes and during the middle years of the century the police generally acted under the Town Police Clauses Act of 1847 (10 and 11 Vict. cap. 89): 'the Police order them out of the streets off their Beats after 11 o'clock, but do not allow them to stand or loiter about at one particular place any time, or importune any passengers . . . We do not interfere with them in their houses if orderly.'[37] Forty years later the Chief Constable of Cambridge was borrowing 'smart young constables' for a few days from neighbouring county forces to tempt prostitutes into soliciting them; the women could then be successfully prosecuted, and the prosecutions, it was hoped, would deter others.[38]

The power of the police in the streets, and their use of this power, probably contributed to the belief among many members of the working class that there was one law for the rich and another,

35. *Hansard*, CCCXVI, 5 July 1887, cols 1796–1823; ibid., CCCXVII, 7 July, cols 74–75; ibid., CCCXVIII, 29 July, col. 551, 4 Aug., col. 1153, and 9 Aug., cols 1715–16.
36. Ian A. Watt, *A History of the Hampshire and Isle of Wight Constabulary 1839–1966* (Winchester: Hampshire Constabulary, 1967), pp. 50–1.
37. Cambs. PA Cambridge Borough, Police Letter Book, 1849–50, Jaggard to Mayhew, 8 Oct. 1851, and to Supt. Combs, Bedford, 21 Nov. 1851.
38. Cambs. PA Miscellaneous letters and correspondence, 228/80, fols 1–5.

harsher, law for the poor. 'The invariable support which the authorities give to the constables has encouraged and tempted them to exercise their power most tyrannically', declared *Fun* in 1866.[39] More than twenty years later Halley Stewart, the radical Liberal MP for Spalding, could still argue in terms reminiscent of some of the early protests against the new police, namely that they found crime where, in reality, there was none:

> If the people were allowed to manage their affairs for themselves, they could do that with half the number of policemen who were now required. By the way in which they were now employed they contrived to make crime instead of diminishing it. They were engaged in the most trivial and unworthy occupations, and many of them were spies and game-keepers for the landed interest of the country. (Cries of 'Oh!')[40]

Few of Stewart's fellow members shared his views, but outside Parliament there was a feeling among many members of the working class that the policeman's word was always believed in court in preference to that of a poor man; and some members of the gentry seemed to think that they stood in a completely different relationship to the police than the working class. When a dragoon officer was prosecuted for knocking a policeman's helmet off at the Edenbridge Steeplechase in 1872, his defence counsel protested that 'it was impossible for a gentleman like Mr Russell to be guilty of such an offence as an assault on the police'.[41] Advanced Liberals and others grew concerned about the expanding regulatory legislation which, in the words of Samuel Blackstone, primarily affected the poor and taught them to know the police 'by the bull's eye of espionage and the truncheon of compulsion'. Such individuals formed organisations to monitor and check the growth of police powers, such as the Vigilance Association for the Defence of Personal Rights, established in 1871 and transformed into the Personal Rights Association fifteen years later. They were also active in endeavouring to bring the Metropolitan Police under the control of the London ratepayers by having the force subordinated to the London County Council.[42]

39. *Fun*, 21 July 1866, p. 196; see also 13 Oct. 1866, pp. 49, 51; and see in general Wilbur R. Miller, *Cops and Bobbies: Police Authority in New York and London, 1830–1870* (University of Chicago Press, 1977), pp. 122–3.
40. *Hansard*, CCCXXVII, 19 June 1888, cols 605–6.
41. Quoted in Carolyn Conley, 'Crime and community in Victorian Kent', Ph.D., Duke University, 1984, p. 251.
42. Petrow, *Policing Morals*, pp. 20–7. The quotation is from Samuel Blackstone, 'Paternal government: wither are we drifting?', *St Paul's Magazine* XII (June 1873).

Yet it would be wrong to conceive of the relationship between the working class and the police in the second half of the nineteenth century as entirely one of mutual hostility. Many members of the working class also sought respectability and desired orderliness and decorum. It is probable that, as Eric Monkkonen has argued for the American experience, the appearance of the police on the streets increasingly led members of the working class to believe that they too had a right to freedom from the annoyance of crime and public disorder.[43] They may not necessarily have liked the police, but the political rhetoric was that the police were there to serve and to protect everyone, so it was perfectly valid to utilise that service, especially as the benefits of the Industrial Revolution percolated down the social scale and enabled members of the working class to have more possessions and more property which, like that of their social superiors, needed protection. Exasperated parents might call in a local constable to deal with a difficult child. In March 1871 P.C. Alexander Hennessy was asked to arrest fourteen-year-old Catherine Driscoll for stealing clothing; the request came from the girl's mother. In October 1883 P.C. Thomas Clark of the Worcestershire Constabulary was reprimanded for 'improperly acceding to the request of a Mr Hollis, to give his son a beating for staying away from school and sleeping out nights'.[44] The police were reluctant to become involved in domestic disputes and the orders issued by some forces instructed constables to steer clear unless the dispute was 'public' or 'serious'.[45] Nevertheless, when the violence of a husband or a parent exceeded the accepted norms, the police were the body to which appeals for help and action were made, and constables acted on these requests. Thus in March 1890, the Chief Constable of Birmingham wrote to the superintendent in charge of Bethnal Green Police Station in London urging him, at the behest of a George Coles, to investigate Joseph Fox who had recently moved from Birmingham to Hackney. Coles, who was Fox's father-in-law, feared that his daughter was being ill-treated. In another case some three months later Detective Constable Frank Wheeler reported:

> that at 4.30 p.m. on the 21st. inst., a man named William Henry Davis . . . called to complain of the ill treatment of a child about 12

43. Eric H. Monkkonen, *Police in Urban America, 1860–1920* (Cambridge: CUP, 1981), p. 154.
44. Metropolitan PA MS Book 1116; West Mercia PA Worcestershire Constabulary, Register and Record of Police Service, 1877–83, no. 99.
45. Alan Bourlet, *Police Intervention in Marital Violence* (Buckingham: Open University Press, 1990), p. 15.

months old believed to be the illegitimate child of a woman, name unknown, who is said to live in Fish Shop Yard, Vauxhall Road, and her mother is occasionally employed as a Charwoman at a Mrs. Clarke's who lives about the third house on the left in Dolman St. from Erskine St. The child appears to be in a filthy condition and is very emaciated, and has a scar on one thigh, and in other ways shows signs of gross neglect . . .'[46]

The police could also be used to search for missing persons, for members of the family with whom contact had been lost and who were believed to be abroad, as well as for lost children;[47] and some children may well have got lost deliberately so that they could spend a short time playing with the few toys kept in the police station for such an eventuality, have a jam sandwich courtesy of the police, and then be taken home.[48] Some police forces also began to establish charitable funds to assist the poor with, most commonly, shoes and clothing. In the late 1870s or early 1880s two superintendents in the Lancashire Constabulary, apparently independent of each other, established soup kitchens for the poor children in their divisions, supplied them with clothes and even arranged summer excursions. 'We looked upon [it] as a mere matter of duty,' declared Superintendent Richard Jervis, 'which we regarded as something more than the prevention and repression of crime.' Jervis's funds, originally collected through police sports days, also contributed to local hospitals, to a local society for the Care and Protection of Young Girls, and to a fund for the widows and orphans of Skelmersdale miners; following the Tawd Vale Colliery Disaster the fund was also used to purchase new tools for the colliers who had lost theirs in the disaster.[49] The Northampton Borough Police established their Good Samaritan Society in 1893 and the Police-aided Clothing Society of Liverpool was set up at about the same

46. West Midlands PA Birmingham Copy Letter Book, Chief Constable's Office, 1890–91, fol. 178, Chief Constable to Superintendent Meering, 18 Mar. 1890, and fol. 567, Wheeler to Chief Constable, 23 June 1890. For police involvement in incidents of male violence see Nancy Tomes, 'A "torrent of abuse": crimes of violence between working-class men and women in London, 1840–1875', *Journal of Social History* 11 (1978), 328–45, esp. at 335–7.
47. See, for example, West Midlands PA Birmingham Copy Letter Book, fol. 97, 22 Feb., and fol. 196, 20 Jan. 1890 (missing persons); fol. 24, 10 Feb., fol. 72, 19 Feb., and fol. 131, 5 Mar. 1890 (letters to New York and Toronto about family members with whom contact has been lost).
48. Raphael Samuel, *East End Underworld: Chapters in the Life of Arthur Harding* (London: Routledge and Kegan Paul, 1981), p. 36.
49. Richard Jervis, *Lancashire's Crime and Criminals* (Southport, 1908), p. 77; James Bent, *Criminal Life: Reminiscences of Forty-Two Years as a Police Officer* (London, 1891), appendix (pp. 273–322).

time.[50] In addition to this kind of help policemen were trained in first aid and consequently could be expected to administer initial assistance to people injured in accidents. In November 1883 *The Times* reported that 1,224 members of the Metropolitan Police, just under a tenth of the force, had received certificates from the St John's Ambulance Association for proficiency in first aid; and it was at about this time that most police stations in London began to be equipped with ambulances.[51]

Edwin Chadwick was all for the police developing what he called their 'collateral services':

> A police force ... must owe its real efficiencies and concurrent action to the great body of the people. It is therefore important, for its moral usefulness as well as on the score of economy, carefully to cultivate its beneficial services and provide for its occupation on occasions of accident or calamity.

He urged that police stations be equipped with stretchers and, if they were close to rivers, with life-saving equipment. He believed that police surgeons should be readily available to anyone in populous districts, and that the police should be trained as fire-fighters. 'These collateral services,' he continued, 'for which there should be the stimulus of distinct appreciation and reward, relieve the monotony of mere sentinel work for any one chief object. As the preventive service against crime prevails, the collateral beneficent services will increase.'[52]

Captain McHardy shared much of Chadwick's vision. He explained to the select committee of 1853 how the police might be employed as collectors of rates and taxes, as postmen and as road surveyors. His men were already acting as inspectors of weights and measures, inspectors of nuisances and common lodging houses under the local boards of health, and as assistant relieving officers under the Poor Law.[53] McHardy believed, like many others, that vagrants were potential criminals; surveying the roads, inspecting common lodging houses and relieving the casual poor was, in consequence, a way of controlling crime. Major William Cartwright,

50. Richard Cowley, *Policing Northamptonshire, 1836–1986* (Studley, Warks: Brewin Books, 1986), p. 175; Sir William Nott-Bower, *Fifty-Two Years a Policeman* (London: Edward Arnold, 1926), p. 99.

51. *The Times*, 23 Nov. 1883, p. 10; Charles Tempest Clarkson and J. Hall Richardson, *Police!* (London, 1889), p. 99.

52. Edwin Chadwick, 'On the consolidation of police force, and the prevention of crime', *Frazer's Magazine* 77 (1868), 1–18, quotations at 16 and 17.

53. PP 1852–53 (603) XXXVI, *First Report of the Select Committee on Police*, qq. 687, 777–8, 780–1, 783.

one of the first of Her Majesty's Inspectors of Constabulary, also believed in close links between vagrancy and crime and was particularly keen to encourage the police into acting as relieving officers. Many chief constables, in both boroughs and counties, often after Cartwright's promptings and/or encouragement from the central Poor Law Board, arranged for their men to act in this capacity.[54] But the experience of policemen acting as relieving officers led some to the conclusion that the role took up too much time and deflected the police from their proper functions, while the results were not always as had been wished or expected. In October 1880 the Hon. H.G. Legge, one of the Inspectors of Constabulary, expressed his concern that 25 of the 196 men of all ranks serving in the police of Cumberland and Westmorland were acting as assistant relieving officers; more seriously, their Poor Law tasks occupied 'fully half the time they should be employed on proper police duty'. Three years later James Kellie-MacCallum, the Chief Constable of Northamptonshire, recommended that the Quarter Sessions rescind the order authorising his men to act as assistant relieving officers:

> It was ... expected that the system would assist the police in the prevention and detection of crime; but it had not done so. The records of the force had been searched for many years past, but he could not find one instance of crime having been thus detected, nor was it reasonable to suppose that a person whose apprehension was sought would wilfully present himself or herself to an officer of police. Tramps as a class were not criminals. Out of 111 persons indicted for crime during the year 1882, only five were described as vagrants, and the returns for the last five years showed a similar proportion. He also pointed out that the relief of tramps was the legitimate duty of the [Poor Law] union officials, and that the police could not be employed in the work uniformly through-out the county without an increase in the present establishment.[55]

In much the same way that they were employed as assistant relieving officers, following the 1870 Education Act some policemen found themselves required to act as school attendance officers and to serve summonses on those parents whose children failed to attend school. The debate in the Hertfordshire Quarter Sessions in April 1884 is indicative of the arguments used for and against this practice. E. King Fordham insisted 'that a police constable was a very

54. Carolyn Steedman, *Policing the Victorian Community: The Formation of the English Provincial Police Forces, 1856–1880* (London: Routledge and Kegan Paul, 1984), pp. 53–9.
55. *Justice of the Peace* XLIV (1880), 30 Oct., 700; ibid., XLVII (1883), 28 Apr., 266.

proper person to perform such duties and that, for the small remuneration afforded, there was great difficulty in getting a better class of men to undertake them'. However, the chairman of the police committee objected 'on the ground that it was not desirable to place the police in a position calculated to make them more unpopular than they were, and he was convinced that nothing would tend to make a policeman more unpopular than his acting in this capacity'.[56]

Policemen also acquired a variety of lesser tasks to do with the general administration of a county or a borough such as collectors of market tolls or auxiliary river watchers under the Salmon Fishery Acts. In a report to his police committee at Easter 1871 the Chief Constable of Hampshire urged that the sanction of the Home Secretary might be required for some of the duties required of his men; he warned that these might lead to the withholding of the Treasury grant and he instanced in particular the tasks of 'inspectors of cattle, impounders of cattle, inspectors of hawkers' licences, inspectors of county bridges, assistant excise officers, and assistant surveyors of the highways'.[57] In the event no force lost its grant for carrying out these additional duties, and they continued to expand at least until the end of the nineteenth century, by which time the increase and developments in urban transport were absorbing more and more police time: during the 1880s, for example, the Birmingham City Police had to detail thirteen men for the inspection of tramcars and the regulation of traffic, and sixteen men had to be transferred from patrolling at night to daytime duty because of the increasing volume of traffic.[58] Some of these tasks fitted in with the traditional responsibilities of local government, and the policeman, perceived as the servant of local government, particularly in the boroughs, was the obvious choice to carry them out. Other tasks were imposed directly by government and began to undermine the local control of the police.

Controlling the police

Three different kinds of police authority had emerged with the new police forces. The commissioner of the Metropolitan Police

56. Ibid., XLVI (1882), 22 Apr., 250; for similar debates see ibid., XLIV (1880), 30 Oct., 705 (Bucks.); ibid., XLV (1881), 15 Jan., 42 (Leics.), 7 May, 305 (Norfolk), 19 Nov., 772–3 (Hants.).

57. Watt, *A History of the Hampshire and Isle of Wight Constabulary*, pp. 28–9.

58. C.A. Vince, *History of the Corporation of Birmingham, Vol. III (1885–1899)* (Birmingham, 1902), p. 219.

was directly responsible to the Home Secretary. The head constables in the boroughs were appointed by, and responsible to, the
watch committees. The chief constables in the counties were appointed by the county magistrates, though the appointment needed
to be ratified by the Home Secretary; the police authority in the
counties, until 1889, was usually a separate committee of members
of the county Bench; after the Local Government Act of 1888,
standing joint committees were established, made up half of magistrates and half of elected county councillors, as the county police
authority. The belief, noisily expressed in the 1830s and again in
the 1850s, that local police forces should be locally controlled continued to be strongly held in the second half of the century; at the
same time there were moves by central government to bypass local
police authorities and to deal directly with chief and head constables.

Given the exceptional status of the Metropolitan Police, it was
understandable that London should be the focus of much of the
debate about local control. The petition drawn up by delegates
from the vestries and presented to the Home Secretary in 1869
urged that a degree of control over the Metropolitan Police be
passed to a 'representative board' along the lines of the borough
watch committees.[59] The issue was brought to the fore in 1888 in
the debates on the Local Government Bill since the proposed legislation provided for the creation of a London County Council.
The debates on the bill followed hard on the heels of the controversy over Bloody Sunday. According to James Stuart, the Radical
MP for Shoreditch, Hoxton 'there was no place in England where
control of the police was more removed from the people than
London, and there was no place in England where there was more
dissatisfaction generally in connection with the police'.[60] Sir Charles
Warren's behaviour as Commissioner of the Metropolitan Police
did not help the government's case and contributed to the continued criticism of the force in Parliament after the demands that the
Local Government Bill give the new London County Council control of the police had been rejected. James Rowlands, for example,
the Radical Liberal member for Finsbury East, insisted that the
criticism of the Metropolitan Police under Warren and the low
level of police–public relations would be considered as 'a municipal
matter' anywhere else in the country 'and ought to be thrashed out
in a County Council composed of representatives of the people of

59. *The Times*, 14 Jan. 1869, p. 12.
60. *Hansard*, CCCXXVII, 15 June 1888, col. 293.

London'.[61] The debates spread from Parliament into contemporary journals. It was urged that the Metropolitan Police performed 'imperial' tasks such as protecting the queen, the royal palaces, Parliament and public buildings, as well as protecting society from the Fenian threat; it was therefore logical that they should remain under the control of the Home Secretary, a member of the imperial government. But there was another concern: as the capital of a large empire, London and the orderly government thereof remained an 'imperial' rather than a local concern:

> It is undeniable that if the London County Council held the control of the police, it would wield a weapon that might be handled with deadly effect against a weak Government, if the majority of the Council chose to make use of it for political purposes.
>
> ... can any reasonable person assert that there will never be a majority of extreme Radicals and Socialists on the County Council?[62]

Such thinking was symptomatic of the concerns among conservative politicians about the direction that local politics in London were taking: the first elections for the LCC in 1889 resulted in a large majority of Progressive and Radical Liberals who campaigned for social reform and criticised privilege and monopoly. But understandably Stuart, and Radicals like him, were outraged by the suggestion that they could not have control of the police because they might use the force against the government:

> This, indeed, is the first time that I have ever heard the claim set up in England that the police are a body for the protection of the Government against the citizens. The fact that such an idea obtains for a moment in Scotland Yard is an adequate condemnation of the present system; and the solidarity between the police systems of Paris and London implied in this ... is too dangerous to be left unnoticed.[63]

Concerns about the activist working class organising to win provincial county council elections, and then seeking to control the police, were also expressed forcibly in the debates on the Local Government Bill both inside and outside Parliament. F.A. Hyeth, the deputy chairman of the Essex Quarter Sessions, feared that the

61. Ibid., CCCXXX, 14 Nov. 1888, col. 1186.
62. H. Evans, 'The London County Council and the police', *Contemporary Review* LV (1889), 445–61, quotation at 449.
63. James Stuart, 'The Metropolitan Police', *Contemporary Review* LV (1889), 622–36, quotation at 629. For the development of local politics in London see John Davis, *Reforming London: The London Government Problem 1855–1900* (Oxford: Clarendon Press, 1988), pp. 115–21.

example of the boroughs needed to be avoided where, for example, victuallers and anti-vaccination supporters had influenced police actions. Moreover, he doubted that in times 'of popular excitement or tumult . . . the County Council will be very ready to call out the Police force against those who are practically their masters'.[64] Stanley Leighton, the Conservative member for Oswestry, was the most outspoken critic in the Commons, warning that

> an elected Body would not be always and altogether in favour of law and order. In certain cases an elected Body would be entirely in the hands of one class of the community and that class might be opposed to the law. In the mining counties, for instance, it would be altogether in the hands of the Miners' Organisation; and the Miners' Organisation was, like every other trade organisation, not always in favour of law and order. These trade organisations, if they used their power, would be able to command a majority in the County Councils. Now, the police ought to have nothing to do with one class of the community or another. Their only business was to carry out the laws passed in that House, and they ought not to be influenced in any way by local feeling.

To the fury of some MPs, Leighton also suggested that some elected town councils, through the watch committees which they appointed, did not always carry out the law in the proper manner.[65]

Since the first appearance of the rural constabularies in 1839 and 1840 county magistrates had controlled the purse strings of their chief constables, but they had rarely sought to issue regular, direct orders to them concerning their duties. Partly this was because, except in an emergency, the police committees of the county Benches only met quarterly and this made it difficult to exercise any rigorous control. They might instruct the chief constable to take action over certain circumstances: at the beginning of 1869, for example, the Bedfordshire magistrates instructed that everyone found committing vagrancy offences in the county should be apprehended, and arrests more than tripled. But the success of such instructions could only be judged when the chief constable presented his quarterly reports to the committee; and there were occasions when chief constables resisted instructions. To take another Bedfordshire example, in 1863 the Chief Constable was opposed to

64. 'The County Government Bill', *Murray's Magazine* III (1888), 738–60, quotation at 755. This article consists of brief statements by 38 chairmen and deputy chairmen of quarter sessions on the Local Government Bill.
65. *Hansard*, CCCXVII, 15 June 1888, col. 279; see also cols 276 and 281, and 18 June, col. 544.

his superintendents making detailed records of beer houses and public houses and keeping these in the police stations:

> I respectfully submit that much Book-keeping and Statistical Returns will occupy the officers more than is desireable or useful. The Books they now keep with the returns they have to make up weekly take up quite as much time as can be spared from their duty in looking after their men and in pursuing crime.[66]

In most instances it would appear that the chief constable and the police committee discussed an issue and came to a conclusion acceptable to both sides. As the chief constables grew into their jobs as professional policemen, so their expertise was recognised by the magistrates. But the relationship was also eased because county magistrates and their chief constables negotiated as social equals. Chief constables in counties were often former military officers and drawn from the landed gentry; indeed, the number of such appointments increased after the 1856 County and Borough Police Act.[67] As such they came from the same social class, and shared the same social outlook, as the gentlemen on the county Bench. There could be problems and concerns: in 1881 the Devon Quarter Sessions had an anxious discussion over the fact that 'the chief constable seemed to have uncontrolled command of the police force', and while there were no complaints over the serving chief constable there were anxieties over his ability to appoint a deputy to act in his absence, especially since the appointment of this deputy, unlike that of the chief constable, was not approved by the Quarter Sessions.[68]

Initially the Local Government Act of 1888 had little impact on the relationship between the county police authority and the chief constable. Henceforward the police authority in a county was to be the standing joint committee, composed half of magistrates and half of elected county councillors; however, the elected county councillors, at least up until the period of the First World War, appear to have been drawn largely from the same social background as the unelected magistrates and they appear also to have conducted their business in the same personal and relatively informal ways as the old committees of magistrates. The divided nature of the standing joint committee originated partly in the belief that the policeman's role was itself divided: it was part administrative and part judicial. There was considerable opposition to the idea of these

66. Beds. RO QEV 4, Chief Constable's Reports, 6 Apr. 1869 and 20 Oct. 1863.
67. Steedman, *Policing the Victorian Community*, pp. 47–9.
68. *Justice of the Peace* XLV (1881), 12 Nov., 754.

committees which split largely between those who wanted police authority to remain in the hands of the magistrates and those who felt that, immediately and entirely, it should be handed over to the elected county councils. Thus the standing joint committees ultimately survived in the legislation as a compromise. A few voices had been raised in favour of the provincial police being taken over entirely by central government: it was believed that shifting the cost of the police to central government would ease the burden on local ratepayers.[69] But such a proposal would have had as little chance in the Parliament of 1888 as in that of 50 years earlier, and a clause in the Local Government Bill enabling the Home Secretary to dictate to local authorities the size of their police forces created such opposition that it was dropped.[70]

The act of 1888 left the control of the borough police in the hands of the watch committees. Unlike the police committees of the county magistrates and the standing joint committees with their quarterly meetings, the watch committees met frequently, often at least once a week. The Municipal Corporations Act of 1835 had given these committees full responsibility for, and authority over, their police forces; while county police constables were appointed by the chief constables, in the boroughs all appointments technically were made by the watch committees. It was possible for such a committee to appoint or to promote men against the advice of their head constable.[71] In Manchester in 1882 William Bannister was appointed Superintendent of D Division in such circumstances, and he turned out to be a particularly bad choice: his division became notorious for corruption and was the subject of a special commission of inquiry in 1897.[72] Yet this incident seems to have been exceptional,

69. Ibid., 20 Aug., 556–7, reports a discussion at the Hertfordshire Quarter Sessions on this issue, and Lord Henneker, the senior chairman of the East Suffolk Bench, argued that the police should be 'an Imperial Force' in his comments in *Murray's Magazine* III (1888), 740. In February 1888 the *Justice of the Peace* reported that, because of the arguments over the proposed standing joint committees, '[i]t has been hinted that the solution will be found by placing the police under the Home Office', *Justice of the Peace*, LII (1888), 24 Feb., 178.
70. For a résumé of the debates on the 1888 legislation see T.A. Critchley, *A History of Police in England and Wales* rev. edn (London: Constable, 1978), pp. 133–8.
71. For much of the second half of the nineteenth century the term 'head constable' was often used for the senior officer of a borough force, though 'chief constable' was becoming more and more common by the mid-1890s. 'Chief constable' was always used for the commander of a county constabulary.
72. Eric J. Hewitt, *A History of Policing in Manchester* (Didsbury: E.J. Morten, 1979), ch. 10. As a result of the inquiry the chairman of the Watch Committee resigned; 13 men from D Division were dismissed, 12 called upon to resign, and 13 others went voluntarily.

at least in the largest towns and cities where the head constable was often recruited from the same pool as his county equivalents. In the smaller boroughs, however, it was common for the head constable to be a man who had risen through the ranks of the police, and this meant that the watch committee members were often his social superiors and tended to regard him very much as their servant. A borough chief constable might stand up to his political masters and get away with it. Superintendent Howe of the Buckingham Police, for example, had a heated meeting with town councillors over the rigorous way in which he enforced the measures relating to weights and measures; he was warned that 'if as a servant . . . [he] took no notice the Council knew the course to be adopted when his re-election came around', and responded that if he had been 'a felon or a vagrant he should have been heard before he was sentenced'. Howe kept his job as police superintendent and as inspector of weights and measures;[73] others may not have been as courageous, or as lucky. In general, however, decisions regarding police operations in the boroughs, as in the counties, were probably the result of discussion and debate, with the watch committee seeking the opinion and advice of their head constable as, increasingly, the expert on police matters. But watch committees might still give direct operational orders to their head constable, ignoring his expertise, and they remained the master: in the words of two analysts of English local government at the beginning of the twentieth century, 'as a matter of law and constitution, the [borough] Chief Constable's authority is very nearly the same as that of every other municipal official – that is to say, he has to act on the instructions of his committee'.[74]

There were two notable confrontations between watch committees and head constables, involving two of the largest police forces in the country, in Birmingham in 1880 and 1881 and in Liverpool in 1890. The initial problem in Birmingham occurred when the Chief Constable, Major E.E.B. Bond, changed the traditional practice of allowing 'quiet drunkards' to proceed on their way without interference and instructed his men to arrest them. The decision was taken without reference to the Watch Committee. More serious was Bond's later decision, again without reference to the committee, to prosecute the manager of Day's Concert Hall for improper

73. Len Woodley, 'Buckingham Borough Police, 1836–1889', *Journal of the Police History Society* 5 (1990), 24–36, at 30.
74. Joseph Redlich and Francis W. Hurst, *Local Government in England*, 2 vols (London, 1903), i, p. 342, and see also ii, p. 305.

performance and for performing plays without a licence. The prosecution failed, and the Watch Committee directed Bond never to take such action again without prior consultation. Bond's response was to inform the committee that his duty to the Home Secretary and to the town magistrates made it impossible that he should give 'an absolute undertaking that I will at no time take any legal steps which may be outside the most elementary criminal proceedings without having previously obtained their approval and authority'. However, neither the Home Secretary nor the town magistrates were prepared to back Bond and he only avoided dismissal by acquiescing in the Watch Committee's demands.[75] In Liverpool there was a long tradition of the Watch Committee taking an active role in directing police operations, though it had ceased its daily meetings in 1847 and had allowed increasing autonomy to its Head Constable. The problem in 1890 occurred when the Vigilance Association won a majority on the Watch Committee and instructed the Head Constable, Captain William Nott-Bower, 'to proceed against all brothels at present known to the Police without any undue delay, and such proceedings shall be by way of prosecution'. Nott-Bower had already warned against taking any such step. He reasoned that a large seaport like Liverpool was, unfortunately, bound to have a number of brothels; proceeding against them would not eliminate the problem, rather it would encourage them to move into hitherto 'respectable' localities and then police time would be taken up in searching for them in their new situations. In the event, however, Nott-Bower did not challenge the order which he received, even though the repercussions were exactly as he had cautioned; the *status quo* was eventually restored, not the least because of the pressure brought to bear by businessmen, shopkeepers and tradesmen who, after the experience of police raids in their neighbourhoods, considered that the 'evil' of prostitution was being spread by police action with potentially disastrous results for their businesses.[76]

Yet while there was a general determination to keep local police forces under local control, there was also a creeping centralisation. The 1856 County and Borough Police Act, by creating the Inspectors of Constabulary and authorising government grants for those forces certified as 'efficient' by the inspectorate, had been a significant move in this direction. The Inspectors began to enforce a degree

---

75. J.T. Bunce, *History of the Corporation of Birmingham*, 3 vols (Birmingham, 1878–1902), ii, pp. 283–7.

76. Mike Brogden, *The Police: Autonomy and Consent* (London: Academic Press, 1982), ch. 2; Nott-Bower, *Fifty-Two Years a Policeman*, pp. 140–5.

of uniformity, specifying what did and what did not constitute proper policing tasks and urging forces to adopt what they considered to be good and sensible practice from elsewhere. Lieutenant-Colonel John Woodford, appointed as one of the Inspectors from the position of Chief Constable of Lancashire, for example considered that the collection of money – 'tolls, rates, taxes or rents' – was not part of police duty, and he was highly critical of the Watch Committee of South Shields for its persistence in using a police inspector as a collector of market tolls.[77] While the result of Woodford's complaints is not recorded, another Inspector, Major-General William Cartwright, was instrumental in persuading forces in the Midlands to employ their men in acceptable administrative tasks such as assistant relieving officers and inspectors of weights and measures.[78] The Inspectors experienced most of their difficulties with the watch committees and the borough forces. Initially, a few boroughs also remained proudly aloof from the government grant: even though their forces were deemed efficient in the early years, Doncaster, Southampton and Sunderland all refused Treasury money. However, the desire to maintain the support of borough electors, who were also ratepayers, ultimately led these to swallow their pride, while others, not yet certified as 'efficient', also sought to fall in with the Inspectors' demands and suggestions.[79] In 1874, precisely to give the Home Secretary greater supervision and control of the provincial police, the Treasury grant was increased from one-quarter to one-half.[80]

Efficiency, in the eyes of the inspectorate, was estimated partly on the men's performance at drill, but primarily on the number of constables in relation to the population, and the number of senior officers available to supervise the constables. It could be difficult for the smaller boroughs to measure up to the Inspectors' demands, but on occasions such boroughs could find unexpected support from the Home Secretary. In January 1883, for example, Sir William Harcourt rejected the Inspectors' recommendation that the Borough of High Wycombe lose its grant as its force was too small. 'The view I have always taken on this matter', he declared, 'is that if local self-government means anything at all it means that local

77. HO 45.7615.

78. For the role of the Inspectors, and of Cartwright in particular, see Steedman, *Policing the Victorian Community*, pp. 38–41, 56–9.

79. Jenifer Hart, 'The County and Borough Police Act, 1856', *Public Administration* XXXIV (1956), 405–17; Henry Parris, 'The Home Office and the provincial police in England and Wales, 1856–1870', *Public Law* (1961), 230–55.

80. HO 45.19,774, Memorandum of 27 Apr. 1874.

authority and not the Government Inspector is the proper judge of the number of police required by them.'[81] However, while a man like Harcourt might side with a local watch committee over numbers, in general the Home Secretaries during the second half of the nineteenth century were, to a man, against the proliferation of tiny borough forces. The Municipal Corporations (New Charters) Act of 1877 forbade the creation of a separate force for any new borough which had a population of less than 20,000. An aborted bill, introduced early in 1884, planned to deny the Treasury grant to any existing borough which had a police force but where the population, by the last census, was less than 20,000.[82] It was suggested that the Local Government Bill of 1888 might be amended to include a similar clause, but in the event the Act of 1888 only abolished those police forces in boroughs with a population of less than 10,000 – a move which reduced the number of separate police forces in England and Wales from 231 to 183.[83]

Some legislation and government directives began to create a direct link between senior police officers and central government, bypassing the local police authorities. There was nothing conspiratorial in this. While it seemed logical for the Home Office circulars dealing with criminal and judicial matters to go first to magistrates and police authorities, and from them to the police, it seemed equally logical that administrative tasks performed on the part of central government which did not involve such matters should be devolved directly to the police. Thus circulars concerning vandalism against telegraph wires and insulators and very sick persons being conveyed to prison by the police regardless of their state of health were sent to magistrates and police authorities.[84] But the Old Metal Dealers Act of 1861 (24 & 25 Vict. cap. 110), the Explosives Act (38 & 39 Vict. cap. 17) and the Adulterated Foods Act (38 & 39 Vict. cap. 63) of 1875 gave executive power directly to the police with no reference to the local police authority. The policing of the serious industrial disorders in the twenty years before the First World War, and the war itself, significantly increased this trend.

81. Quoted in Hart, 'County and Borough Police Act', 411.
82. *The Times*, 18 Feb. 1884, p. 4.   83. Critchley, *A History of Police*, p. 133.
84. *Justice of the Peace* LVI (1892), 3, 10 and 17 Sept., 570–1, 585–6, 602.

CHAPTER FIVE

Professionalisation, Politics and Public Order

Identity and unionisation

In May 1893 the Home Secretary was asked about the case of an Englishwoman, a member of the Society of Friends of Russian Freedom, allegedly treated 'with rudeness and even violence' by a member of the Metropolitan Police. The police had denied the charge and H.H. Asquith responded: 'I do not see any reason for doubting the accuracy of the police statement.'[1] The following year, when it was suggested that policemen in Barnsley had fabricated evidence against two miners for being drunk and disorderly and that one police witness was two miles away from the alleged offence, Asquith saw 'no reason to doubt the truth of the constable's evidence'.[2] The Bobby was now firmly established as a part of the model British Constitution. According to John Burns, a former labour activist but, by 1900, an Independent Radical MP, the City of London and the Metropolitan Police were 'the best police force[s] in the world'.[3] For Captain Melville Lee, in his *History of Police in England* published in 1901, '[h]owever numerous and outrageous may be the theoretical imperfections of our method for maintaining the peace, its practical superior has yet to be discovered'.[4] Captain Nott-Bower, now Commissioner of the City of London force, considered 'that on the testimony of foreign countries, England was, in police matters, *facile princeps*'.[5] The investigations of *The*

1. *Hansard*, XII, 15 May 1893, cols 906–8.
2. Ibid., XXIV, 24 May 1894, cols 1178–9.
3. Ibid., LXXXV, 13 July 1900, col. 1559.
4. W.L. Melville Lee, *A History of Police in England* (London: Methuen, 1901), p. xii.
5. *The Times*, 13 Feb. 1906, p. 10.

Times 'prove[d] beyond all cavil or doubt that our police force is a credit to the men who are responsible for it, and a source of pride to every Englishman who is acquainted with police administration in other countries'. It was 'a great human mechanism, perhaps the greatest of its kind'.[6] The three different kinds of police authority remained established, with the Metropolitan Police answerable only to the Home Secretary, the county police responsible to the standing joint committees, and the borough police directed by the watch committees, yet the idea that there was a single, and peculiarly English, style of policing had taken hold of the imagination of the respectable classes. The police themselves, while recognising that they belonged to different forces and often evincing pride in their separate force identities, were also developing a corporate identity. The creation of the Chief Constables' Association in 1893 was one manifestation of this: the members of the association were the chief constables of the boroughs, and although senior members of the watch committees attended the annual meetings, it was, first and foremost, a professional policemen's organisation as the name itself implies. Another manifestation of corporate identity, far less popular with the authorities, was moves towards police unionism.

It is difficult to conceive of any workforce in which there will not be discussions about the rates of remuneration and the conditions of the job. The new police were established in England in a period which witnessed the emergence of trade unionism with an increasing degree of legal recognition. The early organisation among the lower ranks of the police was *ad hoc* and localised; policemen were not, after all, skilled craftsmen and it was among such groups that trade unionism initially developed significant strength. This *ad hoc* organisation appears also to have affected only urban forces. Possibly the isolated nature of the rural policeman's posting militated against such organisation; so too, perhaps, did the more military ethos of many county forces. In the urban areas some policemen lived in police barracks, which gave the opportunity for regular discussions on pay and conditions. In the urban areas too policemen could see at close quarters the lifestyles of respectable artisans, whom they were expected to emulate, and the power of their craft organisations.

Policemen first sought improvements in pay and conditions by the age-old method of petitioning their superiors. Thus in November 1848 a group of third-class constables in the Metropolitan Police

6. Ibid., 24 Dec. 1906, p. 6.

petitioned for a pay increase on the grounds that a recruit with a wife and three children had difficulty in existing on weekly pay of 16 shillings and 8 pence. 'Most of the married men on joining are somewhat in debt, and are unable to extricate themselves on account of rent to pay and articles to buy which are necessary for [the] support of wife and children.'[7] Seven years later constables of D Division at Paddington complained to Palmerston about the vindictiveness of their Irish sergeants, about the petty discipline, the deductions from wages, and about being ordered to go to church 'like so many schoolboys'.[8] In June 1853 the Manchester Watch Committee rejected the petitions from four divisions of the borough police for a pay rise on the grounds of 'their duty to the ratepayers' to keep costs down. The police response was a mass resignation by 250 of the 435 men and an address to the 'Gentry, Trade and Ratepayers in General' outlining the long hours they worked, the 'colds, rheumatism, asthma . . . insults, sarcasm' which they suffered in the job, and the low pay which left insufficient for

> food and raiment becoming the family of a police constable, who should appear as respectable members of society. Where are domestic utensils, household clothing, and lastly – though not least – the children's schooling to come from? It is very much to be doubted whether our authorities would be very anxious to appoint our sons as police constables, who had been educated and reared on so small a pittance.

The Watch Committee refused to be moved and after a week most of the men who had resigned requested reinstatement.[9] However, early in the following month a major dispute in the cotton trade gave the Manchester policemen an opportunity for exerting real pressure on the Watch Committee: 238 of them resigned, leaving those of their former colleagues who remained on the streets as prey to marauding gangs, and forcing shopkeepers to shut and board up their premises. The Watch Committee awarded a pay increase of 2 shillings a week within a day of the resignations, and all but fifteen men promptly returned to work.[10] Also in June 1853 the police in Hull had a petition for a wage increase drafted by two

7. Metropolitan PA 'The First Pay Claim'.
8. HO 45.6093, and see in general Ronald Charles Sopenoff, 'The police of London: the early history of the Metropolitan Police 1829–1856', Ph.D., Temple University, 1978, pp. 197–203.
9. *Manchester Guardian*, 4, 8, 11, 15 and 18 June 1853; quotation from 11 June.
10. Carolyn Steedman, *Policing the Victorian Community: The Formation of the English Provincial Police Forces, 1856–1880* (London: Routledge and Kegan Paul, 1984), pp. 133–4.

lawyers in the town. Again the Watch Committee refused to budge, and when a strike was threatened the committee interviewed each man separately about his intentions and required the immediate resignation of any man who was contemplating resignation or strike action over the refusal to augment pay. Forty-seven of the 116 constables in the force did resign; as in Manchester, after a week most of them requested reinstatement, but, unlike Manchester, there was no immediate opportunity for a resumption of the campaign with a successful outcome.[11]

Agitation over pay, pensions and conditions occasionally broke surface in the Metropolitan Police in the last 30 years of the nineteenth century. In 1872 a widespread petitioning campaign for improved pay shocked the Commissioner and his senior officers, especially when, on 17 October, over 3,000 sergeants and constables turned up for a mass meeting to discuss the demands. Sir Edmund Henderson communicated his concerns to the equally alarmed and surprised Home Office; a pay rise was rapidly granted and the hours of duty were made less onerous. At the same time it was decided to make an example of PC Henry Goodchild, who had acted as secretary for the divisional delegates organising the policemen's action. Goodchild was ordered to give information to his superiors about the proceedings of the delegates' committee and he was transferred to a different part of his division; he refused to comply with the former order and challenged the latter on the grounds that he was being punished when he had committed no offence. Goodchild claimed that he was denied the opportunity to speak in his defence and, at the conclusion of an interview to which he was summoned at Scotland Yard, he was summarily dismissed. In response to Goodchild's dismissal 180 men refused to go on duty on the night of Saturday 16 November; all were suspended, and 109 were then dismissed. After a few days, however, the majority were reinstated with a reduction in rank or the loss of a week's pay. The Commissioner also warned that future meetings of constables could only be held with his permission.[12]

The Commissioner's ruling seems to have fallen into abeyance by the beginning of the next decade when Parliament began discussing legislation on police pensions. From early 1881 PC Robert Birnie was active in collecting information and organising meetings and petitions on the pension issue. According to his glowing obituary in

11. HO 45.4780.
12. Gerald W. Reynolds and Anthony Judge, *The Night the Police went on Strike* (London: Weidenfeld & Nicolson, 1968), Appendix 1, pp. 202–12.

the *Police Review*, Birnie's activities were instrumental in the rejection of clauses objectionable to the police in a bill presented in 1882; moreover, he always cautioned his fellow constables against taking strike action.[13] The first claim is problematic, but since Birnie was promoted to sergeant in 1890, and, in spite of participating in the agitation of that year, since he survived the resulting dismissals, the second claim is probably correct.

Rumours of meetings between Metropolitan policemen and socialist and trades union leaders began to circulate towards the end of 1889. There were also rumours of new petitions over pay and conditions. To some extent these activities may have been encouraged by the sympathy of the Commissioner, James Monro, who, in the early summer of 1890, instructed his superintendents to get the opinion of their men on the Police Superannuation Bill then going through Parliament. Monro resigned in mid-June and his successor, Sir Edward Bradford, sought to put the lid on the growing agitation. Bradford's actions resulted, once again, in suspensions, followed by a brief strike for union recognition. The new Commissioner reacted rapidly and ruthlessly: 39 men were dismissed and 91 transferred.[14] However the Police Act of 1890 removed one of the main areas of complaint among the men: it guaranteed a pension after 25 years of service, or after only fifteen years if retirement was forced on medical grounds.

Agitation in 1889 and 1890 was also present in the City of London Police,[15] and the whole needs to be considered in the context of the appearance of the 'new unionism'. The late 1880s witnessed a growth of militant trade unionism among semi-skilled and poorly paid workers with a leadership of young men, many of whom had been influenced by socialist ideas. In 1889 gas workers and dockers in London had fought and won in significant industrial confrontations. The police agitation coincided with attempts to organise a union among the postmen. Men like Robert Birnie may have warned against strike action, but the rumoured links between policemen and trades union leaders towards the end of 1889 were said to involve John Burns, an early member of the Social Democratic Federation who had been prominent in the agitation surrounding 'Bloody Sunday' and the strike for the Docker's Tanner. Furthermore,

13. *Police Review*, 1 May 1908, pp. 210, 215. There was a petitioning campaign in favour of another superannuation bill in 1883: see *The Times*, 12 Feb. 1883, p. 12.
14. Reynolds and Judge, *The Night the Police went on Strike*, Appendix 2, pp. 213–25.
15. *The Times*, 11 June 1890, p. 12.

meetings of police delegates held during 1890 took place both in working men's clubs and on the premises of the SDF, and the police received vocal support from trades union activists.[16]

If the attempt at establishing a police union in London in 1890 failed, so too did several of the other attempts at creating new unions; but the idea did not die. The matter was discussed in the correspondence columns of the *Police Review*. In January 1908, for example, 'A Policeman' maintained that it was the agitation of 1889 which had led to the passing of the Police Superannuation Act; 'Cui Bono' opposed a union as it 'would be based on the assumption that it could drive, frighten, coerce or persuade . . . authorities to become gracious and grateful against their inclination'; while a third correspondent insisted that 'Unions of to-day obtain facilities through friendly negotiation, and force is their very last resort' and he pointed to the enormous public sympathy on the side of recent striking railwaymen.[17] Advocates of an English police union were encouraged by the success of Paul Rigail whose determination and organisational abilities led to the creation of the Association Générale Professionnelle du Personnel de la Préfecture de Police in Paris in June 1912, and in September the following year a notice appeared in the *Police Review* declaring that a union was being formed in the Metropolitan Police and that men could join secretly. The notice was inserted by the 'John Syme League', the friends of John Syme, a dour Presbyterian and former inspector of the Metropolitan Police who had been dismissed in 1910 for insubordination and who, ever since, had kept up a steady barrage of protest about oppression and injustice in the force. John Kempster, the editor of the *Police Review*, had been a strong supporter of Syme, but he disapproved of a union with the right to strike. In December 1913 he refused to accept any new union advertisements in the *Police Review* and he proposed, as an alternative organisation, a Police Federation which would specifically eschew the right to strike. Kempster's Federation was massively rejected by his readers: of some 21,000 forms issued inviting men to join the Federation, only about 100 were returned. But if the rank and file had little interest in the idea of a federation, many were sympathetic to the idea of a fully fledged union. A directive from the Home Secretary to provincial chief constables that men who joined the union were liable to dimissal, and an order by the Metropolitan Police Commissioner,

16. Ibid., 26 May, p. 8; 2 June, p. 10; 13 June, p. 9; 21 June, p. 7.
17. *Police Review*, 31 Jan. 1908, p. 58; 17 Jan., p. 34; 24 Jan., p. 45.

Sir Edward Henry, threatening dismissal to any man who joined either the federation or the union, had little deterrent effect. Large meetings of the union's supporters were held in London in December 1913 when Syme claimed a membership approaching 5,000; whatever the accuracy of this claim, by the end of 1913 and beginning of 1914 the union had established itself firmly and clandestinely within the Metropolitan Police.[18]

In addressing a meeting of supporters of the union in Trafalgar Square in December 1913, Syme had declared that the police in Liverpool were also organising.[19] Organisation among the rank and file, and petitions for improved pay and conditions, had continued within provincial police forces in the closing decades of the nineteenth century and the early years of the twentieth. In Birmingham in 1871 the constables made a request to the Watch Committee, for improved pay and increased leisure time, through their sympathetic head constable;[20] but in Hove, in 1899, constables who presented a list of grievances to the Watch Committee were reduced in rank and pay.[21] The organisation for these petitions continued to be localised and *ad hoc* until, in defiance of the Home Secretary's ruling, the new union began to spread into the provinces. Yet before the union established a particular form of identity among some policemen, a national corporate identity was being deliberately fostered by newspapers aimed specifically at the professional policeman.

The *Police Service Advertiser* first appeared in 1866 as 'A Journal for the Police and Constabulary Forces of Great Britain and the Colonies'. Initially it carried some general news, but from February 1867 it began to focus entirely on police matters. 'Probably no public servant is so ill-used by his employer as the policeman', proclaimed an early leader. 'Placed by the public to protect the peace, the first thing the public does is to bring its officers into ridicule, and the next to ill-treat them.'[22] The *Advertiser* saw it as its duty to rectify this situation. Critical of the lack of a proper system of superannuation, it helped in the formation of the Police Mutual Assurance Association. In imitation of other professional journals it printed columns

18. *The Times*, 19 Dec. 1913, p. 8; 20 Dec., p. 8; 22 Dec., p. 10; 29 Dec., p. 2; Reynolds and Judge, *The Night the Police went on Strike*, ch. 2; V.L. Allen, 'The National Union of Police and Prison Officers', *Economic History Review* 11 (1958–59), 133–43.
19. *The Times*, 22 Dec. 1913, p. 10; Ron Bean, 'Police unrest, unionization and the 1919 strike in Liverpool', *Journal of Contemporary History* 15 (1980), 633–53, at p. 636.
20. Steedman, *Policing the Victorian Community*, p. 135.
21. *Hansard*, CXL, 24 Mar. 1899, col. 322.
22. *Police Service Advertiser*, 26 Jan. 1867.

of legal notes on problems of day-to-day policing and answered readers' queries. It opened its correspondence columns to lively debates about whether or not the policeman had the right to vote, and whether or not he should be armed, as well as to complaints about wages and terms and conditions of service. Its partisan leaders probably sharpened its readers' perceptions of such matters; while the information which it gave about conditions in different forces gave serving constables the opportunity to make comparisons and may, in consequence, have fostered some of the *ad hoc* organisation and petitioning. The *Advertiser*'s change of name to the *Police Guardian* in 1872 implicitly reflected both how it perceived of the policeman in relation to society, and how it perceived its own role in relation to the police.

John Kempster published the first edition of *Police Review and Parade Gossip* in January 1893. It was intended as a forum for the interchange of ideas among policemen. Like the first editor of the *Advertiser*, Kempster believed that the policeman was not accorded his full worth by society, and he perceived 'a tendency, all too prevalent, as evidenced on the stage and in the comic Press, as well as on the public footpath, to treat a policeman with less regard for his own self respect than should prevail amongst men towards their fellow-men in all ranks of life'. The policeman, he insisted, should not be regarded 'as a mere chattel or machine: he is a man and a citizen'. Kempster argued that new recruits were now better educated, having 'shared the advantages of our modern Board Schools'; as a consequence they needed 'some means of continuous culture . . . [and] healthy sources of information upon matters specially bearing upon their useful and honourable career'.[23] The *Review* printed poems by policemen, ran essay competitions and gave instruction on the kind of elementary maths that were necessary for promotion exams. Its correspondence columns debated pay and promotion. Both in leading *Review* articles and elsewhere Kempster lobbied for the policeman's right to vote in local elections, for a day of rest, for a more fair system of promotion. He championed individuals whom he believed to have been treated unfairly: in November 1907, for example, in the *Review* and at a public meeting in Abercan, he took up the case of Inspector George Groves who had been dismissed from the Monmouth Constabulary for allegedly requesting merely that a gentleman reimburse him for a penny stamp.[24]

23. *Police Review*, 2 Jan. 1893, p. 1.
24. Ibid., 15 Nov. 1907, pp. 547–9, and 22 Nov., pp. 559–60.

Most of the *Review*'s campaigns were fought in conjunction with the Police and Citizens' Association which Kempster had also been instrumental in creating in 1893. The Association provided education for self-improvement and helped men prepare for promotion exams. Its president, Charles E. Swann, the MP for Manchester North, regularly spoke up in Parliament for the rights both of individual policemen and for policemen as a group.[25] During the discussions in the *Review*'s correspondence columns in 1908 on whether or not a police trade union should be established, it was mooted that the Police and Citizens' Association might even take over the tasks of a union.[26]

Alongside his criticisms of abuses and his desire to win what he considered to be a fair deal for his readers, Kempster was also concerned to create a positive image of policemen. While he was a partisan for the ordinary policeman against unfairness by superior officers and the parsimony of local authorities which deprived men of their rightful due, Kempster's positive image was that of the respectable classes and much like that urged by Home Office officials since the middle of the nineteenth century. The policeman's 'worst enemy' was 'the spirit of arbitrary and dictatorial supremacy, so often misnamed discipline' which could make a man on the beat appear 'an overbearing bully, a cross-grained, ill-bred, tyrannical curmudgeon'.[27] The individual policeman should not be armed: 'for whenever the preventive arm is sharpened thus the desperate hand of crime rises, with a deadlier weapon, to the occasion . . . If the burglar feels all right with his "jemmy", let us not force on him a revolver.'[28] Furthermore, while the policeman had the right to vote like any other citizen, he was strictly to separate his civic function from his civic duty; thus when a letter appeared in a London newspaper claiming to come from members of the City and Metropolitan forces and arguing that police control be transferred to the LCC, the *Police Review* denied the existence of the society which sent

25. It was Swann who raised the disciplining of the constables in Hove (see above, n. 21); see also *Hansard*, XV, 31 July 1893, col. 877, and ibid., XXVII, 16 July 1894, cols 21–2. Swann used the Germanic spelling of his name, 'Schwann', until the First World War.

26. *Police Review*, 31 Jan. 1908, p. 57; 7 Feb, p. 70; 14 Feb., p. 81.

27. Ibid., 31 Jan. 1908, p. 55.

28. Ibid., 23 Jan. 1893, p. 37. In fact precisely the opposite had occurred ten years earlier when a scare about armed burglars had led to the arming of some men on the beat: see Clive Emsley, ' "The thump of wood on a swede turnip": police violence in nineteenth-century England', *CJH* 6 (1985), 125–49, at pp. 136–41.

the letter: 'As men, [policemen] can think and judge for themselves; as citizens, they can vote; but as members of the public service they deem it a wise policy to maintain neutrality.'[29]

Police and politics

Kempster's insistence that the police should maintain a strict neutrality in political matters was in keeping with the respectable classes' perception of the Bobby. Political policing can be taken to mean at least two separate things: on the one hand overt political partisanship on the part of the police; on the other the surveillance of politically suspect groups or individuals. Both were regarded as alien to the evolving police system in England. In 1867, during a lengthy debate conducted in the correspondence columns of the *Police Service Advertiser* on whether or not policemen should be allowed the vote, one serving policeman explained:

> Anyone who has travelled abroad cannot have failed to be struck with the inconvenience – to use a mild term – resulting from the system under which the police become either political agents or partizan politicians. In France not only are they obliged to vote or canvass for the Government candidates, but they are required to distribute their addresses and voting papers, while in the United States they attach themselves to one or other of the great political factions for which that country is distinguished, and, instead of acting impartially as the police of this country do, they may be not unfrequently seen, while 'on duty' at the polling booths, shamelessly impeding those whom they know to be opposed to their party while endeavouring to deposit their voting papers in the ballot box.[30]

A few months before the outbreak of the First World War the Home Secretary, Reginald McKenna, bridled when asked if 'the special or political branch' of the Detective Department at Scotland Yard was part of the Metropolitan Police. 'There is no "political" branch of the Criminal Investigation Department', he protested. 'As regards the special branch, the answer is in the affirmative.'[31] Overt political partisanship was kept to a minimum, but a degree of political surveillance was maintained during the nineteenth century and increased in the years immediately before 1914.

29. *Police Review*, 9 Jan. 1893, p. 18.   30. *Police Service Advertiser*, 6 Apr. 1867.
31. *Hansard*, LXI, 30 Apr. 1914, col. 1874; see also ibid., LXII, 5 May 1914, col. 121.

104   *The English Police: A Political and Social History*

Of course, during the nineteenth century the government at Westminster wanted to keep an eye on those it considered to be potential political trouble-makers. The eighteenth-century belief that spies and informers were inimical to English liberty was maintained, indeed it had been boosted as a result of the use of spies during, and immediately after, the revolutionary and Napoleonic wars. In two particularly notorious incidents, the Pentrich Rising of 1817 and the Cato Street Conspiracy of 1820, it appeared that men had been executed at least partly because of the activities of *agents provocateurs*. These anxieties had contributed to the resistance to detective police on the part of Rowan and, particularly, Mayne. Three years after the creation of the Metropolitan Police there was an outcry which suggested that all of the worst fears about the police as a reservoir of spies and *agents provocateurs* were confirmed. In 1832 Metropolitan Police Sergeant William Popay, a former schoolmaster born in Norfolk, interpreted his instructions to investigate the radical National Political Union to mean that he could disguise himself as an impoverished revolutionary and participate vociferously in political meetings. Concern was such that a parliamentary enquiry was set up, and Popay himself was dismissed from the force.[32] The incident helped to ensure that Metropolitan Police infiltration of Chartist groups later in the 1830s and 1840s was limited and, to a remarkable degree, open. In April 1840, for example, two officers attended a Chartist committee meeting in plain clothes; rather than give false names and addresses, they left the meeting and returned later, in uniform, requesting formal permission to be present. Probably there were also some undercover agents, and at least one self-appointed police spy in Greenwich attempted to act as an *agent provocateur*. The provincial police appear to have enjoyed a much greater freedom in this respect than the Metropolitan Police.[33] But it was always difficult to have regular police constables infiltrating radical committees without fear of their being recognised. Plain clothes constables joined the crowds at mass political meetings to keep the uniformed officers informed of the sentiments of the crowds and the likelihood of trouble developing; and such men, on occasions, found themselves on the wrong end of police truncheons when the uniformed constables were directed to disperse a meeting

32. *PP* 1833 (627) XIII, *Report from the Select Committee on the Petition of Frederick Young and Others.*
33. F.C. Mather, *Public Order in the Age of the Chartists* (Manchester: University Press, 1959), esp. pp. 192–8; and for the Greenwich spy see Geoffrey Crossick, *An Artisan Elite in Victorian Society* (London: Croom Helm, 1978), pp. 209, 239.

or clear a street.[34] However, the uniformed constable, openly taking notes for all to see, was a feature of political meetings during the 1850s and 1860s.

While reluctant to establish a secret, political police, the British governments of the mid-nineteenth century also operated an open-door policy for political refugees. The aftermath of the European revolutions of 1848 saw the arrival of many such, notably Louis Blanc, Louis Kossuth, Alexandre Ledru-Rollin, Joseph Mazzini and Karl Marx. European governments jumped at the invitation to send representatives of their own police to London to assist the Metropolitan Police in supervising the Great Exhibition of 1851. The invitation was meant to help identify foreign thieves and pickpockets; but the European governments saw it as an unprecedented opportunity to investigate the activities of their political opponents in exile. At the same time the Metropolitan Police began some limited surveillance of political refugees, but the British government was always insistent that if foreign governments wanted any discreet information about their political exiles, then they must enquire through diplomatic channels and never directly to Scotland Yard; any replies to the enquiries were to be returned in the same way. During the 1850s the British government used Secret Service money to assist some 1,500 French, Italian and Polish refugees in emigrating to the United States. This action appears to have been popular with European governments; it was kept secret from the British public.[35]

The peculiarly English attitude to political surveillance continued into the second half of the nineteenth century. When the Home Office wanted details of refugees from the Paris Commune its officials decided that the best way to collect such information was to write to those who were most involved; a letter was consequently sent to Karl Marx who responded by sending full details of the International Workingmen's Association.[36] But while the ideas of English liberty were sincerely held, the political, social and economic structure of mid-nineteenth-century England also contributed to the continuance of this attitude to political policing. Until

34. David Goodway, *London Chartism 1838–1848* (Cambridge: CUP, 1982), pp. 114–15, 123–4.

35. Phillip Thurmond Smith, *Policing Victorian London: Political Policing, Public Order and the London Metropolitan Police* (Westport, Conn.: Greenwood Press, 1985), ch. 4.

36. Christopher Andrew, *Secret Service: The Making of the British Intelligence Community* (London: Heinemann, 1985), pp. 42–3; Bernard Porter, *The Origins of the Vigilant State: The London Metropolitan Police Special Branch before the First World War* (London: Weidenfeld & Nicolson, 1987), pp. 9–10.

the last quarter of the century the British economy dominated the world. Politicians and jurists liked to think that the constitutional and legal structure of Britain provided a model for other, less fortunate, nations to follow; in the same way the British economy, based on industrialisation and free trade, was also thought to provide a model. Britain may have had Chartism, but it did not experience revolutions like other European powers; nor were there men lurking at home, or waiting in foreign exile, with alternative constitutional structures to unify or to restore a nation-state (as in the case of some Germans, Italians and Poles), to re-establish an old government (as in the case of Bonapartists, Royalists, or Republicans at different times in France), or to establish something new (as, in particular, with the socialists in Germany and a variety of terrorist groups in Russia). As an under secretary at the Home Office put it just two months after the Versailles troops had surprised the Communards at Porte St Cloud and fought their way into Paris: 'We can safely rely on the good sense of the great bulk of our own working-classes to check and defeat the wild and impractical designs of the few.'[37] In the following year *The Times* boasted that until English working men were fools, fanatics, or something worse, 'we have little fear of the International'.[38] Yet events were not to allow this relaxed and self-satisfied attitude to continue. Terrorist campaigns by the Irish Republican Brotherhood, or Fenians, which spilled over from John Bull's other island in 1867 an again in the early 1880s, led the government to authorise the development of the Metropolitan Police Special Branch working in co-operation with the more practised political policemen of Ireland; indeed, the original name of this section was the Special Irish Branch. There were other pressures too. Foreign governments continued to be worried about the political exiles who sought refuge in England, and more importantly there were calls for international action against anarchists, nihilists and socialists. The new Special Branch began to maintain surveillance of such suspects: in December 1893, for example, the Librarian of the British Museum received a request for an admission ticket to the Reading Room from a Scotland Yard detective: 'I do not require it for the ordinary purpose but as I understand that certain persons (who are certainly not above suspicion) frequent the rooms it would perhaps be of assistance to me. Under ordinary circumstances one cannot enter

37. Quoted in Porter, *The Origins of the Vigilant State*, p. 10.
38. *The Times*, 15 Apr. 1872, p. 11.

without disclosing his identity and worse still that of the suspect.'[39] 'Immorality', generally in the sense of homosexual behaviour, and political subversion were targets for the Branch,[40] and it is probably significant that the major developments in the Special Branch during the 1880s and 1890s coincided not only with the threats from Fenian terrorists and international anarchists, but also with a declining confidence in Britain's international superiority which led to anxieties about the future. There were fears that the British 'race' was somehow being undermined; and it was becoming obvious that the economy was losing its premier position to the burgeoning industries of Germany and the United States.

The turn of the century witnessed further concerns about foreign anarchists and doubts about the policy of offering asylum to foreign exiles. The murder of one policeman in the Tottenham Outrage of January 1909, and of three more in Houndsditch in December 1910 in the run-up to the Siege of Sidney Street, brought the climax to these anxieties, though, as Bernard Porter has pointed out: 'Foreign anarchists in London perpetrated no crimes against British political targets in the 1900s, and no overtly "terrorist" acts. They did not, so far as one could tell, shoot policemen out of principle, but simply in order to avoid being caught.'[41] But the concerns were not confined to London: early in 1909 the Birmingham Police were in secret communication with the Special Branch about a suspected German anarchist who taught at the Berlitz School of Languages in the city and who was, allegedly, seeking to subvert a young man who worked in the telegraphic section of the Post Office.[42] The scope of the Special Branch widened significantly in the period immediately preceding the First World War to include suffragettes and British socialists. These moves were encouraged by successive Home Secretaries, first Winston Churchill and then Reginald McKenna, and enthusiastically directed by Basil Thomson, the colonial civil servant who became head of the Special Branch in June 1913. Churchill also brought the first head of the future MI5, Vernon Kell, into close contact with the country's chief constables during the pre-war spy scare. This scare seriously infected the embryonic Secret Service and, through the chief constables,

---

39. British Museum Central Archives, Confidential Papers, Francis Powell, Scotland Yard, to the Librarian, the British Museum, 12 Dec. 1893. My thanks to Christopher Date of the British Library for this reference.

40. Porter, *The Origins of the Vigilant State*, p. 99.   41. Ibid., p. 162.

42. West Midlands PA Birmingham Police, Superintendents' Reports and Confidential Letters, 1901–23, fols 335–8, 341.

Kell arranged for the supervision of aliens and the preparation of a secret Register of Aliens. The chief constables used their men to investigate suspects on Kell's behalf and directed them to be on the lookout for the spies and secret agents of potential enemies.[43] The directions were sometimes couched in terms which appear silly, but their comic nature is, in itself, illustrative of the extent of the spy scare. In May 1909 the Chief Constable of the East Riding asked his superintendents: 'Are any "Foreigners" ever seen in your district, such as "Organ Grinders", "Waiters", or servants of any kind, "Bandsmen", travelling "Photographers", or in fact "Foreigners" of any class, or acting in any capacity?' In January 1912 he was warning that 'Secret information' had been received 'that a number of Foreign Naval Officers [had been] given special leave to England with a view of making themselves acquainted with the Harbours and Landing places along the East Coast'. He expected them to go 'cruising about in small boats, making enquiries from Fishermen and others, and making extensive notes'.[44] With the fear of subversion during the First World War and in the aftermath of the Russian Revolution, the provincial English police, the Metropolitan Police Special Branch and MI5 were to build on their pre-war links and take much more positive steps in the direction of political surveillance.

While the reluctance to develop a police for political surveillance gradually seeped away, the public determination to prevent police partisanship remained as strong as ever. Yet partisanship on the part of the police was not unknown during the nineteenth century. There were allegations that police sided with Protestants against the Catholic Irish on several occasions; and such allegations in mid-

43. Andrew, *Secret Service*, pp. 103–4. Some of the surviving archives of the police forces give a tantalising glimpse of one side of these investigations. In December 1912, for example, the Chief Constable of the East Riding issued a 'STRICTLY CONFIDENTIAL CIRCULAR MEMORANDUM' to his superintendents along with 'Notes on the work and methods of Foreign Secret Service Agents'. The latter is, unfortunately, no longer with the surviving memorandum; the superintendents were advised that 'this paper must always be kept carefully under lock and key', and were warned of 'the extreme necessity of constant vigilance and attention respecting [aliens]' (Humberside PA East Riding Constabulary, Memo Book, 1912–16, fol. 27). In Birmingham the police carried out enquiries for Kell into Gustav Adolf Strasser in April 1913, and Paul Metz from May to September 1913; the former seems to have been innocuous, the latter was rather more interesting since he seems to have been a purveyor of dirty postcards as well as having a son in the Royal Flying Corps (West Midlands PA Birmingham Police, Superintendents' Reports and Confidential Letters, 1901–23, fols 379–81, 387–90, 392–3).
44. Humberside PA East Riding Constabulary, Memo Book, 1912–16, fols 90, 188.

nineteenth-century Liverpool were not unfounded.[45] Rather more common were the allegations that the police were partial towards brewers and publicans. When the smaller boroughs, with police forces of no more than a few dozen men, became embroiled in arguments over the temperance issue, with Liberal supporters of the Temperance Movement lining up against Tory brewers, then the police, as agents of the politically appointed watch committees, could not help but become involved. It was this involvement which some of those hostile to the county police being subordinated to county councils had in mind in the Local Government Bill debates of 1888. '[T]he Licensed Victuallers are pretty sure to be largely represented in the new Councils', warned the deputy chairman of the Gloucestershire Bench. 'This will not tend to as thorough or impartial supervision of public-houses as heretofore. A hint to a policeman that he has been over-zealous in his watch on a particular house will be readily taken when given by one whom the policeman recognises as his employer.'[46] But even under the standing joint committee system there could be problems: in November 1901 the Chief Constable of Staffordshire informed the Home Office that in parts of his jurisdiction magistrates could not be guaranteed to convict in cases of breaches of the licensing laws:

[I]t is certain that licensing administration would be better in Lichfield if so many people were not interested in the local breweries which own many of the too numerous licensed houses, and it is also certain that the subordinate members of the police force will not go on reporting offences if magistrates discourage them. It is however hopeless to expect that the general body of borough magistrates in a small place like Lichfield should be superior to the pressure of local interests.[47]

Considerable disquiet was expressed in the pages of *Police Review* in 1908 when a superintendent of the Portsmouth Police, on his retirement, received a cheque and a letter of thanks from the local brewers.[48] In the following year the Home Secretary stepped in to advise the Eastbourne Watch Committee that the entertainment offered by local licensed victuallers to a police football team after

45. Frank Neal, *Sectarian Violence: The Liverpool Experience, 1819–1914* (Manchester: University Press, 1988), pp. 144–5.
46. 'The County Government Bill', *Murray's Magazine* III (1888), 738–60; at p. 755.
47. Staffs. PA Staffordshire Chief Constable's Letter Book, 1900–1908, fols 229–31, Anson to Under Secretary of State, 18 Nov. 1901.
48. *Police Review*, 6 Mar. 1908, pp. 115, 117; 27 Mar., p. 148; 29 May, p. 255; 5 June, p. 271; 12 June, p. 292.

a charity match was 'open to very serious objection'. At the 'meat tea' Councillor Major S. F. Cooke had declared that the match

> evidenced the nice harmonious feelings that existed between [the victuallers] and the police of the borough. He also maintained that the police and the licensed victuallers, if they put their heads together, could do more to prevent drunkenness than any number of those extravagant temperance lectures they had heard so much of lately (applause).

In response to the Home Secretary's complaint the Watch Committee instructed the Chief Constable that such entertainments would not be permitted in future.[49] On some occasions policemen were accused of partiality towards the temperance side: in the summer of 1908 the licensed victuallers of Clay Cross in Derbyshire ganged up to bring accusations of discourtesy and incivility against a police inspector who appears to have been enforcing the licensing laws with a new determination and rigour.[50]

Strenuous efforts were made to ensure that policemen were not seen to be partial in local politics. In 1841 Superintendent Jesse Maynard was dismissed from the Brighton Police after it was revealed, and after questions had been raised in Parliament, that he had instructed members of the force to 'guard' some Lewes voters in a public house, thus influencing the outcome of a parliamentary election.[51] A few men in the early borough forces, as ratepayers, were able to exercise their rights as electors, but the members of the county police were disfranchised from the very beginning. Only in 1887, following the Police Disabilities Removal Act, were men who qualified under the franchise legislation allowed to vote in parliamentary elections; a second Act, passed in 1893, permitted them to vote in municipal elections. But large numbers of policemen, especially single men living in section houses, remained unenfranchised.[52] Even when the vote had been granted to some, there was disquiet over whether or not a retired policeman should be permitted to be a member of a standing joint committee.[53] The most glaring instance of political partiality came during the general election of 1900 when Sir John Dunne, the Chief Constable of Cumberland, appeared on the hustings alongside the Conservative

49. *Eastbourne Chronicle*, 17 Apr. 1909, p. 6; 3 July, pp. 5–6.
50. *Police Review*, 15 May 1908, p. 232; 19 June, p. 292.
51. D.J. Oakenson, 'The origins and development of policing in Brighton and Hove, 1830–1900', Ph.D., University of Brighton, 1995, p. 252.
52. *Hansard*, LXIII, 11 June 1914, col. 575.
53. *Justice of the Peace*, LIX (1895), 9 Mar., p. 154; 11 May, p. 296.

candidate and spoke in his favour. It was the second occasion that Dunne had tested the limits of the law relating to police behaviour in elections; his defence in 1900 was that there had been 'very extraordinary attacks made upon everybody nearly who took the side of good government [by] the pro-Boers, the revolutionists, the anarchists, and the Socialists'. The Home Secretary considered that Dunne's actions were 'not only . . . a contravention of the [Constabulary] Act of 1839, but . . . prejudicial to the interests of discipline'. But he advised the Standing Joint Committee against taking proceedings against their Chief Constable.[54]

The Boer War brought other accusations of partiality. It was suggested in Parliament that the police were tardy in assisting critics of the war when, at public meetings, they became the objects of assault and riot.[55] In the by-election held in Stratford-upon-Avon in the summer of 1901 there were complaints that the Warwickshire county police had failed in their duty to protect the Liberal candidate and his supporters during a meeting at the Corn Exchange (Bolton King, the Liberal candidate, was known as a critic of the war and he had also been critical of some of the behaviour of the British army). A sub-group of the Standing Joint Committee recommended an enquiry; the Chief Constable was furious and, at a meeting of the full committee, he forced a vote which divided largely on party lines and which negated the recommendation. The *Stratford Upon Avon Herald* lamented the Chief Constable's 'melodramatic action':

> By taking the course he did he raised the suspicion that something might transpire that would scarcely agree with his reported assertions that the police were in the right in the action they pursued. Now that the enquiry is burked there will be lurking suspicions that the police favoured the disturbers of the meetings and Mr. Bolton King adduces evidence which shows that perfect fairness was by no means shown. Others are in a position to contribute strength to this belief.[56]

The *Warwick and Warwickshire Advertiser* was also disappointed: 'It is of vital importance that we should preserve the English right of

54. Ibid., LXV (1901), 24 Apr., pp. 267–8. See also *Cumberland Pacquet* (1900), 25 Oct., p. 8; 8 Nov., p. 8; ibid. (1901), 8 Apr., p. 8; *Penrith Times* (1900), 30 Oct., p. 6; 13 Nov., p. 7.

55. *Hansard*, LXXIX, 2 Mar. 1900, cols 1614–26; ibid., LXXX, 5 Mar., col. 44; 8 Mar., col. 391; 15 Mar., col. 950.

56. *Stratford Upon Avon Herald* (1901), 19 July, p. 8; see also ibid., 12 July, pp. 2, 8.

free speech, even to express unpopular opinions, and that we should not allow questions of the conduct of the police to be decided by political bias.'[57] A week later the *Advertiser* published an extract from the Unionist *Birmingham Daily Post* which, while it suggested that Bolton King's injudicious language had provoked the trouble, also believed that the Standing Joint Committee had made a wrong decision which 'could only provoke a suspicion of political bias'. The *Post* then contrasted the watch committees of the towns with the county standing joint committees, regretting that the latter did not give 'the community that direct control [of the police] which they ought to have'.[58] Before the end of the year a serious riot had erupted in Birmingham when David Lloyd George, the fiery young Welsh MP who like Bolton King had been critical of the South African War, attempted to speak in the city. The police had expected trouble; but the disorder was such that the meeting was halted and Lloyd George had to be smuggled out of the Town Hall disguised in a police uniform. A police baton charge was considered necessary to clear the streets, and a young man was killed, apparently as a result of a blow from a police truncheon. Several respectable citizens protested about the behaviour of some constables, and Lloyd George himself believed that there was a particularly ferocious aspect to the police baton charge because the city force contained Irishmen who were 'strong pro-Boers'. Almost as if to prove the point made by the *Birmingham Daily Post*, the Watch Committee arranged for those who claimed to be victims of police brutality to attend identification parades of the police divisions involved and mounted a major enquiry into the 'Lloyd George Riot'. However, the promise of the investigation was far greater than the yield: as the proceedings rumbled on the chairman of the Watch Committee lost his council seat in an election, and the whole matter was allowed to subside.[59]

Police and the pre-war strike wave

Arguments about the respective merits of watch committees and standing joint committees continued in the decade before the First

---

57. *Warwick and Warwickshire Advertiser* (1901), 13 July, p. 5.

58. Ibid., 20 July, p. 5.

59. West Midlands PA Birmingham Police, Lloyd George Riots, Documents and Statements, December 1901. For Lloyd George's comment see Peter Rowland, *Lloyd George* (London: Barrie and Jenkins, 1975), p. 161 note.

World War. In 1908 the West Riding County Council promoted an unsuccessful parliamentary bill to transfer control of county police forces from standing joint committees to the elected county councils. E.J. Crossley, the vice-chairman of the West Riding Council's Law and Parliamentary Committee, believed that 'magistrates as administrators of the law would find their hands strengthened if the police, who were apt to be regarded in some quarters as their servants, were controlled by an independent body'.[60] Early in the following year a reporter for *The Times* rehearsed the old arguments about the need for the Metropolitan Police to remain under the direct control of the Home Secretary, and he even enlisted the evidence of a German government functionary who had studied the English system.[61] Yet while the arguments continued, centralisation increased and local police authorities were increasingly by-passed; industrial disorder was the cue for much of this.

It was not unknown for senior police officers to take a particular interest in radical working men. Following the Chartist disorders of 1842 the Chief Constable of Glamorgan persuaded local iron masters to dismiss radicals and advised other employers to take care in their selection of agents and overmen.[62] It was also quite possible for a senior police officer to obtain information on an individual which would be of interest to that individual's employer. In 1857 the Chief Constable of Bedford gave confidential information to a local employer about one of his workmen. The employer, a Mr Howard, made the information public, and the Watch Committee lamented that he 'should have acted with so much indiscretion in this matter as the circumstance is likely to produce an ill feeling unnecessarily against the Police on the part of the Class of Persons to which the individual in question belongs'. The committee resolved that the police should never impart such information again 'where no violation of the Law has taken place or is to be apprehended, and even then it should not be given except in furtherance of the ends of justice'.[63] In 1863 the Chief Constable of Lincolnshire protested that his men were 'constantly receiving letters from private enquiry offices seeking information as to the character, respectability, and money value of persons residing in

60. *Police Review*, 10 Jan. 1908, p. 15. The Local Government (Transfer of Powers of Standing Joint Committees) Bill was printed in ibid., 21 Feb., p. 88.

61. *The Times*, 13 Jan. 1909, p. 4.

62. David J.V. Jones, *The Last Rising: The Newport Insurrection of 1839* (Oxford: Clarendon Press, 1985), pp. 224–5.

63. Beds. RO, Bedford Borough Records, B 3/2 Watch Committee Minutes, 1856–74, 20 Mar. 1857.

the Towns and villages'. He believed that the police of some counties and boroughs had given such information when requested, and had been paid for it. The Chief Constable of Huntingdonshire instructed his superintendents and inspectors to find out whether such enquiries had been made to members of his force, and he ordered that any such requests in future should be referred to him immediately.[64] How often such information was requested and the extent to which it was given is impossible to assess; it seems probable that such incidents were most likely to meet with success where an employer seeking information was himself a member of a watch committee, a magistrates' police committee or, later, a standing joint committee.[65] Throughout the Victorian period the law favoured the employer. Most obvious in this respect was the Master and Servant Act of 1823 (4 Geo. IV cap. 34), which enacted that if an employer broke a contract he could only be sued in the civil courts, while if a workman broke a contract he could be pursued by the full force of the criminal law including, of course, the police. Conservative governments mitigated the severity of this legislation in 1867 and abolished it eight years later; thereafter, police involvement in industrial relations generally occurred during a lock-out or a strike when the police had the responsibility for maintaining the peace. In theory, and in the Victorian liberal parlance of equality before the law, this was an impartial task; in practice it often meant confrontation with strikers or those locked out.[66]

The incidence of what Eric Hobsbawm characterised as 'collective bargaining by riot', by which strikers sought to coerce an employer by damaging his plant and property, may have declined during the nineteenth century as trades unions became better organised, permanent, and received a degree of legal recognition;[67]

64. Cambs. PA Huntingdonshire Constabulary, Chief Constable's Memos, 1857–99, No. 26, 23 Sept. 1863.
65. In the summer of 1890 the Chief Constable of Birmingham was investigating the morals of a member of the staff of the city's Clerk of the Peace. In 1904 he requested the Metropolitan Police CID to 'make quiet enquiry' into the background and circumstances of a woman on behalf of the city's stipendiary magistrate. However, in the following year, in response to the request from a man, whom he did not know, to make enquiries into a certain individual, he replied: 'Police enquiries can only be made in criminal cases or in connection with crime, and it is contrary to the regulations of the Police Service to make private enquiries as to the standing of persons, for the information of individuals': West Midlands PA Birmingham Copy Letter Book, Chief Constable's Office 1890–91, fol. 527; Superintendents' Reports and Confidential Letters, 1901–23, fols 153, 186, 195.
66. Trygve Tholfsen, *Working Class Radicalism in Mid-Victorian England* (London: Croom Helm, 1976), pp. 179–89.
67. E.J. Hobsbawm, 'The machine breakers', *Past and Present* 1 (1952), 57–70. David Philips has suggested that the general trend away from violence in industrial

but strikes still contained the potential for disorder. The Conspiracy and Protection of Property Act of 1875 and the Trade Disputes Act of 1906 authorised a degree of peaceful picketing by members of a trade union involved in industrial action. But the definition of peaceful picketing remained murky and it was largely left to the discretion of those policemen present to ensure that a picket line did not lead to obstruction or a breach of the peace. It was claimed in Parliament in 1914 that in some instances members of the Metropolitan Police 'themselves have decided that not more than one picket shall be allowed'.[68] Ugly confrontations began when employers sought to bring in what they called 'free labour', and what strikers called 'blacklegs' or 'scabs'. Such confrontations saw the police deployed to prevent intimidation and violence, but in practical terms this meant the protection of the strike-breakers. There were others who might need police protection in a trade dispute, and whose protection, in turn, made the police appear partial. The trouble at Silksworth in 1891 began primarily because the police were present to protect the bailiffs, or 'Candymen', evicting strikers from company housing; there were also allegations that the police were instructed to prevent desertion on the part of those 'Candymen' disgusted with their job. The Home Secretary was able to argue in Parliament that the Durham Constabulary were nothing to do with him; and the subsequent complaints that partiality within the Durham Standing Joint Committee prevented discussion of the affair and that partiality on the part of local magistrates led to the dismissal of assault cases against the two superintendents on the occasion of the incident also fell on deaf ears.[69]

Two years after the Silksworth incident a miners' strike in West Yorkshire resulted in fatalities, and, in consequence, more precise instructions were issued to the civil power about how to respond to

disputes applied to industries, like mining, which had a secure future in the industrial age and which, therefore, enabled the workforce to negotiate with some strength; it did not apply, in contrast, to those industries like handloom-weaving and nailmaking which were under threat from industrialisation and were ultimately destroyed by it. David Philips, 'Riots and public order in the Black Country, 1835–1860', in John Stevenson and Roland Quinault (eds), *Popular Protest and Public Order: Six Studies in British History, 1790–1920* (London: Allen & Unwin, 1974), pp. 162–3.

68. *Hansard*, LXIII, 23 June 1914, col. 1639. This may have been the result of a particularly strict interpretation on instructions issued to the Metropolitan Police by the Home Office in 1911 and again in 1913 which said that a worker was not to be approached by more than one 'persuader' at a time, and then only with the worker's consent. See Barbara Weinberger, *Keeping the Peace? Policing Strikes in Britain 1906–1926* (Oxford: Berg, 1991), p. 108.

69. *Hansard*, CCCLI, 5 Mar. 1891, col. 285; 13 Mar., col. 925; 16 Mar., cols 1058–9, 1073–4.

disorder. Early in September 1893 the Chief Constable of the West Riding found his force of 1,042 men impossibly stretched by the demands of the strike and the crowds expected at the Doncaster races. Unable to spare any constables when strikers entered Ackton Hall Colliery at Featherstone to force an end to continuing surface work, he arranged for a squad of 28 soldiers to rendezvous with a magistrate at the scene. The appearance of the soldiers at the colliery inflamed the situation: the soldiers were stoned and they responded, eventually, by firing on the crowd, leaving two dead and fourteen wounded. The shootings were a profound shock. No-one had been shot by troops during a riot since the Chartist period, and it had confidently been assumed by most of late Victorian society that, over the preceding half-century, the police had replaced the army when it came to deaing with disorder. An enquiry was set up to investigate the incident,[70] and in the following year a departmental committee was appointed to define the responsibilities of policemen and soldiers in the event of a riot, and particularly to consider the circumstances in which the military might aid the police.[71] The committee urged police forces to enter into mutual aid agreements with each other as a means of bringing greater constabulary force to bear in the event of riot. While, as has been explained above, police forces had aided each other from the middle of the century, and while the Police Act of 1890 had recommended formal mutual aid agreements, very few such agreements had been made by 1895. The committee suggested that, in the counties, the chief constable was the man best placed to recognise the need for requisitioning troops in an emergency; but in the boroughs, acknowledging the authority of the mayors and the watch committees, it was suggested that the requisitioning of troops should go through the mayor. These recommendations were not always followed over the next decade. Perhaps it was just too much trouble to organise mutual aid agreements but in 1908, when there was a total of 187 police forces in England and Wales, only 30 county and 27 borough forces were a party to such. Some county chief constables appear to have preferred having troops available rather than relying on their own, and their neighbours', police constables. Some magistrates, possibly also large-scale employers who were party to a dispute, preferred to use their power under the common law to requisition troops as and when they considered it necessary. In

70. *PP* 1893–94 [C. 7234] XVII, 385, *Report of the Committee Appointed to inquire into the Circumstances Connected with the Disturbances at Featherstone on 7th. September 1893*.
71. *Report of the Inter Departmental Committee on Riots* (London: HMSO, 1895).

1908 the Home Office issued a circular to police forces attempting to limit calls for troops; it instructed that any request for military aid should be telegraphed to the Secretary of State for War as well as to the local army commander, and it also suggested that the recruitment of temporary, special constables might be considered in an emergency.[72] It was the wave of strikes between 1910 and 1912 which, thanks to a determined and interventionist Home Secretary, Winston Churchill, brought about an erosion of the local direction of police and army in industrial disorder.

In the spring of 1910 a new and aggressive shipping company, Houlder Brothers, upset the well-established relations between unions and employers on the docks at Newport, Monmouthshire. An agreement reached between the employers and the unions was repudiated by Houlder Brothers who sought to bring free labour into the port, and who demanded police protection for that labour. The Watch Committee feared that serious disorder and even bloodshed could result. It sought the advice of the Home Office, then refused police protection to Houlder's men and threatened, instead, to use the police to prevent the arrival of any free labour in the docks. The Home Office, in turn, sought the advice of the Crown Law Officers who concluded that the grave nature of the situation had justified the action taken since protecting the free labour could have been provocative; however, they went on to warn that such emergencies should be considered as very rare.[73]

A more serious and protracted dispute broke out in the South Wales coalfield in November 1910. Captain Lionel Lindsay, the Chief Constable of Glamorgan, borrowed police from his neighbours and also requisitioned troops. Churchill stopped the troops en route and sent, in their stead, 300 Metropolitan policemen. These were put under the command of the principal army officer in the area, General Sir Nevil Macready. While the appearance of the London police and Macready's own troops may, in some ways, have aggravated the feelings in the mining districts, in others they probably eased it. Lindsay had a close relationship with the local colliery owners; he frequently dined with one of them, shared horses with him, and even took his advice on police matters. Macready, in contrast, refused all invitations to himself and his officers that were received from the local coal owners. The Glamorgan Standing Joint Committee objected to the way that Lindsay had borrowed police

---

72. Jane Morgan, *Conflict and Order: The Police and Labour Disputes in England and Wales 1900–1939* (Oxford: Clarendon Press, 1987), pp. 39–40.

73. Ibid., pp. 43–4: Weinberger, *Keeping the Peace?*, ch. 2.

without its authorisation, and it objected to Churchill sending Metropolitan constables; the objections were due, at least in part, to the fact that the cost of the imported police would fall on the county. A court action by one of the colliery owners, to recover the costs of the police quartered on the owners' property during the trouble, resulted in Glamorgan being ordered to pay for the police summoned by Lindsay. The decision implied an increasing independence of the chief constables from their police authority since they could now call for aid and incur additional expense without consultation. In the event, however, Glamorgan did not have to pay for the Metropolitan police; and Churchill withdrew, before its second reading, a bill which would have given him the retrospective authority to send police or military personnel anywhere in the country in an emergency, and charge local authorities for the cost. But, even though there was no new legislation and no legal precedent established, the dispute in the South Wales coalfield was to have significance in increasing Home Office authority over the police and, correspondingly, in undermining that of the local police committees. This was not because of any concerted plan on the part of the Home Office in general or Churchill in particular; but it was greatly assisted by the generally weak nature of local government bureaucracy where matters were often still run on a personal and informal basis. Almost inevitably, when confronted by a crisis, such a system would find itself bypassed by the professionalism of the Home Office civil servants in London and the growing professionalism of the police forces themselves.[74]

A similar situation developed in the summer of 1911 when the entire railway network was brought to a halt after the railway owners, who refused to recognise the railwaymen's union, refused to negotiate with union officials. Churchill again acted decisively, dispatching troops around the country to protect railway lines and stations and, in some instances, to run emergency services. He also urged the recruitment of a reserve of special constables so that mutual aid agreements between police forces could more easily be fulfilled. The reserve was to be divided into two: the First Police Reserve would be made up of retired policemen or soldiers who would wear a uniform, be paid, and receive a pension in case of injury; the Second Reserve would be a body of special constables who might be paid if and when called upon, but who would

74. Weinberger, *Keeping the Peace?*, ch. 3, esp. pp. 63–5; Roger Geary, *Policing Industrial Disputes 1893–1985* (Cambridge: CUP 1985), p. 36; Morgan, *Conflict and Order*, pp. 44–9.

otherwise only receive expenses and an allowance for loss of wages. The Inspectors of Constabulary were advised that they should take account of the existence of a reserve when assessing a force's efficiency. The whole proposal infuriated several watch committees who complained that the Home Office, once again, was encroaching on their authority. Some borough forces implemented the proposal; others ignored it. In the counties too the response was patchy, and provided another opportunity for chief constables like Lindsay to clash with their police authority: the Glamorgan Standing Joint Committee believed that 60 men would suffice for the reserve, but Lindsay wanted 2,000–3,000.[75]

There was a logic to Churchill's actions. National emergencies and nation-wide strikes seemed to him to demand a national and nation-wide response which was best co-ordinated from Westminster and which the existing system of local police forces scarcely allowed for. Yet such emergencies were rare; and the situation could look very different from the provincial perspective, where local authorities worried about having to pay the costs of imported police, or about their own districts being stripped of police protection because of problems many miles away. Mutual aid agreements could also put considerable pressure on police forces when a nation-wide emergency threatened, or when a series of local disturbances coincided. In August 1911, for example, the Chief Constable of Bedfordshire sent a sergeant and thirteen men – 13 per cent of his force – to Bootle to assist the local police with a strike by transport workers and dockers, but within a week he was forced to recall them since he felt that he needed all his men to protect the Midland Railway line during the rail strike.[76] Huntingdonshire was a small county; it was not industrial and was not known for a turbulent workforce. In 1912 the county constabulary consisted of only 60 men. In February of that year the Chief Constable wrote to his counterpart in Nottinghamshire:

> I hardly like to promise to send you any of my force in the event of a coal strike as I am under obligation by written agreement to assist four of my neighbouring forces. If I am not asked for assistance by any of them, and should I not apprehend any trouble at home, I would endeavour on receipt of a wire from you [to] dispatch a Sergt. and 15 men, and an Inspector if required, at 24 hours notice.[77]

75. Ibid., pp. 579.
76. Andrew Francis Richer, *Bedfordshire Police 1840–1990* (Bedford: Paul Hooley, 1990), p. 93.
77. Cambs. PA Chief Constable of Huntingdonshire, Letter Book, 1906–15, fol. 271.

Two years later, however, the national emergency of war was to put undreamed of pressures on the police and seriously to reduce the numbers of men available for both normal and extraordinary duties.

CHAPTER SIX

War, 'Mutiny' and Peace

The Great War and the police 'mutinies'

For many years the Whiggish view of war as an interruption to the natural development of society dominated the interpretation of British history. More recently a younger generation of historians have stressed that economic, political and social developments do not stop because of a war, and they have urged that war can both accelerate change within a society and even propel it in new directions.[1] The strains of the First World War affected police development in several ways: they contributed to the unrest which resulted in the police strikes or 'mutinies' of 1918 and 1919; they fostered further encroachments by central government upon the influence of local police committees; and, together with the fears generated by the Russian Revolution, they raised political surveillance by the police to a level unknown at least since the struggle against Revolutionary and Napoleonic France.

In 1914 the police forces of England and Wales amounted to just over 53,000 men, and most of these men were of military age. Some of them had already served in the armed forces, and a percentage of these were reservists. The Boer War had seen reservists in the police recalled to the colours; but the British military in the First World War needed men in far greater numbers than they had for the conflict in South Africa. By the end of the first year of the world war about one man in five had gone from the provincial forces to the military, and the depletion of the Metropolitan Police was even greater, with just over a quarter of the men being recruited.

1. The seminal text for such an argument with reference to Britain during the First World War is Arthur Marwick, *The Deluge: British Society and the First World War* (London: Bodley Head, 1965).

Lieutenant-Colonel Chichester, the Chief Constable of Huntingdon-shire, wrote to Sir Leonard Dunning, one of His Majesty's Inspectors of Constabulary, as early as November 1914 explaining that, out of the 60 men in his force, 'besides those Reservists who have been called to the Colours, I have lent two to the Military as Drill In-structors, and allowed five of my best young men to enlist, making a total of 13; so I think we have done our share'. However, in the following April he addressed a memorandum to the bachelors in his force stating that he did not wish to act differently from other constabularies 'and will therefore have no objection to bachelors in the Force joining Kitchener's Army and should they wish to do so [I] will endeavour that they shall join Regiments where other mem-bers of the Force are serving'.[2] Towards the end of 1915 Chichester took over command of the Cambridgeshire force, the Standing Joint Committee believing that the middle of the war was an in-opportune moment to recruit a new chief constable; he was to lead the two forces until the restoration of peace. On assuming com-mand he found the Cambridgeshire Police as depleted as that of Huntingdonshire, and while he did not object to men attesting under the Derby scheme, he could see little point, informing the Home Office 'that all men who can be spared have already joined the Army'.[3] In November 1915 the Commissioner of the Metropol-itan Police was expressing his concerns about the impact of military recruitment on his force in a letter to the Home Office: 'The Force has now become so reduced in number that any further depletion would be attended with grave risk.'[4] However, periodic trawls of the police for men for the army and navy continued throughout the four years of the war.

The gaps in police ranks were filled by a variety of expedients. At chief constable level it was always possible to fill a gap by inviting the chief constable of one force to assume temporary command of a neighbouring force. This happened with Colonel Chichester in 1915, and with Captain J.H. Mander, of the Isle of Ely force, who, in the same year, was asked to take temporary command in Norfolk

2. Cambs. PA Chief Constable of Huntingdonshire, Letter Book, 1906–15, fol. 559, Chichester to Dunning, 9 Nov. 1914, and fol. 742 'To the Bachelors of the Hunts Constabulary', 14 Apr. 1915. In the early stages of the war Major W.H. Dunlop, the Chief Constable of the East Riding, was arranging for recruits from his force to be kept together in the Seaforth Highlanders, and specifically in the company of his son, Lieutenant Douglas Dunlop: Humberside PA East Riding Constabulary, Memo-randum Book, 1912–16, fol. 109.
3. Cambs. PA Cambridgeshire Constabulary, Circulars 1915–39, fol. 4.
4. HO 45/10792/301945/7, Henry to Troup, 2 Nov. 1915.

when that county's chief constable rejoined the colours.[5] But other ranks in the wartime police could not be filled by such invitations. The Police (Emergency Provisions) Act of 1915 contained a clause suspending a man's right to retire except with the consent of his chief constable. The special constables organised during the pre-war strike wave were called upon to perform ordinary police tasks. But the specials were of variable quality. His Majesty's Inspectors of Constabulary commented in 1915 that, because of the other calls on their time, it took between six and ten specials to perform the same hours of duty as an ordinary police constable. Sir Edward Henry thought that they gave a degree of reassurance on the streets, but he doubted their efficiency in serious disorder; while the Chief Constable of Dorset found them 'not in any sense of the word useful Constables . . . They just fill up the gaps.' The army could be asked to provide support in incidents of severe disorder, but ministers were increasingly nervous of this, recognising that most of the troops in the country during wartime were recruits undergoing training and fearing that they would be insufficiently disciplined to cope with rioters.[6]

Commenting on an overall reduction in the crime figures early in 1916 the *Justice of the Peace* concluded that there were four reasons for this happy state of affairs: many criminals were serving in the army, and some were making very good soldiers; the war had put much greater restrictions on undesirable aliens; the booming wartime economy had reduced poverty and want, and therefore the inclination to steal; and wartime regulations had put stringent controls on drink.[7] There was also probably a far more prosaic reason for the decline in the criminal statistics which the journal ignored: the war forced the police to shift their priorities away from petty theft and the general problems of order on the streets. Dunning recognised this in the Inspectorate's report for 1915: 'if the police are reduced in number, or are withdrawn from ordinary to special duties, offences escape notice, and prosecutions drop as surely as they would in the case of an actual decrease of offence'.[8] In April 1918 the Standing Joint Committee of the East Riding heard an application for police assistance in the inspection of places of

5. F. Slack, *The Norfolk Constabulary* (Norwich: Norfolk Constabulary, 1967), p. 15.
6. *Report of H.M. Inspectors of Constabulary for 1915*, p. 4; and for quotations see David Englander, 'Police and public order in Britain 1914–1918', in Clive Emsley and Barbara Weinberger (eds), *Policing Western Europe, 1850–1940: Politics, Professionalization and Public Order* (Westport, Conn.: Meckler, 1991), pp. 97–8.
7. *Justice of the Peace* LXXX, 18 Mar. 1916, pp. 133–4.
8. *Report of H.M. Inspectors of Constabulary for 1915*, p. 5.

entertainment and rejected it on the grounds that 'the Police could not undertake any further work at the present time'.[9]

The additional tasks began the moment war broke out. On 5 August 1914 Major Dunlop issued an order to the East Riding Constabulary detailing ten immediate wartime duties:

1. MOBILIZATION
a) Posting mobilization notices in every village and hamlet.
b) Personally warning all Army and Navy Reservists to return to their Mobilization Stations.

2. BILLETING
a) To provide billets for all Officers, Soldiers and Horses, in pursuance of 'Orders' by Commanding Officers. If victualling houses are not available to provide billets in public buildings, warehouses and private dwellings.

3. REQUISITIONING of HORSES and VEHICLES
a) To assist the Military Authorities to provide horses and Transport on emergency requisition, and if objection is raised by owners to take compulsory action.

4. PROTECTION of VULNERABLE POINTS
To co-operate with the Military Authorities, Railway Companies etc in preventing outrages by explosives to Bridges, Railways etc.

5. ESPIONAGE
To carry out the provisions of the 'Official Secrets Act' in the matter of watching persons who may be suspected of being spies.

6. CONTROL of ALIENS
To keep careful watch on the movements of undesirable Aliens.

7. DETENTION of ENEMIES' MERCHANT SHIPS
To assist the Customs Officers in the detention of certain ships and their crews.

8. WATCHING WIRELESS STATIONS
To assist the Post Office Authorities in the matter of protecting Wireless Stations and preventing private persons from erecting or using Wireless installations.

9. PROTECTION of DEFENCE WORKS
To assist the Military Authorities to prevent obstruction by Landowners and others on the matter of constructing Field Defences.

10. INTELLIGENCE
On occasions where Hostile Vessels or Aircraft may be observed to watch and report their appearance and movements to the nearest Coast Guard Officer or the Officer in Command of the nearest Military Body of Troops.[10]

---

9. Humberside PA East Riding Constabulary, Memorandum Book 1916–20, fol. 101.
10. Humberside PA East Riding Constabulary, Memorandum Book 1912–16, fol. 94.

Additional orders required the constables to list the number of Belgian refugees in the district and collect any atrocity stories which they had to tell, to encourage recruiting, enforce the blackout, prevent photography, sketching or note-taking in sensitive areas, to ensure that soldiers and sailors on leave reported on arrival in their district, and to carry out various wartime censuses. Often there was little central direction on where the priorities should be placed for the new wartime tasks, or even what some of the tasks actually involved. In August 1914 Chichester wrote to the Home Secretary: 'I should be glad to know what you mean by attack *from outside.* You also mention that points should be "quietly watched" *for a short time* so as to prevent any risk of serious outrage.' Did this mean that he could soon hand over watching such points to the army? Chichester had already brought his men into divisional police stations and had left the villages in charge of the old parish constables; over the next few weeks he issued a deluge of orders about stopping and checking cars, and guarding reservoirs and vulnerable points, particularly those on the railways. In October he wondered what to do about the arms that his men were carrying in the event of invasion, as 'in my opinion, it would be a mistake for the police to be found in the possession of arms'.[11]

Before the First World War the police had investigated army pensioners and their wives to see if there were any questions about their eligibility, or whether their morals were such that they remained deserving of a pension.[12] In October 1914 the Home Office wrote to chief constables forwarding a request from the Army Council that the police investigate and forward evidence of 'serious misconduct' on the part of any woman in receipt of a separation allowance because her husband was in the armed forces. The problem in the eyes of the military authorities was that the separation allowance was now so liberal that some women might be tempted to squander it all on drink, especially since they were now 'deprived of the company and guidance of husbands'.[13] The Army Council stressed the need for 'discreet and tactful' action, but the task does not appear to have been a popular one even among the most senior of police officers. Sir Edward Henry protested that the Metropolitan

11. Cambs. PA Chief Constable of Huntingdonshire, Letter Book, 1906–15, fol. 444, Chichester to McKenna, 10 Aug. 1914, and fol. 504, same to same, 12 Oct. 1914.
12. West Midlands PA Birmingham Copy Letter Book, Chief Constable's Office, 1890–91, fols 201, 332, 621; Staffs. PA Staffordshire Chief Constable's Letter Book, 1900–08, fols 277–8.
13. Greater Manchester PA Manchester Police, General Orders, vol. 3, fols 460, 482.

Police did not 'want to drag the policeman into anybody's life' and he disliked being given the details of all women in receipt of a separation allowance. Henry and his men were fully aware that a prosecution for drunkenness could result in a woman losing her allowance and generally seem to have admonished such offenders rather than prosecuting them, at least for the first offence.[14] Quite how much snooping went on into the morals and private affairs of soldiers' and sailors' wives by the police in wartime England is impossible to assess; however unpopular the tasks, there is evidence of such investigations being carried out and the information being passed on.[15] Yet, in the early stages of the war at least, policemen, as the representatives of authority, were also the men approached by soldier's wives when they had queries about their allowances.[16]

Wartime food shortages provoked unrest and disorder, as well as a black market, all of which had to be policed. Xenophobia and an exalted loyalty to King and Country fostered the anti-German riots of 1915, the localised anti-Jewish riots of 1917, and fed into the confrontations which aggressive loyalists had with pacifists and those who called for a negotiated peace. Large military camps created other problems of public order. There had been a long-standing problem for the police over how to deal with groups of drunken, rowdy soldiers or sailors throughout the nineteenth century; attempts at arrest then had led to small-scale riots and general mayhem, but the military camps of 1914–18 held far larger numbers than the garrison towns and fleet anchorages of the Victorian period. Military camps and booming naval towns offered opportunities for prostitution. In November 1914 Chichester replied to a letter from the Home Office about 'keeping young girls straight', but he was concerned that they seemed 'more to blame than the military, as they appear to run after [the soldiers] in a most indecent manner. I have, through my officers, taken the names of such girls and have sent a list (confidentially) of them to the Clergyman of the parish.' Four months later he was expressing his concerns to one of his inspectors about the immorality between 'females and soldiers at St. Neots . . . I have heard of respectable people having to turn back in their walks to avoid indecent sights in the

14. HO 185/258, Women's Advisory Committee, Reports and Correspondence. Women's Service Committee Report. Evidence of Sir Edward Henry, 17 Nov. 1915.
15. Cambs. PA Chief Constable of Huntingdonshire Letter Book, 1906–15, fols 593, 638, 684.
16. Ibid., fol. 450.

lanes etc. and I also think that there are other brothels which you may possibly be able to put your finger upon with plain clothes officers.'[17]

Part of the problem of morality policing in the vicinity of military camps, as well as policing munitions factories with their large numbers of women workers, was taken over by Women Police patrols. Since at least the last quarter of the nineteenth century there had been increasing pressure for some kind of policing by women. This pressure came from those involved in voluntary organisations active in rescue and preventive work among women and was steeped in the tradition of social purity; but there were also active feminists urging the creation of women police as part of their campaign to change the nature of society and carve out a full political role for women. In 1883 the Metropolitan Police began to employ a female visitor to visit women convicts on licence and under police supervision; three years later a second such visitor was appointed. In March 1889 fourteen more women were employed to act formally as Police Matrons. Their duties, hitherto undertaken largely by the wives of policemen, were to supervise and search female and child offenders while in police stations and the courts. Other forces also began to employ such matrons, but there remained considerable hostility to women working in this way, commonly couched in terms of the deleterious effects that the foul language, drunkenness, and violence of prisoners would have on respectable women. The outbreak of war gave the opportunity for two separate groups to organise women police patrols: the Women Police Volunteers, who became the Women Police Service in February 1915, were organised by former militant suffragettes and the morality campaigner Margaret Damer-Dawson; the Voluntary Women Patrols were organised by members of the National Union of Women Workers. Both groups were particularly concerned with the control of the public, and at times even the private, behaviour of working and working-class women. Moreover, they both appear to have recognised little distinction between what they perceived as immoral behaviour and what the law defined as illegal. Some of the Voluntary Women Patrols were incorporated into police forces as women police in 1918, and in May of that year Lady Nott-Bower addressed the Annual General Meeting of the Chief Constables' Association on the

17. Ibid., fol. 565, Chichester to the Under Secretary, Home Office, 21 Nov. 1914, and fol. 709, Chichester to Insp. Storey, 15 Mar. 1915.

subject of 'Women Police'; but many watch committees and standing joint committees remained implacably opposed to the idea.[18] The nature of industrial warfare as fought between 1914 and 1918 necessitated mobilisation on the home front, particularly with regard to the economy. The need to keep the men in the trenches fully supplied brought the government into direct involvement with industrial relations and made ministers especially sensitive to strikes and stoppages. The early years of the war saw the police urged to watch for spies and, as with the pre-war spy scare, paranoia led to suspicions of the most unlikely people in the most unlikely places;[19] but by the middle of the war concern had switched to the anti-war activist and the industrial agitator. The latter were more tangible than the spies, and though probably few of them seriously sought the overthrow of the government, that was not how they were perceived in government directives. Lists of 'hostile leaflets', most of which had been published by the No Conscription Fellowship, were continually updated and circulated by the Home Office; these were passed on down to the constables on the beat who were urged to watch out for them and, in some instances, seize and destroy them

18. Philippa Levine, '"Walking the streets in a way no decent woman should." Women police in World War One', *Journal of Modern History* 66 (1994), 34–78; Lynn Amy Amidon, 'Ladies in blue: feminism and policing in Britain in the late nineteenth and early twentieth centuries', Ph.D, State University of New York, Binghampton, 1986, passim; *Chief Constables' Association, Annual General Meeting, 31st. May, 1918*, pp. 9–14. T.A. Critchley, *A History of Police in England and Wales*, rev. edn (London: Constable, 1978), pp. 215–16. One hundred women were incorporated into the Metropolitan Police in the autumn of 1918. Outside London, for example, two women constables were appointed to the Northampton Borough Force in Sept. 1918, but none were recruited for the county force (Richard Cowley, *Policing Northamptonshire 1836–1986*, Studley, Warks., Brewin Books, 1986, p. 179); two women were appointed to the Shropshire force in March 1918, but the Watch Committee of Shrewsbury believed that the recruitment of women was 'unnecessary and impractical' (Douglas J. Elliott, *Policing Shropshire 1836–1967*, Studley, Warks., Brewin Books, pp. 143–7).
19. On 6 Oct. 1914, for example, Dunlop issued the following circular: 'A man representing himself as a Scout Master height 5ft. 10ins. slight build, fair complexion, clean shaved, scar on right eye, speaks German, has been selling pills and liquor to soldiers on duty. A most dangerous character, fully armed. He is to be arrested *on suspicion* wherever seen . . .' (Humberside PA East Riding Constabulary, Memorandum Book, 1912–16, fol. 105). On 19 Oct. 1914 Chichester sent a detailed letter to Vernon Kell about the proprietor of a cinema in Huntingdon whose name was Reach '(or Reich)', who had been seen talking to soldiers until the early hours, and whose wife was overheard asking a soldier details of his home town of Dundee at a cinema performance – the whole conversation being dutifully spelled out in the letter: 'What I want to know is, whether you consider these questions are sufficient to hand the woman over to the Military for safe keeping, or to enquire into, and if so, whether the man Reach should be also arrested?' (Cambs. PA Chief Constable of Huntingdonshire, Letter Book, 1906–15, fols 505–6.)

then and there under Defence of the Realm Regulation 51.[20] Strikes early in 1917 were feared to be part of 'an organised attempt to create trouble in munition works which has more than local importance'. In consequence, chief constables were circularised with a list of individuals who had come to the notice of Sir Basil Thomson and Special Branch, and they were urged, personally, to send him any information which they considered relevant. Thomson's list of 40 names included a Leeds alderman, a Sheffield councillor, and two parliamentary candidates.[21] In Birmingham, apparently at the prompting of the Watch Committee, the police visited the homes of munitions workers when they were absent from work to enforce industrial discipline.[22] Across the country any rumour likely to undermine morale on the home front was promptly to be scotched. The Chief Constable of Hull went so far as to authorise: 'Plainclothes men may occasionally travel on the Tram routes for the purpose of detecting offences of this kind, and may also, with the permission of the Superintendent or Divl. Inspr., enter and remain in the Bars and Lounges of licensed premises for this purpose.'[23]

The wartime tasks of the police strengthened still further the developing links between senior police officers and the representatives of central government, at the expense of those between those officers and local authorities. Before the outbreak of hostilities a small section had been established within the Home Office to draw up preparations for war; once the conflict began, this section, consisting principally of Arthur Dixon and C.D. Carew Robinson reporting to a permanent under secretary, became the War Duties Division. Dixon recalled that, during the war, 'this Division had, perforce, to keep in touch with the Police, including the Borough as well as the Metropolitan and County Forces, by correspondence, telephone and conferences on many aspects of the war measures, and so was able to establish much closer relations with the Forces generally and their work than the Home Office had ever had before'.[24]

During the war also the country was divided into special administrative areas each under an Authorised Competent Military Authority

20. Humberside PA East Riding Constabulary, Memorandum Book, 1916–20, fols 10, 11, 13, 58, 59, 63, 69, 70, 73, 77, 107.

21. Humberside PA Hull City, Chief Constable's Memos, 1916–26, fol. 77.

22. Richard Shackleton, 'The 1919 police strike in Birmingham', in Anthony Wright and Richard Shackleton (eds), *Worlds of Labour: Essays in Birmingham Labour History* (University of Birmingham, Dept. of Extramural Studies, 1983), p. 66.

23. Humberside PA Hull City, Chief Constable's Memos, 1916–26, fol. 22.

24. Sir Arthur L. Dixon, 'The emergency work of the police forces in the Second World War' (unpublished, 1963), pp. 6–7.

(ACMA) who was directly responsible to General Headquarters. The ACMA enforced the regulations made under the emergency, wartime legislation; chief constables acted in a subordinate role to this officer, while their constables undertook most of his routine investigative work.[25] In March 1918 the District Conference system was inaugurated to improve the flow of information between the Home Office and the police. The country was divided into eight districts and the chief constables of both the counties and boroughs in these districts were to meet from time to time in conference and also to appoint members to a central committee which was to confer with representatives of the Home Office and the military. This established the first formal forum for borough and county chief constables to meet and discuss matters of mutual interest; it also drew the Home Office directly into such discussions. But even before the system was formally established the Home Office was recommending district conferences, which could seek Home Office advice and even meet on Home Office premises, to resolve the vexed question of police pay:

> it will be of great importance that after the war the inducements offered by the police service should be sufficient to attract recruits of a good class, and for this purpose it is clearly necessary that a permanent scale of pensionable annual pay should be settled for each force at as early a date as possible and at all events before the war is ended and the demobilization of the army begins. It seems to the Secretary of State tolerably clear that it will be necessary after the war to fix the pay of the police permanently on a higher scale than was authorized before the war, but the amount of the permanent increase is a very doubtful question. A rivalry in this matter between different police Authorities is much to be deprecated as likely to be the cause not only of extravagance in expenditure, but also of unrest and disquiet in the police service itself.[26]

At the time that this letter was written, there was already widespread 'unrest and disquiet' among the police, and not only because of pay.

Wartime police duties put enormous strains on the ageing, depleted workforce which remained to carry them out. The weekly rest day, achieved by Act of Parliament in 1910, was one of the first

---

25. David Englander, 'Military intelligence and the defence of the realm: the surveillance of soldiers and civilians in Britain during the First World War', *Bulletin of the Society for the Study of Labour History* 52 (1987), 24–32.

26. Merseyside PA Liverpool Police Strike, 1919, General Papers, Under Secretary of State to Town Clerk, Liverpool, 4 Jan. 1919.

casualties: in Shropshire, for example, after an initial period with no rest day, the men were granted one day off in every fourteen, but early in 1916 this was reduced to one day off in a month. In Hull, since men were required to work seven days a week, the chief constable authorised an extension in the lunch break from 20 to 30 minutes, but even this was hedged with qualifications and limited

> (1) To men who can get their lunch at a place where there is a telephone conveniently near. In this case a man will ring up the Station when he goes to lunch, and will ring up again when leaving.
> (2) When arrangements can be made for men to have their lunch at a place which can be supervised by the Station Sergeant.

In London the rest day completely disappeared, hours of duty were lengthened, and so too were beats.[27] In addition to the increased workload, the policemen had to cope with wartime inflation. Some men resigned because they could get better wages elsewhere, and some took part-time work in their off-duty hours.[28] Early in 1915 Chichester was fearful of agitation in the different county forces for a pay increase. He wrote to several of his counterparts and to the secretary of the County Police Constables' Club to find out how the problem was being handled elsewhere; he visited the Home Office, in the wake of a deputation of borough chief constables with similar concerns. At the same time he urged his men to be patient and await the end of the war, and he sought to persuade his Standing Joint Committee to pay the men for loss of holidays.[29] Dunlop received several petitions for a pay increase, some even before the end of 1914, 'in consequence of the ever increasing cost of living, longer hours and increased duties, more responsibility etc.'. In April 1916 he proposed that each division make a formal application to him which he would then take before the Standing Joint Committee.[30] Sir William Nott-Bower recalled going to the Home Office with Sir Edward Henry *'begging* for a very small increase in wages,

27. Elliot, *Policing Shropshire*, p. 149; Humberside PA Hull City, Chief Constable's Memos, 1916–26, fols 137, 140; Gerald W. Reynolds and Anthony Judge, *The Night the Police Went on Strike* (London: Weidenfeld & Nicolson, 1968), ch. 3.

28. HO 45/10792/301945/13, Chief Constable of Birmingham to Dunning, 22 Sept. 1915; Greater Manchester PA Manchester Division, Misconduct Book, 1912–35, fol. 42.

29. Cambs. PA Chief Constable of Huntingdonshire, Letter Book, 1906–15, fols 717, 722, 729, 759. *Chief Constables' Association: Annual Meeting, 13th. May 1915*, pp. 26–31, contains an 'Abridged Report of the Deputation from a Conference of Watch Committees to Sir Edward Troup (Permanent Under Secretary of State to the Home Office)' dated 24 Mar. 1915.

30. Humberside PA East Riding Constabulary, Memo Book, 1916–20, fol. 4.

and receiving the reply, "Impossible, impossible"'. [31] The authorities, both central and local, were concerned that any agreement for a wartime increase in basic pay could create problems in a different economic climate after the war; the remedy commonly decided upon was to award the police non-pensionable wartime bonuses. But this was an accountant's remedy, and it did little to alleviate the discontent among the police.

The dissatisfaction over pay and conditions provided the ideal recruiting ground for the Police Union; and the activities of the union increased anxieties among senior officers and government officials. Early in 1917 it was decided to exclude policemen from the schedule of reserved occupations, and early in the following year the union alleged that some police authorities were deliberately selecting union members when preparing new police drafts for the armed forces. The evidence suggests that the allegations were correct and that the Home Office was fully aware of such selection. But such activities, together with the additional trawls for the armed forces, only served to provoke trouble – much as the withdrawal of exemptions from skilled engineers had done in 1917.[32] On 25 August 1918 PC Thomas Thiel, an ex-Guardsman and Boer War veteran, was dismissed from the Metropolitan Police for his union activities; this was the spur to the first strike.[33]

The police strike of August 1918 was confined to London; it lasted less than a week, but it was almost total, involving both the Metropolitan and City forces. Sir Edward Henry was made the scapegoat; he was replaced by General Macready. Lloyd George met the union leaders at 10 Downing Street. The outcome of the meeting was positive for the union in most respects: Thiel was reinstated, and a pay rise, war bonus and widows' pensions were promised. The strike also convinced the Home Office that it would be inadvisable to press ahead with the plans for a further trawl of recruits from the provincial police for the army.[34] But a problem arose over the status of the union itself. Lloyd George declared that he could not recognise a police union in wartime. The union leaders at the Downing Street meeting believed that the statement implied that recognition would follow with peace – especially since it was agreed

31. Sir William Nott-Bower, *Fifty-Two Years a Policeman* (London: Edward Arnold, 1926), p. 284.
32. Englander, 'Police and public order', pp. 118–19.
33. Unless otherwise stated, the information on the two strikes is drawn from Reynolds and Judge, *The Night the Police went on Strike.*
34. HO 45/10792/301945/234, Minute of A.L.D[ixon], 21 Sept. 1918.

that a representative board would meet at Scotland Yard. This is undoubtedly what Lloyd George intended them to think, but it is probable that he never had any intention of granting such recognition. The union claimed that its success in August 1918 boosted its appeal in the provinces, but it is difficult to gauge its provincial membership. There were problems in organising members of the rural constabularies simply because of their dispersal throughout the countryside. Chichester

> with confidence, assure[d] the members of the Hunts, and Cambs, Constabulary that, as in the past, their welfare [was] safer in his hands than that of any Union and [felt] sure that he [could] rely on the loyalty and good feeling of the Forces to approach him as their friend and guide, and show other forces that this [was] their way of assuring themselves and the public that their loyalty and self respect [was] above suspicion.

In Cambridgeshire at least his confidence seems to have been well placed, and in August 1919 he was able to congratulate the men on 'abstaining' from the union.[35] However, in the big cities the union appears to have won considerable support. In Liverpool, where there was a dictatorial chairman of the Watch Committee and a Chief Constable who had little respect from his men, poor accommodation, suspicion of favouritism in the way promotions were made, and a variety of other local factors, combined with the wartime problems of pay and conditions to make the city's police a fertile ground for union recruiters. The union's successes greatly concerned government ministers and officials, and many chief constables. Prompted by a confidential report from Sir Basil Thomson on Bolshevism in England, Sir Charles Rafter, the Chief Constable of Birmingham, believed that the methods being adopted to promote the union merited 'very close enquiry'. He believed that there had been an attempt to organise union activity in his force during the railway strike of 1911, but matters seemed far more serious in 1919.

> The movement is fostered in Birmingham by the Trades Council, who represent the Independent Labour Party. The president of the Trades Council is Frank Spires, who is a lieutenant of J.W. Kneeshaw, and who assisted Kneeshaw in the Anti-Conscription campaign. Kneeshaw is a Labour member of the City Council, and is described

35. Cambs. PA Cambridgeshire Constabulary, Circulars 1915–39, fols 16–17, 28; Chief Constable of Huntingdonshire, Letter Book, 1918–64, fol. 67.

as a bricklayer. He has been associated with Ramsay Macdonald . . .
The ultimate object of this is to organise a strike of all trades, in
which the police would take part, so that it may assume the form of
a revolution.[36]

The Birmingham Trades Council had indeed become very left-wing
by 1918 since a 'patriotic' minority had walked out critical of the
increasingly anti-war stance of the majority. The Council gave considerable support and encouragement to the police union, but it
was hardly Bolshevik. Nevertheless the suspicious Rafter, and the
like-minded chief constables of Leeds and Glamorgan, refused to
allow any members of their forces time off to attend a mass meeting of the union held in the Albert Hall in January 1919.

The union came to dominate the elected delegates to the representative board established in the Metropolitan Police; both in this
forum, and elsewhere, it was bitterly critical of Macready. When the
new Commissioner named Brigadier General Horwood as his assistant there were charges that the police were being militarised. In
May, following a confrontation in Hyde Park between police and
members of the National Federation of Discharged Soldiers, the
union issued a press statement blaming the militarisation of the
police for the violence and urging closer links between the police
and organised labour. The leadership of the union began to split
between moderates and radicals, and against this background the
committee of Lord Desborough, appointed by the government to
investigate the pay and conditions of the police, presented its
findings to the Home Secretary.

Towards the end of May the Home Secretary, Edward Shortt,
sought leave to introduce a bill which, following the recommendations of Desborough, would prevent the police from belonging to
a union and establish alternative consultative machinery. At the
same time he announced an immediate, and significant, pay rise
for all the police in the country. On 8 July he introduced his Police
Bill providing for a Police Federation, as a replacement for the
union, and a Police Council as the consultative body. The bill was
an obvious challenge to the union; as one police activist put it at
a meeting in Liverpool: 'They had fought for liberty in France but
now they were fighting for themselves, and the oath they must be

36. West Midlands PA Birmingham Police, Superintendents' Reports and Confidential Letters, 1901–23, fol. 505, Rafter to Thomson, 26 Nov. 1918; see also fol. 506,
same to same, 10 Feb. 1919, and fols 499–504, Rafter to Under Secretary of State,
2 and 7 Nov. 1918. For the police union in Birmingham see Shackleton, 'The 1919
police strike in Birmingham'.

loyal to, was that of the Police Union, nothing else mattered.'[37] In Birmingham the union urged others to take warning from the government's assault: 'This is not solely the policemen's fight but an effort to safeguard the elementary rights of citizenship and freedom.'[38]

The strike of August 1919 was a disaster for the men who took strike action and for the union. It covered a larger geographical area than its predecessor, with men coming out on Merseyside and in Birmingham as well as in London. But most of the men in Birmingham and London refused to strike, and only in Liverpool was the action particularly solid.[39] Elsewhere in the country many men responded to the call by burning their union cards: the pay rise had satisfied them and they were not prepared to jeopardise this, and their pensions, for the sake of the union. Promises of support from other trade unions yielded little in the affected localities, and nothing at the national level. The strikers were all dismissed, no matter how long or how distinguished their service; and not one was ever reinstated. A principal concern of central government and of senior police officers during the period of the union's existence had been the possibility of it siding with other trade unions during a major industrial dispute,[40] and while the strike had been a disaster for the union there were those at the centre of government, and particularly in the Secret Service, who continued to be concerned about police reliability in labour disputes.[41]

---

37. Merseyside PA Liverpool Police Strike, General Papers, 1919, Report of John Leatham Flood, 1 Aug. 1919.

38. Quoted in Shackleton, 'The 1919 police strike in Birmingham', p. 72.

39. Some 1,056 men struck work in the Metropolitan Police, 57 in the City of London, 954 in Liverpool, 119 in Birmingham, 114 in Birkenhead, 63 in Bootle, and one in Wallasey. Among the strikers in Birmingham was Police Sergeant Edward Taylor, a veteran of 22 years' service and the man who, as a constable, had escorted 'Constable' Lloyd George from the Town Hall during the riot of 1901.

40. Chichester suggested to the Home Office: 'if it was put to the forces generally "do you wish to tie yourselves down to the sometimes oppressive measures of the various labour unions, and possibly have to strike in sympathy with any of them, or do you prefer to stand aloft [sic] having now got representative boards and good pay, conditions of service, pensions etc." I feel sure the majority of the members would prefer the latter': Cambs. PA Chief Constable of Huntingdonshire, Letter Book, 1918–64, fol. 130, Chichester to Dixon, 4 Mar. 1919. See also Nott-Bower, *Fifty-two Years a Policeman*, pp. 301–2. Critchley, *A History of Police*, p. 187, suggests that the confrontation between Macready and the union 'seems to have been a struggle between organised labour to secure control over the police in a way that would encourage their sympathy in industrial disputes, and the determination of the Government to preserve their neutrality'.

41. Christopher Andrew, *Secret Service: The Making of the British Intelligence Community* (London: Heinemann, 1985), pp. 331, 518.

The Police Federation, created by the Police Act of 1919, was designed to provide a veneer of consultation and to impede industrial militancy. Every policeman, from constable to inspector, automatically became a member of the Federation which was funded, frugally, by a Home Office grant. Industrial action was prohibited, as were affiliation or association with outside bodies. At both force and national level there were branch boards elected separately from and for the ranks of inspector, sergeant and constable. The joint boards, which met at both local and national level, had equal numbers of representatives from the three ranks, and this prevented any domination by the constables, who were the most numerous in the police but who had also shown themselves the most militant. The central committee of the Federation could submit representations to the Home Secretary, but overall the new organisation was only authorised to concern itself with welfare and efficiency; discussion of promotion and discipline, areas which had generated much of the anger and militancy in the past, was explicitly denied.

Peacetime emergencies

Peace with Germany did not bring economic plenty: the immediate postwar years witnessed a wave of serious industrial disorder, while the Depression brought the hunger marches; and the 1930s saw the police deployed to keep the peace when Fascists and their opponents faced each other on the streets. The traditional view is that the police acted throughout these years, and particularly during the General Strike of 1926, with 'good humour . . . impartiality and forbearance'.[42] There is something in this, but there is also another side. The industrial and social problems of the inter-war years witnessed continuing encroachment by central government on the local authorities' control of their police: like Winston Churchill confronted by the pre-war strike waves, members of central government and their civil servants during these years felt that national action by trade unions required a co-ordinated national response. Chief constables also maintained their links with the Secret Service and some of them developed the kind of political ideas which had been expressed by Sir John Dunne in the general election of 1900. They considered that it was part of their duty to protect 'the English

---

42. Critchley, *A History of Police*, p. 200; almost identical terms are used in Cowley, *Policing Northamptonshire*, p. 76, and Elliott, *Policing Shropshire*, p. 164.

way of life' from alien creeds; the problem was that for some chief constables, particularly during the 1920s, the most threatening alien creed was that espoused by people on the political left and here they lumped together members of the Labour Party and the Independent Labour Party as well as communists. Such reasoning naturally brought them into conflict with left-wing councillors and members of standing joint committees, but in such confrontations they were always able to count on the backing of the Home Office.

The concerns about industrial unrest in the immediate aftermath of the war coalesced with fears of revolutionary upheaval and encouraged central government to develop further the links with provincial chief constables. In February and March 1919 several senior police officers were called to conferences at which the government's general plans for dealing with emergencies were outlined and discussions were held on local arrangements in the event of a general strike by miners and transport workers. On 21 March a confidential Home Office circular gave chief constables instructions on requisitioning military aid, on the protection of food convoys, on a system for sending daily intelligence reports to the Home Office, and on arrangements for sending documents by aeroplane – the latter was actually employed in the railway strike during September and October 1919.[43] In the following year the government responded to the miners' national strike by introducing the Emergency Powers Bill which swept through Parliament in the last week of October. The new Act enabled the executive to make regulations 'for the preservation of the public peace' and 'for any other purposes essential to the public safety and the life of the community'. Emergency Regulation 26 authorised the Home Secretary to require any police force to aid another with up to 10 per cent of its total strength; and Regulation 27 authorised him to deploy contingents of up to 10 per cent of a force outside its own district, not necessarily for mutual aid. At the same time chief constables were informed confidentially of the names of the civil commissioners who were to assist and co-ordinate local authorities in the event of an emergency: there was a chief commissioner named for London, and one each in the eleven districts defined earlier in connection with road transport arrangements. This machinery was left untouched by the Labour government of 1924, and was used to effect during the General Strike of 1926. Its significance was later noted

43. Sir Arthur L. Dixon, 'The Home Office and the police between the two world wars' (unpublished, 1966), pp. 237–8.

by Sir Arthur Dixon who, during the 1920s, was one of the two civil servants responsible for F Division, the Police Division, of the Home Office: 'these experiences established the [Police] Service in what was virtually a new, and certainly important, role as an executive Force, efficient, trustworthy and versatile, and ready at a call to guide, assist or restrain the civil population in a wide variety of ways'.[44]

Alongside this strengthening of the links between the Home Office and the chief constables there was an ideological pressure which encouraged tough police action, less because of actual offences committed in industrial and economic disputes, and more because of the character and motives which could be attributed to offenders. Superintendent Parker of the Metropolitan Police justified a baton charge against a procession of unemployed in October 1920 on the grounds that the crowd was 'obviously composed of the lower class of alien Jews'.[45] Twelve years later a senior officer commenting on a deputation by the unemployed to Parliament could lump together 'the unemployed and the hooligan element', and report that his men had stopped and turned back 'persons of doubtful appearance'.[46] The National Unemployed Workers' Committee Movement in particular was singled out as 'communist' and therefore 'subversive'; in his orders for policing a march by the unemployed in November 1936, for example, the Chief Constable of Staffordshire instructed his superintendents to get 'the names of any known Communists among the marchers, or other persons likely to cause breaches of the peace'.[47]

The fear of an enemy within ensured the continuation of the links between the police and MI5. In 1931 Kell's department virtually took over the Metropolitan Police Special Branch;[48] and Kell himself was a regular guest at the dinners of the Chief Constables' Association.[49] Some chief constables appear to have responded to

44. Ibid., p. 251.

45. Barbara Weinberger, 'Police perceptions of labour in the inter-war period: the case of the unemployed and of miners on strike', in Francis Snyder and Douglas Hay (eds), *Labour, Law, and Crime: An Historical Perspective* (London: Tavistock, 1987), p. 152.

46. MEPO 2/3066, SDI, Kennington Road, M Division, 2 Nov. 1932, fol. 12.

47. Staffs. PA Staffordshire Constabulary Memo Book, 1935–40, fol. 48; and see in general Weinberger, 'Police perceptions of labour'.

48. Andrew, *Secret Service*, p. 513.

49. Introducing Kell at the dinner in 1936, for example, the Chief Constable of Bradford commented that, of course, Kell was well known to everyone present and added that his 'style of correspondence is well-known to all of us – it is so delightfully shorn of official jargon that it almost becomes a pleasure to make enquiries for him': *Chief Constables' Association: Annual Report, 10th. June 1936*, p. 79. Kell addressed the conference on 'Co-operation between the Police Forces of the Country and

the threat of subversion with the same kind of nervousness they showed to the fear of spies before and during the First World War. At the end of 1924, for example, Chichester wrote to Kell about a London firm which was proposing to set up a hosiery factory in Huntingdon: 'Do you know anything about these people . . . I do not like the sound of their names.'[50] Yet the evidence collected by the police for Kell appears to have been broadly accurate and sober, and often perceptive. The different chief constables' remarks on the role and influence of communists on the General Strike, for example, are far more restrained and believable than the official and overall conclusion prepared at Scotland Yard that 'had there been no communist propaganda, there would have been no general strike'. Furthermore, while most chief constables reported little or no communist influence on the strikers in their jurisdiction, MI5 considered it of the utmost significance that 'the ten months preceding the General Strike witnessed a considerable intensification of Communist effort to tamper with the loyalty of the Forces'.[51]

In June 1921 Sir Basil Thomson addressed the Annual General Meeting of the Chief Constables' Association on the subject of 'The Revolutionary Movement and the Third International'. He stressed what he saw as a problem for moderate labour leaders under pressure from 'younger and more irresponsible elements among their own men', but in the discussion that followed several watch committee representatives, who were also labour leaders, showed dissatisfaction at what they took to be his warnings about revolution.[52] Yet Thomson's comments were moderate, especially when put alongside those of some chief constables. V.F. Bosanquet, Captain Lionel Lindsay and W. Picton Phillips, the Chief Constables of Monmouthshire, Carmarthenshire and Glamorganshire respectively, were particularly loud in the condemnation of communists and those whom they considered to be subversives. Their jurisdictions were set in the midst of the South Wales coalfield where there was a

M.I.5' in 1924: *Chief Constables' Association: Annual Report, 5th. June 1924*, pp. 29–35. See also Andrew, *Secret Service*, pp. 349–51, 525–7.

50. Cambs. PA Chief Constable of Huntingdonshire Letter Book, 1918–64, fol. 440.

51. *Aspects of the General Strike, May 1926* (New Scotland Yard, June 1926), Part I 'Communism and the General Strike', p. 23, and Part III 'Communist Effort to Undermine Loyalty and Discipline in His Majesty's Forces During the Strike: Contributed by M.I.5', p. 1; for the chief constables' assessments see Part II 'Summaries of Information Regarding the Strike Furnished by Chief Constables in England, Scotland and Wales'.

52. *Chief Constables' Association: Report of the Annual General Meeting, 9th. June 1921*, pp. 14–19.

tradition of militancy tinged with syndicalism, but their authoritarian attitudes and their open hostility to left-wing politics in general, and communism in particular, served only to aggravate matters. During the miners' strike of 1921 Lindsay called in troops, stopped meetings, and raided homes for seditious literature. In August 1925 Picton Phillips's men fought the day-long 'battle of Ammanford' with striking miners. All of this was a far cry from the 'good humour . . . impartiality and forbearance' described by Critchley; and things were no better during the General Strike, when each of the three clashed with their standing joint committees. In Monmouthshire the committee called for Bosanquet's resignation 'in as much as his actions in times of emergency are calculated to disturb the peace of the country'. Describing the county council representatives on the committee as 'my little lot of Communists', Bosanquet refused to resign. He was backed by the Home Office which declined to issue the force with a certificate of efficiency for the year ending September 1926, and withheld the police grant until the force was increased.[53]

Not every chief constable acted like the three in South Wales, and in some areas local labour leaders were keen to work with the police rather than simply confront them. In Lincoln, for example, the Chief Constable, William Hughes, worked amicably with the local strike committee in May 1926.[54] The Chief Constable of the North Riding reported that in several instances in his jurisdiction 'the workmen asked to be allowed to protect their own works and I accordingly swore in large numbers of them as Special Constables for duty at their own works'.[55] In Shrewsbury a local councillor, who could boast of being 'one of those terrible fellows who has been on

53. Jane Morgan, *Conflict and Order: The Police and Labour Disputes in England and Wales 1900–1939* (Oxford: Clarendon Press, 1987), pp. 133–4, 192–201. There is no mention of 'inefficiency' in Monmouthshire in the Report of H.M. Inspectors of Constabulary for 1926. It is worth noting that Bosanquet had been seriously criticised earlier in 1926 when, in spite of his force's inability to come up with any leads in a case of suspected murder, he steadfastly refused to call any assistance from larger detective forces, notably that of Scotland Yard. This had prompted the *Police Review* to urge that 'the powers of County Chief Constables be limited in like manner to those possesed by Borough Chiefs. This is not the age for autocrats': *Police Review*, 1 Apr. 1926, p. 211.

54. Morgan, *Conflict and Order*, pp. 122–3. However, Morgan goes on to state that the events in Lincoln during the General Strike led to an enquiry by the Inspector of Constabulary which resulted in the forced resignation of both Hughes and the chairman of the Watch Committee. This is a mistake, as the Lincoln Watch Committee Minute Books in the Lincs. Record Office show that both Hughes and Councillor Charles T. Parker continued to hold their posts into the 1930s.

55. *Aspects of the General Strike*, Part II 'Summaries and Information', North Riding.

strike', praised the town police for their behaviour during the General Strike and lauded the Chief Constable as an 'absolute brick'.[56] However, another borough chief constable, A.K. Mayall of Oldham, expressed some concerns about the overall effects of the strike: he feared that it had contributed to a belief that 'the Police are controlled by political elements'.[57] The Home Office made no obvious attempts to encourage the more conciliatory tone in preference to the aggression exhibited, most notably, by the police in South Wales. Indeed, by the Trade Disputes Act of 1927, which widened the meaning of the term 'intimidation' and forbade mass picketing and house-to-house picketing, the police were encouraged to take more vigorous action against strikers.[58]

During the 1930s the Home Office urged the police to take an even-handed approach towards political extremists on the Left and the Right, yet this in itself led to charges of partiality and to disquiet among some senior police officers who considered that the real problems of street disorder emanated largely from the British Union of Fascists. 'Even-handedness' in this Home Office definition could mean taking action against left-wing street politicians who were little trouble, simply because action had been taken against Blackshirts who were serious trouble. Some senior provincial policemen ignored such directives and, with the full support of their local police authority, acted against those whom they considered to be the trouble-makers. John Maxwell, the Chief Constable of Manchester, was notable in this respect, authorising his men to enter 'private' Fascist meetings when hecklers were brutally ejected, and banning political uniforms and marches through certain districts of the city some four and a half months before the Public Order Act of 1936 became law. Furthermore, when allegations were made that his men had been interfering unnecessarily with Labour Party meetings, Maxwell demanded that his superintendents furnish him 'with any known instances of where any member of the Manchester

56. Elliott, *Policing Shropshire*, pp. 164–5.
57. *Report of the Royal Commission on Police Powers and Procedure. Minutes of Evidence, Part II* (London: HMSO, 1929), p. 577.
58. Morgan, *Conflict and Order*, pp. 217–19. It should be noted that some of the chief constables' reports on the General Strike expressed concern about picketing. The Chief Constable of Manchester, for example, protested that 'in effect there is no such thing as "peaceful picketing". What is known as "peaceful picketing" leads to more trouble than anything else the Police have to deal with in trade disputes as the pickets, when they see a favourable opportunity, will and do resort to means which certainly cannot be regarded as peaceful': *Aspects of the General Strike*, Part II 'Summaries and Information', Manchester, and see also Cumberland and Westmorland, and Bristol.

City Police Force has in any way interfered with a Labour Party Meeting in the streets of Manchester'.[59]

Some of the violence meted out by the forces of order during the General Strike can be blamed on undisciplined Special Constables sworn in for the duration of the emergency, but by no means all; and police violence was not confined to the General Strike. There were probably a variety of reasons for this violence, and the argument that the police were simply acting as the shock troops of capitalism when they broke heads is the least convincing.[60] Policemen confronting crowds could themselves be frightened. They might be angry at losing a rest day. They could also just lose their tempers and, with that, all discipline. Men called away to give mutual aid could prove less restrained for other reasons: they might resent being taken from their families and homes; they might find themselves abused and challenged as outsiders by the local community;[61] and while billeted together in uncomfortable conditions in a strange district, they might respond rather like soldiers in alien territory, with little liking or respect for the local community. All discipline appears to have been lost in Liverpool in September 1921 and in Birkenhead in September 1932; in the first instance only local police were involved, in the second it was both local police and reinforcements drafted in from outside. In neither case would the Home Office, or the local authority, sanction an investigation.[62]

Violence by the English police during the inter-war period, while less life-threatening than elsewhere in Europe or the United States, was an issue on which central government and official journals were both smug and touchy. The implicit argument was that, since the English police were 'the best in the world', they could never, as a body, be unnecessarily violent. The National Council for Civil Liberties was established partly out of concerns over police actions against left-wing demonstrations, and the Home Office concluded that its *modus operandi* was 'to vilify the police on all possible occasions'.[63] A London newspaper's description of mounted police

59. Paul Cohen, 'The police, the Home Office and surveillance of the British Union of Fascists', *Intelligence and National Security* 1 (1986), 416–43; Greater Manchester PA Manchester Police, General Orders, vol. 27, fol. 204.

60. Clive Emsley, 'Police forces and public order in England and France during the inter-war years', in Emsley and Weinberger (eds), *Policing Western Europe*.

61. There is clear evidence of this happening in 1911 in both Cardiff and Liverpool: see Barbara Weinberger, *Keeping the Peace? Policing Strikes in Britain 1906–1926* (Oxford: Berg, 1991), pp. 83, 91.

62. Weinberger, 'Police perceptions of labour', pp. 159–60; Allen Hutt, *The Post-War History of the British Working Class* (London: Gollancz, 1937), pp. 223–25.

63. MEPO 2/3112, fol. 14.

dispersing a demonstration by the unemployed using their 'sword-sticks' brought forth a sharp correction from the *Justice of the Peace*:

London policemen do not carry swordsticks. A swordstick is usually considered to be a walking stick which conceals a sword. The mounted constable carries a long wooden truncheon, about the length of a sabre furnished with a hand guard, but quite innocent of steel. It is a useful, efficient weapon, but it certainly is not a swordstick, and we hope that no foreigner will imagine that London policemen charge crowds with drawn swords, or even that their sticks conceal swords.[64]

Critics of the police involved with the extreme left-wing press could find themselves in court. In May 1926 Edward Wilson, a miner, was prosecuted for circulating *Northern Light*. The edition in question had made allegations of police brutality during a baton charge in Gateshead. In sentencing Wilson to three months' hard labour the chairman of the Bench declared: 'Why you and those who are associated with you don't go off to Russia I don't know. I am sure the Government and I, personally, would subscribe willingly to get rid of the whole lot of you.' *The Labour Monthly* called the case 'fairly typical'.[65] Ten months later the editor and proprietor of the *Workers' Weekly* were found guilty of libelling the Durham police after accusing them of brutality towards a procession in Chester-le-Street. The Lord Chief Justice, summing up for the jury, explained that if the report was criticising a single policeman, then this should have been made plain:

In the passage complained of there was an allegation of police brutality and not brutality by an individual policeman, and a clear suggestion that the police, so far from doing their duty, had allowed themselves to be animated by the basest motive and had done something which was entirely wrong.[66]

When the ILP's James Maxton raised the question of police brutality against demonstrations by the unemployed in Sheffield and Manchester in 1934, the Home Secretary, Sir John Gilmour, replied that he had received reports from the chief constables and saw no reason to take action. Lady Astor enquired: 'Is not the word of a chief constable better than that of a Communist?'[67]

64. *Justice of the Peace* XCV (1931), 5 Dec., p. 756.
65. 'The police persecutions: a document of the General Strike', *The Labour Monthly* 8 (June 1926), 379–84; the journal quoted the court case verbatim from the *Blaydon Courier*, 22 May 1926.
66. *Justice of the Peace* XCI (1927), 12 Mar., p. 184.
67. *Hansard*, CCXCVIII, 21 Feb. 1935, cols 537–8.

Disquiet was voiced in the popular press during the 1920s following allegations, not of violence, but of corruption in the policing of night-clubs and bookmakers, and of policemen using their powers in an arbitrary fashion; the arbitrariness, it was sometimes suggested, was a legacy of the extensive police powers under the wartime Defence of the Realm Regulations. In 1926 Major R.O. Sheppard was mistakenly arrested and then mistreated in Vine Street Police Station in central London. Two years later a similar fate befell Major Graham Murray; and in the same year officers of the Metropolitan Police were accused of bullying Irene Savidge after she was caught in a compromising situation with Sir Leo Chiozza Money, a well-known writer on financial matters.[68] These cases led ultimately to the creation of the Royal Commission on Police Powers and Procedure, but not before Sir William Joynson-Hicks, the Home Secretary and an ardent supporter of the police, suggested that 'the public abstain from criticising the police for the next twelve months':

> It is an indisputable fact that the British police force is one of the finest – if not the finest – in the world, it frequently receives tributes from European and American States, and while the satisfaction of knowing this should not be allowed to degenerate into complacency, it should surely call for vigorous inquiry when sweeping attacks, unsupported by any semblance of evidence, are made upon it.[69]

The Royal Commission concluded that 'black sheep' were responsible for the 'isolated incidents' of misconduct, and from the testimony of 'responsible and judicial authorities' its members formed a favourable opinion 'of the conduct, tone and efficiency of the Police Service as a whole'.[70]

The Savidge case, the exposure of Metropolitan Police Sergeant Goddard's involvement with night-club and brothel owners, and the widespread corruption involving bookmakers and members of the Liverpool Police, which all hit the headlines in 1928 and 1929,[71] were not typical of the policeman's portrayal in the press. By and large the official view that the English Bobby was honest and

---

68. J.B. Lopian, 'Crime, police and punishment: Metropolitan experiences, perceptions and policies', Ph.D., University of Cambridge, 1987, pp. 45–50.

69. *Justice of the Peace* XCII (1928), 28 July, p. 501. Even H.A. Taylor, the contemporary biographer of Joynson-Hicks, suggested that his subject's enthusiasm for the police was somewhat excessive: H.A. Taylor, *Jix, Viscount Brentford* (London: Stanley Paul, 1933), p. 220.

70. *Report of the Royal Commission on Police Powers and Procedures, 16th. Mar. 1929*, Cmd. 3297, pp. 99, 111.

71. Alan Doig, *Corruption and Misconduct in Contemporary British Politics* (Harmondsworth: Penguin, 1984), p. 91.

moderate in his behaviour, and thus different from his continental neighbours, especially when it came to dealing with strikers and demonstrators, was also that taken by the newspaper press and, subsequently, by cinema newsreels. This is probably best explained by the essentially integrationist attitude of the news media. At the beginning of the twentieth century the Home Office and the Commissioner were determined to keep secret the number of disciplinary cases in the Metropolitan Police, and magistrates were advised not to make public statement which might be detrimental to the police; the situation astonished a former commissioner of the New York City Police who recalled having to give almost hourly reports to the press.[72] In 1919 an official was appointed at Scotland Yard to give information to the press on cases of public interest, and a press information bureau was established eight years later.[73] But the Metropolitan Police remained extremely cautious about 'leaks' to the press. In 1932 this was put forward as a reason for not circulating daily crime figures to police stations; and four years later, when the Commissioner was expressing concerns to his superintendents about some police officers' truthfulness in giving evidence and statements, he warned that 'it was of course essential that the terms of the Memorandum should not be allowed to leak to the press'.[74]

The leadership of the Labour Party also subscribed to this official view of the English Bobby as unique, impartial and non-political. It made little fuss over the dismissal of the strikers in 1919, and no attempt to reinstate them during its brief spells in office. While some of the party's members clashed with chief constables on standing joint committees or watch committees, while some had links with the National Council for Civil Liberties, and while others criticised anything which smacked of militarisation in the police, the party as a body studiously avoided making either the police or policing an issue of national political debate. Perhaps the Labour leadership sincerely believed that the official view of the Bobby was an accurate one; perhaps too, in their determination to present a respectable and responsible image themselves, they were reluctant to criticise those hailed as guardians of the public and of the English way of life. Perhaps also some of the Labour leadership shared

72. Clive Emsley, 'The English Bobby: an indulgent tradition', in Roy Porter (ed.), *Myths of the English* (Oxford: Polity Press, 1992), p. 123.

73. *Justice of the Peace* XCI (1927), 30 April, p. 332.

74. MEPO 2/10402, Superintendents' Conference, 20 Jan. 1932; MEPO 2/10406, Superintendents' Meeting, 29 April 1936.

concerns about police loyalty and did not wish to cause any alienation on the part of the police.

In part, the determination to protect the police from criticism, together with the continuing praise of the unique qualities of the Bobby, may have been prompted by a perceived need to maintain police loyalty. The concerns generated by the strikes of 1918 and 1919 were never completely assuaged. After the report of Sir Eric Geddes's committee on the best ways to cut government expenditure, the government contemplated recalling the Desborough Committee and reopening the issue of police pay. The idea was dropped, partly it seems because of the mood manifested at a mass meeting organised by the Police Federation in January 1924.[75] However, following the May Committee Report on National Expenditure of July 1931, with its recommendations for reductions in unemployment benefit and expenditure on the civil service and the military, police pay was cut by 10 per cent in two equal, annual tranches. Again there was anger and frustration. A regular contributor to the *Police Review* commented cynically:

> Ever since 1919, when we first received a reasonable wage for the work we do (except for a short period following the General Strike, in 1926, when we were acclaimed as super-men, worthy of the highest remuneration), the trend of opinion in certain quarters has been to the effect that a Policeman's job was, financially, second only to a Cabinet Minister's; the only difference being that a Cabinet minister had a certain amount of responsibility.

As a result of the pay cut, he went on, it would now be necessary for the police 'to give up our racing stables and dispose of our yachts . . . sell our country seats and retain no more than two town houses each'.[76] The Home Secretary, conscious of the anger, banned public meetings by the Police Federation, considering it inadvisable 'that there should be anything in the nature of a public propagandist campaign through-out the country. It was considered that that would be exceedingly disturbing to the Police Force and would not serve a useful purpose.'[77]

For a short period in the early 1920s a group of dismissed police strikers published *The Bull's Eye*, a radical journal which regularly carried articles warning against the militarisation of the police and urging policemen to get to know 'and therefore to love their fellow

75. *Police Review*, 18 Jan. 1924, pp. 26–31, and 1 Feb., p. 55.
76. Ibid., 25 Sept. 1931, p. 781.
77. *Hansard*, CCLXV, 2 May 1932, cols 863–4.

workers'.[78] Pamphlets and handbills were also prepared by different groups urging the police not to act against their fellow workers. Towards the end of 1921, for example, Lilian Mary Thring was prosecuted for circulating a pamphlet called *Out of Work* which contained an address 'To the Coppers'.[79] In November 1932, following the pay cut, the married men at Commercial Street and Arbour Street Police Stations in London were circulated with 'AN APPEAL TO THE POLICE' which began:

> We, the unemployed workers, are fighting for Bread, for Work, Against the Means Test, for No More Economies.
> You London Police know what the Government's Economies have meant for us. As you walk the streets you see on every side of you the hunger, the misery, the bitter suffering forced on us and our families.[80]

The 'Appeal' went on to draw attention also to the way the government's economies were affecting the police. Lord Trenchard mentioned such attempted subversion in his annual report, but the Home Secretary did not think 'it would be in the public interest' to present any details to Parliament.[81]

In addition to the need to preserve police loyalty given the economic situation, it was also increasingly recognised from the 1920s that there was a need to maintain middle-class support for the police. The development of the motor car, and its increasing availability to middle-class families, was, even by this date, bringing members of a social group, who hitherto had had virtually no contact with the police, into regular conflict with them. In the summer of 1928 the Home Secretary made 'a pressing personal appeal' to all chief constables that they should urge caution on their men in the way they behaved towards the public on the roads.[82] Stressing the Bobby's unique qualities, his good humour and impartiality was an additional way of seeking to check the new and damaging confrontations between policemen and members of the middle class on the roads.

78. *The Bull's Eye*, No. 2, Aug. 1920, p. 3; see also No. 7, 29 Oct. 1920, pp. 1–3, No. 11, 24 Dec. 1920, p. 4.
79. *Justice of the Peace* LXXXV (1921), 3 Dec., p. 561.
80. MEPO 2/3066, fols 37, 40, 41.
81. *Hansard*, CCLXXVII, 4 May 1932, col. 988.
82. Staffs. PA Staffordshire Constabulary Memo Book, 1926–31, fol. 23; and see in general Clive Emsley, ' "Mother, what *did* policemen do when there weren't any motors?" The law, the police and the regulation of motor traffic in England 1900–1939', *HJ* 36 (1993), 357–81.

CHAPTER SEVEN

Policing Mid-Twentieth-Century England

Face to face with change

The motor car was only one of a series of developments which, during the twentieth century, forced changes in policing. From the moment that motor vehicles appeared on the roads it was apparent that they presented a new and distinctive problem for the police. 'Criminals' had been perceived as mobile in the early nineteenth century, and there were concerns that the railways gave them greater mobility; the motor car increased such concerns many times over,[1] even though most crime remained petty and apparently local.[2] But the police had also, from their creation, been responsible for the smooth running of the streets: the motor car caused far greater problems than the occasional runaway horse, the carter driving without reins, or the 'scorching' cyclist. By the early 1920s chief constables and His Majesty's Inspectors of Constabulary were expressing anxiety about the amount of time now taken up with the supervision of the roads: in 1924, for example, Chichester complained to Dunning that in the county town of Huntingdon 'the only men I have here – with the exception of the Sergeant – have

1. On 18 Oct. 1931, for example, the Chief Constable of Bedfordshire informed his men: 'Crime in this county is increasing and nearly all of it is done from the stealing of fowls to large robbery with the help of a motor car. Small robberies committed by tramps make it difficult for the police to detect because these men get lifts on lorries': Beds. PA Beds. Constabulary Order Book, 1930–35.
2. Whatever the claims of the Chief Constable of Bedfordshire, the Departmental Committee which examined detective work during the 1930s noted that 'in 73 per cent of the cases in which the offences were detected the offender was found to live in the police district in which the crime was committed. In the county forces 85 per cent of the offenders lived within the police district or within 20 miles of it': *Report of the Departmental Committee on Detective Work and Procedure*, 5 vols (London: Home Office, 1939), i, p. 30.

to be continually on point duty, and with them the work cannot be efficiently done, and . . . practically no ordinary patrol duty can take place'.[3] The motor car forced an immediate response from the police, but they were much slower in recognising, and grappling with, other, more gradual changes.

The police began to use motor vehicles themselves from the first decade of the century, but in many other instances they made little or no attempt to reap the benefit of scientific and technological advance, partly because of expense, partly because of their organisational structure, but also probably because of an institutional conservatism. At the turn of the century, for example, there was a general reluctance to authorise patrols by bicycle, though this was not always the fault of conservative chief constables: in Norfolk in 1896, for example, it was the Standing Joint Committee which turned down the Chief Constable's request for the purchase of six bicycles, authorising him only to hire a bicycle 'in case of emergency . . . to be ridden at the rider's risk'.[4] The Metropolitan Police had begun using telegraphic communication in the early 1850s and by the end of the following decade police stations in London were linked into a telegraph network.[5] At the turn of the century there was considerable reluctance to replace the system with the new telephone: 'the existing efficient system of telegraphic communication between all the police stations which is entirely under police control, meets all police requirements', declared the Home Secretary on two separate occasions.[6] But experiments had begun to be made with police boxes which enabled constables on the beat to receive information and summon assistance. At first these involved telegraph equipment, but the first phone box was tried out in 1897 and ten years later there were 33 police phone boxes or fixed points with telephone links in the outer divisions of the Metropolitan Police district.[7] Elsewhere when the outlay was made on telephones, there were concerns about the expense. In Staffordshire in the summer of 1902 the Chief Constable was authorised by his Standing Joint

---

3. Cambs. PA Chief Constable of Huntingdonshire Letter Book, 1918–64, fol. 402.

4. *Hansard,* LXII, 26 July 1898, col. 1302; Cambs. PA Huntingdonshire Constabulary, Chief Constable's Memos, 1857–1907, No. 93, 21 Sept. 1893; F. Slack, *The Norfolk Constabulary* (Norwich: Norfolk Constabulary, 1967), p. 12.

5. Phillip Thurmond Smith, *Policing Victorian London: Political Policing, Public Order, and the London Metropolitan Police* (Westport, Conn.: Greenwood Press, 1985), p. 42.

6. *Hansard,* LXVII, 23 Feb. 1899, col. 293; ibid., XCV, 20 June 1901.

7. John Bunker, *From Rattle to Radio* (Studley, Warks.: Brewin Books, 1988), pp. 136–47.

Committee to have six of his police stations connected to the telephone exchange; the following year he wrote to the National Telephone Company suggesting that his force was being charged too much for the facility and pointing out the benefits which the company itself received from the county.[8] In the aftermath of the First World War the telephone system was greatly extended amongst the police and most large towns also developed systems of phones in pillars or in police boxes for beat constables; indeed, some of the police boxes were almost miniature stations with wash basins or enough room to park a bicycle.[9] In July 1933 Sir John Gilmour, the Home Secretary, could report that:

> Telephones are installed in practically every police station in the country, and in about one half of the houses of constables on rural beats, which are over 5,000 in number. The police authorities of a few counties in which the telephone facilities appeared to be inadequate have already been urged to improve these facilities, and improvements have already been made, and His Majesty's Inspectors of Constabulary, in the course of their inspections, are drawing attention to such deficiencies as remain.

The principal problem was the high cost of installing telephones in remote districts, and for this reason Gilmour felt it was not possible for him to lay down hard and fast regulations for police authorities.[10]

The aftermath of the First World War also witnessed developments in wireless which opened up still more opportunities, but many chief constables were slow to recognise the potential which such communications offered their forces.[11] It was not until 1932 that the Chief Constables' Association heard an address from the Director of Telegraphs and Telephones at the GPO on 'The Possibilities of the Telegraph, Telephone and Teleprinter Services as Affecting the Police and Fire Brigades'.[12] The discussion arising out of a similar paper presented three years later highlighted some of the problems which the structure of policing presented to some of

8. Staffs. PA Staffordshire Constabulary, Chief Constable's Letter Book, 1900–8, fols 298, 430.

9. Bunker, *From Rattle to Radio*, pp. 149–50.

10. *Hansard*, CCLXXX, 3 July 1933, col. 15. A telephone in a police station or in a rural police house could prove a boon to the local community. For example, PC George Cordy noted in his Journal for Sunday 24 April 1932: 'Recd. telephone message 12.45 a.m. from Addenbrook's Hospital Cambridge r.e. condition of Mrs Bennett of Feltwell. Relatives informed': Norfolk PA Feltwell Beat Journal 1931–33.

11. Sir Arthur L. Dixon, 'The Home Office and the police between the two world wars' (unpublished, 1966), p. 167.

12. *Chief Constables' Association: Reports of the General Conference and Special General Conference, 1932*, pp. 43–54.

those interested in developing radio communications. J.A. Wilson, the Chief Constable of Cardiff, pointed out

> the difficulty of some of us in isolated cities surrounded by Counties which possibly do not take the interest in scientific work that the Boroughs do. One knows of places having adopted or being prepared to adopt effective wireless systems, but this is negatived because adjoining County areas do not adopt systems of their own. That happens in Glamorgan. We have offered to co-operate but without success, and as long as things are like that it is impossible to carry out an efficient system of wireless.

Wilson explained that there would be no difficulty for him in getting the necessary money from his Watch Committee. However, Alderman Thraves of Sheffield 'was very concerned about the cost of these things . . . We have to think of the number of unemployed men there are to provide for, and on that account we cannot afford to undertake any experimental work.'[13] A matter of days after this discussion, the Home Secretary, now Sir John Simon, could inform the Commons that, in the Metropolitan Police district, 'a complete service of rapid wireless communication with police officers patrolling in motor vehicles has now been developed, and is proving of great value for the detection and the apprehension of criminals'.[14]

The potential for scientific aid in criminal detection was explored by a few enthusiastic chief constables, and most notably before the First World War by Sir Edward Henry when, building on the work of others, he developed a system for the classification of fingerprints.[15] During the inter-war years energetic chief constables in Nottingham and Sheffield linked with biologists and pathologists in local universities to develop methods of forensic detection. There were similar moves in Cardiff, Hull and Liverpool, but there were also chief constables who lacked such vision: when Eric St Johnston became Chief Constable of Oxfordshire in 1940 he found a force which had no specialist sections at all, not even a Criminal Investigation Department.[16] Dixon, at the Home Office, was eager to see the creation of a police college which could be the focus for police research; and there were others keen to see some scientific training for police constables, and especially for detectives. Lord Trenchard,

---

13. *Chief Constables' Association: Reports of the General Conference and Special General Conference, 1935*, pp. 72, 75.
14. *Hansard*, CCCIII, 27 June 1935, col. 1287.
15. David Ascoli, *The Queen's Peace: The Origins and Development of the Metropolitan Police 1829–1979* (London: Hamish Hamilton, 1979), p. 181.
16. Eric St Johnston, *One Policeman's Story* (London: Barry Rose, 1978), p. 65.

as Commissioner of the Metropolitan Police, urged the creation of a Medico-Legal Institute to put the English police on a level with their neighbours, but the project foundered on the Treasury's reluctance to provide any funding.[17] Eventually, in 1939, a Common Police Services Fund was established through which the Home Office was to finance crime clearing houses, laboratories, and wireless depots; half of the Fund came from the government, and the remainder from those forces using the facility, each contributing in proportion to its size.[18]

For much of the nineteenth century, 'criminals' were perceived as coming from a particular social group at the bottom layer of the working class. The task of the police was to contain this group within its teeming rookeries. 'We look upon it', declared Rowan in a much-quoted phrase, 'that we are watching St James's and other places while we are watching St Giles and bad places in general.'[19] Rough districts continued to exist for the police to contain; the relationship between the police and the communities in these districts was never simply one of oppression since the police could be called in to aid the weak against the strong, to protect wives and children, possibly to use their first aid training, and to help in times of tragedy or crisis.[20] But the old rookeries had been destroyed well before the end of the nineteenth century, and while the 'criminal classes' may have continued to lurk primarily in inner city areas, the growth of the suburbs gave the police a much extended 'St James' to guard.

A key element in the creation of the new police forces in nineteeth-century England had been the increased demand for order and decorum in public places. The imposition of the new level of order had meant the police 'moving on' street traders, prostitutes and drunks, and anyone else who sought to loiter in the street. Street traders and loiterers had little or no public voice in the nineteenth century; nor did those members of the working class for whom the street was a principal centre of entertainment and leisure. At least

17. Dixon, 'The Home Office and the police', pp. 126, 147, 161–5, and Appendices 12 and 13. *Chief Constables' Association: Reports of the General Conference and Special General Conference, 1930*, pp. 23, 38–47.

18. T.A. Critchley, *A History of Police in England and Wales*, rev. edn (London: Constable, 1978), p. 214.

19. *PP* 1834 (600) XVI, *Select Committee on the Police of the Metropolis*, q. 166.

20. Jerry White, *The Worst Street in North London: Campbell Bunk, Islington, Between the Wars* (London: Routledge and Kegan Paul, 1986), pp. 114–15; Joanne Marie Klein, 'Invisible working-class men: police constables in Manchester, Birmingham and Liverpool 1900–1939', Ph.D., Rice University, 1992, pp. 73–80 and, in general, ch. 8.

up until the Second World War the street continued to provide this facility with, on occasions, street gambling games, the bookies' runners available to take bets, and street fights, sometimes involving the police, which could still be described in the local newspapers as 'exciting', 'interesting' or 'thrilling'. Moreover, as motor cars remained beyond the reach of the majority, many people still walked in the streets both on the way to and from work, and for pleasure. However, as the increasing availability of motor transport gradually drew pedestrians from the streets, so too did the enormous expansion of spectator sports: the inter-war years witnessed a tremendous growth in licensed boxing, dog-track racing, speedway and, of course, association football. Cinemas and dance-halls provided new centres for organised leisure; the development of the radio and the gramophone provided new opportunities for entertainment at home.[21] Football crowds showing hostility towards opposing teams and fans had begun to cause trouble for the police from the 1880s.[22] Poor facilities inside the grounds could also provoke trouble; and after these were improved, other developments could create difficulties, sometimes outside the stadiums. In October 1926, for example, the Chief Constable of Lincoln informed the City Watch Committee:

> that, owing to serious complaints made to the police concerning motor vehicles standing in Sauthsthorpe Street and Sincil Bank during the time football matches were being played on the ground of the Lincoln City Football Club, he gave instructions to the Police on Saturday last that they were to serve a notice on each motorist who left his vehicle standing in the street to the effect that instructions had been given that motor vehicles were not to be allowed to remain there in future.[23]

Senior police officers had backed the legislation of 1906 prohibiting street betting in the belief that betting was having a corrosive effect on the working class and that it could be eradicated by strong

21. Eric Dunning *et al.*, 'Violent disorders in twentieth-century Britain', in George Gaskell and Robert Benewick (eds), *The Crowd in Contemporary Britain* (London: Sage, 1987), pp. 29–34; J.E. Cronin, *Labour and Society in Britain 1918–1979* (London: Batsford, 1984), pp. 84–6; John Stevenson and Chris Cook, *The Slump: Society and Politics during the Depression* (London: Cape, 1977), pp. 27–8.
22. Tony Mason, *Association Football and English Society 1863–1915* (Brighton: Harvester, 1980), esp. pp. 163–7.
23. Lincs. RO Lincoln Watch Commitee Minutes, 1926–34, fol. 14. The following year, following a deputation to the Watch Committee from the directors of the Football Club, it was agreed to permit parking on one side of the road: ibid., fol. 62.

laws and vigorous enforcement. But the legislation created more problems than it solved, while the development of forms of mass betting with football pools and on-course betting at horse races and dog tracks made enforcement seem more and more an exercise which was serving to undermine police authority rather than enhance it. The police responded to the difficulties created by the street betting legislation with an unofficial policy of minimum enforcement and at times unofficial arrangements were also entered into with the bookmakers.[24]

Some chief constables clung to the idea of the tramp as a probable criminal, or at best an object of suspicion, into the early twentieth century. In March 1908, for example, Chichester was still keen to have his men serve as Assistant Relieving Officers: 'I feel it my duty to point out it is for the good of the public that these duties should be performed by the police as it brings the tramping community under their notice and thereby enables them to be in touch with their movements, which are not always satisfactory.'[25] However fear of the tramp appears to have declined alongside the fear of the residuum during the First World War. The supervision of tramps was increasingly seen as a welfare role, albeit performed by the police, rather than essentially a problem of crime prevention. In 1926 the Annual Meeting of the Chief Constables' Association was addressed by Edward Waugh, solicitor and secretary to the East Sussex Joint Vagrancy Committee, who stressed that many more of the men on the roads were 'bona-fide working men who were genuinely in search of work'. He was keen that the police should distribute Vagrancy Way Tickets 'to men whom they know to be of good character and in search of work'.[26] In the following year the Conference resolved that the Poor Law Authorities were in a better position to deal with the issue than the police; nevertheless, during the Depression the police did find themselves responsible for the issue of such tickets.[27] Clifford Jeeves, a police constable in the Borough of Bedford, recalled how vagrants coming into the town 'had to go to the police station to get a ticket to go to the workhouse ... you were detailed to that after you'd had your tea,

24. David Dixon, 'The state and gambling: developments in the legal control of gambling in England, 1867–1923', paper presented to the Fifth National Conference on Gambling and Risk-taking, Caesar's Tahoe Hotel and Casino, 22–25 Oct. 1981, pp. 16–24, 71–2.

25. Cambs. PA Chief Constable of Huntingdonshire Letter Book, 1906–15, fol. 102.

26. *Chief Constables' Association: Annual Report, June, 1926*, p. 46.

27. *Chief Constables' Association: Annual Report of ... Conference, June, 1927*, p. 34.

5 o'clock time, you'd get to go to the office at the rear and dish out tickets ... and you had to put them all down on a piece of paper and you used to take that to the workhouse'.[28]

Like the supervision of vagrants, the organisation and co-ordination of charitable relief by the police, and the running of clubs and sports for working-class boys, fell between the stools of crime prevention and welfare. Police charities supplying boots and clothing to the poor continued well into the twentieth century. As Chief Constable of Plymouth H.H. Saunders, a former detective in the Metropolitan Police, established a Widows and Orphans Fund in his jurisdiction in 1917; in the middle of the following decade he showed himself progressive enough to use the new medium of the cinema to advertise his society, demonstrate its work, and request cinema patrons to contribute to its efforts.[29] His Majesty's Inspectors of Constabulary believed that the policeman should be 'encouraged to interest himself in schemes which will give him a wider outlook on his opportunities for doing good' and suggested that 'active participation in works of charity or social betterment, such as police Aided Clothing Associations or Boys' Clubs, give him an influence for good over those who might grow up to regard him as their enemy'.[30] In 1926 C.H. Dain, the Chief Constable of Norwich, urged the Conference of the Chief Constables' Association 'to listen to ... the call of the BOY'. The state, he explained, sought to prevent sickness and promote good health through its physical welfare departments, and to combat ignorance with schools. 'Why not then, using the same logic, attempt to prevent moral delinquencies?' Throughout his address he extolled the virtues of the Boys' Clubs which he had founded in Norwich in 1918. He was received sympathetically by his audience, and Councillor Melling, the vice-chairman of the Sheffield Watch Committee, was probably voicing the thoughts of many in suggesting that 'Boys trained in the right direction were the best cure for Bolshevism'.[31] In the early 1930s George Lansbury paid tribute to the example set by the police of Norwich and Brighton in organising clubs for boys, and he urged

28. Taped interview with ex-PC Clifford Jeeves, Feb. 1987.
29. Clive Emsley, 'The blue-coated social worker' (conference abstract), *Social History Society Newsletter* XV/1 (Spring 1990), 11–12. The films have been deposited with the British Film Institute. See also *Police Review*, 7 Mar. 1924, p. 134.
30. *Report of H.M. Inspectors of Constabulary for 1923*, p. 7; see also ibid. for 1929, pp. 5–6.
31. *Chief Constables' Association: Report of the Annual General Meeting, June, 1926*, pp. 26–32. 'The call of the BOY' was urged by Dain before a variety of audiences: see, *inter alia*, *Police Review*, 23 Apr. 1926, p. 247, and 12 June 1931, p. 496.

other forces to follow their lead.[32] Police involvement with youth
clubs and with organised sports for boys continued after the Second
World War,[33] though gradually shedding the ostentatious paternalism
of Dain. The welfare assistance for the poor also continued, sometimes through official action like the clothing funds, or like the
holiday home established for poor children at Lytham by the
Preston Police,[34] but also simply by virtue of the police being there.
Harry Daley, who served in the Metropolitan Police from 1925 to
1950, recalled how many Londoners used their local police station
as a kind of unofficial welfare centre and citizen's advice bureau:

> Scores of people called for money, often thinking there was a fund
> for doling out in emergencies. This was not so. We could issue Rail-
> way Travel Warrants to poor people called upon to make long jour-
> neys in unusual circumstances – to visit a wounded soldier son for
> instance; but all money paid out came from the pockets of compas-
> sionate coppers and was seldom paid back. Each case was dealt with
> on its merits, deserving cases often got up to a couple of bob, but
> naturally most people were refused.[35]

The Widows' and Orphans' Funds, like that run by Saunders
in Plymouth, were regulated by gender division: Saunders ran the
organisation, his constables looked for deserving cases, while Mrs
Saunders and other 'ladies' sewed and knitted. Similarly, in the
early decades of the twentieth century, while the encouragement of
boys in healthy, sporty pursuits was perceived as a way of preventing
crime and Bolshevism, when it came to suggestions that women
police might provide a similar preventive to girls and young women,
a double standard was applied. The excuse was often to keep costs
down, but male prejudice was also apparent. In part, the women
who had been responsible for organising the women police patrols
in the First World War were motivated by the double standard in
the courts, which left women and children victims of sexual or
domestic assault in a vulnerable position, and also by the fear that
young women could easily be tricked into 'White Slavery' and prostitution. Many were open in their aspirations that their wartime
example would enable the peacetime development of professional

32. *Hansard,* CCLXV, 2 May 1932, col. 875.
33. *Justice of the Peace* CXXIV (1960), 26 Mar., pp. 197–8.
34. *Police Review,* 2 July 1926, p. 372.
35. Harry Daley, *This Small Cloud: A Personal Memoir* (London: Weidenfeld & Nicolson, 1986), p. 209; see also pp. 81, 201, 208. For the similar situation in Liverpool
after the Second World War see James McClure, *Spike Island: Portrait of a Police
Division* (London: Macmillan, 1980), pp. 167, 342.

women police.[36] Macready had authorised a nucleus of 110 women police attached to the Metropolitan Police in 1919; significantly, he drew his women police from the Voluntary Women Patrols rather than the Women Police Service which, though more professional, had a cadre of former militant suffragettes. A very few chief constables, impressed by the role played by women during the war, also kept tiny numbers of women on their strength. Essentially, these women were expected to maintain their gender role and deal primarily with women and juveniles. Committees which reported on their efficiency during the 1920s urged that women police should be expanded across the country, while recognising that the final decision remained in the hands of the chief constables and the police authorities. His Majesty's Inspectors of Constabulary were similarly complimentary. But when the 'Geddes Axe' fell in 1922 the Home Secretary, Sir Edward Shortt, proposed the complete abolition of the women's section of the Metropolitan Police. His insistence that the work of the women police was 'welfare work . . . not police work proper', and that they only kept down crime 'with the sense in which the schoolmaster keeps down crime, and the clergyman and the Sunday-school teacher',[37] roused some MPs to fury, notably Nancy Astor. In the end Shortt was persuaded to leave a squad of 24 women constables attached to the Metropolitan Police. A less public example of the determination to keep the police a male preserve and of the prejudice faced by women is to be found in a memorandum sent by the Chief Constable of Staffordshire to his superintendents in March 1928:

> No possible risk must be taken of any woman being put into a cell and not being attended to by a woman, however short the time of detention. A great deal of attention is given to this matter at the present time, and there are a number of women's organisations the members of which are actively on the look out for any excuse for pressing for the appointment of women police and special 'police matrons' at stations. In any special emergency, at any station where for any cause the services of the woman who would usually attend to a female prisoner may temporarily be not available, the officer in charge must have a free hand to make the best arrangement he can without being tied down as to cost: the same care to avoid any reasonable

36. Lynn Amy Amidon, 'Ladies in blue: feminism and policing in Britain in the late nineteenth and early twentieth centuries', Ph.D., State University of New York, Binghampton, 1986, esp. pp. 67–91; Jill Radford, 'Women and policing: contradictions old and new', in Jalna Hanmer, Jill Radford and Elizabeth A. Stanko (eds), *Women, Policing and Male Violence* (London: Routledge, 1989).

37. *Hansard*, CLII, 28 Mar. 1922, col. 1280; ibid., 10 May, col. 2343.

cause of complaint must be taken whether the female arrested is a tramp or a woman of good position.

He added as a postscript that the memorandum was '[n]ot to be exhibited where any female "Nosey-Parkers" can read it'.[38] The situation improved marginally with the recommendations of the Royal Commission on Police Powers and Procedure in 1929, and in October 1931 the Home Office issued a set of regulations defining the function and status of police women wherever and whenever they were employed; but there was still no compulsion to recruit women and many continued to believe that police work was men's work and that women in police uniform, especially dealing with unpleasantness on the streets, somehow lost their femininity.[39] It took the depletion of the ranks of male policemen during the Second World War to see any marked expansion in women police, and on this occasion there was a more determined decision to continue their recruitment after the war. In 1939 there had been a total of 246 women police officers, 20 of whom were not sworn in; this amounted to less than 0.4 per cent of the total police establishment in England and Wales. Ten years later their numbers had quadrupled and the Police Federation reluctantly agreed to women police becoming members. By 1963 there were just over 3,000 women police officers, comprising about 3.5 per cent of the total police establishment.[40]

Well before the policewoman received gradual and grudging acceptance among her male colleagues and male superiors, small changes in the ethnic structure of English society were producing new problems with which some police forces had to come to terms. Immigrants had long been perceived as a problem by the police. During the Victorian period many Irish communities had been labelled as 'criminal'. Irish peasant immigrants brought habits with them which offended the indigenous inhabitants: in particular they sought to keep their animals in tenement buildings, and they continued to indulge in their traditional faction fights. Indeed, the criminality of the Irish communities appears to have stemmed much more from their inter-personal and anti-police violence, rather than

38. Staffs. PA Staffordshire Constabulary, Chief Constable's Memo Book, 1926–30, fol. 17, 6 Mar. 1928.

39. Amidon, 'Ladies in Blue', pp. 145–6, 148; Radford, 'Women and policing', pp. 37–8. Amidon notes that some historians have also tended to take this view in their portrayal of the first policewomen.

40. The only history of women police in England is Joan Lock, *The British Policewoman* (London: Robert Hale, 1979).

from any general propensity to thieve.[41] Yet the Irish immigrants could also assimilate with relative ease, and numbers of Irishmen even became English policemen. Towards the end of the nineteenth and at the beginning of the twentieth centuries an influx of Jews from eastern Europe created ghetto districts in some English cities, notably in parts of London's East End. The Jews were not 'criminal' as the Irish had been, something which policemen patrolling Jewish districts tended to explain once again by a resort to prejudice: the Jews were 'tricky', but 'not man enough to be rough'.[42] But these districts seemed impenetrable to the police compared with the old Irish immigrant districts since, even if they were not as violent and dangerous, the Jews stuck to their own language. The problem became more acute when, as a result of the Aliens Act of 1905, the police were compelled to take a close interest in the Jewish immigrant communities. In 1905 the Metropolitan Police began voluntary classes in Yiddish for men patrolling the Jewish districts, and prizes were offered for proficiency.[43] The problems of knowing what was going on in these communities continued both during and after the First World War when the alien population was perceived as a threat to national security and public order. Furthermore, the police, unable to comprehend the different customs of eastern European Jewish immigrants, tended to equate their unregistered marriages with mock marriages to enable foreign prostitutes to avoid deportation.[44] This lack of comprehension may have contributed to the anti-Semitism which Harry Daley described among some of the young constables in the Beak Street Section House at the beginning of the Second World War.[45] But immigrant communities were a very minor problem for police forces during the inter-war period. Where such communities did exist, as in the seaport of Liverpool with its Afro-Caribbean, Chinese and West African residents, there is evidence of racism on the part of the police. In part this probably stemmed from a generally assumed superiority on the part of white Britons as creators of an empire,

41. Frances Finnegan, *Poverty and Prejudice: A Study of Irish Immigrants in York, 1840–1875* (Cork: University Press, 1982), ch. 9; Roger Swift, ' "Another Stafford Street row": law, order and the Irish presence in mid-Victorian Wolverhampton', *Immigrants and Minorities* 3 (1984), 5–29.

42. David Englander, 'Booth's Jews: the presentation of Jews and Judaism in *Life and Labour of the People in London*', *Victorian Studies* XXXII (1989), 551–71, at 563–6.

43. *Hansard*, CXLIII, 23 Mar. 1905, col. 953; ibid., CLII, 1 Mar. 1906, col. 1305.

44. David Englander, '*Stille Huppah* (quiet marriage) among Jewish immigrants to Britain', *The Jewish Journal of Sociology* XXXIV (1992), 85–109, at 101–2.

45. Daley, *This Small Cloud*, pp. 172–4.

though there seems also to have been a reluctance among Afro-Caribbeans to play the game of deference to a police uniform.[46] However, the difficulties of penetrating and policing these communities, together with the problems of racial prejudice within the police, were as nothing compared with those which emerged with the growth of Black communities from the late 1950s.

The steady march of centralisation

The idea of a single English police service, largely based on the Metropolitan model, had been emerging in the mid-nineteenth century among politicians, journalists, and professional policemen. Greater degrees of uniformity were encouraged among the different forces by the reports and recommendations of the Inspectors of Constabulary; while the independence of the police forces from their local political masters was gradually fostered by the conferences of chief constables and by the preference of members of the central government bureaucracy to bypass local police committees and to deal directly with chief constables in matters of administrative regulation or national emergency – Sir Arthur Dixon recalled that certain confidential matters were not passed on to the chief constables of boroughs during the inter-war years because of their close links with their police authorities.[47] There were some calls for a national police during the inter-war period, though more common were the calls for a national criminal investigation department, to deal with the contemporary perceptions of increasingly sophisticated and mobile criminals, or for a national traffic police to cope with the increasing number of motor vehicles on the roads.[48] The watch committees and the standing joint committees continued to function; governments and civil servants continued to support the idea of local control of the police, except in London; and all the while the actions of central government, the interpretation of legal rulings, the continuing development of police professionalism, and then the emergency brought about by the Second World War, served to undermine the system.

46. Mike Brogden, *On the Mersey Beat: Policing Liverpool Between the Wars* (Oxford: OUP, 1991), pp. 148–55.
47. Sir Arthur L. Dixon, 'The emergency work of the police forces in the Second World War' (unpublished, 1963), p. 6.
48. *Hansard*, CXCVI, 7 June 1926, col. 1124; *Justice of the Peace* LXXXIX (1925), 1 Aug., pp. 451–2; ibid., XCI (1927), 12 Feb., pp. 103–4.

The Desborough Committee of 1919 recommended a series of measures to bring greater uniformity to the police in the interests of efficiency and good order. It proposed the establishment of uniform and improved rates of pay, and of standard conditions of service throughout the nation's police forces; at the same time it urged that the government grant to efficient forces should be increased from one-half of the cost of pay and clothing to one-half of the total cost. It recommended setting up both a Police Council and a Police Federation. The former was to include representatives from the police authorities and all ranks of the police under the chairmanship of the Home Secretary or one of his senior officials; its task was to advise the Home Office on matters relating to police and policing. All policemen were to become members of the Federation, and through their elected representatives they could bring matters of welfare and efficiency before police authorities or the Home Office; members of the Federation were not to be permitted the right to strike. In order to cope with the anticipated extra work which these recommendations would bring, it was also proposed to establish a specific police department, which became F Division, within the Home Office. Each of these proposals was accepted and rapidly implemented; each also served to strengthen the idea of a single police service, albeit divided into separate local units, ultimately responsible to the Home Office. Various other proposals by the Desborough Committee, which took a little longer to organise, also worked in this direction, notably the recommendations that co-operative arrangements should be developed further between the different forces, and that training might be improved and unified. Training was particularly a problem for the smaller forces, but during the inter-war years they began to send their recruits to the training establishments of the larger forces. The training school in Birmingham developed a high reputation due, in no small measure, to the enthusiastic Deputy Chief Constable in the city, C.H.H. Moriarty, the author of the instructional manual and guide *Police Law*, which was studied by generations of police constables.[49]

The Desborough Committee also proposed a rationalisation of the borough police forces in the name of efficiency. It recommended that the forces in any boroughs with a population of 50,000 or less be amalgamated with the surrounding county constabularies, and that the powers of appointment, discipline, and promotion in the

---

49. For the Birmingham Police Training School see ibid., XCII (1928), 17 Nov., p. 750. The first edition of Moriarty's *Police Law* appeared in 1929.

boroughs be brought into line with the counties and be transferred from the watch committees to the chief constables. These recommendations, like similar proposals in the Victorian period, provoked anger and resentment among the municipalities. The second proposal fell at the first hurdle; the amalgamation of the smallest forces continued to be advocated throughout the inter-war period by both the Home Office and the Inspectors of Constabulary, but to little effect.[50] The Economy (Miscellaneous Provisions) Bill of 1922 would have enabled the Home Secretary to force amalgamations in the interests of economy, but the bill was abandoned. In their report for 1929 the Inspectors of Constabulary lamented that talks about the merger of the eleven men in the Borough of Tiverton force with the Devonshire Police had failed; 'little island police districts like Tiverton are anachronisms in these days of modern facilities of travel, fenced in as they are by boundaries of which nobody but the police takes notice'. The Inspectors suggested that they might be squeezed out of existence by administrative action such as appraising their claim to the Treasury grant 'on a standard which would be reasonable for larger districts'.[51] The suggestion was not taken up. The Home Office proposed the abolition of forces in boroughs with a population of less than 75,000 to both the Royal Commission on Local Government, which met during the 1920s, and a parliamentary select committee of the early 1930s. On the first occasion the Association of Municipal Councils organised themselves for action with a committee established from the representatives of three of the threatened boroughs – Dudley, Exeter, and Rotherham – and funded by all of the others.[52] The Select Committee of 1932 recommended the abolition of the forces in boroughs with a population of less than 30,000, but nothing was done, partly because of concerns about provoking local opposition. In July 1935 Colonel J.C. Wedgewood, speaking in terms redolent of both local pride and laissez-faire liberalism, warned the Home Secretary against tampering with the Englishman's 'cherished rights' of decentralisation and local control. Any attempt to amalgamate police forces would, he believed, be blocked by the MPs representing places which had such forces.

> I prefer my local police force, though it may not be so efficient and may be a bit more extravagant, because, after all, the police there are

50. Critchley, *History of Police*, pp. 240–1.
51. *Report of H.M. Inspectors of Constabulary for 1929*, p. 4.
52. Lincs. RO Lincoln Watch Committee Minutes, 1926–34, fols 85–6, 105–6.

not doing the work of the bureaucracy up here. They are more human, even open to the hard cases and the people know them. One thing I would ask the Home Secretary to avoid, and that is more centralisation of authority. Let us remember that the movement towards liberty means decentralisation. In every case, whether it is the Home office or the church or a trade union, the cry is, 'The bigger we can make it the better it will be.' They do not understand how much is lost by lack of local knowledge, local interest and local control.[53]

He might also have added that even in large forces efficiency could not be guaranteed since liaison between the different divisions was not always forthcoming.[54] But the attitude of central government and senior civil servants was largely set. The Departmental Committee on Detective Work reported five years after Wedgewood's speech. It noted the value of local forces for police–public relations; it shied away from extending its terms of reference to discuss amalgamations, but it also drew attention to the Desborough Commission's recommendations for rationalisation and insisted that 'from the point of view of the detection of crime there can be no doubt that the existence of so many small forces introduces a serious element of difficulty and complication'.[55]

Increasingly from the 1920s the Home Office and various legal authorities were arguing that the constable was not, first and foremost, a servant of local government. Answering a question put by a 'Town Clerk' in 1926, *Justice of the Peace* considered that, following a legal ruling of 1877, a county police constable was 'the servant of the police authorities who were then quarter sessions'. The journal concluded, however, that the constable's position in this respect was 'not altogether free from doubt'.[56] In 1928 the matter was discussed in the same journal by O.F. Dowson, a barrister and Assistant Legal Adviser to the Home Office. Dowson explained that the police officer, because of his powers and duties under Common Law, was much closer to being a servant of the Crown than a servant of the police authority.[57] The crucial judicial ruling came two

53. *Hansard*, CCCIV, 16 July 1935, col. 960.
54. In October 1930 the Chief Constable of Manchester was furious at the 'complete lack of co-ordination on the part of Station Officers and Detective Officers in checking and tracing stolen and abandoned motor vehicles': Greater Manchester PA Manchester Police, General Orders, vol. 20, fol. 222.
55. *Departmental Committee on Detective Work*, i, p. 43.
56. *Justice of the Peace* XC (1926), 15 May, p. 303; see also 6 Mar., p. 158.
57. Ibid., XCII (1928), 13, 20, 27 Oct. and 3 Nov., pp. 663–4, 679–80, 695–6, 710–11.

years later in the celebrated case of *Fisher* v. *Oldham Corporation*. A man named Fisher, having been mistakenly identified, was arrested on a warrant in London and taken to Oldham. Here, once the error was recognised he was released, but he promptly began an action seeking damages for false imprisonment. Probably fearing that the policemen involved would not be able to pay damages, he directed his action against their employers, Oldham Corporation. In his ruling Justice McCardie quoted extensively from precedent and concluded that 'a police constable is not the servant of the borough. He is a servant of the State, a ministerial officer of the central power, though subject in some respects, to local supervision and local regulation.' The ruling has been the subject of much critical comment, particularly with reference to the confusing way in which McCardie drew on previous cases involving other 'servants' yet apparently denying them the special constitutional status of the constable; McCardie was also apparently ignorant of the powers which watch committees possessed over the police as specified in the 1856 County and Borough Police Act. In the early 1960s the Association of Municipal Corporations disputed the precise meaning of the ruling in its evidence to the Royal Commission on the Police; however, the understanding of central government politicians and subsequent refinements by the judiciary confirmed it as limiting the powers of local authorities over the police particularly with reference to operational matters.[58]

In spite of the greater powers of watch committees over chief constables, the St Helens affair, which reached its climax three years before the *Fisher* v. *Oldham* ruling, demonstrated that it was not only standing joint committees who could find it difficult to remove such an officer. A.R. Ellerington had become Chief Constable of the borough of St Helens in 1905. For over a decade he appears to have been given a free hand, but trouble began in the aftermath of the First World War when a group of Watch Committee members began to challenge his authority. During industrial disorders in 1926 police from Liverpool were brought into the borough to assist the local force; the Watch Committee objected and sought to take direction of the Liverpool men. Watch Committee meetings became chaotic and the situation was only resolved following an enquiry by Sir Leonard Dunning. The following year the conflict flared again with members of the Watch Committee

58. Laurence Lustgarten, *The Governance of Police* (London: Sweet and Maxwell, 1986), pp. 56–61; *Royal Commission on the Police. Final Report, 1962*, Cmd. 1728, pp. 27–8.

complaining of Ellerington's behaviour towards them, as well as towards local magistrates, his men, the Police Federation, and the general public. The committee sought his dismissal but Ellerington appealed to the Home Secretary and was reinstated after another enquiry. This was the only one of 103 appeals under the Police (Appeals) Act of 1927 to be granted by the Home Secretary between 1927 and 1935; it was also the only appeal by a chief constable. But even this did not end the affair. The Watch Committee produced new statements, some of which suggested misconduct on Ellerington's part, and a new enquiry, this time with the possibility of evidence being given on oath, was appointed. Although there was considerable evidence against the Chief Constable the enquiry found in his favour and drew attention to the way in which he had been baited by members of the Watch Committee. The enquiry doubted 'whether the Chief Constable of a borough should be at the mercy of a temporary majority of a Watch Committee acting perhaps on party lines, either in reference to breaches of discipline in the force, or in regard to his own tenure of office'. The Watch Committee was instructed by the Home Secretary to reinstate Ellerington and to maintain proper relations with him so that the certificate of efficiency could be awarded and, by implication, the Treasury grant paid. For the *Justice of the Peace* the affair was another demonstration of the need to abolish the smaller forces.[59]

In addition to their resentment of any attempts to reduce their authority over their local police, the municipal authorities were also out of sympathy with the proposal for a Police College which was drafted by Dixon at the Home Office and given wide publicity in 1930. The intention was to provide opportunities for serving policemen to develop their knowledge of police subjects and of other matters with a bearing on policing. Candidates were normally to be men who had served in the police for five years, who had passed the examination for promotion to sergeant, and who were still under 35 years of age. Such men were perceived as the future leaders of the police, and developing their abilities would, it was assumed, reduce the need to look elsewhere for senior officers: the continuing recruitment of former military officers and of officers from paramilitary colonial forces was unpopular with the Police Federation, and probably also the rank and file, and it fuelled the charges of creeping militarism. Dixon outlined the scheme to the

59. Jane Morgan, *Conflict and Order: The Police and Labour Disputes in England and Wales 1900–1939* (Oxford: Clarendon Press, 1987), pp. 135–6; *Justice of the Peace* XCII (1928), 26 May, p. 355.

Chief Constables' Association in June 1930 and faced a barrage of questions, some sympathetic, but others raising again the suspicion of militarisation, and the fear that the college would be the 'thin end of the wedge' towards the creation of 'one big Police Force in this Country'.[60] In the event the financial crisis ensured the collapse of the proposal but, under the forceful personality of Lord Trenchard as Commissioner of the Metropolitan Police, a college was established for that force in 1934. Trenchard was looking for 'officer material' and was prepared to accept direct entry from well-qualified young men who were immediately given the new rank of junior station inspector along with the other students who were already police officers. The Home Office had misgivings; the Police Federation was openly hostile, and so were those who had been expressing concerns about militarisation – it was bad enough that Trenchard was a military man and had surrounded himself with senior officers who were also military men, now it looked as if a military ethos was being created by the search for officer material. F.S. Cocks, the Labour MP for Broxtowe in Nottinghamshire, even managed to find a suspicious element in the modern history exam for candidates to the college: why were they required

> to pay special attention, amongst other matters, to Frederick the Great and the rise of Prussia, Bismarck and the union of Germany, and the ambitions of Louis XIV? . . . Does this mean that the Government wish to inculcate the spirit of Prussianism in the police force; if not, will the [Home Secretary] consider substituting the execution of Charles I, the downfall of the Kaiser, and the rise of English liberty?

He concluded by asking whether it was being arranged 'to allow instruction to be given in these subjects by Herr Hitler's agents in London'.[61] In the event Hitler's war brought about the demise of the college; ultimately it also brought about the opportunity for the abolition of the smaller police forces.

Together with the Home Office, the police, in the shape of chief constables, had been planning their response to a new war since the early 1930s. Determined to ensure that there was no repetition of the problems which had resulted from the disappearance of so

---

60. *Chief Constables' Association: Reports of the General Conference and Special General Conference, 1930*, pp. 20–37. For the hostility of the municipal authorities see, for example, Lincs. RO Lincoln Watch Committee Minutes, 1926–34, fols 238, 242. See also *Police Review*, 9 Jan. 1931, pp. 31–2.
61. *Hansard*, CCLXXXIII, 7 Dec. 1933, cols 1807–8.

many men into the armed forces during the First World War, it was resolved that no reservists serving in the police should be recalled to the colours until three months after the outbreak of war. When war did come, the recruitment of other police officers was carefully controlled, and a system of give and take was developed whereby while some men were recruited into the armed forces, the army also released other men to return to policing duties. In addition some 35,000 auxiliaries were ready to assist as special constables on the outbreak of war. As in the previous conflict, the police found themselves with a variety of additional duties brought about by the emergency. Many of these concerned air-raid precautions; but rationing, and the accompanying black market, needed to be policed, while military absentees and deserters, billeting, aliens, and the guarding of 'vulnerable points' all ate up police time. The additional burdens of wartime policing meant that, once again, some traditional police tasks received less attention than was usual. There were isolated instances of disaffection, notably over the refusal to accept resignations from the police in wartime,[62] and those men who continued to serve again found their purchasing power diminished by wartime inflation; but the situation, and any disaffection, never became as acute as in the earlier war.

The system of local control by watch and standing joint committees continued throughout the Second World War, but the Defence Regulations, and particularly Defence Regulation 39, gave the Home Secretary extensive if temporary powers over chief constables. He could issue direct instructions relating to the maintenance of public order, public safety, the defence of the realm and the prosecution of the war. He could also give precise orders concerning mutual aid from one force to another, even to the extent of specifying the number of men to be involved. A regional organisation was established under the direction of civil commissioners rather like that of the early 1920s. These commissioners were responsible for civil defence and possessed an elaborate command structure involving the Inspectors of Constabulary, now backed up by police staff officers, linking with the Home Office, the regional civil commissioners and regional military liaison officers. At the same time, however, the Home Office was anxious to ensure that its developing relationship with the chief constables should be maintained and consequently a memorandum was drafted in the summer of 1939, shortly before the outbreak of war, declaring:

62. *Justice of the Peace* CIV (1940), 14 Nov., p. 634, and CV (1941), 13 Sept., p. 510.

it is essential to bear in mind that the police service and Chief Officers of Police are in a fundamentally different position from the other local services associated with air raid precautions. Chief Officers of police and the constables under their control are not servants of the local authorities, but carry out their functions as constables by virtue of the offices they hold and in the exercise of Common Law and statutory rights and obligations which are special to their office as constables . . .

Chief Officers of police have in peace-time unfettered rights of access to the Home Office on any question affecting themselves or their forces. This practice would be maintained in time of war, so far as circumstances might permit, and they should be given similar right of access to Regional Commissioners . . .[63]

Such statements were at variance with much nineteenth-century practice and belief, yet were in keeping with the claims being made from the 1920s, as well as with the *Fisher* v. *Oldham* ruling.

The question of force amalgamations came up particularly in 1941 with reference to those areas which were considered most vulnerable to invasion and which contained large numbers of troops undergoing training. In July 1942 the Association of Municipal Councils and the County Councils Association were officially informed that the Home Secretary was contemplating amalgamations in such districts; and towards the end of the month, under the Emergency Powers (Defence) Act, the regulation was made authorising the Home Secretary to force amalgamations. A motion critical of the regulation was introduced in Parliament in October, but it was withdrawn following a promise, similar to one given to the two associations of councils, that any amalgamations made would be for the duration of the war only. Early in 1943 26 separate forces on the south coast of England were amalgamated into six.[64] The chief constables who headed the new amalgamations considered the exercise a great success particularly with reference to efficiency

63. Dixon, 'The emergency work of the police', p. 65. Dixon's unpublished monograph is the best analytical study of the police during the Second World War, but see also Critchley, *History of Police*, ch. 7. There is also a lively popular study, Roy Ingleton, *The Gentlemen at War: Policing Britain, 1939–1945* (Maidstone: Cranborne Publications, 1994).

64. Guildford and Reigate forces were amalgamated with the Surrey county force; Penzance was amalgamated with Cornwall; East Sussex, West Sussex, Brighton, Eastbourne, Hastings and Hove were brought together into one single force; Salisbury was amalgamated with Wiltshire; the Isle of Wight and Winchester were amalgamated with Hampshire; nine borough forces in Kent were united with the county force. At the same time the tiny borough of Tiverton voluntarily united with Devon. The idea of extending the amalgamations into Norfolk and Suffolk was eventually deemed unnecessary. See Dixon, 'The emergency work of the police', pp. 191–4.

and economy in matters of control, communications, records and staffing; they also stressed the advantages for their men in improved promotion prospects and a broadening of experience. Chuter Ede, the Home Secretary in the Labour government which came to power in 1945, was also impressed with the amalgamations. In spite of complaints from the municipal authorities and their supporters in Parliament, on 15 April 1946, almost exactly a year after Labour's election victory, a new Police Act provided for the abolition of 45 borough forces. The Act came into effect on 1 April 1947 and with four other voluntary amalgamations agreed in that year the number of police forces in England and Wales was reduced to 131.

Other amalgamations gradually whittled the number of separate forces down to 125 by 1960, and over the same period there was some tinkering with the system in the name of rationalisation to increase efficiency. In addition to the Metropolitan Police Training School at Peel House, eight district training schools were established in the aftermath of the war to provide a uniform instructional grounding for all recruits. In June 1948 a police college was opened at Ryton-on-Dunsmore in Warwickshire to train able young officers to fill the higher ranks of the different forces. But training schools and colleges need students, and the major problem for the police in the two decades following the Second World War was finding recruits. New pay scales and new rates of pay were introduced at intervals, but did little to solve the problem. In 1954 Sir Harold Scott, who had recently retired as Commissioner of the Metropolitan Police, argued that the problem had arisen because of the better wages available in other walks of life, dissatisfaction over the prospects for promotion, the lack of police housing, and the tough and restrictive nature of the job. He believed that the situation was improving, but police strength did not come up to establishment until the significant increase in pay granted during the 1970s.[65]

The shortfall in police numbers in the two decades following the Second World War corresponded with a steady increase in the statistics of crime. Yet for most of this period public perception appears to have been that crime was low, or at least within manageable limits, and it was during these years that the image of the avuncular English Bobby was to reach its apogee with the creation of the fictional character of PC George Dixon. Dixon first appeared in a feature film, *The Blue Lamp*, made with the co-operation of Scotland

65. Sir Harold Scott, *Scotland Yard* (London: Andre Deutsch, 1963), ch. 3.

Yard and premiered in 1950. He was shot dead in the film but was resurrected in 1955 for a television series, *Dixon of Dock Green*, which ran for 434 episodes over 21 years. Dixon knew everyone on his beat, and was known by everyone. He was always polite, whatever the circumstances, and always ready to offer friendly help and advice even to those on the wrong side of the law. He cared for his colleagues and his family. Above all he was honest and dependable. The film critic of *The Times* commented in 1950 that the character of Dixon was the reflection of 'an indulgent tradition' rather than any reflection of reality, and more recently a sociologist has suggested that he 'gave a good impression of a classic boy scout'.[66] Nevertheless it was the character of Dixon which began to be used as a benchmark against which the behaviour of police later in the century was to be measured.

66. *The Times*, 20 Jan. 1950, p. 8; Alan Clarke, ' "This is not the boy scouts": television police series and definitions of law and order', in Tony Bennett, Colin Mercer and Janet Woollacott (eds), *Popular Culture and Social Relations* (Milton Keynes: Open University Press, 1986), p. 225.

CHAPTER EIGHT

Local Bobby or State Lackey?

The 1960s: change all round

The 1960s heralded a marked change in the seemingly good relations between police and public and witnessed significant developments in police organisation. A key indication of the growth of affluence and the consumer society was the enormous increase in private motor vehicles; all the attendant problems of regulation and supervision meant a major extension of road traffic duties for the police. The decline in deference and the general inclination to question authority which, together with the spread of education, appeared to characterise much of the cultural development of the decade, probably contributed to growing suspicions about the unique nature of the English Bobby. So too did the glorification of youth culture, the incidence of civil disobedience and protest demonstrations, and the emerging self-consciousness of Afro-Caribbean and Asian immigrants and of their British-born children. But the most immediate and tangible changes were to be found in police organisation and structure.

In the second half of the 1950s there were a succession of scandals involving chief constables and another serious confrontation between the chief constable of a borough and his watch committee. In 1957 H.J. Phillimore, QC was asked by the Home Secretary to investigate a row between the Chief Constable of Cardiganshire and his Standing Joint Committee which had led to eleven disciplinary charges against the former. Phillimore concluded that there were bound to be problems when a slack chief constable was in command of a small force in a tightly-knit, parochial community: 'if a police is to exist as a unit . . . both incorruptible in the widest sense and known by the public to be so, it must be based on a wider framework and be less dependent on immediate local authority'. The following year the Cardiganshire force was amalgamated with that of Carmarthen. Also in 1958, while the Chief Constable of Brighton was acquitted, the second in command of his CID, together with a detective sergeant, was found guilty of corruption and sentenced to five years in prison; a few months later the Chief Constable of Worcester was found guilty of misappropriating Police Club funds and sentenced to eighteen months' imprisonment.[1] In the following year Captain Athelstan Popkess, the Chief Constable of Nottingham, approached the Director of Public Prosecutions with his suspicions of corruption in the city's government. Acting on the advice he was given, Popkess called in the Metropolitan Police to make enquiries, but the result of the investigation led the DPP to advise that no further action be taken. The Nottingham Watch Committee were informed of the investigation by the town clerk and asked Popkess for a report, but this he refused to give, stating that criminal law enforcement was his duty and no business of the Committee. The Committee responded, in turn, by suspending him; and the Home Secretary stepped in to support Popkess's interpretation of his independence. The Chief Constable was reinstated, reluctantly, but retired at the end of the year.[2] These events combined with a further well-publicised incident to suggest that the control, and the constitutional position, of the police needed some clarification. The final incident involved the civil proceedings begun by a civil servant for assault and false imprisonment against a constable of the Metropolitan Police. The case was settled out of court with a £300 payment to the plaintiff, though the police admitted no fault on their part. MPs, and others, wanted to know why the payment had been made if the PC involved had done nothing wrong; and why, if he had done something wrong, he had not been disciplined. The Home Secretary, R.A. Butler, reported that the question of disciplinary proceedings was a matter for the Commissioner, but acknowledged that important issues had been raised. It was to resolve these issues that a Royal Commission, chaired by Sir Henry Willink, QC, was appointed in January 1960.[3]

1. Alan Doig, *Corruption and Misconduct in Contemporary British Politics* (Harmondsworth: Penguin, 1984), pp. 121–3, 232–4.
2. T.A. Critchley, *A History of Police in England and Wales*, rev. edn (London: Constable, 1978), pp. 270–2; Laurence Lustgarten, *The Governance of Police* (London: Sweet and Maxwell, 1986), pp. 49–50.
3. Critchley, *History of Police*, pp. 273–4. Critchley, who served as Principal Private Secretary to R.A. Butler and then as secretary to the Royal Commission, provides a thorough résumé of the Commission's work and its reception, pp. 275–93.

The fundamental question which the Royal Commission found itself having to confront was where the ultimate control of the provincial police should reside. Most witnesses drawn from central and local government, as well as from senior police officers, considered that the existing system was working successfully. The Association of Municipal Corporations, however, continued to be unhappy about the significance which was given to the *Fisher* v. *Oldham* ruling and argued that a ruling in a case of civil liability should not be used as the basis for a doctrine of police independence. Eric St Johnston, now Chief Constable of Lancashire, raised the central issue of the precise meaning of 'local policing'. He became the spokesman for a section within the police, including some chief constables and the Police Federation, who argued for full centralisation or, at least, regional amalgamation. Such suggestions, in turn, raised once again the spectre of continental police systems and particularly those of the recently defeated fascist dictatorships. The Commission itself considered that 'the creation of a national police service . . . [was not] constitutionally objectionable or politically dangerous'; however, it believed that 'there is much value in a system of local police forces' and concluded that the best policy was to develop the existing system in accordance with the demands of the modern, fast-changing world.[4] The Commission accepted the verdict of the *Fisher* v. *Oldham* ruling as the basis for police authority and its recommendations were to deprive local police committees of the legal responsibility for the efficient policing of an area. It urged that police authorities be as small as possible and be uniformly composed, with two-thirds of their membership drawn from the appropriate local council or councils and one-third co-opted from the local magistracy. In the boroughs the watch committees' powers of appointment, discipline and dismissal were to be handed over to the chief constables, thus bringing them into line with the position in county forces. There was one dissenting voice on the Commission. A.L. Goodhart, Professor Emeritus of Jurisprudence at the University of Oxford, proposed the creation of a Royal English and Welsh Police, administered regionally. His minority report found considerable favour with sections of the press and with some MPs on both sides of the House; the government, however, resolved to move on the majority recommendations.

The Police Act of 1964 incorporated most of the recommendations

---

4. *Final Report of the Royal Commission on the Police*, Cmd. 1728 (London: HMSO, 1962), p. 141.

of the Royal Commission. It repealed and replaced the nineteenth-century legislation upon which the police system had been built, and it attempted to define, for the first time, the functions and responsibilities with regard to the police of the Home Secretary, of local police authorities, and of chief constables. The latter, in both boroughs and counties, were given uniform, full 'direction and control' of their forces including full powers regarding appointment, discipline and promotion. The local police authorities, now established uniformly along the lines proposed by the Royal Commission, were responsible for maintaining an 'adequate and efficient' police force which was properly housed and equipped. They were to receive annual reports from their chief constable, and they were responsible for his appointment and, if necessary, his dismissal, subject to approval by the Home Secretary. The Home Secretary himself could call for reports from chief constables, and as well as approving their appointment and dismissal he could also compel retirement on grounds of inefficiency. His supervisory role was strengthened with new powers to promote the ever-popular, but ill-defined, idea of police efficiency.[5] In the name of efficiency he was required to ensure uniform service arrangements and promote co-operation between forces; and he was also given the power to amalgamate forces.

The Act was the last significant measure relating to home affairs passed by the Conservative government under Sir Alec Douglas Home. The power to amalgamate police forces was used vigorously by Roy Jenkins, the Home Secretary in Harold Wilson's Labour government. In May 1966 Jenkins announced a programme which would cut the number of provincial police forces from 117 to 49, and though there were the usual squeals of protest, the amalgamations were largely achieved by the end of the decade. The Local Government Act of 1972 subsequently reduced the number of provincial forces yet again, to 41.

The amalgamations effected by Jenkins were in keeping with the image which Wilson's government projected of itself as the architect of structural change and planning. Also in keeping with this image was the way in which Jenkins fulfilled the growing aspirations of the Police Federation by bringing it into discussions about police efficiency. In March 1965 the Federation had published a document

5. In their genrally favourable assessment of the meaning of the Act, Tony Jefferson and Roger Grimshaw note that 'efficiency' is nowhere defined: Tony Jefferson and Roger Grimshaw, *Controlling the Constable: Police Accountability in England and Wales* (London: Muller, 1984), p. 19.

called *The Problem* in support of its pay claim. *The Problem*, presented simultaneously to the press and the official side of the Police Council, warned that because of the shortage in police numbers they were 'in grave danger of losing the battle against crime'. In 1966 Jenkins appointed Federation representatives to working parties on police manpower, equipment and efficiency. At the same time he successfully pressed for the police to be made a special case and exempted from the proposed pay freeze of July 1966. When the working parties reported in 1967, the Federation was ecstatic: it considered that the proposals for new management systems, new equipment and the introduction of the Unit Beat System were largely the product of the arguments presented in *The Problem*. 'Those who are talking about a "revolution" are quite right . . . the working parties have pointed the way to modernisation and to a status for the constable never achieved in the past.'[6]

Wilson and his ministers also spoke of the nation's need to embrace technology, and the police took them at their word with increasing fervour. Ben Whitaker's *The Police*, researched and written in the first part of the 1960s, revealed how much of the general factotum of the Victorian period still remained. In a small number of forces policemen were still collecting money due under maintenance orders, acting as civic mace-bearers, court ushers, market inspectors, mortuary attendants, keeping registers of domestic servants, licensing and inspecting hackney carriages, and performing various duties under legislation affecting poisons, shops, and weights and measures. Her Majesty's Inspectors of Constabulary made perfunctory inspections which were well advertised and rarely revealed even the most serious problems. Neighbouring forces used different wireless frequencies, and there was no access to computer or data-processing equipment. Many technological developments and experiments continued to be hampered by lack of finance, and where successful innovations were introduced, such as the use of radar, or pocket transistor radios, and a quarterly bulletin evaluating new police equipment, it was usually the result of the initiative of a particularly forceful chief constable.[7]

Forceful chief constables were still important, but with greater co-ordination from the Home Office new ideas and new technology were more easily disseminated. The Unit Beat System was a good example of this. It developed out of experiments in the Lancashire

6. Quoted in Robert Reiner, *The Blue-Coated Worker: A sociological study of police unionism* (Cambridge: CUP, 1978), p. 33.
7. Ben Whitaker, *The Police* (London: Eyre and Spottiswoode, 1964), ch. 2.

Constabulary to cope with a large new town built on the outskirts of Liverpool. The town of Kirby was built, initially, with no plans or thought for anything other than houses. Moreover, many of the families moved into the town were identified by the police as problem families: in the words of the then chief constable, they were 'working class people, the majority of whom had lived in slum areas the whole of their lives and who were, to say the least, very anti-social'.[8] The use of special crime patrol cars had begun in Lancashire in 1958; within four years it was being popularised in the television series 'Z' *Cars* set in a new town modelled on Kirby. However, the complete reorganisation of policing in Kirby did not begin until 1965:

> Although we had divided the town into eleven beats we were unable to find enough policemen to send to Kirby, and we had at the most only six uniformed men patrolling the town at any one time, and this in a community which had risen to 60,000 by 1963. We decided the foot patrol beat must go, and in May 1965, the eleven foot patrol beats were re-organised into five mobile beats patrolled throughout the twenty-four hours by a policeman in a car . . . More important, each man carried in his pocket a personal radio which enabled him at all times, whether in the car or out of it, to keep in touch with his station, so that wherever he was he could summon speedy help or be directed to the scene of any incident.[9]

Similar experiments were tried in London involving small teams of officers working on the beats in the localities where they lived, and who maintained communications with personal radios known as 'bat-phones'.[10] By 1968 two-thirds of the population of England and Wales were covered by the Unit Beat System which had evolved from its Lancashire beginnings to involve a foot policeman with 24-hour responsibility for his area, a patrol car covering two such areas, and a collator analysing the information collected by the patrols for the detection of offences. The system was generally welcomed as providing improved efficiency and job satisfaction for the police, and also as a means of bettering relations with the public.[11]

8. Sir Eric St Johnston, *One Policeman's Story* (London: Barry Rose, 1978), p. 168.
9. Ibid., p. 169; for the origins of 'Z' *Cars* see pp. 181–5.
10. David Ascoli, *The Queen's Peace: The Origins and Development of the Metropolitan Police 1829–1979* (London: Hamish Hamilton, 1979), pp. 291–2.
11. Critchley, *History of Police*, pp. 307–8; Robert Reiner, *The Politics of the Police* (Brighton: Wheatsheaf, 1985), pp. 63–4. For an example of the praise heaped on the system see *Hansard*, 14 Dec. 1967, cols 603–4.

In 1964 Whitaker had noted the police's lack of access to computer and data-processing equipment; yet this was changing even as he wrote. Initially provincial forces used the facilities of the local authorities, but as the potential of the computer began to be realised, police forces began to press for their own equipment. Command and control systems were developed and large databases were constructed providing quick and easy access to information on known offenders. In 1964 a study was begun to assess the feasibility of centralising police records in a national computer system, and five years later the Labour government announced plans for a national Police Computer Unit to be based in the Metropolitan Police training centre at Hendon in North London. As ever, the official emphasis was on the use of technology to improve efficiency, yet liberals and radicals increasingly began to express concerns about the kind of information that might be stored, who was to have access, and how long it was to be kept.[12]

The decade also witnessed a growing degree of disquiet over other aspects of police behaviour. Social surveys conducted during the 1950s had shown a high degree of satisfaction with the police and good police public relations.[13] The Royal Commission concluded that 'the findings of the [Government Social] Survey constitute an overwhelming vote of confidence in the police, and a striking indication of the good sense and discrimination of the bulk of the population in their assessment of the tasks that policemen have to carry out'.[14] But even as the Commission was deliberating, the police were considered by many to be behaving in a heavy-handed way against passive demonstrations by members of the Campaign for Nuclear Disarmament. Towards the end of the decade there were violent confrontations between the police and non-passive demonstrators against the war in Vietnam and the apartheid regime in South Africa; and if, as some demonstrators complained, there were instances of rough treatment by the police, these confrontations

---

12. Tony Bunyan, *The History and Practice of Political Police in Britain* (London: Julian Friedmann, 1976), pp. 80–7; Sarah Manwaring-White, *The Policing Revolution: Police Technology, Democracy and Liberty in Britain* (Brighton: Harvester, 1983), ch. 3.

13. Geoffrey Gorer, *Exploring the English Character* (London: Cresset Press, 1955), ch. 13; Gabriel A. Almond and Sidney Verba, *The Civic Culture: Political Attitudes and Democracy in Five Nations* (Princeton, NJ: Princeton University Press, 1963), pp. 106–13.

14. *Final Report of the Royal Commission* (1962), pp. 102–3. It has been argued that the Royal Commission put rather too sanguine an interpretation on the findings of this survey: see John Benyon, 'Policing in the Limelight', in John Benyon and Colin Bourn (eds), *The Police: Powers, Procedures and Proprieties* (Oxford: Pergamon, 1986), p. 7.

also revealed that, in spite of their passionate embrace of new management and technology, the public order training and equipment then available to the police was woefully inadequate. The arrest of a member of the National Council for Civil Liberties during a demonstration against Queen Frederika of Greece in the summer of 1963 began the process which exposed Detective Sergeant Harold Challenor for having framed a succession of innocent men, carried out illegal arrests, and assaulted men in custody. Yet with the exception of a new recruit to the Metropolitan Police, at the ensuing public enquiry no police witness was prepared to admit that Challenor had done anthing wrong.[15] In November 1969 *The Times* published an article suggesting widespread corruption within the Metropolitan Police CID. The paper printed the story within hours of submitting the details of its investigations to Scotland Yard, and it urged 'that the most stringent enquiry . . . be made'. An inquiry was made within the Metropolitan Police, though its results were hardly satisfactory and the investigating officer was himself later to be charged, along with others, with corruption, and sentenced to twelve years in gaol.[16]

One of Challenor's victims was Harold Padmore, an ex-cricketer and, at the time he was assaulted and charged, a shunter working for London Transport. Padmore, born in Barbados, was black.[17] Unfortunately, other policemen appear to have made the equation between immigrant and criminal, and to have let traditional prejudices cloud their perceptions with the arrival of Afro-Carribeans in the 1950s, and the subsequent arrival of Asian immigrants. The problem was scarcely perceived when Whitaker published his critical appraisal of the English police in 1964. He noted a policeman recounting with pride 'how he and some colleagues once extorted a confession from two West Indians by staging a mock trial at the police station, sentencing them to death, and leading them to an adjoining room where they were told they would be hanged immediately'; but Whitaker quoted this in a broad discussion of the problem of police violence. He recognised that there was a problem in that while 1 per cent of the population was black, there was not a single black policeman; and he concluded that the excuses of the white population not being ready for black policemen and of black applicants being below the normal standard for white recruits were really masks for the 'internal difficulties' that would arise if

15. Mary Grigg, *The Challenor Case* (Harmondsworth: Penguin, 1965).
16. *The Times*, 29 Nov. 1969, pp. 1, 6–7. See also Barry Cox, John Shirley and Martin Short, *The Fall of Scotland Yard* (Harmondsworth: Penguin, 1977).
17. Grigg, *The Challenor Case*, pp. 63–6.

any black constable was sworn in.[18] It was largely left to a novelist, Colin MacInnes, to describe racial prejudice within the police in *City of Spades* and *Mr Love and Mr Justice*, more than a decade before the resulting tensions exploded into riot.[19]

A crisis of confidence

While elements of 'kitchen-sink' realism and toughness were introduced into the media image of the police with the television series 'Z' Cars – elements which upset several members of the Lancashire Constabulary who had assisted with the series[20] – disquiet about aspects of police behaviour in the 1960s remained muted. Over the following two decades, however, concern became louder and more extensive as revelations of corruption, violence and racism continued. Also, the police appeared to become more and more associated with a strident law and order lobby and the abrasive policies of Margaret Thatcher's government. The fact that the police did better in terms of pay and resources than other groups within the public sector under Thatcher's government tended to aggravate such concerns.

The Times's suggestion that its revelations of November 1969 were only the tip of a rather nasty iceberg was to be confirmed by subsequent scandals involving first the Drugs Squad and then the Obscene Publications Squad.[21] A new Commissioner, Robert Mark, was appointed to the Metropolitan Police in 1972, and he set out to cleanse the detective department of the force. Mark developed better, more open relations with the press. He established an elite department whose task was to investigate complaints against police officers. He moved detectives from one posting to another and back into uniform; and during his five years as Commissioner nearly 500 men were dismissed or required to resign.[22] But the problem was not solved. In the year that he followed Mark as Commissioner, David McNee was confronted by allegations about members of his Robbery Squad and this led to a four-year investigation of more

18. Whitaker, *The Police*, pp. 147, 100–2.
19. *City of Spades* was published in 1957, *Mr Love and Mr Justice* in 1960. A third novel, *Absolute Beginners*, published in 1959, dealt with the race riots in Notting Hill and Nottingham in the summer of 1958; these were directed against Blacks, unlike the disorders of the 1980s which were, in many respects, directed against the police.
20. Taped interview with ex-Chief Superintendent Tom Andrews, Sept. 1987.
21. Cox, Shirley and Short, *The Fall of Scotland Yard*.
22. Ascoli, *The Queen's Peace*, p. 321, n. 2.

than 200 officers in Operation Countryman. The investigation resulted in only two convictions, but closed with a series of recriminations between McNee and the Chief Constable of Dorset who had led the enquiry, the former alleging that the enquiry had let itself be swamped by dubious information, the latter protesting that the operation had been sabotaged by members of the Metropolitan Police.[23] Accusations of police corruption, of framing suspects and extorting confessions, continued, and were not confined to London. An IRA bombing campaign in the mid-1970s put the police under tremendous pressure to get results; but the results which they got in the cases of the individuals convicted of bombing public houses in Guildford and Birmingham created much disquiet and long campaigns which ended in the convictions being quashed. In August 1989 the entire Serious Crime Squad of the West Midlands Police, some of whom had been involved in the affair of the Birmingham bombers, was disbanded amid allegations of framing and corruption. Early in the following year *The Independent* identified at least 40 cases in England and Wales where police forces were being investigated by officers from other forces: 'In individual complaints, most forces will not disclose detailed information unless it is made public. This makes it difficult to assess the seriousness of many investigations ... A relatively formal inquiry into a death in custody cannot be distinguished from a corruption inquiry.'[24] The fact that the investigators were other policemen only added to the disquiet.

In addition to the allegations of corruption and framing, a series of notorious cases in which individuals died as a result of police action or while being held in police custody gave rise to suspicions about the police use of physical force. The decision by the Director of Public Prosecutions not to start proceedings against any police officer in connection with some 30 such deaths during the 1970s and early 1980s served only to fuel the suspicions.[25] In the mid-eighties there were serious allegations of harassment and assault on students made against the Greater Manchester Police following police behaviour at a demonstration outside the Manchester University Students Union. The inquiry by the Avon and Somerset Force left many unsatisfied, including the Manchester University Senate, which called for a judicial inquiry; but no further action was taken.[26]

23. Reiner, *The Politics of the Police*, p. 67.
24. *The Independent*, 30 Apr. 1990, p. 2.
25. Steven Box, *Power, Crime and Mystification* (London: Tavistock, 1983), pp. 82–91.
26. Martin Walker, *With Extreme Prejudice: An Investigation into Police Vigilantism in Manchester* (London: Canary, 1986).

The most persistent complaints of police violence and harassment came from the Black communities. In 1979 McNee proposed that a wide-ranging study be carried out on the relations between the Metropolitan Police and the community: the resulting report by the Policy Studies Institute made uncomfortable reading on the subject of race relations. The researchers found 'that racialist language and racial prejudice were prominent and pervasive and that many individual officers and also whole groups were preoccupied with ethnic differences'. While this did not necessarily prevent friendly and relaxed relations between the police and Blacks, they concluded that 'police hostility towards people of West Indian origin is connected with the belief that they are rootless, alienated, poor, unable to cope and deviant in various ways'.[27] Suspicion of, and hostility towards, the police on the part of young Blacks exploded into violence in the inner-city riots of 1981 and 1985. The savage killing of PC Keith Blakelock in the latter disturbances on the Broadwater Farm Estate in North London resulted in the conviction of three young men for murder. But in this instance too questions were raised about the manner in which the police conducted investigations, and prepared the case which secured the convictions. At the end of the decade a poll commissioned by the BBC suggested that two-thirds of the population believed that the police bent the rules to gain convictions, and newspapers at opposite ends of the political spectrum were concluding that public esteem for the police was at an all-time low.[28]

Alongside concerns about police abuse of their authority, the 1970s and 1980s witnessed an inexorable increase in the statistics of crime. The Police Federation, continuing the policy which it had launched with *The Problem*, and several chief constables persisted in making public statements about law and order. While they continued also to insist on the non-partisanship of the police in politics, these statements grew similar in content and tone to those made by the Conservative Party. The similarities reached a peak first in the run-up to the general election of 1979, and then early in 1982, the latter instance being seen by some as an attempt to head off reforms in police policy and organisation, and as a police counterattack against Lord Scarman's report on the riots of 1981 with its criticisms of police behaviour.[29] The alliance between the police

27. David J. Smith and Jeremy Gray, *Police and People in London* (London: Gower, 1985), pp. 388, 390.
28. *The Guardian*, 18 Nov. 1989, p. 22; *The Sunday Times*, 19 Nov. 1989, p. B3.
29. Reiner, *The Politics of the Police*, pp. 73–6.

and the Conservative Party appeared to many to be further cemented by the way in which the Thatcher government treated the police in contrast to other public sector employees. Whereas the latter found their pay, their numbers and their resources squeezed, the police enjoyed the opposite experience. Of course there could still be tensions over pay, and William Whitelaw, the Home Secretary, was given a hard time by the Metropolitan Branch of the Police Federation in November 1982;[30] but between 1979 and 1989 police pay increased in real terms by 41 per cent, significantly above average earnings. There were also warnings that the police were not to be exempt from the stringencies being imposed elsewhere and were expected to demonstrate value for money. This was underlined in Home Office Circular 114/1983, 'Manpower, Effectiveness and Efficiency in the Police Service', which noted that substantial resources were given to the police and that there was a need to show that they were being used effectively. The Circular outlined key principles for the future assessment of efficiency. It proposed first, that police officers be released for active duty by the recruitment of civilians to all posts that they could fill economically and properly; and second, that the police service adopt systems of rational management developed in the commercial sector.[31] Yet for most of the period of the Thatcher government the changes which these proposals heralded were masked by the Tory generosity towards the police and the high profile acquired by public order policing. To many, and to the regret of many police officers, they appeared to have become 'Maggie Thatcher's private army'.[32]

The 1970s and 1980s witnessed the widespread use of police in industrial disputes and a more aggressive police response to disorder. In the latter decade this looked like a further manifestation of a bond between the police and the Thatcher government, and reawoke the fears of militarisation. The demonstrations against the Vietnam War outside the United States' Embassy in Grosvenor Square in 1968 had shown the police to be unprepared for coping with enormous numbers of determined demonstrators of whom some might not shrink from violence. The Metropolitan Police were ultimately successful in containing the trouble in Grosvenor

30. *The Guardian*, 20 Nov. 1982.

31. Les Johnston, *The Rebirth of Private Policing* (London: Routledge, 1992), pp. 52–6.

32. The words are those of a senior Metropolitan Police officer quoted in Terence Morris, *Crime and Criminal Justice since 1945* (Oxford: Blackwell, 1989), p. 160; see also Roger Graef (ed.), *Talking Blues: The Police in their Own Words* (London: Collins Harvill, 1989), p. 74.

Square, but six years later, during the miners' strike of 1972, provincial police in Birmingham were forced to give way to the demands of a crowd. For a week in February 1972 miners' pickets and their supporters sought to close Saltley Coke Depot and the police sought to keep it open; on 10 February, with 800 police confronted by a crowd of about 15,000, the police agreed to close the gates in the interests of public safety.[33] As a direct result of the Saltley incident the National Reporting Centre was established in New Scotland Yard. The Centre was only to be opened and staffed in an emergency, but it was then to be responsible for co-ordinating mutual aid between the different police forces. For the police and the Home Office the new Centre seemed the obvious answer to mass, mobile pickets in national industrial disputes; their logic was the same as that of Winston Churchill in the disputes before the First World War, but their means were far more extensive and sophisticated.

There was similar mass picketing in the dock strike of 1972, in the dispute at the Grunwick Processing Laboratory in 1977, and in the steel strike of 1980. These incidents, together with the inner-city riots of the summer of 1981, prompted a string of new developments designed to deal more professionally, and hence more effectively, with public disorder. The concept of the Police Support Unit (PSU) had been introduced as a result of perceived civil defence needs in the early 1970s: the original PSUs were to deal with wartime contingencies, but they were rapidly adapted into the basic organisational unit for dealing with disorder. A PSU was commanded by an inspector and consisted of two 'serials' each made up of a sergeant and ten constables. Long shields were introduced in 1976; and short, generally round ones became available for PSUs required for rapid movement in the following decade. The traditional helmet was redesigned in 1976 with a strengthened interior and chinstraps to be worn in an emergency; a protective crash helmet with visor, together with flame-retardant overalls, first appeared in 1981. By the summer of 1983 new public order tactics had been devised and outlined in the *Tactical Options Manual.* This had been read and approved by the Home Secretary, but was restricted to the 270 officers of the ACPO (Association of Chief Police Officers) rank. The secrecy which surrounded the *Manual* fostered conspiracy theories and the idea that a new kind of paramilitary policing,

33. Roger Geary, *Policing Industrial Disputes 1893 to 1985* (Cambridge: CUP, 1985), p. 76.

hitherto confined to British colonies, was being developed furtively for Britain herself.[34]

During the year-long miners' strike of 1984–85 pickets found themselves confronted by police organised very differently from the previous decade. Police mutual aid was co-ordinated across the whole country by the National Reporting Centre. Pickets seeking to travel from the Kent coalfield to areas of confrontation in the Midlands and the north were stopped at police road blocks at the Dartford Tunnel under the Thames and ordered home. In the early summer of 1984 the miners sought to repeat the Saltley incident by closing Orgreave Coke Depot in South Yorkshire. They found themselves confronted by policemen drawn from a dozen or so different forces, but uniformly kitted out in riot overalls with helmets and visors, shields and long batons. Police tactics were also new. Lines of men carrying long shields took the brunt of any missiles hurled at the police; the lines then parted to release either squads of men carrying small, round shields and batons, or mounted police – the former, according to the new *Manual*, were to 'disperse and/or incapacitate' demonstrators, the latter 'to create fear'. The principal battle of Orgreave was fought on 18 June, and to the extent that it ensured that Orgreave remained open throughout the dispute, it was a victory for the police. However, the case against every miner arrested and charged with riot during the incident collapsed, and the court cases brought the existence of the new *Manual* to the attention of the public, and of Parliament, for the first time.[35]

Police organisation and behaviour during the 1984–85 miners' strike fuelled the concerns being expressed by liberals and radicals. The Association of Chief Police Officers, formed in 1948 by a fusion of the separate associations of borough and county chief constables,

34. Gerry Northam, *Shooting in the Dark: Riot Police in Britain* (London: Faber & Faber, 1988), pp. 38–43, stresses the significance of a presentation to the ACPO annual conference in September 1981 of the tactics developed by the Royal Hong Kong Police to deal with the disturbances provoked in the colony by the Cultural Revolution in China. P.A.J. Waddington, *The Strong Arm of the Law: Armed Police and Public Order Policing* (Oxford: Clarendon Press, 1991), pp. 213–15, disputes the significance of the Hong Kong presentation and points out that British police officers were in regular and constant contact with many police institutions throughout the world. In a personal communication (13 Aug. 1994) he noted that work on the *Manual* commenced in the aftermath of the Bristol, St Paul's riot of April 1980 and was virtually complete by the summer of 1981; furthermore, in 1985 the Metropolitan Police sent a delegation to study riot-control methods in Hong Kong, Japan and Singapore, and rejected almost all the methods peculiar to these countries as inappropriate in a British setting.

35. Northam, *Shooting in the Dark*, pp. 52–61.

became one object of criticism. It was pointed out that the body had no formal constitutional status and was answerable to no-one, yet its members met together to agree policies and had regular meetings with officials and ministers from the Home Office. Equally serious, it was the current president of the ACPO who directed the National Reporting Centre when it was called into being. At best, critics of the Centre saw it as a surreptitious step on the road to a national police force; at worst it was a major step towards an authoritarian state. What particularly worried those police authorities with a left-wing majority which supported the miners was their inability to get either details about the numbers deployed from their forces during the strike or the eventual financial cost. Margaret Simey, chairperson of the Merseyside Police Authority, protested that when her committee passed a resolution requesting that the Chief Constable cease sending his men to the strike picket lines, 'he laughed out loud at us and said he wasn't going to take any notice'. The committee's request was naive, especially given the powers which successive Home Secretaries had been amassing in respect of police mutual aid, but the Chief Constable also refused to give a daily breakdown of the deployment of his men and the numbers receiving overtime:

> We know ACPO told all chief constables in writing that they had the Home Secretary's assurance that resources for policing the miners' dispute were not a problem. In other words they were given a blank cheque. But he [the Home Secretary] never told us that. He just walks about saying it's nothing to do with him. It seems ACPO can communicate with the Home Secretary about spending money but not with us. ACPO, in fact, has become an executive limb of the state, without any authorisation and without being under any control. It's incredible.[36]

This ignoring of the police authority when and if chief constables and the Home Office wished is probably better seen, not as something startlingly new, but as a culmination of a situation developing from the nineteenth century, and which had already been manifested in some districts during the inter-war period.

Again as in the inter-war years, there were chief constables who had the unfortunate habit of aggravating situations by speaking out against agitators and extremists who they saw as being behind every incident of disorder and every criticism of the police. In a letter to

36. Quoted in Phil Scraton, *The State of the Police* (London: Pluto Press, 1985), pp. 157–8.

The Guardian in November 1979 Michael Dummett, the Wykeham Professor of Logic at Oxford, rebuked McNee for such comments:

> The word 'extremist' should be dropped from the police vocabulary. When the word is used in speaking about race, it is unclear whether opinions about politicians or about race itself are meant (the two need not go together); and, if the latter, it is unclear what would be counted as 'extremist' (the views of the Commission for Racial Equality perhaps?).
>
> In any case, mere *opinions* are in general of no concern to the police. The intended suggestion is that 'extremists' indulge in violence; but holding opinions which stand at the end of the political spectrum in no way implies approval of violence.[37]

But there were senior officers who ignored the rebuke and continued to show publicly that they considered opinions to be their affair. Little more than a year after Dummett's letter a former chief constable of South Yorkshire was explaining on television that it was 'common sense' to have files on anyone with an affinity to communism, as well as anyone who was 'decrying family life . . . pushing drugs or advocating the acceptance of certain drugs, homosexuality, indiscipline in schools, weak penalties for anti-social crimes . . . things . . . pecking away at the foundations of society'. And James Anderton, the Chief Constable of Greater Manchester, who put forward his fervent Christian faith with all the righteous certainty of a biblical prophet, could also be relied upon for a quotation about the moral descent of society and 'extreme left wing groups, and factions in the ethnic minorities. People who are permanently hostile to the police.'[38] Comments like these only served to strengthen the beliefs of those who thought the police partisan and out of democratic control. Left-wing councils began to establish police monitoring units, while some radical groups urged that the police no longer be given access to schools with the opportunity to talk formally to the children in the classroom. In London some Labour councillors urged that their borough's financial contribution to the Metropolitan Police be withheld, while the majority Labour group elected to the Greater London Council at the beginning of the 1980s pledged to seek to establish a police authority

37. *The Guardian*, 13 Nov. 1979. At the time Professor Dummett was chairing an inquiry, sponsored by the NCCL, into the events during a demonstration against a meeting by the National Front at Southall in West London during which Blair Peach, a teacher, had been killed, apparently the victim of a weapon wielded by a policeman.
38. Quotations in Walker, *With Extreme Prejudice*, pp. 189–90 and 12 respectively.

'consisting solely of elected members of the GLC and London boroughs to have control over the Metropolitan and City police'.[39]

Reinventing the Bobby

However, alongside the criticism of the police and the fears expressed about the decline in public esteem there was also evidence of much sympathy and continuing support. The police continued Mark's policy of openness with the media and this appears to have paid dividends. There were documentaries showing police training and day-to-day life on the beat. There was a succession of books by journalists who were given the run of police stations and who went on patrol with ordinary policemen.[40] A variety of special articles and series in newspapers also focused on the problems of contemporary policing, generally highlighting the increase in crime and disorder, but also the problems raised by international and IRA terrorism. 'Thank God for the Thin Blue Line' declared *The Sunday Mirror*, a tabloid with Labour Party affiliations, in one such six-page 'Special Report' published in March 1987:

> The Job, as the police call it, is getting tougher . . . Many of them are bewildered by the conflicting demands that our changing society makes on them. In spite of that they show patience, tact and courage in conditions of extreme provocation. The overwhelming majority of Britain's policemen and policewomen are devoted to their duty, in spite of its difficulties. We acknowledge that dedication, and are proud of them.[41]

Furthermore, while some expressed their doubts about tough policemen who bent and broke the rules, and while some such appeared before the courts, the hero of one of the most popular television police series of the 1970s, repeated during the 1980s, was cast in such a mould. But Detective Inspector Jack Regan in *The Sweeney* was always shown to be ultimately in the right; he only kicked against bureaucracy and pettifogging functionaries who impeded the apprehension and punishment of 'real criminals'.

---

39. *The Guardian*, 19 Apr. 1980; Box, *Power, Crime and Mystification*, p. 110.

40. Among the best of these books are Andrew Brown, *Watching the Detectives* (London: Hodder & Stoughton, 1988), and Robert Chesshyre, *The Force: Inside the Police* (London: Sidgwick & Jackson, 1989). Roger Graef, who made two of the most significant television police documentaries during the 1980s, *Police* and *Operation Carter*, edited an interesting collection of police interviews on different aspects of the job: *Talking Blues: The Police in their Own Words* (see n. 32 above).

41. *The Sunday Mirror*, 15 Mar. 1987. *The Times* carried a series on 'The Thin Blue Line', 10–13 Nov. 1986.

While some senior policemen inflamed the fears of an authoritarian state by their public statements, there were other police officers who showed genuine concern about racism in their ranks, about the sexist treatment of women police officers, the fabrication of evidence against 'known' offenders, the militarisation engendered by the new public order tactics, and about the way that police deployment in industrial disputes implied political partisanship.[42] In the hope that it would restore community links and act as a better preventive of crime and disorder, there was much talk of community policing and of taking policemen out of the cars into which they had so willingly climbed during the 1960s, and putting them back on foot and bicycle beats. Some of this was done, and community liaison was developed with Black communities; indeed, it is arguable that a contributory factor in the rioting at Broadwater Farm was the temporary absence of the leaders of the Youth Association with whom the local police superintendent regularly liaised.[43] There were recruitment drives among the Black communities, highlighted by the BBC televison series *Black in Blue* transmitted in the summer of 1990. The series also showed serious attempts being made in training recruits to warn them of the dangers of racism and sexism. Yet later in the year an industrial tribunal decided that a police officer of Asian origin had been racially discriminated against when he tried to become a detective in the Nottinghamshire Police. The written decision of the tribunal, running to some 500 pages, concluded that there was no overt racism in the force, but it was highly critical of some officers and contained many allegations of racial 'banter' directed at Black officers; and similar problems were exposed periodically in other forces.[44]

The Conservative government's attempts to reduce public sector spending, and to bring commercial management techniques and value for money assessments into the police, ultimately ruptured the close links which appeared to be developing between the party and the police during the 1980s. Early in 1990 the Thatcher government proposed changes to the liberal housing allowance then granted to police officers. The Home Secretary was received by the Police Federation Annual Conference in an icy silence.[45] Two years

42. See comments throughout Brown, *Watching the Detectives*, Chesshyre, *The Force*, and Graef (ed.), *Talking Blues*.

43. Jennifer Davis, 'From "Rookeries" to "Communities": race, poverty and policing in London 1850–1985', *History Workshop Journal* 27 (1989), 66–85, at 77.

44. *The Guardian*, 31 Oct. 1990, pp. 22–3. For similar allegations against the Metropolitan Police in 1995 see, *inter alia, Police Review*, 24 Nov. 1995, pp. 4–5.

45. *The Sunday Times*, 27 May 1990, p. A7.

later a leading businessman, Sir Patrick Sheehy, was appointed chairman of a committee to examine the rank structure, remuneration, and conditions of service of the police. In the summer of 1993 the Sheehy Inquiry issued its report with 272 recommendations including proposals for fixed-term appointments (initially ten years, renewable thereafter for five-year periods), for pensions payable after 40 years' service or at the age of 60, for the freezing and subsequent abolition of the housing allowance, for a new pay structure including points for ability, performance and the toughness of the job. The Police Federation was incensed, called a mass demonstration at Wembley which was attended by an estimated 23,000, and rejected the recommendations outright.[46] A new Home Secretary, Michael Howard, set aside the more contentious recommendations, but the suspicion remained that he intended to impliment Sheehy 'in disguise'.[47] Furthermore, the system of appraisal-related pay, which the government was keen to introduce and which was piloted in thirteen forces during 1994–95, began to be regarded with similar suspicion. It was, declared the Chief Constable of Humberside, 'an expensive and time-consuming exercise in political dogma':

> Officers should not be motivated by financial rewards. . . . The Government has failed to grasp the fundamental ethos underpinning British policing. We are not a production line to be paid by results, we are a public service.[48]

The idea of service began to be stressed more and more as senior officers latched onto the rhetoric of consumerism which began to sweep the public sector as part and parcel of the Thatcher reforms. The public began to be perceived, and occasionally even referred to, as 'customers'; no matter that, as one of the most perceptive analysts of policing warned, 'policing is not about the delivery of an uncontentious service like any other'.[49] Yet, whatever the validity of such concepts, their impact was positive. Senior officers recognised that, during the 1980s especially, the priorities of the police and public appeared to have diverged – the police had stressed enforcement, while the public seemed to prefer more of a community orientation. At the beginning of 1990 the Metropolitan Police launched its Plus Programme, a conscious attempt to change

46. *Police Review*, 23 July 1993, pp. 4–5, 12–17. On 2 July, just 'after the report was published, the *Police Review* published a special pull-out section detailing the recommendations.
47. Ibid., 5 Nov. 1993, pp. 14–16, 'Howard's sleight of hand'.
48. Ibid., 3 Dec. 1995, p. 6.
49. Reiner, *The Politics of the Police*, p. 269.

police culture and to remould it in the image portrayed by the Whig historians and by Dixon of Dock Green. As part of the programme a statement of common purpose and values was posted on noticeboards in New Scotland Yard and in police stations throughout London:

> The purpose of the Metropolitan Police Service is to uphold the law fairly and firmly; to prevent crime, to pursue and bring to justice those who break the law; to keep the Queen's peace, to protect, help and reassure people in London: and to be seen to do this with integrity, common sense and judgement.
>
> We must be compassionate, courteous and patient, acting without fear or favour or prejudice to the rights of others. We need to be professional, calm and restrained in the face of violence and apply only that force which is necessary to accomplish our lawful duty.
>
> We must strive to reduce the fears of the public, and so far as we can, to reflect their priorities in the action we take. We must respond to well-founded criticism with a willingness to change.[50]

The programme was a precursor of the Statement of Common Purpose and Values which emerged from a meeting of the Joint Consultative Committee of the three police staff associations (the Federation, the Superintendents' Association and the ACPO) at the end of the same year. Many of the aspirations of such programmes could have been voiced when police forces were first created in the nineteenth century, and of course a restatement of fundamental aims is a useful exercise for any institution. Yet there is little doubt that it was the anxieties, events and revelations of the recent past, together with the new consumer rhetoric, which had prompted a deal of heart-searching, and became the driving force behind these statements.

50. Quoted in *The Guardian*, 21 Feb. 1990, p. 21.

CHAPTER NINE

A Life in the Force

The recruits

Sir Robert Peel had very clear ideas about the men that he wanted for his new police in 1829. Applications from military officers on half pay and from gentlemen in reduced circumstances were rejected. The recruits were to be respectable young men from the working class. They were to be at least 5 feet 9 inches tall and aged under 35 years, fit, literate, and blessed with a perfect command of temper. Such men were to fill all of the ranks up to commissioner; ability and merit were to be the sole criteria for promotion. The legislation establishing the county constabularies made similar requirements, though initially permitting the recruitment of men up to the age of 40. The height requirement in the Metropolitan Police was raised by two inches towards the end of the nineteenth century, but the recruitment regulations drafted in the beginning largely governed police recruitment for the next century and a half; the first commissioner of the Metropolitan Police to rise from the rank of police constable was Sir Joseph Simpson, who was appointed to this rank in 1958.

The traditional view is that recruits to the English police forces in the nineteenth century were agricultural labourers. Superintendent F.W. Mallalieu told a select committee of Parliament in 1852 that the best recruits to the Metropolitan Police were to be found among 'the intelligent part of the agricultural labouring community'.[1] Similar comments can be found well into the twentieth century and, following the popular image of rural society, there was a perception among many senior officers that the agricultural labourer

---

1. *PP* 1852–53 (715) XXXVI, *Second Report of the Select Committee on Police*, q. 2,872.

was the ideal recruit since he was fitter than the man born and bred in the city and thus better able to endure the rigours of the job, he appeared more readily to accept the social hierarchy, and to be more malleable in the hands of the police institution.[2] Such beliefs led to specific campaigns to recruit rural workers in the period immediately before the First World War. These beliefs and campaigns, together with the large number of recruits who gave their trade or calling as 'labourer', encouraged some historians to conclude that all such 'labourers' came from the land. However, as will be shown below, while there were significant numbers of agricultural labourers who joined the Victorian and Edwardian police, the pool of recruits was much wider and deeper. Another common, though largely unspoken assumption, has been that all police forces recruited the same kinds of men. Yet, as Carolyn Steedman's work on the Buckinghamshire and Staffordshire forces has shown, while the local economic background was central to recruitment, the different backgrounds could produce different results.[3]

The following discussion is based on details given in the personnel registers of three borough forces (Birkenhead, Hull and Ipswich), two county forces (East Suffolk and Worcester), and in the warrant books of eight divisions of the Metropolitan Police. These cover, very broadly, the period from 1840 to 1940, though the fullest detail here is for the period 1880 to 1920.[4]

In all of these registers labourers form the largest single group. But 'labourer' was the general term used by the unskilled in Victorian society and not simply by those who worked on the land. As the nineteenth century wore on even labourers appear to have become more specific in their job descriptions to the recruiters. In Ipswich, among the 35 men recruited between 1880 and 1889 there were

2. Haia Shpayer-Makov, 'The appeal of country workers: the case of the Metropolitan Police', *Historical Research* 64 (1991), 186–203.
3. Carolyn Steedman, *Policing the Victorian Community: The Formation of English Provincial Police Forces, 1856–1880* (London: Routledge and Kegan Paul, 1984), chs 2 and 3. For other discussions of police recruitment see: Wilbur R. Miller, *Cops and Bobbies: Police Authority in New York and London, 1830–1870* (University of Chicago Press, 1977), pp. 25–8; W.J. Lowe, 'The Lancashire Constabulary, 1845–1870: the social and occupational function of a Victorian police force', *CJH* IV (1983), 41–62; Haia Shpayer-Makov, 'The making of a police labour force', *Journal of Social History* 24 (1990), 109–34; idem, 'A portrait of a novice constable in the London Metropolitan Police around 1900', *CJH* XI (1991), 133–60.
4. All of these records remain in the hands of the police except for the registers for Ipswich and East Suffolk, which have been deposited with the Suffolk RO and are catalogued as DF 2/1, RO 1465/3 and RO 1465/4. For a more detailed discussion of this information see Clive Emsley and Mark Clapson, 'Recruiting the English policeman c. 1840–1940', *Policing and Society* 3 (1994), 269–86.

thirteen 'labourers' but also a 'labourer and fisherman' and a 'labourer and farmer's son'; in East Suffolk in the following decade a 'farm labourer' was identified separatly from 46 'labourers'; in Hull the registers began to list specific 'farm labourers' from 1907, and then 'bricklayer's labourer' and 'builder's labourer' were also identified. Besides the farm labourers the registers also show a large number of men whose previous trade or calling was linked with agriculture. Large numbers of recruits were drawn from the old handicraft and artisan trades such as butchers, bakers, carpenters, shoemakers and tailors, and from the building trades. But, as might be expected given the shifting patterns of employment over the nineteenth century, the old trades gradually decline from the personnel registers, to be replaced, in the early twentieth century, by a plethora of new jobs ranging from 'chocolate worker' to 'tube screwer', and from 'cinema operator' to 'thermometer maker'. The large number of men drawn from the coal and metalwork trades recruited into the Worcestershire force appear to have drifted down from the Birmingham area – a significant illustration of the influence of the local economic background. In the Metropolitan Police and the East Suffolk force, there was a noticeable increase in the number of recruits from non-manual backgrounds who were often categorised simply as 'clerks'. The police appears also to have been seen as a logical organisation to join from other sections of the uniformed working class such as the railways or the post office.

The army in Victorian and Edwardian England, like the police, valued agricultural workers as recruits, and for much the same reasons. Yet there were always concerns about publicly drawing parallels between soldiers and policemen, and several senior police officers expressed concerns about recruiting former soldiers as police. Mallalieu admitted that many soldiers had been recruited at the beginning, but he declared them to be far fewer in numbers by mid-century and stressed that they made poor policemen. Captain W.C. Harris, the Chief Constable of Hampshire, informed the 1852 select committee that the problem with soldiers was that after three or four years of military service they were 'invariably addicted to drinking'.[5] However, in spite of these concerns, there appears to have been an increasing percentage of men with military experience recruited into the police as the nineteenth century wore on. The short service enlistment introduced by Edward Cardwell in 1870 may have had some impact here. Men were now leaving the

---

5. PP 1852–53 (715) *Second Report of the Select Committee on Police*, qq. 225–6.

TABLE 9.1 *Principal trades of recruits, c. 1840–1900*[a]

Force	Total recruit sample	'Labourers'	Agricultural work	Traditional trades	Building and decorating	Merchant sea service	Clerks	Coal/metal trades	Railway workers
Metropolitan	5 056	1 843 (36.4)	574 (11.3)	742 (14.7)	179 (3.5)	112 (2.2)	121 (2.4)	61 (1.2)	73 (1.4)
Birkenhead	430	166 (38.6)	54 (12.5)	23 (5.3)	10 (2.3)	18 (4.2)	16 (3.7)	11 (2.5)	9 (2.0)
Hull	665	396 (59.5)	26 (3.9)	63 (9.5)	18 (2.7)	21 (3.1)	18 (2.7)	4 (0.6)	26 (3.9)
Ipswich	355	134 (37.7)	23 (6.5)	45 (12.7)	16 (4.5)	11 (3.1)	1 (0.3)	—	—
East Suffolk	208	93 (47.7)	38 (18.2)	13 (6.2)	4 (1.9)	8 (3.8)	2 (0.9)	—	5 (2.4)
Worcestershire	449	159 (35.4)	79 (17.6)	61 (13.6)	21 (4.7)	3 (0.7)	9 (2.0)	35 (7.8)	8 (1.8)

[a] The figures in brackets show the trade group as a percentage of the total.

TABLE 9.2 *Principal trades of recruits, 1901– c. 1930*[a]

Force	Total recruit sample	'Labourers'	Agricultural work	Traditional trades	Building and decorating	Merchant sea service	Clerks	Coal/metal trades	Railway workers
Metropolitan	2 700	294 (10.8)	311 (11.5)	249 (9.2)	97 (3.6)	78 (2.9)	212 (7.8)	80 (2.9)	87 (3.2)
Hull	587	221 (37.6)	88 (14.9)	28 (4.8)	18 (3.0)	15 (2.5)	13 (2.2)	5 (0.8)	23 (3.9)
Ipswich	39	8 (20.5)	15 (38.5)	2 (5.1)	—	—	1 (2.6)	—	4 (10.2)
East Suffolk	333	35 (10.5)	62 (18.6)	29 (8.7)	5 (1.5)	19 (5.7)	43 (12.9)	4 (1.2)	13 (3.9)
Worcestershire	401	85 (21.2)	72 (17.9)	31 (7.7)	16 (3.9)	1 (0.2)	9 (2.2)	23 (5.7)	36 (8.9)

[a] The figures in brackets show the trade group as a percentage of the total.

army after a relatively short period; they were still young and, perhaps, had grown attracted to life in a disciplined, uniformed, hierarchical institution. Furthermore, some chief constables, themselves former military men, maintained an interest in recruiting former soldiers, particularly, it seems, for the bearing and smartness which the army had given them. The recruitment of soldiers into the Ipswich force during the 1870s and 1880s was not marked with much success: fifteen of the 24 soldiers recruited during these years did not serve for more than ten months each, and thereafter the number of ex-soldier recruits declined. However, in Hull, of the 782 men recruited between 1880 and 1910, 169 (22 per cent) were former soldiers, and about one-third of these served for at least twenty years and until retirement. In part the successful record of these men may have stemmed from the improving conditions in the army, though it is also probably significant that 66 (39 per cent) of these ex-soldiers gave their calling as 'musician': the skills of army bandsmen no doubt set them apart from the ordinary rankers, but also made them particularly attractive to any chief constables and watch committees eager to develop the pomp of their forces with police bands.

Guardsmen were especially popular with some chief constables. Colonel Chichester in Huntingdonshire corresponded with the Guards Employment Office in his search for recruits, though he was deeply disappointed with one man who seemed to consider that his new police uniform was designed primarily to attract young women.[6] The Desborough Committee considered that men who had served a short period in the army would make excellent policemen[7] and, during the inter-war period, several chief constables took them at their word. Some men enlisted in the army, particularly the Guards, during the 1920s specifically to join police forces when their three years' short service was over.[8] Between 1927 and 1938 just over 50 per cent of the recruits to the Bedfordshire Police were former soldiers, most of whom had served in the army for just three years; two-thirds of these ex-soldiers came from the Brigade of Guards.[9] In contrast to Bedfordshire, however, of the 101 recruits to the East Suffolk force over the same period, only nine were former

6. Cambs. PA Huntingdonshire Constabulary, Chief Constable's Letter Book, 1884–1908, fols 431, 459.

7. *PP* 1920 [Cmd. 574] XXII, 539 *Report of the Committee on the Police Service, England, Wales and Scotland, Part II*, p. 543.

8. Taped interviews with ex-PC Harry Bleasdale (Westmorland Police), Apr. 1987, and ex-PS Horace Rogers (Bedfordshire Police), Feb. 1987.

9. Beds. PA Bedfordshire Constabulary, Force Conduct Book, 1927–40.

soldiers. If nothing else, it is unwise to generalise about police recruiting policies from the example of one force.

The notion of using strangers to police a community had obvious attractions in that such men were less likely to find themselves
in a situation of conflicting loyalties. In some districts chief police
officers and watch committees made it a policy to recruit largely
from outsiders: such a policy appears to have been followed in
Birmingham in the late nineteenth and early twentieth centuries.
But more often the police drew on what they could get from the
local pool of labour. In some cases this could result in a large
number of outsiders being recruited, especially where a force was
situated on a busy travelling route or, like the metropolis, acted as
a draw for people from all over the country. What is surprising,
perhaps, about the Metropolitan Police is quite how many of the
recruits were born in London or Middlesex; and the number of
local men increased from around 10 per cent in the second half of
the nineteenth century, to around 25 per cent in the first 40 years
of the twentieth, with particularly large numbers in the decade
following the First World War when the pensioning of those elderly
men kept on during the war and the dismissal of strikers created a
large and acute need for recruits. Of the men listed in the personnel registers of the Birkenhead Police as having been recruited
between 1866 and 1901, 26.7 per cent were born in Ireland; only
ten were natives of Birkenhead, and when the other 78 men born
in Cheshire are added to them, this still only accounts for a fifth of
the men who served in the force. On the opposite side of the
country, in Hull, 17.9 per cent of the men listed in the personnel
registers from 1856 to 1920 were natives of the city and just over
another third were born in the East Riding. The number of recruits
native to Hull gradually increased over the period, suggesting,
perhaps, a greater local acceptance of the police as a career and an
organisation. In Worcestershire, for the same period, just over half
of the recruits had been born in the county, while another third
came from the neighbouring counties of Gloucestershire, Herefordshire, Shropshire, Staffordshire and Warwickshire. In more remote,
quieter districts, such as East Anglia, an even greater proportion of
the recruits were local. Three-quarters of the East Suffolk force
were born in Suffolk, and most of these came from the east of the
county; another 15 per cent came from neighbouring Cambridgeshire, Norfolk and Essex. Similarly, three-quarters of the Ipswich
recruits who gave a county of origin were from Suffolk, with about
16 per cent from the three neighbouring counties.

TABLE 9.3 *Birthplace of recruits, c. 1840–c. 1930*[a]

(a) Metropolitan	Total sample	Metropolis (including Middlesex)	Counties bordering Metropolis (Berks, Bucks, Essex, Herts, Kent, Surrey)	Other English counties	Ireland[b]	Scotland	Wales	Abroad	Unknown
	7 756	1 391 (17.9)	1 874 (24.2)	3 232 (41.7)	588 (7.6)	263 (3.4)	128 (1.6)	23 (0.3)	257 (3.1)

(b) Borough forces	Total sample	Borough	Surrounding county	Other county	Ireland	Unknown
Birkenhead	430	10 (2.3)	78 (18.1)	210 (48.8)	115 (26.7)	17 (3.9)
Hull	1 251	225 (17.9)	421 (33.6)	546 (43.6)	23 (1.8)	36 (1.9)
Ipswich	394	1 (0.2)	220 (55.8)	67 (17.0)	3 (0.8)	103 (26.1)

(c) County forces	Total sample	County	Neighbouring county	Other county	Unknown
East Suffolk	541	408 (75.4)	88 (16.3)	43 (7.9)	2 (0.4)
Worcestershire	860	438 (50.9)	303 (35.3)	116 (13.5)	3 (0.3)

[a] The figures in brackets show the number as a percentage of the total.
[b] Only six of these Irishmen were recruited after 1921; the 582 men recruited before this date represent 8.3 per cent of the total who joined before that year.

The number of Irish recruits in Birkenhead and London is worth some comment. Irish policemen were prominent in those areas of Victorian and Edwardian England with a significant Irish population; but the numbers joining the police were greater in percentage terms than the numbers in the local population as a whole. The place of origin of these recruits is in keeping with that of the general pattern of Irish emigration, but recruits to the police were supposed to be literate and, since most Irish emigrants were illiterate, this must have marked the police recruits off from their fellows. Indeed, a study of the careers of recruits in the Metropolitan Police in the early twentieth century suggests an impressive tendency on the part of Irish recruits to get on.[10]

While legislation permitted men to join the police in their thirties, the recruits were generally young men in their twenties. W.J Lowe found that the mean age of recruits to the Lancashire Constabulary fell from 27.8 years in 1845–50 to 24.8 years in 1866–70.[11] The evidence from the forces surveyed here suggests that such a fall continued as the nineteenth century wore on. By the turn of the century most of the recruits were men in their early twenties, suggesting, perhaps, that men were joining the police increasingly with a view to a career.

Probably few of the first recruits to the new police joined with the idea of a career in mind. Policing was just another job to be tried when trade was depressed. In the recession of 1847–48, for example, there was a significant rise in the number of married men who sought employment in the Lancashire Constabulary.[12] Timothy Cavanagh joined the Metropolitan Police in 1855 when he was out of work, and he believed that 'nine-tenths of all who have ever joined ... from its formation in 1829 to the present [1893] have done so through "stress of weather"'. Cavanagh was one of only 37 accepted out of 140 applicants.[13] Many men failed the simple educational tests or could not pass the medical examination: Rowan and Mayne reckoned that only a third of the applicants actually made it into their force, and many of these resigned after two or three days.[14] Half a century later the chief surgeon to the Metropolitan Police,

10. Emsley and Clapson, 'Recruiting the English policeman', 278–9; Haia Shpayer-Makov, 'Career prospects in the London Metropolitan Police in the early twentieth century', *Journal of Historical Sociology* 4 (1991), 380–408, at 397.

11. Lowe, 'The Lancashire Constabulary, 1845–1870', 46.   12. Ibid.

13. Timothy Cavanagh, *Scotland Yard Past and Present: Experiences of Thirty-Seven Years* (London, 1893), p. 2; Metropolitan PA MS 844.85, 'The Memoirs of Chief Inspector John Monk', p. 5.

14. *PP* 1834 (600) XVI, *Select Committee on the Police of the Metropolis*, q. 46.

Alexander MacKeller, estimated that he rejected about half of the applicants that he examined, and that townsmen were more often rejected than countrymen. The medical examination was, he considered, far more rigorous than that conducted on army recruits.[15]

For some of the men who passed the literacy test and the rigours of the medical, the rigours of police life proved too much and they resigned after a short time. Some who joined through 'stress of weather' may have taken advantage of an upswing in the economic cycle to return to their old trade. Many were required to resign, or were simply dismissed, for disciplinary offences which, during the nineteenth century, were invariably related to drink. Early in 1834 Rowan and Mayne informed a parliamentary select committee that of the 2,800 constables serving in May 1830, only 562 remained. They also reported that four out of five dismissals were for drunkenness.[16] Thirty years later it was estimated that there was an annual turnover of about one-sixth of the Metropolitan Police, which led to London being burdened with 'a large number of inexperienced and almost useless men'. One critic's solution was for fixed-term enlistments like the army and the navy which would ensure that the best men were kept on, though he recognised that some would still have to be dismissed for disciplinary offences.[17] Similar problems of a high turnover in manpower and dismissals for drunkenness affected the provincial forces, though the situation improved as the century wore on. By the inter-war period, admittedly when employment was often difficult to find, resignations were greatly reduced, and so too were the dismissals. The provincial forces increased during these years from about 36,500 men to some 37,500. On average, 1,800 recruits were admitted annually giving a turnover of slightly over 5 per cent. The number of men dismissed or ordered to resign never rose above 200. The figures were roughly the same for the Metropolitan Police. This force had an established strength of approximately 20,000 throughout the inter-war period; about 1,000 men left each year, but some two-thirds of these were taking their pensions, generally after service of 25 years or more. The numbers dismissed or ordered to resign fluctuated, but taken together never amounted to as many as 100 in any one year, and on three occasions during the 1930s were below twenty.

But even from the outset there were some men who saw the police

---

15. *PP* 1890 (c. 6075) LIX, *Metropolitan Police Superannuation*, qq. 1305, 1313–14.
16. *PP* 1834 (600) XVI, *Select Committee on the Police of the Metropolis*, qq. 105, 107–8.
17. 'Custos', *The Police Force of the Metropolis in 1868* (London, 1868), p. 13.

TABLE 9.4 *Metropolitan Police: establishment and departures, 1921–37*

Year	Establishment	Left force	Pensioned	Discharged in probationary year	Ordered to resign	Dismissed
1921	21 230	973	659	—	72	15
1922	20 987	947	649	11	64	18
1923	20 464	1 022	747	—	44	16
1924	20 381	1 017	737	1	30	20
1925	20 360	976	693	7	35	17
1926	20 058	1 024	717	16	46	8
1927	20 061	1 038	772	12	38	24
1928	20 029	1 019	708	19	54	13
1929	20 245	962	686	18	27	24
1930	20 274	1 226	964	46	25	7
1931	20 650	1 074	866	13	18	39
1932	20 496	945	754	10	8	6
1933	20 074	1 000	794	8	13	14
1934	19 659	1 010	782	4	21	19
1935	19 364	1 088	856	7	13	29
1936	19 439	1 050	783	8	7	9
1937	19 436	1 067	717	9	10	7

Based on figures in the Annual Reports of the Commissioner.

TABLE 9.5 *Provincial police: establishment and recruitment, 1921–34*

Year	Establishment	Dismissed	Ordered to resign	Recruits	Left in first years
1921	36 439	not given	not given	3 785	378
1922	36 415	not given	not given	1 126	302
1923	36 415	not given	not given	1 486	128
1924	36 448	not given	not given	2 484	167
1925	36 562	not given	not given	2 467	178
1926	36 604	not given	not given	2 317	189
1927	36 751	not given	not given	1 948	204
1928	36 751	47	122	1 834	163
1929	36 895	71	75	1 915	160
1930	37 187	73	114	1 949	183
1931	37 187	50	91	1 868	164
1932	37 352	33	73	1 267	159
1933	37 294	49	65	1 646	132
1934	37 368	47	56	2 035	187

Based on figures in the Annual Reports of HM Inspectors of Constabulary.

as a career and as a means of social, perhaps also geographical, mobility. In the 1830s men were moving from the Metropolitan Police to a promotion in another force. The police also became a family trade from early on as brothers and sons enlisted. Henry Tooms was the son of the parish constable of Donington in South Lincolnshire. His father had taken his tasks seriously and had educated Henry in the trade. Henry served in the Hull Police for six years before returning to take over his father's old post. He then moved to Swineshead and, steadily building up reputation in South Lincolnshire, in 1852 he was appointed as policeman by the town of Horncastle where he served until the new county force took over in 1857.[18] Richard Jervis joined the Lancashire Constabulary in 1850 aged only 18: his father was then an inspector stationed in Southport.[19] Hector Macleod joined the Northamptonshire force in 1886: his father, who had served in a Scottish police force, advised him in terms of which Peel himself would doubtless have been proud:

> Never be tyrannical in any case towards any human being, whether rich or poor. Above all, have a perfect command over your own temper. You will find it very hard at times to keep your coolness, but in losing it you cannot perform your duty and will give your opponents the advantage over you. Being harsh, you lose public sympathy; being cool and firm, and having made yourself thoroughly conversant with your instructions, fulfil these instructions to the letter as far as your ability goes. But bear in mind, overstepping these instructions in over zeal in doing duty, whatever it is, always carries its own punishment, if not pecuniary, then the loss of the Public Confidence, and of your own superior officers.
>
> I put the public first because you are the community's servant, among whom you are placed for the time being, and it is your duty to please them as well as your commanding officer. The great evil in many when they are appointed as P.C.s is that they don't look at the public as their supreme masters, and sneer at them.
>
> A P.C.'s conduct should be to control his conduct and duty so that the public would see and appreciate his efforts to protect life and property, the main duties of a Police Constable.
>
> Study often and well your instructions, and the Law, so that in a case of emergency you have only to act and be sure that you are within the Law. There is a certain cunning necessary sometimes to overcome the breaker of the law when plain courses won't succeed. This cunning should be used with extreme caution. Bear in mind

18. B.J. Davey, *Lawless and Immoral: Policing a Country Town 1838–1857* (Leicester: University Press, 1983), pp. 161–3.
19. Richard Jervis, *Lancashire's Crime and Criminals* (Southport, 1908), pp. 11–12.

not to put a case against anyone stronger than it really is in giving evidence in court. Give it unhesitatingly and straightforward, at once showing the prisoner's counsel that you have but one evidence to give, that being the truth. When in uniform, be smart, especially in court, but always be smart and clean. Make yourself as intelligent as you can. If you intend to follow the Police Service, you cannot learn too much about it.

Macleod clearly took the advice to heart, and rose through the ranks to end his service as Deputy Chief Constable of Northamptonshire.[20]

Career prospects were enhanced by the guarantee of a pension by the Police Act of 1890. Before that date the decision as to whether or not a man received a pension depended often on his chief constable and several of the superannuation schemes established for the different forces in the middle of the century had got themselves into a mess. Under the 1890 Act a man received his pension automatically after 25 years' service, or after only fifteen years if there were medical grounds for his retirement. The increased uniformity in the police forces, which followed the recommendations of the Desborough Committee, also probably made the police a more attractive career for young men. Equally attractive to recruits, if not always to their employers,[21] in the inter-war period were the then relatively high rates of pay, and the security of the employment. It was, recalled Bob Edmondson, 'a "safe" career'; one chief constable thought it useful to encourage his men by pointing out in Police Orders that 'a very large number of really good men are asking to join the Police today [1931] so that any man who is not keen in his work cannot be retained', while another urged sobriety on his men over Christmas and the New Year, reminding them 'of the existing industrial stagnation and the difficulty in obtaining employment'.[22] There was, however, some controversy as

20. My thanks to Annabel Macleod for a copy of this letter and for permission to cite it.

21. *Police Review*, 9 May 1924, p. 254, for example, quotes the Mayor of Stalybridge protesting to his Town Council about the equality of police pay introduced following the Desborough Committee: 'I think it is wicked that a Policeman in Stalybridge, where rents are so low and where they can live so near to their work, should have to be paid the same as London Constables, who have a long distance to travel from home to their work, and where rents are much higher.'

22. *Bob's Beat: The Story of a Lancashire Policeman (1934–1963)* (Manchester: Neil Richardson, 1985), p. 9; Beds. PA Bedfordshire Constabulary, Order Book 1930–35, 18 Mar. 1931; Greater Manchester PA Manchester Police Order Books vol. 16, fol. 56. See also Mike Brogden, *On the Mersey Beat: Policing Liverpool Between the Wars* (Oxford: OUP, 1991), pp. 76–8. The *Interim Report of the Royal Commission on the Police* published in 1960 estimated that for much of the inter-war period the maximum of the constable's pay scale was some 55 per cent higher than the earnings

to whether the unemployment of the inter-war period led to an influx of better recruits. In 1923 the Inspectors of Constabulary found some chief constables claiming that they were getting better men than ever before, and others arguing the opposite; they concluded that possibly 'the former are mostly those who in old times were handicapped by a comparison of conditions, but now, when pay is standardised, secure their fair share of the better recruits'.[23] Many men continued to be rejected as physically unsuitable sometimes even before they saw the doctor, but by the early 1930s the number of recruits with secondary school qualifications was increasing.[24] A degree of friction sometimes developed between the better educated, new recruits and the older men who could boast of having survived the hard times of the war and the strikes and who felt that they had won the advantages of the 1919 Police Act.[25]

In the aftermath of the Second World War, in spite of shortages of police manpower, Sir Harold Scott estimated that only about a quarter of the applicants who were interviewed for the Metropolitan Police progressed successfully through that interview, the medical examination, the educational test and the character inquiry. The men continued to be recruited largely from social class III in the Registrar General's classification: that is, they were drawn from skilled manual and low-grade non-manual workers. But a relatively high proportion were the sons of policemen, and it appeared also that policemen serving in the early 1970s had done rather better at school than the manual working class as a whole.[26] The 1970s and 1980s were marked by an increase in the number of graduates in the police, some of whom were encouraged to take their degrees while serving, others encouraged by a graduate entry scheme with a special course and accelerated promotion. The substantial pay rises awarded in the latter decade and the decline in the pay and prestige of careers elsewhere in the public sector may also have acted as a spur to such recruits. Although the graduates tended to rise to the more senior ranks, they were also twice as likely to resign

of the average adult male industrial worker: T.A. Critchley, *A History of Police in England and Wales*, rev. edn (London: Constable, 1978), p. 249.

23. *Report of H.M. Inspectors of Constabulary for 1923*, p. 4.

24. Ibid. for 1924, p. 5; ibid. for 1934, p. 8.

25. Joanne Marie Klein, 'Invisible working-class men: police constables in Manchester, Birmingham and Liverpool, 1900–1939', Ph.D., Rice University, 1992, pp. 150–4.

26. Sir Harold Scott, *Scotland Yard* (London: Andre Deutsch, 1954), pp. 41–2; Ben Whitaker, *The Police* (London: Eyre & Spottiswoode, 1964), p. 96; Robert Reiner, *The Blue-Coated Worker: A Sociological Study of Police Unionism* (Cambridge: CUP, 1978), pp. 149–52.

as the officers without degrees, dissatisfied with what they considered to be poor management and a lack of career prospects.[27]

Police life

Most nineteenth-century policemen received such training as they got on the job. The Metropolitan Police was probably the most advanced in the instruction of recruits, but instruction in the mid-nineteenth century lasted for only two weeks, largely concentrated on drill and sword exercise, with two afternoon lectures by a superintendent, and a considerable amount of legal material to learn by rote. Following this, the new constable patrolled with an experienced man for about a week; he was then moved to his division and sent out on his own. A section house reserved for candidates to the force was opened in 1886 with an assistant chief constable appointed as instructor, and when Benjamin Leeson joined in 1890 the training at Kennington Lane Section House lasted 'from three to five weeks' beginning each morning with two hours' drill on the Guards' paradeground at Wellington Barracks. It was not until May 1907 that a proper training school was established for the Metropolitan Police with the opening of Peel House.[28] By the 1920s recruits studied at Peel House for ten weeks; there continued to be drill and rote learning, but there were also regular lectures, instruction on first aid, self-defence, how to draft reports, and even mock accidents were staged. After this initial training the new constable was again introduced to patrolling in his division by going out with an experienced man.[29]

On-the-job training was much the same in the provincial forces of Victorian and Edwardian England. Some borough forces employed local schoolmasters to give instruction in reading, writing and arithmetic, but elsewhere chief constables relied largely on exhorting their men to study hard. In February 1895 the Chief

27. Alan Smithers, Susan Hill and Geoff Silvester, *Graduates in the Police Service* (University of Manchester, School of Education, 1990).

28. Phillip Thurmond Smith, *Policing Victorian London: Political Policing, Public Order, and the London Metropolitan Police* (Westport, Conn.: Greenwood Press, 1985), pp. 39–40; Charles Tempest Clarkson and J. Hall Richardson, *Police!* (London, 1889), p. 88; Ex-Det. Sergeant B. Leeson, *Lost London: The Memoirs of an East End Detective* (London: Stanley Paul, 1934), p. 24; David Ascoli, *The Queen's Peace: The Origins and Development of the Metropolitan Police 1829–1979* (London: Hamish Hamilton, 1979), p. 184.

29. Metropolitan PA MS Book 175.88, Arthur Battle, 'This job's not what it used to be', pp. 7–12; MS Book 159.88, Edward Lyscom, 'London policeman', pp. 5–10.

Constable of East Sussex set an examination for those men wishing promotion to Constable First Class; he was concerned that several candidates passed because their high marks for dictation compensated for very low marks on Police Duties and he promised to change the marking scale for the future. Twelve years later the Chief Constable of the East Riding proposed that each member of his force 'devote not less than half-an-hour each day . . . to the study of "The Police Manual" with which he has been provided'; the superintendents and inspectors were periodically to test the men, especially the junior constables, on their knowledge.[30] G.H. Totterdell recalled that when he joined the Essex force in November 1912 he had to pick up the job as he went along. There was a month's training at the headquarters in Chelmsford which included drill, police law and procedure, but there was no library or rest room in which to study. 'The more ambitious among us as time went on kept personal records of our cases, filled them in against the Act which applied so that we could refer to them in the future.' Frank Bunn found similar problems, and self-help solutions, in Norfolk: he used his retainer as an army reservist to buy copies of the instruction books.[31] Correspondence colleges, notably the Bennett College in Sheffield and the institution established by Thomas Walton, also in Sheffield, developed courses specifically for policemen and regularly advertised in the *Police Review* during the interwar years and later; the former styled itself 'the Policeman's University', the latter, less grandiosely, 'the Policeman's College'.

The Desborough Committee recommended that a training officer be appointed in each force, though such appointments were not always made. However, the development of half a dozen training schools during the inter-war period did lead to a greater uniformity in training, especially when the smaller forces began to take advantage of them. Also in the inter-war years some forces began to recruit boy clerks who could progress, rather like cadets, to the rank of police constable when they reached the appropriate age. However, it was not until after the Second World War that police training was fully sytematised across the whole country, and not until the 1960s that a formal system of police cadets was established.[32]

30. Clarkson and Hall, *Police!*, p. 141; East Sussex RO SPA 2/2/3 fol. 38; Humberside PA East Riding Constabulary, Memorandum Book 1900–12, fol. 40, see also fol. 149.

31. G.H. Totterdell, *Country Copper* (London: Harrap, 1956), p. 41; Frank L. Bunn, *No Silver Spoon* (Stoke on Trent: F.L. Bunn, 1970), p. 85.

32. Critchley, *A History of Police*, p. 322; Sir Arthur L. Dixon, 'The Home Office and the police between the two world wars' (unpublished, 1966), p. 200.

While in the training centres the recruits were generally quartered together in barracks and, in the inter-war period at least, the discipline, not to mention the haircuts, was remembered as unpleasantly military. Henry Holm, who had served a marine engineering apprenticeship but could not find work during the 1920s, joined the Cumberland Constabulary in 1927 and was sent for training with the Lancashire force at Lancaster Castle; it was, he thought, 'very much the same as a Guards depot'. Arthur Almond, sent to the Birmingham Training School by the Cambridgeshire Police in 1928, described the officers as 'fond of bullying tactics'. Fred Fancourt, who joined the Birmingham Police from his native Lincolnshire the following year, remembered the inspector in charge of that force's training school as appearing to want to create 'an atmosphere of terror in which no mercy was shown'.[33]

Young single men recruited into the larger urban forces commonly lived in section houses, sometimes, in spite of the military connotations, referred to as 'barracks'.[34] Initially they slept in dormitories, though by the early twentieth century many, perhaps most, had been converted to provide each man with a separate cubicle. The section houses contained common rooms, drying rooms, and sometimes libraries, where the books, especially in the Victorian period, were carefully selected to avoid criticism of the political and social system and to emphasise morality and improvement. There was also a shared kitchen, but the residents of each house usually negotiated their own practice for buying and cooking the food. During the Victorian period, the men were required to attend church on Sunday, and well into the twentieth century single women were prohibited from entering the section houses.[35]

The section houses were popular with senior officers who saw them as a way of keeping their men together and limiting the temptations to immorality. But bringing groups of young men together inevitably led to boisterousness and horseplay. Timothy Cavanagh described the men in his first section house pelting each

33. Taped interview with ex-PC Henry Holm (Cumberland Constabulary), May 1987; Clive Emsley (ed), 'The recollections of a provincial policeman: Arthur Ernest Almond', *Journal of the Police History Society* 3 (1987), 53–66, at 53; 'The police service of George Frederick Fancourt: Birmingham City Police 1929–1960', MS deposited at the Open University. Both Almond and Fancourt vividly remembered their Birmingham haircuts.
34. See, for example, Clarkson and Hall, *Police!*, pp. 140–1; *The Times*, 27 Oct. 1900, p. 14; *Hansard*, CXXXI, 3 Mar. 1904, cols 64–5.
35. Ronald Charles Sopenhoff, 'The police of London: the early history of the Metropolitan Police, 1829–1856', Ph.D., Temple University, 1978, pp. 182–90; Clarkson and Hall, *Police!*, pp. 88–98.

other with eggs, ducking an awkward comrade under the station pump and tipping a bucket of whitewash over another. Tom Divall remembered courts for those who did not conform to the section house rules, and arguments settled by fisticuffs. Such behaviour sometimes spread beyond the section house. For a joke Benjamin Leeson threw and smashed a bottle of beer at the feet of what appeared, in the night-time gloom, to be a drowsing constable; he was alarmed when the constable turned out to be his section sergeant, but was able successfully to deny responsibility.[36] In April 1903 a constable in the Cambridge Borough force twisted his ankle during a bout of horseplay in the station parade room; the Chief Constable ordered that he receive no pay for as long as he could not work and urged his senior officers to prevent such behaviour in future.[37] But, of course, pranks continued. Ted Lyscom and a comrade acquired a naked female dummy while on their beats one night and used it to play a trick on a station sergeant 'renowned for his appreciation of the female form'. Arthur Battle remembered a variety of night-time wheezes:

> At one time a craze developed among us of using catapults when on night duty, and it would be a common thing to be walking down a quiet street lined with deep doorways in that semi-conscious state one develops on night duty to be suddenly brought back to life by a whining 'Wheee-e-e-e' as a catapult missile ricocheted off a nearby wall. All would be quiet for a time, and one resumed one's patrol, only to be followed by a pellet fired from an unknown direction. Childish, but all good clean fun!
>
> Black thread, helmet high, tied to two milk bottles placed on opposite window sills in a narrow alley provided another diversion. Another variation was to suspend a milk bottle or old electric light bulb filched from a dustbin from the arm of a nearby gas lamp by means of a long black thread, the other end of which was held by a P.C. lurking in a dark doorway. Immediately the P.C. on the beat had passed the lamp standard the thread would be released, and the bottle fell to the ground with a splintering crash behind the luckless victim.[38]

36. Leeson, *Lost London*, pp. 68–9.

37. Cavanagh, *Scotland Yard Past and Present*, pp. 39–45; Tom Divall, *Scoundrels and Scallywags* (London: Ernest Benn, 1929), p. 24; Cambs. PA Cambridge Police, General Orders, 1894–1927, 10 Apr. 1903. See also Harry Daley, *This Small Cloud: A Personal Memoir* (London: Weidenfeld & Nicolson, 1986), pp. 90–1.

38. Lyscom, 'London policeman', pp. 76–7; Battle, 'This job's not what it used to be', p. 38. C.H. Rolph recalled playing the same prank of using black thread to knock a policeman's helmet off when he was a child at the beginning of the century: C.H. Rolph, *Living Twice: An Autobiography* (London: Victor Gollancz, 1974), p. 29. For other pranks, this time in Liverpool, see Brogden, *On the Mersey Beat*, pp. 59–60.

Similar 'good clean fun' continued long after the Second World War. A sociologist interviewing police in Islington during the early 1970s was struck by how much they enjoyed the comradeship of the force and how this was exemplified by the community of the section house with its horseplay, petty pilfering and strenuous parties.

> While they displayed deference to the symbolisms of Authority, these working-class youths were quite active in a whole culture of insubordination, with its own quite elaborate rituals of misrule. All this seemed to be officially tolerated, though not encouraged, as a necessary safety valve for young men subject to rigorous discipline at the bottom of the command structure . . . Just as it served as a defence against what was perceived as social ostracism by the local community.[39]

Even in the cities not all men, and especially not married men, could be accommodated in section houses. These had to find, or were sometimes found, lodgings. Nineteenth-century and early twentieth-century police pay may have been regular, but it rarely measured up to that of the skilled working class with whom the police were meant to identify. The problem was compounded by regulations, varying from force to force, which either limited or prohibited a constable's wife contributing to the family budget by working. In the East Riding in July 1909 the Chief Constable informed his men that the idea that their wives could not work was mistaken. If they were 'domestic servants, dressmakers etc.' he had no objection to them taking temporary employment 'without neglecting their houses and families'; but they were not to keep shops.[40] Nor were wives permitted to take lodgers, sometimes even from among members of their own families, or to have any employment on licensed premises. It was not until the Second World War that the restrictions on the work which could be undertaken by police wives were eased, and even in 1946 at least one chief constable had to be instructed by the Home Office to permit the wife of one of his men to work as a teacher.[41]

Low pay and the restrictions on a wife's opportunities for contributing to the family budget was behind much of the discontent in the mid-nineteenth-century police forces. Towards the end of

39. Phil Cohen, 'Policing the working-class city', in Bob Fine *et al.* (eds), *Capitalism and the Rule of Law: From Deviancy Theory to Marxism* (London: Hutchinson, 1979), p. 135.
40. Humberside PA East Riding Constabulary, Memorandum Book, 1900–12, fol. 92.
41. Ibid., Memorandum Book, 1912–16, fol. 65; Merseyside PA Birkenhead Police, Disciplinary Report Book, 1920–30, fol. 182; Sir Arthur L. Dixon, 'The emergency work of the police forces in the Second World War' (unpublished, 1963), p. 166.

the 1860s *The Times* expressed sympathy with the recruit to the Metropolitan Police who had to be of good character and literate; who, if married when joining, was not to have more than two children, and whose wife could no longer follow her trade. 'Yet for fulfilling all these conditions, which manifestly . . . imply a first-rate man of the working classes, the remuneration is only 19s. a week, with a hope of gradual promotion to 21s., 23s., and 25s. weekly.'[42]

For all the problems, policemen clearly sought to keep up appearances. When Charles Booth and his investigators embarked on their massive survey of London some twenty years later, they listed most of the policemen they found as living in those streets defined as 'comfortable working class'.[43] At the turn of the century, however, the plight of London's policemen was being raised in the correspondence columns of *The Times* and in the House of Commons. In particular it was alleged that they were having difficulty in finding accommodation close to their stations because of high rents. A rent allowance was agreed for men posted to the centre of the city, where rents were highest, but in August 1901 Captain Cecil Norton, the Liberal member for Newington, protested that the recent demolition of tenement housing in Marylebone meant that some men were having to walk an eight-mile round trip to and from work.[44] The following year Captain Claude Hay, a Conservative MP well known for his interest in working-class housing, reported that in his constituency of Hoxton some police were compelled to live in accommodation which had been built for the poor.[45] Rent aid to members of the Metropolitan Police was extended early in 1904, but the problem of rents continued to be a bone of contention up to and during the First World War. Again it was the Desborough Committee which brought a resolution to the problem with its recommendation that policemen be provided with rent-free accommodation or paid a rent allowance in lieu. Over time, however, this solution created a new problem, especially when, towards the end of the 1970s, police pay began to outstrip that of people in skilled

42. *The Times*, 30 Jan. 1868, p. 6.
43. This is based on information from the Booth Database at the Open University. Listing the streets containing members of the 'uniformed' occupations up to Notebook 67 reveals 86 streets with police residents: of these, 56 are Pink (comfortable working class), four are Red (middle class), four are Pink–Red, ten are Purple (mixed), five are Orange (upper middle class) (but in each case here the policeman is described as a 'Policeman caretaker'), two are Light Blue (poor), and one is Dark Blue (casual, very poor).
44. *Hansard*, XCVII, 2 Aug. 1901, col. 1043; see also *The Times*, 27 Oct. 1900, p. 14; 8 Jan., p. 12; 9 Jan., p. 8, and 25 Jan. 1901, p. 9.
45. *Hansard*, CVIII, 30 May 1902, col. 1051.

manual work as well as in some professions. Well-paid policemen were buying their own houses and the rent allowance was a considerable help towards the mortgage. In 1974 it was estimated that 70 per cent of serving officers were receiving the rent allowance which, on average, amounted to some 20 per cent of their pay.[46] It was suggestions by the Conservative government that such allowances might be looked at and revised, which contributed to the anger shown at the Police Federation conference in 1990.

Lodgings could create problems of security for the constable especially when beat journals and other documents had to be kept. In February 1905, for example, a general order was issued in the East Riding warning that such constables who were unmarried and who lived in lodgings must 'carefully keep their *Journals, Duty Scales, Weekly Reports,* and *all* other *official papers,* safely *under lock and key* when not in use by them'.[47] There were also the difficulties of having to dry wet uniforms in time for the next duty since, unlike the section houses, lodgings were unlikely to provide drying rooms. For some there could be the occasional complications of nubile landladies or their daughters.[48]

Rowan and Mayne considered that married men were steadier policemen particularly because they were less susceptible to the temptations from 'the women of the town'.[49] Nevertheless, in many forces men were not allowed to marry until they had served for a period of two or three years in the force. In the Metropolitan Police during the inter-war period a man had to have served for four years before he could marry. 'Some such condition is necessary', declared the Home Secretary in 1933, 'in order to prevent the number of single men in police quarters falling too low, and I am satisfied that its introduction is in the interests of efficiency.' 'Even if the right honourable gentleman considers it is in the interests of efficiency,' quipped William Lunn, 'does he think it is in the interests of morality?'[50] The Home Secretary did not respond. But when a constable did seek to marry, his fiancée had to have suitable references and be approved by his senior officers. In West Sussex as late as the end of the 1930s Nat Taylor recalled:

46. J.V. Boothman, 'The historical development of the modern contract under which a police constable is employed in England and Wales', Ph.D., University of Leeds, 1982, p. 244.

47. Humberside PA East Riding Constabulary, General Orders, 1905–10, fol. 7.

48. 'Recollections of . . . Almond', p. 55; Merseyside P.A. Birkenhead Police, Disciplinary Report Book, 1920–30, fols 268–9.

49. *Select Committee on the Police of the Metropolis,* qq. 148–9.

50. *Hansard,* CCLXXXIII, 23 Nov. 1933, col. 243.

You had to be single to join. You had to work two years probation before you could get married ... When the time came we had to produce bankbooks to say we'd got a specified sum, and that we could afford to get married without going into debt, and ... she had to produce three references as to character to be a policeman's wife.[51]

Furthermore, the constable's wife had to keep her good character, or the constable might find himself brought before a senior officer to answer for her behaviour.[52]

In some rural forces the marriage might not be allowed until suitable accommodation was available, usually in a village where there was a police house.[53] Such police houses had to be kept clean, neat and tidy by the constable's wife, and they were subject to visits by sergeants, inspectors and even chief constables.[54] The wife of a rural policeman stationed in a village and living in a police house could find herself acting as a police auxiliary. While her husband was out on his beat she was expected to take messages and enter details of, for example, any reported lost property; clearly one reason why some rural chief constables objected to their men's wives working was that there would be no-one in the village police stations to perform these tasks. Yet in return the system offered a degree of protection to a constable's wife. Policemen were expected to treat their wives and families with respect and consideration; the slightest hint of scandal, of ill-treatment or abuse, led to a disciplinary hearing with the possibility of anything from a caution to dismissal.[55]

Police life could be hard on a constable's wife and family given the unsociable hours that he worked and the regular upheavals of new postings in rural districts. In some neighbourhoods too the very nature of the job could make both the policeman and his

51. Taped interview with ex-PS Nat Taylor (West Sussex Police), Dec. 1987; for Essex in the 1880s see Totterdell, *Country Copper*, p. 10; and for questioning whether such rules on permission to marry should exist see *Police Review*, 5 Feb. 1926, p. 84. Such bans ended in 1939, partly as a result of increasing criticism, but primarily because of recruitment difficulties in several forces: see Barbara Weinberger, *The Best Police in the World: An Oral History of English Policing from the 1930s to the 1960s* (Aldershot: Scolar Press, 1995), pp. 103–4.
52. Greater Manchester PA Manchester Division, Misconduct Book, 1912–35, fol. 34.
53. *Justice of the Peace* XLV (1881), 19 Nov., p. 771; Humberside PA East Riding Constabulary, General Orders 1905–10, fol. 12.
54. Weinberger, *The Best Police in the World*, p. 107.
55. Greater Manchester PA Manchester Division, Misconduct Book, 1912–35, fols. 31, 33, 78, 89; Merseyside PA Birkenhead Police, Disciplinary Report Book, 1920–30, fols 99, 114.

family outsiders. Flora Thompson remembered the constable in her Oxfordshire village as 'a kindly good-tempered man; yet nobody seemed to like him, and he and his wife led a somewhat isolated life, in the village but not entirely of the village'.[56] But in the recollection of former village and small town policemen who served in the middle two quarters of the twentieth century, while they recalled the life as often being hard for their wives, they considered that they were accepted from the beginning as a part of the community. Horace Rogers met his wife while on his beat, checking the pigs on her father's farm. When Arthur Pickering was recalled to the colours in 1939 the village community delivered cut firewood to his wife, dug his allotment, and helped her to pack when she had to move from the village police house. Yet Pickering confessed to cuffing local youths who stepped out of bounds, or swinging at them with his cape. Henry Holm chastised youthful offenders with the walking stick, known as 'William the Conqueror', that he carried on his beat: 'The following day it was quite common for one of them to say, "You were a rough old bugger last night." I said "Don't you think you deserved it?" "We probably did." '[57]

In the big towns and cities, where there were much larger concentrations of police, the situation could be different. Even outside the section house policemen and their families might often tend to associate largely with their peer group. Looking back on his career in the Birmingham Police, Fred Fancourt explained:

> A policeman's life is different from the ordinary man in the street. He is always working different shifts. He is either on first watch or second watch or night-duty, so you can't get a true rhythm to how you live. Because of that, getting to know other people in the street was restricted and, furthermore, you weren't encouraged to get to know other people socially very much ... I remember when the wife and I first set up home, we were living on the Dudley Road side of the city ... There was a big factory ... in Smethwick within walking distance of us. With one or two policeman colleagues we used to go there once a month to a Whist Drive, which we used to enjoy very much. But we would never, even in that case, mix up with any of the other individuals, not because we didn't want to, but it just didn't happen.[58]

On 31 May 1890 John Hill resigned from the Worcestershire Constabulary 'on account of his wife who threatened to leave him

56. Flora Thompson, *Lark Rise to Candleford* (Harmondsworth: Penguin, 1973), p. 484.
57. Taped interviews with Rogers, Holm and Pickering.
58. Taped interview with Fancourt.

if he remained in the police service'.[59] Such evidence is rare, but while there is no way of measuring the precise impact of the pressures of the job and the occasional isolation of the policeman and his family, it is probable that all of these contributed to the high turnover in manpower.

The harsh discipline also probably contributed to the turnover. Policemen always had to appear with military smartness throughout the nineteenth century. In most forces, they were expected always to wear uniform; in Devon the only exceptions allowed were when a man had special permission or when he was working in his garden.[60] Hair had to be neatly and regularly cut, and men were expected to shave every day before going on duty.[61] As in any hierarchical institution, some men who achieved senior rank were tempted to abuse their authority and bully some subordinates while showing favouritism to others. Again it is impossible to assess the incidence of such behaviour, but complaints, concerns, and even disciplinary cases against senior officers can be found testifying to its existence. From early on there were complaints about the oppression of sergeants and other more senior officers in the Metropolitan Police.[62] According to Superintendent Jaggard of the Cambridge Borough force, the men in the Cambridgeshire County Police gave their first chief constable 'a very queer character, especially for bullying the men'.[63] Captain John Frost, who commanded the Hampshire Constabulary from 1856 to 1891, had a reputation for harsh treatment and partiality – a reputation which prompted adverse comment in the local press.[64] At the turn of the century the Chief Constable of Staffordshire was worried about the situation at Old Hill Police Station. Constables were showing considerable reluctance to be posted to the station; one had even resigned to avoid the move. The problem appeared to be the local inspector.[65] In the aftermath of the police strikes of 1918 and 1919 C.H. Rolph

59. West Mercia PA Worcestershire Constabulary, Register and Record of Service, 1888–93, no. 53.

60. Devon and Cornwall PA Devon Constabulary, M Division Order Book 1865–1910, 21 Feb. 1874 and 17 Apr. 1884.

61. Ibid., 15 Mar. 1867; see also East Sussex RO SPA 2/2/2, fol. 13.

62. Sopenhoff, 'Police of London', pp. 201–3; Shpayer-Makov, 'The making of a police labour force', 118.

63. Cambs. PA Cambridge Police, Letter Book, 1849–52, Jaggard to Superintendent Smith, Police Office, Ringwood, Hants., 21 Dec. 1851.

64. Ian A. Watt, *A History of the Hampshire and Isle of Wight Constabulary 1839–1966* (Winchester: Hampshire Constabulary, 1967), pp. 20–2.

65. Staffs. PA Staffordshire Police, Chief Constable's Letter Book, 1900–08, fol. 86.

believed that there remained for many years a 'top brass' which distrusted and victimised men 'who . . . were believed to have left-wing views and had been seen with the *Daily Herald* or, what was much worse, *The Freethinker*'. This tendency infected the sergeants also, who gave the suspect men all the worst duties.[66] John Wainwright considered that his promotion chances were checked because of a long feud with a detective chief superintendent.[67] Of course in such instances most of the advantages lay with the senior men, but on occasions senior officers were brought to book for 'oppressive conduct' towards their subordinates.[68]

But while there were drawbacks to a life in the police, there were also compensations. Some of these are difficult to compare in strict monetary terms with other jobs: what, for example, was the value of work clothing in the form of the policeman's uniform? There was also the opportunity of buying old uniforms when the regular replacements were issued. Free medical assistance was introduced in some forces at a very early stage, and this might also be extended to members of the policeman's family.[69] Benefit societies or benevolent funds could be organised within forces to pay medical or funeral expenses, or to grant sums to widows and orphans.[70] The policeman's pay may not have measured up to that of the workers with whom he was expected to identify, but from the beginning there was provision for a pension. The problem was that for 60 years there was no guarantee of the pension since it depended on the recommendation of the chief constable. This situation was aggravated by the reluctance of local authorities to finance such pensions out of the rates; the small superannuation deductions from the men's pay, together with the various other monies collected from fines and fees, were not always sufficient to keep the pension funds solvent. The matter was raised in Parliament throughout the 1870s and 1880s, and while there was anxiety that old and infirm policemen were being kept on just so that they might receive a pension,

66. Rolph, *Living Twice*, pp. 84–5.
67. John Wainwright, *Wainwright's Beat; One Man's Journey with a Police Force* (London: Macmillan, 1987), pp. 158–9, 161–2, 212–14.
68. Merseyside PA Birkenhead Police, Discipline Book, 1920–30, fols 260–1. Of course disciplinary authority had to be maintained, and Major Dunlop warned his superintendents never to admonish a sergeant in the presence of a constable: Humberside PA East Riding Constabulary, Memorandum Book 1900–12, fol. 1.
69. Cambs. PA Huntingdonshire Constabulary, Chief Constable's Memos 1857–99, No. 15, 15 July 1858.
70. See, for example, the detailed constitution of the East Riding force's benevolent fund organised by the Chief Constable in 1911: Humberside PA East Riding Constabulary, Memo Book, 1900–12, fol. 150.

there remained the problem of the finances of the local authorities.[71] The guarantee of a pension by the Police Act of 1890 resolved the issue and added to such attractions as the job had in comparison with others during the late Victorian and Edwardian periods. Cheap lodgings and the various allowances granted, especially following the recommendations of the Desborough Committee, contributed to these during the inter-war years. Finally, on retirement, and with his pension, a policeman could expect a reference from his chief constable which would stand him in good stead for another, less physically demanding job in his fifties and sixties. Occasionally prospective employers might write to a chief constable for the name of a pensioner who would be suitable for them to employ; sometimes such requests might offer employment to the children of policemen.[72] Local government jobs were occasionally found for ex-policemen, much to the annoyance of some who, in the inter-war years, could find no work, let alone a paid job while in receipt of a full pension.[73]

Police culture

Barrack life and, to a lesser extent, the community of the police station tended to foster a rough, masculine culture. The pranks and the horseplay have already been described. Drinking and gambling also figured in this culture, though men were disciplined for both activities. C.H. Rolph, on joining the City of London Police in the aftermath of the First World War, 'believed for a few months that [he] had arrived among the most sex-absorbed body of men in the country'.[74] As well as group discussions and boasts about sexual prowess, some men appear to have hoped to take advantage of the glamour of their uniform to make conquests; sometimes they were successful, like the Worcestershire constable dismissed for 'having sexual intercourse . . . with a girl on two occasions on Sunday afternoon April 18th. 1880, in full uniform and broad daylight . . . and his misconduct being witnessed by two men and some children'.[75]

71. See, *inter alia, Justice of the Peace* XLVI (1882), 28 Jan. p. 59, 6 May pp. 281–2, 15 July p. 442, 29 July p. 473.

72. Humberside PA East Riding Constabulary, Memo Book, 1900–12, fol. 109; ibid., 1912–16, fols 125, 179, 180, 195.

73. *Hansard*, CCCIX, 5 Mar. 1936, cols 1641–2.

74. Rolph, *Living Twice*, pp. 57–8.

75. West Mercia PA Worcestershire Constabulary, Register and Record of Police Service, 1877–83, no. 36.

Equally, some men abused the power which their position gave them over women in their charge: there were, protested one woman reformer to the Manchester Watch Committee in 1909, instances 'of roughness and insolence, petty persecution which women hardly ever speak of but suffer under very acutely'.[76] Such abuse, and the fear of such abuse, led to the appointment of police matrons and later contributed to the perceived need for women police, but these did not solve the problem. The records of the police in Birmingham, Liverpool and Manchester reveal that, between 1900 and 1939, over 250 officers were involved in cases of sexual misconduct. Most of these occurred during the 1920s when there were particularly large numbers of young constables, and most of the incidents suggest young men using the advantage of being a policeman to seek out the company of women and/or to force their attentions on them.[77] Sociological research undertaken towards the close of the twentieth century suggested that many policewomen found it easier to accommodate rather than confront the aggressively masculine attitudes of many of their male colleagues.[78]

Strenuous heterosexual sex was the order of the day in this culture and Harry Daley recalled the cruel treatment meted out to those branded as 'Nancy-Boys' when they were brought into the police station. Daley himself was homosexual; he was victimised by some of his comrades because of his 'lack of interest in women', but also because of his interest in books and music which did not accord with the norms of the culture.[79]

This kind of culture was likely to emerge in any male work organisation. But the strength of police culture was probably fostered by the nature of the institution itself. Besides the 'barrack' communities, the hierarchical nature of the police gave an additional bonding to the constables at the bottom of the pyramid, as did the nature of the police job which often set the men apart from, and sometimes at odds with, the surrounding community. A trade argot developed, often varying from force to force, which became both

76. Greater Manchester PA Watch Committee Papers, vol. 44, fols 277a–278. For disciplinary charges apparently resulting from such behaviour see West Mercia PA Worcestershire Constabulary, Register and Record of Police Service, 1877–83, no. 172, and Merseyside PA Birkenhead Police, Disciplinary Report Book, 1920–30, fols 152–4.

77. Klein, 'Invisible working-class men', pp. 219–20, 223.

78. David J. Smith and Jeremy Gray, *Police and People in London* (Aldershot: Gower, 1985), pp. 372–8. (This is the single-volume version of the four-volume Policy Studies Institute Report.) See also Roger Graef (ed.), *Talking Blues: The Police in their Own Words* (London: Collins Harvill, 1989), ch. 6.

79. Daley, *This Small Cloud*, pp. 101, 112–13.

a part of the work culture and helped to cement the police community. Thus, to members of the Metropolitan Police an ordinary
member of the public became 'chummy', a prostitute was a 'tom'
and her trade 'tomming', a pickpocket was a 'dip', a summons a
'blister', an arrest a 'knock' or a 'knock off', the truncheon was
'Charley Wood', the police station 'the nick', and the area covered
by the station or an individual constable 'the manor'. 'Once you
picked up these terms', recalled Ted Lyscom, 'you never used the
correct ones again.'[80] Such terms also spread to cover different
sections of the police. In London from the 1950s a cadet became
'a gadget'; in the following decade the black equipment of motor-
cycle officers, together with their reputation for not excusing fellow
members of the force for traffic offences, earned them the soubri-
quet of 'black rats', and the elite Special Patrol Group (SPG) were
'Snatch, Punch and Grab'. The long-standing rivalry between the
uniformed branch and the CID led the former to speak disparag-
ingly of the 'Creeping Insect Department'.

Old sweats – tough, brave, and knowing all the dodges – passed
on their experience, and probably often their attitudes, to recruits.
Personnel registers and personal reminiscences give hints of this
process in action. Harry Owen joined the Worcestershire Constabulary in 1877. In his 26 years' service he received two commendations for courage in stopping runaway horses, but he never rose
above the rank of Constable First Class and he was demoted on six
occasions for a variety of offences ranging from being drunk to
falsifying his journal and going out shooting without a licence.
Towards the end of his police career there were two demotions
which suggested that he was passing on his perception of the job,
and his way of doing it, to recruits. In March 1898 he was disciplined for 'drinking in two public houses when on duty, and taking
a young constable with him'. In December 1900 the offence was
'telling idle and foolish untruths to young constables respecting
petty larcenies and poaching alleged to have been committed by
himself'. William Henry Cooper, who served for 24 years in the
same force and made the rank of sergeant, had a similar record of
commendations and demotions.[81] Early on in his Metropolitan Police

80. Lyscom, 'London policeman', p. 19. Police television series particularly have
popularised several of these terms, but it is worth noting that in the comments on
the shooting script of the film *The Blue Lamp* a member of the British Board of Film
Censors wrote: 'I do not know what a "nick" is, but the context suggests it is a
church': British Film Institute Library, BBFC Scenario Reports, 1948–, 24a.

81. West Mercia PA Worcestershire Constabulary, Register and Record of Police
Service, 1839–77 and 1877–83.

career Ted Lyscom was assisted by an old sweat nicknamed 'Chelsea' when dealing with a domestic disturbance. A young widow had been beaten up by her brother-lodger. 'Chelsea' instructed her to run a cold bath in which he repeatedly totally immersed the offender; he then gave the young man a lecture, and left the house confident that the man would not make a complaint and that he, 'Chelsea', had no need to write a report on the initial disturbance.[82]

Considerable solidarity developed among the men which again both contributed to, and drew strength from, the police culture. Once a case was 'solved' there was reluctance to reopen the investigation if there was the implication that a mistake had been made. When the celebrated burglar Charlie Peace confessed to the murder of a Lancashire policeman, for which William Hebron had been convicted, the Chief Constable and his assistant preferred to stick to the circumstantial evidence collected by Superintendent Bent against Hebron. When it was proved that the bullet from PC Cock's body had been fired from Peace's gun, Hebron was released with £800 compensation, but even then Bent could write in his autobiography about Hebron's 'supposed erroneous conviction'.[83] Policemen stood up for each other and closed ranks to shield individuals from criticism or charges of wrong-doing. Sometimes such behaviour was officially sanctioned as when, in 1913, the Chief Constable of the East Riding authorised members of his force to subscribe to a fund to pay the legal expenses of an inspector who had been accused in a local newspaper of unlawful wounding.[84] In other instances the solidarity had no such sanction and could impede disciplinary investigations: thus in 1904 a Worcestershire constable was reduced in rank for 'conspiring with other Police officers in telling untruths to the Commission of Enquiry in order to defeat the ends of justice, relative to the birching by Supt. Pitt . . . of two youths . . .'.[85] John Monk was 'sent to Coventry' for some weeks after contradicting the false reports of some twenty colleagues, and he also recalled

82. Lyscom, 'London policeman', pp. 87–8.
83. Bob Dobson, *Policing in Lancashire 1839–1989* (Nelson: Landy Publishing, 1989), pp. 35–6; James Bent, *Criminal Life: Reminiscences of Forty-Two Years as a Police Officer* (London, 1891), p. 243.
84. Humberside PA East Riding Constabulary, Memorandum Book 1912–16, fols 67, 71.
85. West Mercia PA Worcestershire Constabulary, Register and Record of Police Service 1877–83. According to the *Justice of the Peace* LXVIII (1904), pp. 510, 521 and 533, Pitt confessed to the chief constable that he ordered some PCs to back his case up. For a less serious example of a constable shielding a comrade on a disciplinary charge, and being admonished for it, see Merseyside PA Birkenhead Police, Disciplinary Report Book 1920–30, fol. 157.

a case in the 1890s when constables conspired to deny that a prisoner had been assaulted in the cells.[86] In December 1908 *The Times* suggested that the days were largely over when police *esprit de corps* led to the men closing ranks in the face of any complaint against one of their number;[87] but it was mistaken. At the beginning of 1922 a London magistrate threw out a charge of insulting behaviour against two men on the grounds 'that it was a charge trumped up by the police in order to protect one of their number from the results of his own impertinence'. Three months later the *Justice of the Peace* was expressing concern about this aspect of police *esprit de corps* and associating it with the perennial bugbear of English policing – 'militarisation'.[88] The PSI study of the Metropolitan Police in the early 1980s found a determination to protect comrades who had done wrong: 'If one of the boys working for me got himself into trouble,' explained a sergeant, 'I would get all of us together and I would literally script him out of it. I would write all the parts out and if we followed them closely we couldn't be defeated.'[89] The Operation Countryman inquiry and the investigations into the West Midlands Regional Crime Squad in the 1970s and 1980s showed this element of police culture in practice, particularly among the detectives who regarded themselves as an elite.

As they began to surround themselves with a professional mystique, so the police began to see themselves as the experts in identifying 'criminals' and keeping track of 'old offenders'. When Henry Smith, a 27-year-old shoemaker of Seven Dials, was sentenced to seven years' penal servitude in October 1866, PC Alexander Hennessy, who had been involved in the case, put a description of Smith in his notebook followed by '66/ 67/ 68/ 69/ 70/ 71/ 72/ 73/ time will expire'.[90] The legislative requirement that the police supervise ticket-of-leave men and 'habitual criminals' in the second half of the nineteenth century increased police consciousness of their expertise in this area, but, in some instances, it also led to victimisation as some policemen pursued their 'property' and made it difficult for men with previous convictions to find steady employment.[91] The scandals of the 1970s and 1980s suggested that a few

86. 'Memoirs of . . . Monk', pp. 18–19, 42.
87. *The Times*, 28 Dec. 1908.
88. *Justice of the Peace* LXXXVI (1922), 7 Jan. p. 4, 18 Mar. p. 127.
89. Smith and Gray, *Police and People in London*, p. 355.
90. Metropolitan PA MS Book 1116.
91. Clive Emsley, *Crime and Society in England 1750–1900*, 2nd edn. (London: Longman, 1996), p. 174. Charged at the Old Bailey towards the end of 1856 with robbery with violence, Charles Hunter, a ticket-of-leave man, protested: 'When I

policemen were 'fitting up' known offenders for crimes which they had not committed because they could not get them for offences which they believed that they had committed. There were times, too, when, in a rather similar way, some policemen saw themselves as the sole experts in understanding and dealing with disorder. They developed the perception of popular disorder as largely the fault of agitators, with the bulk of the participants being either misguided dupes or dangerous riff-raff. The problem of where these ideas could lead, particularly in the case of preparing cases against 'known criminals', prompted the Chief Inspector of Her Majesty's Constabulary to call in 1992 for 'a radical reworking of police culture' and the need for a police code of ethics which would encourage officers not only to seek the truth but always to tell the truth.[92]

But English police culture did not just have a dark side. In addition to the tough masculine attitudes and the determination to keep 'police property' in its place and under tight surveillance, there was also the avuncular, caring, George Dixon image. This was manifested, for example, in the letter quoted above which Hector Macleod received from his father on joining the Northamptonshire Police. The traditional image of the English Bobby may have been an indulgent middle-class myth, but myths are often rooted in fact. It was this image which was stressed by the police newspapers, particularly the *Police Review*, at the end of the nineteenth and beginning of the twentieth centuries. It is an image which is to be found in several police memoirs.[93] The difficulty lies in measuring the extent to which the absorption of this image into English police culture affected police behaviour. Good behaviour and civility has

came home from transportation, I obtained a situation at a beer house in the Waterloo-road, where I was getting a comfortable living, and supporting my wife and aged mother; I had been there a few weeks when sergeant Broad came and told the landlord that I was a ticket-of-leave man, and if he allowed such characters in his house he should indict it; he told me to go; after that I drove a costermonger barrow and he followed me about the streets, telling my customers to see that their change was good, for I was a ticket-of-leave man; I was compelled to give that up; I went to live with my parents, and worked at tailoring, and every time I came in or out of the court where I lived, he would stop and search me, if any of the neighbours or their children were about; so that at last I could get nobody to trust me with anything; what had I to do? I would work if they would let me, but they will not': Central Criminal Court Sessions Papers 1856–57, No. 87, pp. 102–3. Of course Hunter may have been angling for a lighter sentence (he was transported for life), but his story at least illustrates the potential power of the police.

92. Sir John Woodcock, 'Why we need a revolution', *Police Review*, 16 Oct. 1992, pp. 1929–32.

93. See, *inter alia*, William Chadwick, *Reminiscences of a Chief Constable* (Manchester: John Heywood, 1901), pp. 147–9; Daley, *This Small Cloud*, esp. pp. 81–3.

never made particularly good copy for the press, while the constant reiteration that the English Bobby was different and 'better', which did appear in the press as well as in parliamentary speeches, has to be viewed with scepticism like any other historical evidence. Yet the constant stress on his differences from other European and North American policemen, and the insistence that he was more approachable, less aggressive, non-military and non-political, probably did encourage a large number of men to behave in precisely such a fashion and to pass on this ideal, as well as other, less savoury, aspects of police culture, to new recruits.

CHAPTER TEN

The Policeman as a Worker

The experience of work

Crime fighting and crime control, the most eye-catching and exciting of the policeman's tasks, have only ever occupied a small percentage of police time. Much of the policeman's experience of work has always been routine and often humdrum, yet his tasks and duties have always been complex and manifold and they have grown significantly since 1829. A study of police manpower conducted during the 1960s estimated that the bulk of police time was still taken up by the routine patrolling of a beat; of the remainder, criminal investigation, traffic and court work accounted for about 30 per cent, 23 per cent and 10 per cent respectively.[1]

Beats varied enormously. The most obvious difference was that between the beats of paved, urban streets and those of the countryside which were often much bigger and could rarely be covered in a single tour of duty. There were also tremendous contrasts between beats in different areas, both rural and urban. During his 25 years in the Metropolitan Police, Harry Daley served in three divisions at three very different police stations: first in West London at the station in the busy Hammersmith Broadway; from there he moved to Vine Street in London's theatreland and was responsible also for the colourful and cosmopolitan district of Soho; finally he was posted to Wandsworth Police Station which covered an area

> vast and varied, ranging from the riverside between Wandsworth and Putney Bridges to as far inland as Wimbledon Parkside. This took in the old-fashioned Cockney districts, sprinkled with slums, of York Road and Garratt Lane, and the big Victorian houses starting at West

1. J.P. Martin and Gail Wilson, *The Police: A Study in Manpower* (London: Heinemann, 1969).

Hill and growing increasingly imposing until one reached the great mansions lining Putney Heath and Wimbledon Common.[2]

Experience could be equally varied in the force of a predominantly rural county. Arthur Pickering began his service in the Bedfordshire Police in 1932 with a posting to the town of Dunstable; from here he was moved to Pulloxhill, a small village just outside Luton marked every weekday morning by an exodus, and every evening by a return of people from their Luton work-places. After war service Pickering was posted to a village in the Bedfordshire brickfields where virtually everyone in employment was an employee of the London Brick Company. His final posting was to Turvey, in some ways the traditional, picturesque English rural village, complete with squire.[3]

Beats were carefully planned and measured. In the Metropolitan Police district in the second half of the nineteenth century the average day beat was seven and a half miles, the average night beat was two miles. These had to be walked at a steady rate of two and a half miles an hour. During the day the constable patrolled on the kerbside of the pavement, at night he walked on the inner side from where he could more easily check bolts and fastenings – 'milking locks' or 'shaking hands with doorknobs' as it was known in different forces.[4] On the much bigger country beats a rural constable's patrols were often varied from day to day to ensure that he visited his entire district at least once or twice a week; but these were also strictly regulated and timed.[5] Much patrolling was done by night. In the built-up areas of the Metropolitan Police district during the 1880s 40 per cent of the available men did split duty of four hours on and four hours off over the sixteen hours from 6 a.m. to 10 p.m.; the remaining 60 per cent of the men patrolled the night beats from 10 p.m. to 6 a.m. This meant that a man did one month of day duty followed by two months on nights.[6] The system continued on a similar pattern into the twentieth century.

2. Harry Daley, *This Small Cloud: A Personal Memoir* (London: Weidenfeld & Nicolson, 1986), p. 183.
3. Taped interview with ex-PC Arthur Pickering, Feb. 1987.
4. Mike Brodgen, *On the Mersey Beat: Policing Liverpool Between the Wars* (Oxford: OUP, 1991), pp. 40–1; taped interview with ex-PS Nat Taylor, Dec. 1987.
5. In Devon it appears that the men were expected to walk at three miles an hour, rather faster than in London: Devon and Cornwall PA Devon Constabulary, M Division, Order Book 1865–1910, 28 Aug. 1880.
6. 'The police of London', *Quarterly Review* CXXIX (1870), 87–129, at 100–1; 'The Metropolitan Police system', *Westminster Review* XLV (1874), 31–56, at 33; Charles Tempest Clarkson and J. Hall Richardson, *Police!* (London, 1889), pp. 86–7.

Harry Daley found night duty 'a pleasure'. As a raw recruit, Ted Lyscom was told by veterans that night duty was 'very relaxing . . . quiet and peaceful, all the people had gone to bed and the traffic was off the streets'. Lyscom took them at their word, failed to take a sensible rest before his first night duty, and fell asleep for 25 minutes when he sat down to rest on the station toilet during the early hours of the morning.[7] After that he was more careful, and got used to night work, but many others found it difficult if only because the time could drag so slowly. William Chadwick left the Metropolitan Police after about two years in the 1850s because he disliked the monotony of night duty. After two months' service with the Worcestershire Constabulary in 1880 John Bateman was caught drinking in a pub when he should have been on night duty, 'his excuse being that he went there to smoke a pipe of tobacco, that it was too hard to walk about all night'. Two years later John Partridge resigned from the same force after only six weeks, protesting that 'the night air did not agree with him'; and Edwin Lowe lasted only six days in October 1888 'as he said he found the night duty did not suit him'.[8] Timothy Cavanagh, looking back on his first night beat from Stone's End Police Station in the Borough, wrote: 'No-one, not having gone through the ordeal, can possibly imagine the dreary work it is tramping about for eight hours in such a filthy neighbourhood.' James Bent recalled his nervousness at the beginning of his night patrols for the Lancashire Constabulary, made worse by his 'reading cheap trashy literature' about ghosts and hobgoblins. A century later, looking back on his night-time beats in the North Riding, Nicholas Rhea could state that constables had to conquer two fears: 'the fear of the dark and . . . a fear of ghosts. There are constables who are subjected to one or both of these terrors, and for them a night patrol is a continuing test of courage and devotion to duty.' In 1903, following an enquiry about watchmen for a Birmingham factory, the Chief Constable of Staffordshire doubted whether any of his pensioners would want the job, 'having already had so many years' of night work.[9]

7. Daley, *This Small Cloud*, p. 141; Metropolitan PA MS Book 159.88, Edward Lyscom, 'London policeman', pp. 24–5.

8. William Chadwick, *Reminiscences of a Chief Constable* (Manchester: John Heywood, 1900), p. 10; West Mercia PA Worcestershire Constabulary, Register and Record of Service 1877–83 nos. 72 and 147, and 1888–93 no. 25.

9. Timothy Cavanagh, *Scotland Yard Past and Present: Experiences of Thirty-seven Years* (London, 1893), p. 28; Nicholas Rhea, *Constable on the Prowl* (London: Robert Hale, 1980), p. 40; Staffs. PA Staffordshire Constabulary, Chief Constable's Letter Book 1900–08, fols 405–6. See also Brogden, *On the Mersey Beat*, p. 44.

At night on rural beats constables sometimes patrolled with their dogs for company. In April 1896 the Chief Constable of East Sussex ordered his men that, while they might keep dogs, they were not to take them on duty, but the practice continued to be followed in other areas.[10] Arthur Battle vividly recalled the night duty men parading at Cheshunt on the Hertfordshire border of the Metropolitan Police district during the early 1930s:

> There were only about six men on parade, but each man had his dog with him, sitting quietly under the parade room seat. Alsatians, Airedales and Labradors seemed to be favourites. Each man wore the skirts of his greatcoat pinned away from his knees, like the old style French infantryman, and all carried heavy ash sticks. These men were all older types, with heavy moustaches, and they looked very impressive as they walked away from the station, with their dogs trotting easily behind, or walking close to heel.

The practice of rural constables patrolling with their own dogs continued at least into the 1950s.[11]

The beat journals of James Jackson, who served in the Hertfordshire Constabulary from 1865 to 1877, are illustrative of the lack of incident and excitement which was the lot of many Victorian rural policemen.[12] For most of his eleven and a half years' service Jackson was stationed alone in the village of Hadham, close to the Essex border. Crime was a rare occurrence here. On three occasions Jackson had to make inquiries about burglaries in the district, but most of the thefts on his particular beat were very petty, often involving food. On several occasions he reported spending time in watching vegetable fields, nut trees and fruit orchards after dark; occasionally such surveillance paid off, as did his watching of coal at the local railway station which led to the arrest and conviction of a railway porter for the theft of 50 lb of coal. Throughout his entire service Jackson recorded the apprehension of 26 persons for theft; he served summonses on another fifteen to attend court in

10. East Sussex RO SPA 2/2/3, East Sussex Constabulary, Chief Constable's Memo Book, 1894–99, fol. 110; Clive Emsley (ed.), 'The recollections of a provincial policeman: Arthur Ernest Almond', *Journal of the Police History Society* 3 (1988), 53–66, note 6 at 45.

11. Metropolitan PA MS 175.88, Arthur Battle, 'This job's not what it used to be', p. 30; Bob Edmondson, *Bob's Beat: The Story of a Lancashire Policeman* (Manchester: Neil Richardson, 1985), pp. 56–7; John Wainwright, *Wainwright's Beat: One Man's Journey with a Police Force* (London: Macmillan, 1987), p. 30.

12. My thanks to Robert C. Webb for letting me borrow and cite these journals, written by his great-grandfather.

connection with thefts. He apprehended four persons for poaching; and served two separate summonses on another individual for poaching offences. There were occasional violent incidents on Jackson's 'patch': the most serious was a stabbing, but no action appears to have followed and the perpetrator was subsequently killed in a railway accident. Jackson reported being assaulted only once himself, his assailant being drunk at the time. The inspection of pubs, and ensuring that they kept their proper licensing hours, was a regular duty; and most of the summonses which Jackson served involved the general orderliness and regulation of society – drunkenness, non-payment of rates, nuisances, riding in carts and waggons without reins, false weights and measures, selling substandard food, deserting an employer or a wife and children. But over the whole period of his service Jackson rarely served more than twelve summonses a year.

The beat journals surviving for the village of Feltwell in southwest Norfolk during the inter-war years give a similar picture of a largely uneventful life, broken periodically by a petty theft, a fire, an individual riding a bike at night without a light, an outbreak of animal disease, or the need to count a farmer's sheep through the sheep dip.[13] From his reports of cautioning youths it would appear that Louis Edwards, who replaced Samuel Tink as the Feltwell village Bobby towards the end of 1921, was rather less tolerant of youthful high spirits than his predecessor; while for George Cordy, a decade later, the principal potential threat to public order appears to have been the dances at the YMCA hut. The overall impression is that an arrest or a summons, the occasional investigation, a fair or a fire to police, relieved the monotony of routine patrolling.

Given his isolation from his colleagues, the rural policeman was much more likely than his urban counterpart to absorb the perceptions and values of those whom he policed. Furthermore, while the village policeman may have felt it necessary to maintain some social distance from local people so as to avoid embarrassment when called upon to make an arrest, prefer a charge, or issue a summons, the relationship between policeman and people in the countryside was much more interdependent than that in urban areas.[14]

Beats in industrial districts, or in the centre of cities or towns, were more lively given the greater numbers of people and, even

13. Norfolk PA Feltwell Beat 1920–22 and 1931–33.
14. Maureen E. Cain, *Society and the Policeman's Role* (London: Routledge and Kegan Paul, 1973), ch. 4.

before the development of the motor car, the greater volume of traffic. By the mid-1890s the Manchester Watch Committee could receive a complaint that 'the Policemen on foot duty do not care at all for foot passengers as they simply devote their attention to the vehicles and leave the public to cross [the road] as best they can'.[15] Alexander Hennessy patrolled parts of central London in the third quarter of the nineteenth century; his beats included the busy thoroughfares of Oxford Street and Tottenham Court Road. Unlike the beat books of village constables, Hennessy's notebook, covering 1857 to 1880, does not record his daily duties but is largely a list of offenders and the offences for which he apprehended or summonsed them. In all the book identifies 107 offenders: a quarter of these had committed theft, generally of a very petty nature; another quarter were drunk and disorderly; a fifth were drunk in charge of a vehicle, and a further fifth were cab or bus drivers loitering and plying for hire. PC Robert Stephens patrolled a similar district to Hennessy between 1891 and 1895. His notebook is more detailed as far as charges go, and he brought many more – 365 in total. Half of these involved cab drivers loitering or plying for hire, almost a quarter involved other vehicular offences; disorderly behaviour, generally involving drunkenness, begging, and soliciting accounted respectively for another 16 per cent, 12 per cent and 8 per cent. The shorter record left by PC Butler for his time at Cannon Row Police Station, Whitehall, from December 1914 to December 1915 and from August 1919 to July 1922, gives a similar picture of the busy life of central London, but now with the added complication of motor vehicles.[16]

Traffic congestion and the potential danger from fast motor vehicles meant that for urban policemen from the late nineteenth century until after the Second World War, the experience of regular beat patrolling was coupled with the experience of regular, static periods on point duty. Standing in the middle of a busy road junction and directing traffic with clear arm and hand signals for several hours gave no opportunity for relaxation. It could be frightening and dangerous. Charles Hanslow remembered the danger of standing in Bond Street: 'we had to watch out very carefully when a bus came along, because, owing to the narrowness of the roadway the wheels came unpleasantly close'. His police overcoat was damaged while he was directing the heavy traffic around Piccadilly Circus;

15. Greater Manchester PA Watch Committee Papers 1895 onwards, vol. 2, fol. 128; see also vol. 3, fol. 197.
16. Metropolitan PA MS Books 1116, 676 and 572.

he had to pay for the repair himself.[17] Arthur Battle recalled the
boredom and the physically tiring nature of such duty:

> for sheer boredom and soul destroying monotony traffic control was
> the worst affliction ever imposed on man. This was especially so in
> winter time, when performing duty from 4 p.m. till midnight. One
> wore the long and enormously heavy greatcoat of the times [1929],
> plus leather belt and heavy Wooton lamp, the whole lot surmounted,
> if it was raining, by a voluminous oilskin traffic coat and leggings.
> There one stood with arms aching enough to drop out of their
> sockets for hour after hour, not daring to relax for a moment.
>
> One was fortunate if the P.C. on the beat was of a charitable
> disposition, as he would come along once or twice during one's tour
> of duty and relieve one for a few minutes breather. Many a penny
> have I spent to go into a public lavatory to sit down for five minutes,
> to smoke a cigarette and try to ease the kinks out of one's spine and
> arms before hurrying back to the point before one's absence was
> noted by a patrolling sergeant or inspector. Point duty came round
> about four times a year. Some periods were for four weeks, some
> five, according to the number of days in the month, and I have never
> met a man who enjoyed it. I am sure if a testimonial fund was started
> for the man who invented traffic lights Police would head the list of
> subscribers.[18]

As Battle's recollections explain, point duty and beat patrols had
to be carried out in all seasons and in all weathers, with only very
rare exceptions; and men found themselves having to go on duty
with clothes still wet from the previous day.[19] The rigours of the job
had a deleterious effect on the health of many men. In a report
prepared for the Home Secretary in 1862 Dr William Farr concluded that of the Metropolitan policemen pensioned between 1840
and 1860 over a quarter had respiratory or rheumatic complaints;
another tenth were suffering from injuries received while on duty.[20]

17. Metropolitan PA MS Book 105.87, 'Anecdotes: memories of Charles Hanslow',
p. 15.
18. Battle, 'This job's not what it used to be', p. 18; Edward Lyscom also described
the physical pain of long periods of point duty: 'London policeman', p. 41; and one
of Brogden's interviewees remembered 'arms and legs like lead': Brogden, *On the
Mersey Beat*, p. 44.
19. In the particularly severe December of 1860 the Chief Constable of Huntingdonshire allowed his men to dispense with their usual conference points because of
the snow and because he considered 'patrolling singly ... fraught with danger to
individual officers': Cambs. PA Huntingdonshire Constabulary, Chief Constable's
Memos, 1857–99, No. 20. For patrolling in wet clothes see Brogden, *On the Mersey
Beat*, pp. 45, 58.
20. UCL Chadwick MSS 16, Folder: POLICE Memoranda etc (1855–69), Printed
report to the Secretary of State ... by William Farr MD, FRS (April 1862).

Evidence and opinion offered to the committees looking into police superannuation later in the century were conflicting as to whether agricultural labourers and coalminers had harder jobs than policemen; but there was agreement among the witnesses that patrolling in all weathers could seriously affect a constable's health, and that the dangers of assault were high.[21] The statistics presented to the 1908 Royal Commission on the Duties of the Metropolitan Police by the force's chief surgeon presented a similar picture: in the half-year January to June 1906, 2,256 men were on the sick list with 'diseases of exposure' – rheumatism, catarrh, bronchitis and tonsilitis; in the second half of the year the number was 1,991. Between 1903 and 1906, on average some 2,500 men were injured as the result of some kind of assault made on them in the execution of their duty.[22]

It is not possible to draw up a balance sheet of the comparative dangers, but it is probably true to say that the beats in the poorer parts of towns and cities, and in industrial districts, were more dangerous for policemen than those in rural areas. Rowan and Mayne reported that from 1 January to 16 October 1847 the Metropolitan Police had lost 1,475 man-days because of the injuries inflicted on constables during assaults; over the same period 835 persons had been charged with assaulting police officers, of whom 764 had been convicted.[23] At the end of the century the figures suggest that each year about one in four London policemen were the victims of assault.[24] Whitechapel in particular was notorious for the way in which its inhabitants 'considered that they had a natural right to get fighting drunk and knock a policeman about whenever the spirit moved them'.[25] In industrial Lancashire there were similar problems. Thomas Smethurst remembered that in the roughest part of Bolton towards the end of the century 'we used to work in couples, one on the main street, the other dodging in and out of

21. *PP* 1875 (352) XIII, *Select Committee on Police Superannuation Funds*, q. 2572; *PP* 1890 (c. 6075) LIX, *Departmental Committee on Metropolitan Police Superannuation*, qq. 362–3, 384, 780, 923–6, 1412, 1860. See also Clarkson and Richardson, *Police!*, p. 366.

22. *Royal Commission on the Duties of the Metropolitan Police*, vol. I 1908, *Report*, Cmd. 4156, pp. 58–61.

23. HO 45.1889.

24. Geoffrey Pearson, *Hooligan: A History of Respectable Fears* (London: Macmillan, 1983), p. 88.

25. Frederick Porter Wensley, *Detective Days: The Record of Forty-Two Years' Service in the Criminal Investigation Department* (London: Cassell, 1931), p. 8; see also Ex-Det. Sergeant B. Leeson, *Lost London: The Memoirs of an East End Detective* (London: Stanley Paul, 1934), pp. 22, 30–2, 40.

the side streets, but always within call of the whistle'. While investigating an assault on a constable at a steel works in Newton Heath, James Bent was savagely beaten and burned with red-hot irons. When Richard Jervis was warned that a group of men whom he had prosecuted for bowling stones along the highway in Colne were intending to ambush him, he took no chances: he crept up on them from behind and set about them with his 'logwood', beating one so severely that his arm was broken.[26] Some rural districts could also be rough. G.H. Totterdell recalled his father patrolling his country beats in Essex armed with stout, heavy walking sticks; sometimes the sticks were brought home broken. Most of the men of Great Wakering worked in local brickfields, and the village was a particularly rough beat for members of the Essex force in the early twentieth century. Sergeant Totterdell brought it under temporary control after a savage night-time battle, and the breaking of yet another stick.[27]

Police reminiscences of the first half of the twentieth century, as well as police statistics,[28] do not imply the same degree of violence directed against them as against their predecessors. But Saturday night fights involving the police were not unknown, and districts dangerous for them continued to exist. There were streets of Liverpool between the wars notorious for 'bobby-beating'.[29] At the Thames Police Court in the summer of 1927 a magistrate lamented:

> Some people go in for parson-baiting and others go in for baiting the police. It is a form of big-game hunting. I hold no brief for the police, but it is dirty and cowardly for a gang to set upon one or two men. It is not English or decent. The people in this district must be taught to find some other amusement other than knocking the police about – there are always the pictures.[30]

Campbell Bunk in Islington was also popularly known as 'Kill Copper Row', and Metropolitan constables do not appear to have relished patrolling there at night during the inter-war years.[31] Even after the

26. Thomas Smethurst, *Reminiscences of a Bolton and Stalybridge Policeman 1888–1922* (Manchester: Neil Richardson, 1983), p. 11; James Bent, *Criminal Life: Reminiscences of Forty-Two Years as a Police Officer* (London, 1891), pp. 75–80; Richard Jervis, *Lancashire's Crime and Criminals* (Southport: 1908), pp. 18–19.

27. G.H. Totterdell, *Country Copper* (London: Harrap, 1956), pp. 12, 20–1, 30.

28. V.A.C. Gatrell, 'Crime authority and the policeman state', in F.M.L. Thompson (ed.), *The Cambridge Social History of Britain 1750–1950* (Cambridge: CUP, 1990), iii, pp. 286–7.

29. Brogden, *On the Mersey Beat*, p. 107.

30. *Justice of the Peace* XCI (1927), 25 June p. 489; for similar assaults and comments see ibid., 23 Apr. p. 308, and 15 Oct. p. 776.

31. Jerry White, *The Worst Street in North London: Campbell Bunk, Islington, Between the Wars* (London: Routledge and Kegan Paul, 1986), pp. 114–21.

Second World War, and before the sensational media reports of violence in the new Black communities, there continued to be rough districts in towns and industrial areas where, even if a policeman was not necessarily in physical danger, his life could be a misery. Having crossed a senior officer John Wainwright, a constable in the West Riding force, was posted to one such beat in a mining district:

It was a 'punishment beat' and, regardless of any disclaimer made by officialdom, they do exist. They are recognised and earmarked as beats with which to tame stroppy coppers . . .

Like any copper who knows his job the first thing I did when we'd settled into our new house was to check on the convictions of those whom I was there to police. I ran a finger down the names on the Voter's Register and pulled the appropriate yellow cards – the Previous Conviction Cards – from the file. I had a full house! You name it, and short of murder, some bastard at Toll Bar had committed it. The emphasis was on violence, with theft running a close second and, more often than not, going hand-in-hand.[32]

Whatever the beat, there was always the bureaucracy. Journals and notebooks had to be kept up to date. Reports of incidents had to be written; at least until the Second World War they began with the formal and respectful 'I beg leave to report . . .'. Different forms had to be completed, or different registers filled in for different occurrences or different requirements; and constables and sergeants had to be aware of which forms and which register to complete as errors and lapses could lead to disciplinary action. Nor was it only the lower ranks of the police who had to participate in a bureaucratic paper chase. As described above, as early as October 1863 the Chief Constable of Bedfordshire declared his reluctance to have his senior officers burdened with yet more paperwork.[33] Some 40 years later the Chief Constable of Staffordshire made a similar complaint to the Home Office when it requested that offences against the intoxicating liquor laws be submitted annually in a new format when his men had already completed quarterly returns in the old way.[34] It was not until after the Second World War that there was any concerted effort to bring civilian clerical staff into police stations to release policemen from some of the burdens of paperwork.[35]

32. Wainwright, *Wainwright's Beat*, pp. 174–5.
33. See above, p. 88.
34. Staffs. PA Staffordshire Constabulary, Chief Constable's Letter Book 1900–08, fol. 665.
35. T.A. Critchley, *A History of Police in England and Wales*, rev. edn (London: Constable, 1978), p. 255.

The other great shared experience of policemen was appearing in court. Here the constable was expected to stand to attention, speak clearly and, given the way that his evidence might be questioned, carefully. In July 1913, for example, Major Dunlop warned the members of his force that in cases of 'Driving recklessly etc . . . on no account are they to state the speed as "So many miles per hour" but they are to say that "The motorist was travelling at a dangerous speed and much faster than a horse could trot or gallop" as the case may be'.[36]

It was, perhaps, the ceremony of the courts which prompted the relatively unlettered nineteenth- and early twentieth-century constable to give his evidence in pompous language which would well have suited Dogberry, and which prompted critical comment from contemporary legal journals. In 1917 the *Justice of the Peace* expressed its irritation with the officer who

> never walks or runs, he always 'proceeds'; he never asks, he always 'requests'; he never finds people quarrelling, they are always 'having an altercation'; for a stable to be behind a house near a church is too simple; it has to be 'situated at the rear of a house in the vicinity of a church'; he never watches, he always 'keeps observation' or 'keeps observation in conjunction with another officer'; if he charges a man with what in our days is considered the indecency of making water in the street, he must describe the action as 'urinating'; he prefers not to speak of a scratch or a bruise, it must be an 'abrasion' or a 'contusion'. The ridiculous state of things sometimes occurs that the court has to translate his pompous phraseology into more homely language which the ignorant can understand. Another disadvantage attached to this special dialect is that when several officers give evidence of the same facts their testimony sounds stereotyped, and this lays them open, often unjustly, to the suspicion of having compared notes.

A little over a decade later the *Solicitors Journal* was making similar complaints at similar length. Both journals included the story of the constable who declared 'that he saw a man and a woman having "intellectual course" together, meaning "sexual intercourse"'.[37] Similar criticism of the use of 'grandiloquent language' and a call for 'clear and concise English' from the constable was also to be found in the *Police Review*, and as late as the 1950s.[38]

36. Humberside PA East Riding Constabulary, Memorandum Book 1912–16, fol. 61.

37. *Justice of the Peace* LXXXI (1917), 10 Feb. p. 64; *Solicitors Journal* LXXVI (1932), 5 Nov. pp. 767–8; see also ibid., LXXIV (1930), 11 Oct. p. 665.

38. *Police Review*, 27 June 1924 p. 348; ibid., 8 Feb. 1952 p. 105, and 22 Feb. pp. 134–5.

For a few senior and experienced police officers, appearance in a magistrates' court could involve much more than giving evidence. Increasingly during the nineteenth century the police replaced the victim as the prosecutor of an offender;[39] in the lower courts this often meant that the prosecution was conducted by a senior police officer. Jealous on the part of their profession, many Victorian lawyers objected and the *Justice of the Peace* was sympathetic to their complaints against those it labelled as 'these amateur advocates'. The objections appear to have quietened after the ruling in the case of *Webb* v. *Catchlove* in December 1886 which decided largely in favour of the legal profession.[40] But in spite of this ruling senior police officers continued to act as prosecutors and the matter was raised again, notably in December 1907 when J.W. Wall, appearing for the defendant in a larceny case at Bootle Magistrates' Court, protested at the Chief Constable's appearance as prosecutor. 'I, as a solicitor, a practising solicitor, and one admitted to the rolls, have to object to any layman prosecuting ... This is a matter that is rising throughout the country; it is no personal matter, it is a matter of principle.'[41] In later years the arguments made tended to be less simply a defence of the interest of the legal profession; rather it was stressed that if the police acted as prosecutors it implied too close a link between the police and the courts, and that police officers could be at a serious disadvantage when confronting trained solicitors or barristers acting for the defence.[42] However, the practice of using prosecuting officers, some of whom were no further up the police hierarchy than the rank of sergeant, continued until the creation of the Crown Prosecution Service in 1986.

Controlling the constable

Whatever the protests of politicians and senior police officers, policemen belonged to an hierarchical institution which was akin

39. Clive Emsley, *Crime and Society in England 1750–1900*, 2nd edn (London: Longman, 1996), pp. 190–3.

40. *Justice of the Peace* XLV (1881), 10 Sept. p. 607; ibid., XLVIII (1884), 9 Feb. p. 94 and 23 Feb. p. 122; ibid., C (1886), 10 Apr. pp. 227–8 and 11 Dec. pp. 295–6.

41. Ibid., LXXI (1907), 21 Dec. pp. 604–5; see also ibid., LXXII (1908), 11 Jan. pp. 16–18, 15 Feb. pp. 75–6, and 24 Apr. p. 196. For another query after the *Webb* v. *Catchlove* ruling see ibid., LIV (1890), 26 Apr. p. 264.

42. Ibid., CI (1937), 6 Nov. p. 720 and 20 Nov. p. 742; ibid., CIX (1945), 27 Oct. pp. 510–11; ibid., CXIX (1955), 26 Mar. pp. 195–6; ibid., CXXXIV (1970), pp. 413–14. John Wainwright recalled a tough and wily chief inspector who, by his theatrical behaviour when appearing as a prosecutor, appears to have been more than a match for any defence solicitor: *Wainwright's Beat*, pp. 40–1.

to the military. The major difference between the police constable and the soldier was that the former was generally expected to act on his own: he patrolled his beat alone, he stood on point duty alone, and he had to act on his own discretion. The point was stressed by 'Custos' in his survey of the Metropolitan Police in 1868, but he also noted that the soldier and the police constable were both 'drawn from the same class, the one not infrequently relinquishing his truncheon that he may be free to enlist, and the other constantly seeking and obtaining admission to the Police after he has completed his limited term of military service'.[43] The problem for senior officers was how to establish and enforce what they considered to be the necessary discipline over their men, particularly to ensure that they carried out their allotted tasks.

The supervision of detective policemen, working in plain clothes, was always a problem. Arguably one reason for the relatively limited development of the detective department of the Metropolitan Police during the early years of the force was the concern that these men, because of the nature of their work, could be so little observed and controlled. The scandal which led to the reorganisation under Howard Vincent underlined such fears; half a century later the Royal Commission on Police Powers and Procedure commented that policemen employed in plain clothes were exposed 'to greater temptations than when they are in uniform'.[44] In most forces the CID came to regard itself as an elite, superior to the uniformed branch; it prided itself on its special expertise, and the lack of set beats and hours. By the early 1970s the Metropolitan Police CID had become something of a law unto itself, when the Commissioner, Sir Robert Mark, brought it under stricter control of the uniformed hierarchy and established a greater measure of personnel interchange between the uniform and CID branches.[45]

Most policemen did not, of course, have the freedom of the detectives: they wore uniforms, and even if they generally acted on their own, there were attempts to maintain a rigorous supervision. In towns throughout the nineteenth, and for much of the twentieth, centuries police sergeants and, less regularly, inspectors patrolled

43. 'Custos', *The Police Force of the Metropolis* (London, 1868), p. 16.

44. *Report of the Royal Commission on Police Powers and Procedure*, Cmd. 3297 (London: HMSO, 1929), p. 40.

45. For a fascinating study of the culture of London detectives, much of it similar to that of those whom they policed, and the reforms of Sir Robert Mark, see Dick Hobbs, *Doing the Business: Entrepreneurship, the Working Class, and Detectives in the East End of London* (Oxford: OUP, 1989).

the beats to ensure that the constables were on their allotted routes and keeping to their timed schedules. The police box enabled a new form of supervision, with men required to ring in to their stations at fixed times; something which, arguably, limited the constable's capacity for crime prevention since he had to be constantly on the move so as not to be late at his next box.[46] In rural districts, of necessity, the system was rather different. Here sergeants and inspectors still made their rounds, but the constable was also expected to meet at fixed times at conference points with the constable on a neighbouring beat. All conference point meetings, together with all meetings with a superior officer, were to be recorded in the rural constable's beat journal and this provided an additional way for senior officers to check that a man was doing his job. Police orders made constant reference to the need for journals to be neatly filled in and up to date, and senior officers were instructed to make regular inspections of the journals. In March 1888, for example, the Chief Constable of Huntingdonshire was instructing his superintendents to examine their men's journals '*at least* twice a month and initial in column of remarks in *Red Ink*'.[47]

If a constable was late for duty, or missing from his beat or a conference point, if he was lax or sloppy in completing his journal, if he failed to notice an unbarred door or a break-in, and had no satisfactory excuse, then he was reprimanded and/or punished. Punishment took a variety of forms and its severity appears to have depended largely on a man's previous record and character. In the Borough of Ipswich, for example, in the mid-1840s, absence from the beat for a long period was punished in very different ways: John Holmes was dismissed, but George Grimsey was only reprimanded for his first offence and fined 5 shillings for the second.[48] The matters brought into consideration were spelled out clearly in the disciplinary reports for the Birkenhead Police during the 1920s. In the case of a PC drunk and absent from his beat in December 1922 the Chief Constable noted taking into consideration 'this offence together with his general character' and dismissed the man. But in a disciplinary hearing brought the following April against a constable who had failed to make the appropriate inquiries in a motor-car

46. Barbara Weinberger, *The Best Police in the World: An Oral History of English Policing from the 1930s to the 1960s* (Aldershot: Scolar Press, 1995), pp. 35–7.
47. Cambs. PA Huntingdonshire Constabulary, Chief Constable's Circulars, 1888–1907, No. 87.
48. Suffolk RO DF 2/1, Ipswich Borough Police (Personnel) Register.

accident, the Chief Constable only issued a severe caution: 'I do this in consideration of [his] previous clean record.'[49]

Dismissal was, of course, the most severe form of punishment. There were several gradations of sanction which could be employed before this, the mildest being a caution or reprimand. A more serious offence, or succession of offences, could lead to a fine or a reduction in rank. On some occasions a man might be moved to a different district with the requirement that he pay the costs of the removal himself. Thus in December 1912 two Lancashire constables were transferred from the Manchester Division to the Bolton and Lonsdale Divisions respectively: the first for 'conduct likely to bring discredit upon the force by being over familiar with a single woman . . . and thereby causing a scandal in the neighbourhood'; the second for 'gossiping with a vindictive spirit, bringing discredit upon the force'.[50] The severity of punishments appears to have declined, particularly in the early twentieth century. In Birkenhead, for example, during the 1920s the most common result of a disciplinary hearing for a man being late for parade was a reprimand, sometimes with the requirement that the time lost be made up in some fashion.[51] But at the same time the evidence from the Order Books of the Manchester Police suggests that there was a general decline in the inter-war period of the number of defaulters charged with lateness on parade or missing unsecured doors, gates and windows while on their beats; this may, of course, have been the result of the recruitment of better, more dependable, men during the Depression.

Beginning in the early twentieth century, in many parts of the country, there was a slight relaxation in the rigidity of the beat system. As early as September 1902 the Chief Constable of Huntingdonshire was of the opinion

> that instead of keeping to the hard and fast hours for duty hitherto detailed, more good might be done by some of the force being from time to time detailed for early duty for a few hours in the morning at which time he considers many offences such as poaching and fowl and egg stealing etc. might be detected.

49. Merseyside PA Birkenhead Police, Disciplinary Report Book, 1920–30, fols 121, 131.

50. Greater Manchester PA Manchester Division, Misconduct Book, 1912–35, fols 4, 5. For similar examples see Cambs. PA Huntingdonshire Constabulary, Chief Constable's Circulars, 1888–1907, Nos. 113, 124, 199, and Humberside PA East Riding Constabulary, General Orders 1905–10, fol. 113, and see also fols 157, 168.

51. Merseyside PA Birkenhead Police, Disciplinary Report Book, 1920–30, passim.

Superintendents and inspectors were directed to take the necessary action.[52] During the early 1930s one of the Inspectors of Constabulary, Lieutenant-Colonel W.D. Allan, was urging such a relaxation in the belief that if the police constable had more discretion in the way he worked his beat, then more offenders would be apprehended. He insisted that the experience of those forces which followed this policy proved the point.[53]

In May 1888 George Biggs, a constable in the Worcestershire Constabulary, was reprimanded and reduced in rank from first to second class for 'falsifying his Duty Journal and making untruthful statements to cover the small fault of having overslept himself, which he should have acknowledged at once, instead of telling lies'. But the unfortunate Biggs had a drink problem and a string of other offences followed over the summer. The Chief Constable tried to get him to take the temperance pledge but at the end of September found no other alternative but dismissal.[54] As early as 1834 Rowan and Mayne highlighted the problem of drink among the police to a parliamentary select committee; they estimated that four out of the five men they had dismissed were dismissed for drink-related offences.[55] Across the country men disappeared from their beats and into pubs; some missed parades, insulted members of the public and/or abused their officers whilst under the influence of drink. The incidence of such offences gradually declined, but drink remained the most serious threat to discipline until well into the twentieth century and the Disciplinary Report Book of the Birkenhead Police for the 1920s still shows the Chief Constable endeavouring to get men to take the pledge and stick to it.[56]

As in any rigorously disciplined institution, men sought ways of making life easier and more satisfying for themselves and of successfully avoiding supervision. Some men simply had a quick drink

52. Cambs. PA Huntingdonshire Constabulary, Chief Constable's Circulars 1888–1907, No. 153.

53. *Report of H.M. Inspectors of Constabulary for 1932*, p. 11; *Report . . . for 1933*, p. 9; *Report . . . for 1934*, p. 11.

54. West Mercia PA Worcestershire Constabulary Register and Record of Service 1877–83, no. 155.

55. *PP* 1834 (600) XVI, *Select Committee on the Police of the Metropolis*, qq. 107–8.

56. Merseyside PA Birkenhead Police, Disciplinary Report Book, 1920–30, fols 135, 145, 149. The Registers of the Hull Police suggest the decline of dismissal for drink-related offences over the late nineteenth and early twentieth centuries: of the men recruited during the 1880s 14.5 per cent were eventually dismissed for such offences, of those recruited in the 1890s 8.5 per cent were dismissed for such, while the corresponding figure for the men recruited between 1900 and 1910 was only 6.8 per cent.

in a pub, or a quick sit-down on their beat, and hoped not to get caught. Others developed more sophisticated ways of getting round the system. Rural constables might make false entries in their journals and even seek to come to an arrangement with their neighbouring colleagues over conference points. In May 1885 PC William Cooper of the Worcestershire Constabulary was reduced in rank and moved at his own expense from Malvern to Bewdley for 'falsely entering in his Duty Journal a Conference Point which he did not make in collusion with P.C. 191 A.H. Wargent'.[57] In order to avoid having to spend time in court or writing a report after a gruelling night duty, some constables shifted drunks from their own beat to that of a neighbour.[58] Arthur Battle described how, if two PCs on night duty wanted a gossip with each other, they would speak round the corner of a building: 'If a sergeant approached from either direction he would only be able to see one P.C. The one whom he saw would approach him boldly and report "All correct", giving his friend time to scuttle back to his own beat, or disappear up some nearby alley.'[59] Both Battle and Charles Hanslow recalled newspaper sellers, bus and cab drivers conniving at constables skipping off for a quick smoke or a sit down by giving warning of an approaching sergeant or inspector.[60] But Battle was probably right in stressing that, apart from the occasional rest and cigarette, most PCs still sought to do their duty:

> From what I have said I would not like to give the impression that a P.C. spent all the night hiding out of sight, or skulking in a shop doorway. He only sat down when he had been over his beat with a fine tooth comb when commencing duty, and this checking was most meticulously carried out again before leaving his beat at 6 a.m. A surprising number of good 'stops' and 'suspects' were accounted for by the fact that a P.C. was standing in a dark doorway . . .
>
> We were never conscious of being the victims of an oppressive system, and the supervision under which we worked kept us on our toes, as it was no doubt meant to. Another point is that if a high standard of conduct was demanded of us an equally high standard was demanded of other ranks. The lot of a section sergeant was no sinecure. Practically the whole of his duty time was spent in patrolling

57. West Mercia PA Worcestershire Constabulary Register and Record of Service 1877–83, no. 173.

58. Cavanagh, *Scotland Yard Past and Present*, pp. 29–31; Leeson, *Lost London*, pp. 35–6; C.H. Rolph, *Living Twice: An Autobiography* (London: Victor Gollancz, 1974), pp. 149–50.

59. Battle, 'This job's not what it used to be', p. 22.

60. Ibid., p. 20; Hanslow, 'Anecdotes', p. 15.

his section. Hanging about in the station fiddling with correspondence would not have been tolerated at all. Even the small section
states [sic] were taken out by the sergeants when they left the station,
usually rolled round their truncheons, and they filled in the details
at any time and place while on their section.[61]

The perks of the job

As well as the dodges to make life easier, there were also some
perks to the job. In some instances these might be officially organised, like the annual excursions enjoyed by the members of the
East Sussex force during the 1890s when 'generous subscriptions'
by the local inhabitants provided trips to London and Portsmouth
for constables and their families, and also provided pocket-money
for the trips.[62] But more often the perks were unofficial and frowned
upon, as, for example, the 'common practice' of Metropolitan Police
constables riding free on trams during the 1880s – a practice which
the senior officers tried to stamp out with heavy penalties.[63] This
particular perk appears to have been institutionalised across the
force, but others varied from beat to beat and from opportunity to
opportunity.

Timothy Cavanagh's first beat in mid-nineteenth-century London was regarded as the best in the division:

There was a good deal of money to be made on the ground – as
many as forty calls belonging to the happy possessor of the beat.
A 'call' meant that a man (and here they mostly belonged to the
Borough Market) wanted calling at four or five, or even earlier, in
the morning, for which service he paid on Saturday night with great
regularity the sum of sixpence. Should he, however, fail to pay up,
matters were soon put right by failing to call him on Monday morning, when, in consequence of losing half a day's work, he was certain
to be in the way with the stipulated 'tanner' the next night. In this
way a good sum was added to the regular pay, and placed a man in
a fairly good position.[64]

An enterprising workman might undercut the police and set himself up as a full-time 'knocker-up',[65] but it was the development of

61. Battle, 'This job's not what it used to be', pp. 23, 24.
62. East Sussex RO SPA 2/2/3, fols 125, 127, 184.
63. Metropolitan PA MS 844.85, 'The memoirs of Chief Inspector John Monk',
p. 8.
64. Cavanagh, *Scotland Yard Past and Present*, pp. 22–3.
65. James Berrett, *When I was at Scotland Yard* (London: Sampson Low, Marston
and Co., 1932), p. 63.

the alarm clock, and its spread down the social scale, which brought an end to this particular perk. Even so, policemen on night duty were still waking colleagues for morning parades during the inter-war years.[66] Of course other perks remained, the most commonly recalled being the pint of beer left at the back door or on the back window-sill of a pub.[67] Harry Daley considered the daytime patrols around Hammersmith Broadway to be boring, but there was always the possibility of slipping into the back room of 'Auntie's' sweet shop for a cup of tea. The dodge was well known to the local sergeants, but when they burst in looking for a missing constable Auntie 'merely poured another cup and brought out the cake'.[68] Officers who were known to cinema or theatre managers might be able to scrounge, or were sometimes simply offered, complimentary tickets.[69]

Rural beats had similar advantages. Both Nat Taylor and Arthur Pickering recalled that it was a foolish constable who, when cycling round his beat, did not have a bag on his handlebars. The bag was ostensibly to carry a pair of leggings for when trudging around farmyards, but it could also be used for carrying home the eggs, vegetables or game offered by local farmers. In Arthur Almond's recollection the 'gentry' usually reserved pheasants for the senior officers.[70] One of John Wainwright's beats in the West Riding was perched on top of a coalfield. The miners all received free coal, and far more than they could use. 'A nod and a wink and, instead of the coal being delivered to the miner it was meant for, it was delivered to a policeman's house.'[71]

Several of the perks described above probably contributed to the policeman's acceptance within the community which he patrolled. The receipt of food and drink especially could demonstrate a constable's friendliness and willingness to comply with the norms and standards of the local community. It was also useful to the policeman, not only because of the respite which the receipt of certain

66. Taped interview with ex-PC Clifford Jeeves, Feb. 1987; Merseyside PA Birkenhead Police, Disciplinary Report Book, 1920–30, fol. 293.

67. 'Memoirs of . . . Monk', p. 8; taped interviews with ex-Chief Constable Anthony Armstrong, Feb. 1988, and ex-PS Nat Taylor, Dec. 1987; Brogden, *On the Mersey Beat*, pp. 110–13.

68. Daley, *This Small Cloud*, p. 94; for similar examples in Liverpool see Brogden, *On the Mersey Beat*, pp. 54–5.

69. Hanslow, 'Anecdotes', p. 22; Lyscom, 'London policeman', p. 329; Wainwright, *Wainwright's Beat*, p. 17.

70. Taped interviews with Taylor, Dec. 1987, and Pickering, Feb. 1987; Emsley (ed.), 'Recollections of . . . Almond', 56.

71. Wainwright, *Wainwright's Beat*, p. 147.

perks provided from the monotony of the beat, but also because it gave him the opportunity to talk with people in a relaxed manner, to learn about them, and to get information from them.[72] Other perks could come as a result of a particular posting. Point duty in Berkeley Square might bring the occasional Christmas gift, such as a cigar, from the wealthy; and Mr Marks of Marks & Spencer's stores according to Hanslow, would 'walk from Bloomsbury and tour the Charing Cross Road area giving us P.C.s packets of peppermints or/and spearmint'.[73] During the inter-war period duty around Olympia at the time of the Motor Shows provided the opportunity of helping gentlemen to park their cars and then making sure that they were protected from damage or theft. The gentlemen usually responded with a tip, and Daley reckoned that it was possible to make as much as £30 in a week from such a posting.[74] A day out policing a race meeting, a fete, or some other public event, besides relieving the routine of the daily beat, also sometimes offered perks such as a good, free lunch and free drink.[75] There were, of course, some men who went too far on such occasions. In June 1880 Owen Thomas was dismissed from the Worcestershire Constabulary for 'pilfering sandwiches and bottled beer or porter at the meeting of the Bath and West of England Society's Show at Battenhall, Worcester, where he was on duty with other Constables'.[76]

Going too far was always a problem with perks. Some men showed an entrepreneurial spirit, like John Gillings of the Ipswich Borough Force who, in August 1868, was reprimanded for taking two people to the police cells to see one of the prisoners, and receiving payment for the same.[77] Members of the Metropolitan Police Thames Division were disciplined early in 1901 for receiving money from wharfingers. Other men took it upon themselves to go round their beats asking for Christmas boxes. When news of this reached Major Dunlop in the East Riding in January 1912 he instructed his men that this was 'entirely contrary to the letter and spirit' of his orders.[78] A few men did not stop at the occasional free pint of beer offered

72. Cain, *Society and the Policeman's Role*, p. 37.
73. Hanslow, 'Anecdotes', p. 15.
74. Daley, *This Small Cloud*, p. 107
75. Emsley (ed.), 'Recollections of . . . Almond', 55.
76. West Mercia PA Worcestershire Constabulary Register and Record of Service, 1877–83, no. 71.
77. East Suffolk RO DF 2/1.
78. *Hansard*, XC, 4 Mar. 1901, cols 379–80; Humberside PA East Riding Constabulary, Memo Book 1900–12, fol. 189.

by publicans, something in itself frowned on by senior officers,[79] but went so far as to demand free drinks or the money for drinks. In February 1879 Edward Hudspith resigned after having been seen 'asking people in the streets to give him drink and insulting them upon their refusal to do so'. In July 1890, after twenty years' service in the Hull City Police, Jonathan Haigh was called upon to resign after a publican complained that Haigh had been obtaining drinks for the last six weeks without paying.[80] Anthony Armstrong remembered that, only half a century later, two detectives in Whitley Bay would occasionally go to the back door of a pub in the early hours of the morning 'where they knew the licensee very well, and they'd thunder on the back door and he'd come down in pyjamas, poor old fellow, and they'd make him open up the bar. He'd be there to about 4 o'clock in the morning!'[81]

The whole practice of perks was on the edge of the grey area which shaded into the taking of bribes. Stories of bribes in the Metropolitan and other forces in the first decade of the twentieth century prompted Colonel Chichester to forbid his men to receive 'Christmas or any other presents from Brewers or tradesmen of any sort'. It was, however, still permissible to accept a present of game from a magistrate or game preserver.[82] 'For a policeman to accept a gift means to put himself on the spot', declared Arthur Almond. He went on, rather lamely, 'but why should it when it is given with a good heart and with no sinister reason behind it?'[83] The problem, of course, was always recognising the motivation behind the gift. Perhaps it was indeed easy to see when something was given openly 'with a good heart', but in many instances the motivation was far from altruistic. In some instances the bribe may even have been suggested by the policeman. For four years the Chief Constable of Manchester denied that any of his men took bribes to turn a blind eye to motoring offences; then, in May 1930, he found himself having to dismiss a constable for precisely such an offence.

79. In March 1895 the Chief Constable of East Sussex called on one of his constables to resign at once for having received beer from a publican while on duty, and early in the following year a general order was issued 'that constables are not to receive any gifts from Publicans either when on or off duty': East Sussex RO SPA 2/2/3, fols 44, 89.

80. West Mercia PA Worcestershire Constabulary Register and Record of Service 1877–83; Humberside PA Hull City Police, Appointment Book 1855–1921.

81. Taped interview with Armstrong, Feb. 1988.

82. Cambs. PA Huntingdonshire Constabulary, Chief Constable's Circulars 1888–1907, No. 232.

83. Emsley (ed.), 'Recollections of ... Almond', 56.

Members of the Force enjoy good conditions of service and are in receipt of pay and allowances of a sufficiently high standard to ensure independent and faithful service and the conscientious discharge of the duties entrusted to them.

The Watch committee and the Chief Constable take a very serious view of what is nothing but a corrupt practice, and any member of the Force who may in future be found guilty of this offence will not only be dismissed the Force but will be taken before the Court and prosecuted.[84]

In the late nineteenth and early twentieth centuries it was alleged that some policemen in central London were either blackmailing or taking bribes from prostitutes.[85] Harry Daley, who was not one to sweep the faults of the Metropolitan Police under the carpet, described the constables of Vine Street Police Station as being on good terms with the prostitutes of the West End. But he believed that, after the scandal of the Sergeant Goddard affair of 1929, there was no bribery in the relationship.[86] Betting was probably the area in which the greatest number of illicit perks was given and received. The legislation of 1906 was unenforceable and police attempts at enforcement were unpopular and detrimental to their relations with the public. Often agreements were reached with the bookmakers which were tantamount to unofficial licences. In such instances bookies' runners were provided when required by the police, arrested, taken to court and fined; the bookie paid the fine, and as often as not paid a fee to the victim who was rarely one of his regular runners. Where the relationship between bookie and police slipped into more murky waters was when constables were tipped for ignoring the runners on their beats, or when police stations received Christmas hampers and crates of whisky.[87]

Poor leadership and poor examples by superior officers probably contributed much to the relationship between some constables and bookies. In May 1908 Lionel Everett was appointed Chief Constable of Preston. A scion of the Wiltshire gentry – his grandfather had been a JP and a deputy lieutenant in the county, his father was a clergyman – Everett had worked his way from constable to superintendent in

84. Greater Manchester PA Manchester Police General Orders, vol. 20, fol. 91.

85. *The Times*, 2 Nov. 1868, p. 11; *Royal Commission on the Duties of the Metropolitan Police*, vol. I 1908, pp. 81–3; and see above, p. 78.

86. Daley, *This Small Cloud*, pp. 149–51.

87. Ibid., pp. 93–6; Battle, 'This job's not what it used to be', pp. 35–7; Raphael Samuel, *East End Underworld: Chapters in the Life of Arthur Harding* (London: Routledge and Kegan Paul, 1981), pp. 180–1; Wainwright, *Wainwright's Beat*, p. 148.

the county force in ten years. Still only 31 he set about his new position in Preston with enthusiasm, but his assault on the local bookmakers uncovered a web of corruption involving his men, bookmakers and publicans. Thirteen of the 120 men in the force were suspended and on Everett's recommendation, following a hearing by the Watch Committee, three were dismissed: a sergeant, a 'warrant officer', and a constable, with twenty, eighteen and eleven years' service respectively. Another constable was called on to resign, and the remaining nine men were reduced in rank.[88]

Police pay cuts during the inter-war years were another spur to temptation. Arthur Battle recalled a comrade with about twenty years' service behind him setting off to collect a pound from a local bookmaker.

> I told him I wanted nothing to do with it at all. He continued 'Well you do as you like, old boy, but I'm going to get mine. I've never taken a penny from them all my service, but now these cuts have come along I'm not going to be the loser.'[89]

There were other temptations for the constable, often poorly paid in comparison with other workers, to make money on the side by turning a blind eye to petty offences. In Worcestershire in December 1890 PC Alfred Jones was severely reprimanded and fined £1 (six days' pay) for 'neglect of duty in not reporting a baker whom he found delivering bread without his scales and afterwards accepting 3 pence from him to obtain drink'. The following February PC William Wallace was dismissed for a similar offence and for accepting a bribe of 1/6d.[90] There were also the temptations that occur in any bureaucracy, such as the cheating on expense claims. In both 1886 and 1896, for example, the Chief Constable of East Sussex warned his men that they would be dealt with severely if they were caught claiming more for rail fares than they had actually spent.[91]

It is impossible to assess the precise extent of fiddling or workplace crime in any trade or profession. The fact that some policemen committed such offences only serves as a reminder that the police are a workforce like any other. In many respects the Victorian policeman was built up as the archetypal worker of his age: the steady,

---

88. *Preston Herald,* 18 Sept. 1909 pp. 4 and 13, and 22 Sept. p. 2. For Everett's career see *Police Review* (1908), 29 May p. 254.

89. Battle, 'This job's not what it used to be', p. 37.

90. West Mercia PA Worcestershire Constabulary Register and Record of Service, 1888–93, nos. 14 and 94.

91. East Sussex RO SPA 2/2/2, fol. 65, and SPA 2/2/3, fol. 147.

machine-like pace of his footsteps on his beat were expected to march in time with the steady pulse of the gospel of work. He was expected to be sober and hard-working, and this would give him the potential of rising, through self-help and diligence, from constable third class to be the chief constable of a borough; by the second half of the twentieth century he could climb to the very top as Commissioner of the Metropolitan Police or as one of Her Majesty's Inspectors of Constabulary. The policeman's time was strictly regulated and, while he generally worked on his own and had to rely on his own discretion, at the outset particularly attempts were made to supervise his every working moment. The rigours of this supervision were alleviated gradually, and especially as the twentieth century progressed, but it is hardly surprising that men kicked against the system and devised ways around it; nor should it be surprising that, for their own advantage, some men were tempted to bend or break the laws which they were sworn to uphold.

Conclusion:
Constabulary, Gendarmerie and
Haute Police

The traditional view of the English police as exemplified by the Whig histories is that there is one 'police service' in England and Wales which sprang, almost fully formed, from the model proposed by a group of farsighted reformers and was established in London in 1829 by Sir Robert Peel. By implication, at least, this view maintains that, first, the Metropolitan Police model rapidly demonstrated its efficiency and was therefore taken up by the majority of the municipalities in 1835 and by sensible, progressive counties after the legislation of 1839–40; those local authorities which failed to adopt the model were myopic, stupid, or worse. A second implication is that the Metropolitan Police model, subsequently the English model, was unique, particularly in so far as the men were non-military, unarmed and non-political. The first of these implications has led to a serious distortion of the history of police and policing in England and Wales; the second ignores the political and social contexts in which the English police were allowed to develop during their formative period and especially in the second half of the nineteenth century.

The Metropolitan Police established in 1829 was a new departure for English policing, not because of what the constables did – efficient watchmen were already patrolling their beats in the way that police constables were to do – but because it was a large body of uniformed men answerable directly to the Home Secretary. It was an instrument of government the like of which, with the exception of the army, had never been seen before in England. The Whig historians have attempted to trace a direct line from the Fieldings and their Runners, through the stipendiary justices established in 1792, to the Metropolitan Police; but the organisation which was established in 1829 was not the obvious outcome of these earlier developments. The logical outcome would have been a much more decentralised organisation directed by the stipendiary magistrates and working out of their offices along the lines of the 'Red Breasts' and the various other patrols based at Bow Street. At the same time all London vestries could have been required to establish watches on a common pattern, but might also have retained control of them.

Police reform was already being contemplated in the provinces before the creation of the Metropolitan Police, and before the Acts of 1835, 1839 and 1840. Some boroughs and counties looked to the new police of London as a model and also for their senior officers; but by no means all did this. Metropolitan policemen who took up positions in the boroughs found a very different situation from that which they had left; they were responsible to elected officials in the shape of the watch committees, and were often regarded as servants of the municipality first, and policemen second. In some counties the magistrates looked to the Royal Irish Constabulary for their model and for senior personnel, reasoning that here was a force established for a rural community rather than an urban one. Elsewhere, magistrates sought to introduce a degree of professionalism into the old parish constable system by the recruitment of superintending constables rather than by creating a fully fledged county constabulary. There were problems with the superintending constables in that the men had too much to do, and they might find themselves pulled between two masters – a local magistrate, who regarded the constable as his man tied to his petty sessional division, and the magistrates of the county police committee who took a county-wide perspective with regard to policing needs. However, several witnesses to the Select Committee on Police of 1852–53 were happy with the superintending constables, and it is probably significant that witnesses were not called from Kent, where the justices had recently been the driving force behind a series of parliamentary proposals to develop the system.

A degree of uniformity was imposed from above by the 1856 County and Borough Police Act and by the appointment of the Inspectors of Constabulary whose task it was to adjudicate annually on a force's efficiency and thus enable it to receive a government grant. This Act was the result of drawn out negotiations between the government, which wanted to impose a degree of uniformity, expecting thus to improve efficiency, and local authorities, especially the boroughs, determined to hang on to their independence and their police. While the differences must not be overemphasised, it nevertheless remains true that, in the century following the 1856 Act, there were three different kinds of police force in England and Wales with three different chains of command. There was the Metropolitan Police, always the largest force in the country, and responsible directly to the Home Secretary. The borough forces, which could range from the very large, like those of Liverpool and Manchester, to the very small, were responsible to watch committees appointed by the local councils. These committees had extensive powers and some were not afraid to use them and to give direct orders to their chief constables. The county forces, again ranging from the very large to the very small,[1] were responsible initially to the police committees of the county bench, then, after 1889, to the standing joint committees of both magistrates and county councillors; the authority of these county committees over their chief constables was much less marked than that of the watch committees. The Police Act of 1964 reduced the kinds of police to two: the Metropolitan force, which remained responsible to the Home Secretary, and the 40-odd provincial forces whose new police committees had far less clout with their chief constable than did the Home Office.

Debate over local control of the police continued in the century and a half following the 1856 Act, and could be heated. Should the Metropolitan Police be responsible to the elected representatives of local government in London? Should the standing joint committees have the greater powers of the watch committees? When these latter bodies were abolished the questions focused on the degree of control which the new police committees ought to exert over the chief constables of the much larger, amalgamated forces. The enfeebled committees established in 1964 were a reflection of the decline in local differences and independence in police matters which had begun at least as early as the 1856 Act, and which had continued with central government increasingly bypassing local government to deal directly with chief constables, and with the increasing uniformity in the terms and conditions of police service and training.

While the unique nature of the English police has often been stressed, a brief glance across the Channel shows that, during the nineteenth and for much of the twentieth centuries, there were also broadly three different kinds of police with three different chains of command: the police of Paris, the municipal police, and the gendarmerie.

The police of Paris, like the Metropolitan Police, were directly

---

1. For the authorised establishments of the Metropolitan, county and borough police forces in 1870, 1910 and 1939 see Appendix 1.

responsible to central government. Probably the political aspects of policing in Paris were overstressed by contemporaries and have been subsequently overstressed by historians. The police of Paris were charged with the day-to-day prevention and detection of crime and general maintenance of order. Nevertheless, the nervousness of different French regimes during the nineteenth and early twentieth centuries – justifiable given the number of revolutions and *événements* which convulsed their capital – did ensure that the police were required to watch and repress political activists and critics in ways, and to an extent, largely unknown in England. Every successful upheaval, and some of the unsuccessful ones, resulted in political purges in the senior police ranks. The open acknowledgement that the police were state agents made government and ministers directly responsible for police actions and behaviour; during the Third Republic ministers, even governments, fell following parliamentary criticism of the police – again, something unknown in England.[2] The turbulence of modern French history, in comparison with modern English history, has ensured that the police of Paris have remained, highly placed, on the political agenda.

The municipal police in nineteenth-century France were generally under split control: the principal officers, the *commissaires*, were appointed from Paris, but they were paid by the municipality; the agents on the streets were recruited by the municipality. The desire to keep costs down meant that municipal police could be thin on the ground; there was no system of national inspection, and policing could become a contentious issue in local government as opposition factions accused the ruling groups of recruiting the police from their own supporters and running them in their own interest. Confrontation between the *commissaire* and the local authority was not unknown, especially when the municipality was socialist and disliked the orders issuing from Paris. But Paris also treated local authorities with circumspection over matters of policing: many posts of *commissaire* were vacant at the beginning of the twentieth century, partly it would seem because local authorities did not wish to pay for them and central government did not wish to force the issue, though it has also been suggested that the areas lacking these

2. Clive Emsley, 'Policing the streets of early nineteenth-century Paris', *French History* 1 (1987), 257–82; Benjamin F. Martin, *Crime and Criminal Justice under the Third Republic: The Shame of Marianne* (Baton Rouge, Louisiana: State University Press, 1990), chs 2 and 3; Jean-Marc Berlière, 'La professionalisation: Revendication des policiers et objectif des pouvoirs au début de la IIIe république', *Revue d'histoire moderne et contemporaine* XXXVI (1990), 398–428, at 406–7.

municipal *commissaires* were relatively well policed with other agents. The turbulent city of Lyon had a state police imposed upon it in 1851; this was under the direction of the departmental prefect who was appointed from Paris. But it was not for another half-century that another city, Marseilles, was given such a police; and the gradual spread of such police in the aftermath of the First World War was met with considerable opposition from some local authorities jealous of their independence.[3]

The centralised nature of the Paris police, the cheesepairing of French municipalities and their reluctance to yield their independence in policing matters to the state, have obvious parallels with the English experience. The policing of the French countryside, however, took a very different form to the English county police. The gendarmerie was a military organisation, and while its primary duties were to aid the civil power, it was responsible to the Minister of War. Why was there such a marked contrast between the policing of rural France and rural England? The answer is to be found in the way that the two states developed and the ways in which central and local government interrelated.[4]

The gendarmerie originated in the *maréchaussée* – the men of the military marshals (*maréchaux*) of France. The *maréchausée* was established in the sixteenth century to control the royal army in France which was as much a danger to the native population as it was to the king's enemies. In England there was never the same trouble with marching armies and discharged soldiers since, although there was a civil war, England was far less involved in wars than her continental neighbours during the sixteenth and seventeenth centuries. The *maréchaussée* acquired its authority over civilian offenders by virtue of the fact that there was no other body, or bodies, to

3. Clive Emsley, *Policing and its Context, 1750–1870* (London: Macmillan, 1983), pp. 88–98; John M. Merriman, *The Red City: Limoges and the French 19th Century* (Oxford: OUP, 1985), pp. 202, 238, 241; Jean François Tanguy, 'Le conflit des pouvoirs de police à Rennes, 1870–1914', in Alain Faure *et al.*, *Maintien de l'ordre et polices en France et en Europe au XIXe siecle* (Paris: Créaphis, 1987); Joan W. Scott, 'Mayors versus police chiefs; socialist municipalities confront the state', in John M. Merriman (ed.), *French Cities in the Nineteenth Century* (London: Hutchinson, 1982); Marie Thérèse Vogel, 'Les polices des villes entre local et national: l'administration des polices urbaines sous la IIIe république', 3 vols, Doctorat de Science Politique, University of Grenoble, 1993.

4. Pierre Miquel, *Les Gendarmes* (Paris: Olivier Orban, 1990), is a popular survey. As yet, there is no good academic history of the gendarmerie, but there are some useful pointers in Howard C. Payne, *The Police State of Louis Napoleon Bonaparte 1851–1860* (Seattle: University of Washington Press, 1966), and Georges Carrot, *Le maintien de l'ordre en France depuis la fin de l'ancien régime jusqu'à 1968*, 2 vols, University of Toulouse, Centre des études et de recherches sur la Police, 1984.

undertake the task for the centralising state.[5] In England, in contrast, while the centralised tax system was amongst the most efficient in Europe, the centralised state was checked and forced into temporary retreat as a result of the constitutional struggles of the seventeenth century. In the aftermath of the Glorious Revolution of 1688 the authority of the local gentry in local government and administration reached new heights. Central government authorised the use of troops in an emergency, but basically left the local magistrates alone to get on with things; and while troops might be used to put down disorder, the rhetoric of the eighteenth-century 'freeborn Englishman', looking back to Cromwell's major-generals, was highly critical of a standing army and its deployment for internal policing. Nineteenth-century England escaped the revolutions of continental Europe, and did not have the continental varieties of Liberals, radicals and revolutionaries aspiring to bring in new constitutions or to create new, unified nation-states. England was already a nation-state and had been probably at least since Tudor times. All of these elements combined to militate against any perceived need for, or preparedness to contemplate, a gendarmerie-style police. But there was also another, crucial element feeding into the equation. The majority of the English population appear to have had some sort of notion of 'Englishness'; as late as the nineteenth century parallel notions of 'Frenchness' were lacking among large numbers of peasants who lived in France but who had little idea of what France was and did not even speak French. Thus in addition to their roles of controlling military offenders and day-to-day policing, *cavaliers* of the *maréchaussée*, and later gendarmes, might also be said to have had a colonising role, showing the flag to Alsatians, Auvergnats, Bretons, Gascons, and helping to transform them into Frenchmen. Other militarised police forces in Europe had similar functions, from the *Santa Hermandad* in the Spain of Ferdinand and Isabella, to the *Carabinieri* of Cavour's united Italy.[6] Gendarmeries were created to patrol the rural districts of the early nineteenth-century German states, both in Prussia, with its tradition of militarism and its new populations of Rhinelanders and

---

5. For the development of the *maréchaussée* see Iain A. Cameron, *Crime and Repression in the Auvergne and the Guyenne 1720–1790* (Cambridge: CUP, 1981), and Claude C. Sturgill, *L'organisation et l'administration de la maréchaussée et de la justice prévôtale dans la France des Bourbons 1720–1730* (Vincennes: Service Historique de l'Armée de la Terre, 1981).
6. The argument here is further developed in Clive Emsley, 'Peasants, gendarmes and state formation', in Mary Fulbrook (ed.), *National Histories and European History* (London: UCL Press, 1993).

Poles, and in the more liberal southern states which disliked having to rely on their armies to maintain order but which, in the aftermath of the upheavals of the revolutionary and Napoleonic wars, felt the need to have some armed force in the countryside to oversee the peasantry and to pursue beggars and vagrants. When it came to colonising, showing the flag, or seeking to turn recalcitrant natives into loyal subjects of the British Crown, then militarised police forces along the gendarmerie model were deployed by those same governments that gloried in the English Bobby's unique nature; these British imperial gendarmeries started as close to home as Ireland. Even before Peel had established the Metropolitan Police, units known as 'mounted police' were being recruited directly from military regiments in the new Australian colonies to patrol the remoter districts. When the North West Mounted Police embarked on their great march into western Canada in 1874 they wore scarlet coats and were armed with lances and carbines; the only thing that identified this cavalry as 'police' was the name.[7]

Pains were taken at the time of the creation of the Metropolitan Police to ensure that they did not look military, and the traditional police historians insist that the English police were always 'non-military'. But what exactly was non-military about them? It is true that they were never responsible to the minister of war and men did not enlist for a fixed term as was generally the case in the army. However, policemen were organised in a strict hierarchical institution. During the nineteenth, and for much of the early part of the twentieth centuries, many of their commanding officers were former soldiers, or men from the colonial gendarmeries. The constables were subjected to a strict discipline, they were given parade-ground drill and sometimes quartered in 'barracks'. They had to make their boots, belts, buttons and badges shine, and wear their uniforms smartly. All of these things were considered necessary, though whether they were, and whether they did make for better police and policing, are moot points;[8] they none of them smack of a civilian nature.

7. Michael Sturma, 'Policing the criminal frontier in mid-nineteenth-century Australia, Britain and America', in Mark Finnane (ed.), *Policing in Australia: Historical Perspectives* (Kensington: University of New South Wales Press, 1987), pp. 23–4; Lorne and Caroline Brown, *An Unauthorized History of the RCMP* (Toronto: James Lorimer, 1978), pp. 14–15; William R. Morrison, *Showing the Flag: The Mounted Police and Canadian Sovereignty in the North 1894–1925* (Vancouver: University of British Columbia Press, 1985), pp. 2–5.

8. Mid-nineteenth-century American city cops appear to have shared the democratic suspicion of uniforms – 'livery' as it was sometimes called. As a result they often opposed uniforms or wore them in flamboyant and individualistic ways: Emsley, *Policing and its Context*, pp. 111–12. *The New York Times*, 9 Dec. 1857, described the

The policeman has a wide degree of discretion on his beat in deciding how to respond to different offenders. The argument could be, and was, advanced that in this respect he differed from the soldier who was commonly under the immediate direction of superior officers. There is an element of truth in this. Yet if the English Bobby differed from the soldier in this respect, so too did the Prussian *Schutzmann*, always an army veteran who patrolled the streets in spiked military helmet and armed to the teeth.[9] The difference here was less the non-military nature of the Victorian Bobby and the military nature of the *Schutzmann*, and more the different traditions and the different ethos of the two societies: on the one hand a broadly liberal England with a suspicion of militarism, on the other an authoritarian Prussian state which glorified the military idea and within which every state functionary could expect to have his orders obeyed as if they were military directives and could respond to defiance accordingly.

'Non-military' seems often used by commentators on the English police as a synonym for 'unarmed'. Fears about the militarisation of the police have sometimes focused on the question of their access to lethal weaponry. Edged weapons and guns may not have been carried as a rule but the former were commonly available to constables on lonely or dangerous beats, and were also issued during confrontations with potentially disorderly crowds. Guns might also be issued; perhaps a little less restraint on the part of the Home Office during the 1830s and 1840s, and a little more violence on the part of Rebecca and her children and the Chartists, would have seen the English police come much closer to a continental gendarmerie. In the 1860s it was the Home Office which restrained those county chief constables who were eager to train their men as auxiliaries to the army; but at the end of that decade guns were being issued to cope with the Fenian threat, and following a rash of armed burglaries in London in the mid-1880s some Metropolitan Police constables began patrolling wearing revolvers in holsters on their belts.[10] This carrying of guns spread to other

city policeman as wearing a uniform 'to be sure, but he disdains to button it in military fashion, and exposes his snowy linen and its California diamond with as much ostentation as a railway conductor. To put one's hands in one's pockets while on duty is a grave military offence. Your New York policeman hardly ever puts them anywhere else.'

9. Emsley, *Policing and its Context*, pp. 101–3.

10. Clive Emsley, ' "The thump of wood on a swede turnip": police violence in nineteenth-century England', *CJH* VI (1986), 125–49. Constables in Devonshire appear to have been issued with revolvers while patrolling coastal landing places during

forces and was still being done by some men on night beats after the First World War, and on special patrols, like the 'Jewellers' Patrol' in the Birmingham Bull Ring, throughout the inter-war period. Proposals for a general issue of revolvers, however, were rejected.[11] The Home Office remained very wary of arming the police and possibly fostered the rhetoric of their lack of arms as a means of restraint. When firearms began to be more widely carried in the perpetration of offences after the Second World War, and when the threat from different terrorist organisations developed during the 1970s and 1980s, the issue of firearms rose in parallel, but only to carefully selected authorised firearms officers (AFOs) trained in the use of a variety of weapons. Accidents and errors excited alarm, notably the shooting of Stephen Waldorf in mistake for a 'known criminal' in January 1983 and, two years later, the shootings of Mrs Cherry Groce and a five-year-old boy, John Short-house. But terrorist outrages, the occasional murder of a police officer, and the appalling Hungerford massacre of 1987, when Michael Ryan randomly shot dead sixteen people in a quiet Berk-shire town before turning a gun on himself, prompted periodic calls for more guns for the police and questionnaires to police officers on whether they now perceived a need for arms. The ques-tionnaires showed that a majority of the police did not wish to be armed; the tradition of the non-military, unarmed Bobby contin-ued to be proclaimed as unique and beneficial to English society by both politicians and most senior policemen, and the issuing of firearms remained restricted to AFOs. But after the Hungerford incident most forces began to deploy Armed Response Vehicles – generally traffic vehicles containing arms locked in boxes, and which in theory could be deployed rapidly to any emergency. For

the Fenian scare at the end of 1867: Devon and Cornwall PA Devon Constabulary, M Division Order Book 1865–1910, 9 Jan. 1868. At the end of 1882 the Chief Con-stable of East Sussex received a complaint that one of his men was carrying a gun, and he ordered the practice to stop forthwith: East Sussex RO SPA 2/2/2, fols 22–3.

11. *Hansard*, CXXV, 19 Feb. 1920 cols 1089–90; ibid., CXXVI, 2 Mar. 1920 col. 259 and 4 Mar. col. 684; ibid., CXXX, 16 June 1920 cols 1295–6, 17 Mar. col. 1452, and 21 Mar. col. 1790; ibid., CXXXV, 1 Dec. 1920 cols 1233–4; taped interview with Fred Fancourt (Birmingham Police), Dec. 1986. A Birkenhead PC was disciplined in April 1921 for firing his revolver 'when he was not attacked by a person with fire-arms or other deadly weapon'. The PC's doctor testified that the man 'was suffering from the effects of shell shock. His condition is such that he is at times in a highly nervous state and is apt to act on the impulse of the moment.' It was resolved that the PC would not be issued with a revolver in future: Merseyside PA Birkenhead Police, Disciplinary Report Book, 1920–30, fol. 31; for another instance of a disci-plinary case involving a man armed with a revolver see fol. 37.

self-protection in the early 1990s, and in the light of fears of a more violent society, several forces began to supply their officers with longer, side-handled batons in place of the short truncheon.[12]

The use of police to keep the peace during industrial disputes or large-scale demonstrations also led to accusations of militarisation, particularly when the police broke up the crowds with baton charges or when they were actually deployed alongside troops. Well might government functionaries and police reformers like Chadwick insist that there was a difference between the policeman and the soldier in these circumstances, but for the follower of Rebecca, the Chartist, for unemployed or political demonstrators, and for strikers and their supporters the difference was probably academic. The soldiers may have had lethal weapons, but they very rarely used them; the police were commonly used well before any recourse to the army, and they had their truncheons. The developments in police riot training during the 1970s brought the English police rather closer to a gendarmerie in their riot equipment and tactics; yet the men and women deployed for riot duty were ordinary police officers whose general duties commonly involved beat patrolling – unlike their continental neighbours, they were not specialised riot squads.

The deployment of police during the miners' strike of 1984–85 brought not only accusations of militarisation, but also the allegation that the police were now being employed in a partisan fashion; even police officers expressed such concerns.[13] But it has always been difficult, if not impossible, for the police to be acknowledged as neutral by both sides in such disputes. Only one side needs to take to the streets to proclaim the justice of its claim and to ensure that 'free labour'/'blacklegs' do not keep a plant functioning. Only one side is therefore in danger of breaching the peace: the decision by the Newport Watch Committee not to assist Houlder Brothers in 1910 was the exception which proved the rule. Policemen, by their very nature as instruments of the state – or servants of the Crown in English constitutional parlance – are required to maintain the dominant conception of public order. This, in itself, in broad terms is a political activity. What the traditional police historians,

12. See especially P.A.J. Waddington, *The Strong Arm of the Law: Armed and Public Order Policing* (Oxford: Clarendon Press, 1991), Part II. For questionnaires on arming see *Police Review*, 7 Dec. 1990 pp. 2405–7, and 14 Jan. 1994 pp. 14–16.

13. Roger Graef, *Talking Blues: The Police in their Own Words* (London: Collins Harvill, 1989), p. 74; Terrence Morris, *Crime and Justice since 1945* (Oxford: Basil Blackwell, 1989), p. 160.

the politicians, and the constitutional lawyers have meant by the English police being non-political relies on the very narrow definition of 'political' as party-political organisation and the administrative apparatus of the state.[14]

The nature of American democracy has often involved American police forces in party politics, and sometimes in ways which have tended to undermine that democracy. In mid-nineteenth-century England men were already boasting how this made American police different from and, by implication, inferior to the Bobby.[15] It would be wrong to say that the English police never became involved in local politics; their use by different factions in borough politics over the Temperance issue is the obvious contradiction. But it is also true that strenuous efforts were made to keep the police out of party politics, first by denying them the vote, and then by repetition of the instructions to avoid political comment. It would also be wrong to assume that police forces never came under the domination of local government officers. When Frank Bunn became Chief Constable of the Stoke-on-Trent force in 1936 he found the Town Clerk used to directing the police over who they should, and should not, prosecute; subordinates of the Town Clerk in particular had immunity. Instilled with the traditions of English policing, Bunn opposed this practice and ultimately brought it to an end;[16] yet his predecessors had allowed it to develop, and elsewhere others, overawed by local functionaries and politicians, had probably acquiesced in similar developments.

One of the advantages of the American system was the openness in comment and criticism which was brought to policing. William McAdoo, a former Commissioner of the New York Police, visited London in the early twentieth century, and while he saw great advantages in the lack of red tape and the exclusiveness of the Commissioner of the Metropolitan Police – 'He is accorded a greater exclusiveness than the Secretary of Foreign Affairs [and] treated on the same plane as a judge of one of our highest courts' – he was amazed by the fact that the press had no access to Scotland Yard and by the way in which magistrates treated the police as 'partners' in carrying out justice.[17] Except in moments of moral panic such as

14. Robert Reiner, *The Politics of the Police*, 2nd edn (Hemel Hempstead: Wheatsheaf, 1992), pp. 1–2.
15. *Police Service Advertiser*, 6 Apr. 1867. See also above, p. 103.
16. Frank Leonard Bunn, *No Silver Spoon* (Stoke-on-Trent: F.L. Bunn, 1972), pp. 165–73.
17. William McAdoo, 'The London police from a New York point of view', *The Century Magazine* LXXVIII (1909), 649–70. In the Third Republic, also proud of its

the garrotting scares of the mid-nineteenth century or the Jack the Ripper murders of 1888, criticism of the English police invariably brought squeals of protest, and complaints that such criticism was unhelpful. When critical comments were made in Parliament in 1881 about the behaviour of Metropolitan Police detectives during the Titley case, the Home Secretary, Sir William Harcourt, protested that 'it is not to the advantage of the public that general aspersions of this character should be cast on the whole body of the police. To do so creates a danger to the cause of peace and order in this Metropolis.'[18] Joynson-Hicks's plea for the public to abstain from criticising the police for a year in 1928 was a similar, if rather more extreme, suggestion; but it continued to have echoes as when, for example, some 40 years later a regular columnist of *Justice of the Peace* lamented: 'I am getting utterly sick of the constant knocking of our police force which is all that stands between us, the citizens, and downright anarchy.'[19] Since the constitution and its appendages were so rarely the focus of criticism, or issues of political debate in late nineteenth- and early twentieth-century England, this condemnation of the critics of the police appears to have generated little question and comment. It became easy to hide behind the claim that the English police were among the finest, if not the finest, in the world, and that while there might be a few black sheep, the institution was functioning well.[20] However, this lack of openness and of receptiveness to criticism may have had a detrimental effect on the prevention and detection of offences. The development of bureaucratic, professional policing in the century and a half following 1829 also saw a marked decline in public vigilance and participation in the pursuit of offenders. The police made little attempt to encourage such vigilance and participation, and while they collected information from victims, they rarely publicised much; the prevention and detection of crime had become their job as the professionals. Only during the 1970s and 1980s, faced with soaring crime statistics and a decline in public confidence, did the police begin to open up links with the community by promoting schemes such as neighbourhood watch, designed to

'democracy', the press was also a significant critic of the police: Berlière, 'La professionalisation', 408–13.

18. *Hansard*, CCLVII, 18 Jan. 1881, col. 942.

19. *Justice of the Peace* CXXXIV (1970), 26 Sept. p. 720. For Joynson-Hicks's comment, see above, p. 144.

20. For examples of the insistence that the English police were the best in the world see Clive Emsley, 'The English Bobby: an indulgent tradition', in Roy Porter (ed.), *Memory, Myths and Monuments* (Oxford: Polity Press, 1992).

bring the public into partnership in the prevention and detection of criminal offences.[21]

As well as underplaying any military aspect of their new police, those who established the police in England, conscious of, and generally sharing, the sensibilities and prejudices of their fellow countrymen, also sought to avoid any implications of spying or political surveillance. If the United States gave nineteenth-century Englishmen good examples of police involved in party politics, almost everywhere in continental Europe offered examples of the police involved in political surveillance and political repression – what the French called *haute police* – and of the use of *agents provocateurs*. After the disorders of the 1830s and the 'Hungry Forties', the Victorians could argue with conviction that this kind of policing was unnecessary and irrelevant to their society. England had not experienced revolutions such as those which wracked Europe in 1830 and 1848; even allowing for the Merthyr rising, her industrial cities witnessed nothing comparable to the Lyon insurrections of 1831 and 1834. In the middle quarters of the nineteenth century in England there were no significant groups seeking to impose completely new constitutional structures. In much of Europe the opposite was the case. Many European liberals and reformers looked to England for their new constitutional models, and their new police; though often, if they achieved power, they felt too unsafe to employ their understanding of the English police model on its own.[22] The change in England came gradually towards the end of the nineteenth century; it was brought about by the Fenian threat, pressure from European governments worried about the various anarchists and socialists continuing their activities from exile in England, and perhaps also by fear for the future as the workshop of the world's economic superiority began to wane. The spy scares before the First World War, the war itself, and the Russian Revolution combined to boost the involvement of the police with secret service and internal security organisations. These links continued

21. See the comments by John Styles, 'Print and policing: crime advertising in eighteenth-century provincial England', in Douglas Hay and Francis Snyder (eds), *Policing and Prosecution in Britain 1750–1850* (Oxford: Clarendon Press, 1989), pp. 94–5.

22. Napoleon III reformed the Paris Police on the lines of the London Metropolitan Police, but he still kept the *haute police* and the gendarmerie: Payne, *The Police State of Louis Napoleon Bonaparte*. Italian Liberals showed a similar desire to employ the model of the English 'Policemens', but to maintain political surveillance and military muscle: Steven C. Hughes, 'Gendarmes and Bobbies: Italy's search for the appropriate police force', paper presented to the Southern Historical Association Meeting, New Orleans, Nov. 1987.

during the inter-war period, yet the reluctance to discuss such matters publicly, and the condemnation and cold-shouldering of those who dared to criticise the police for 'political' activity, helped to perpetuate the idea of the non-political Bobby through the 1920s and 1930s. The growth of political protest groups in the 1960s, the activities of terrorist groups in the 1970s and 1980s, and the heavy-handedness of the Conservative government over matters of internal security during the 1980s, all served to make more explicit the involvement of the English police in matters of *haute police.*

That the English police were able to maintain a non-political, non-military and unarmed nature for so long owes less to the far-sightedness of the early police reformers and more to the special circumstances of mid-nineteenth-century England when the police system was spread across the whole country. The young men who grew up in the second half of the nineteenth century, and who went on to run the country either as politicians or Home Office officials, or who went on to command the police forces, were steeped in this tradition of policing and, even as it was changing under their direction, they continued to stress its unique nature. The circumstances following the Second World War, and generations brought up in a less stable and secure environment than that of Victorian England, have combined with the developments within the police to make the image of the English Bobby become less different from that of his continental and American neighbours, or from colonial-style gendarmes.

Police duties have always covered a variety of tasks. *Haute police* and gendarmerie-style policing represent the most dramatic of them; they can be both controversial and exciting, romantic and sinister. Picking up drunks, sorting out traffic jams and accidents, watching sheep through the sheep dip, are not the stuff of great political speeches, nor are they likely to provide plots for novels or newpaper revelations; yet day-to-day policing has involved the prosaic latter far more than the dramatic former. The men largely responsible for the creation of the English police during the nineteenth century, sensible of the attitudes of their fellow countrymen, wanted to limit the political and military nature of the new police, but the economic, political and social nature of Victorian England was instrumental in helping them to achieve their aim.

Appendix 1: The Authorised Establishment of the English and Welsh Police Forces in 1870, 1910, and 1939

No. on Map	Force	No. of men in 1870	No. of men in 1910	No. of men in 1939
1.	Metropolitan	9 160	19 418	19 358
2.	City of London	705	1 095	1 162
3.	Bedfordshire	92	164	162
	Bedford	16	46	64
	Dunstable	3	—	—
	Luton	—	47	111
4.	Berkshire	116	235	300
	Abingdon	6	—	—
	Maidenhead	4	—	—
	Newbury	8	—	—
	Reading	34	98	131
	Windsor	13	21	39
5.	Buckinghamshire	124	186	378
	Buckingham	4	—	—
	Chepping Wycombe	4	19	41
6.	Cambridgeshire	70	76	74
	Cambridge	44	65	120
	Wisbeach	11	—	—
7.	Cheshire	258	516	791[1]
	Birkenhead	85	171	220
	Chester	36	54	62
	Congleton	5	11	18
	Hyde	—	34	41
	Macclesfield	18	35	47
	Stalybridge	25	32	35
	Stockport	28	105	145
	Wallasey	—	—	127

1. Includes a temporary increase of 107 men for Experimental Motor Patrol Scheme.

No. on Map	Force	No. of men in 1870	No. of men in 1910	No. of men in 1939
8.	Cornwall	193	230	302
	Falmouth	3	—	—
	Helston	1	—	—
	Launceston	1	—	—
	Liskeard	3	—	—
	Penryn	2	—	—
	Penzance	7	14	24
	St Ives	1	—	—
	Truro	6	12	—
9.	Cumberland	146[2]	197	286
	Carlisle	33	61	82
10.	Derbyshire	178	386	521
	Chesterfield	14	40	89
	Derby	52	134	177
	Glossop	8	30	31
11.	Devonshire	345	434	524
	Barnstaple	10	14	—
	Bideford	2	—	—
	Devonport	46	88	—
	Exeter	44	63	90
	Plymouth	83	142	299
	Southmolton	2	—	—
	Tiverton	7	11	11
	Torrington	2	—	—
	Totnes	3	—	—
12.	Dorset	133	190	298
	Blandford	3	—	—
	Dorchester	7	—	—
	Poole	12	—	—
	Weymouth	12	32	—
13.	Durham	357	750	1 119
	Durham	14	19	—
	Gateshead	40	137	156
	Hartlepool	13	26	26
	South Shields	40	127	143
	Sunderland	105	201	219
14.	Isle of Ely	52	69	88
15.	Essex	251	479	831[3]
	Colchester	24	54	65
	Maldon	3	—	—
	Southend-on-Sea	—	—	247

2. Cumberland and Westmoreland forces were combined in this period.
3. Includes a temporary increase of 71 men for Experimental Motor Patrol Scheme.

No. on Map	Force	No. of men in 1870	No. of men in 1910	No. of men in 1939
16.	Gloucestershire	288	388	511
	Bristol	303	567	670
17.	Hampshire	258	464	646
	Basingstoke	5	—	—
	Portsmouth	95	257	315
	Southampton	64	146	272
	Winchester	16	33	38
18.	Herefordshire	62	81	102
	Hereford	28	36	49
	Leominster	8	—	—
19.	Hertfordshire	117	277	386
	Hertford	6	—	—
	St Albans	8	25	51
20.	Huntingdonshire	52	54	71
21.	Kent	300	540	793
	Canterbury	21	30	40
	Deal	8	—	—
	Dover	28	62	65
	Faversham	7	—	—
	Folkestone	11	45	73
	Gravesend	26	44	59
	Hythe	2	—	—
	Maidstone	26	47	64
	Margate	12	43	71
	Ramsgate	13	48	63
	Rochester	28	47	59
	Sandwich	1	—	—
	Tenterden	4	—	—
	Tunbridge Wells	21	59	66
22.	Lancashire	931	1 652	2 526[4]
	Accrington	—	47	52
	Ashton-under-Lyne	23	47	61
	Bacup	—	26	28
	Barrow-in-Furness	—	71	96
	Blackburn	70	145	175
	Blackpool	—	91	169
	Bolton	71	187	234
	Bootle	—	86	115
	Burnley	—	115	130
	Clitheroe	—	13	15
	Lancaster	13	45	60

4. Includes a temporary increase of 331 men for Experimental Motor Patrol Scheme.

No. on Map	Force	No. of men in 1870	No. of men in 1910	No. of men in 1939
	Liverpool	1 097	1 508	1 821[5]
	Manchester	753	1 249	1 511[6]
	Oldham	55	150	180
	Preston	83	120	152
	Rochdale	41	89	136
	St Helens	—	108	152
	Salford	151	360	345[7]
	Southport	7	72	115
	Warrington	28	82	113
	Wigan	42	96	118
23.	Leicestershire	109	183	253
	Leicester	86	274	312
24.	Lincolnshire	269	359	461
	Boston	15	22	31
	Grantham	5	19	29
	Grimsby	12	82	120
	Lincoln	25	56	98
	Louth	9	10	—
	Stamford	9	—	—
25.	Monmouthshire	99	201	300
	Monmouth	6	—	—
	Newport	37	115	153
26.	Norfolk	231	254	352
	Great Yarmouth	36	68	76
	King's Lynn	19	23	30
	Norwich	93	136	156
27.	Northamptonshire	115	166	223
	Daventry	2	—	—
	Northampton	44	114	131
28.	Northumberland	145	248	381
	Berwick-on-Tweed	6	15	—
	Newcastle-upon-Tyne	165	370	426
	Tynemouth	37	74	87
29.	Nottinghamshire	140	258	447
	Newark	12	16	27
	Nottingham	104	339	408
30.	Oxfordshire	101	119	148
	Banbury	5	14	—
	Oxford	36	72	134

5. Includes a temporary increase of 53 men for Experimental Motor Patrol Scheme.
6. Includes a temporary increase of 53 men for Experimental Motor Patrol Scheme.
7. Includes a temporary increase of 15 men for Experimental Motor Patrol Scheme.

No. on Map	Force	No. of men in 1870	No. of men in 1910	No. of men in 1939
31.	Peterborough Liberty	21	10	10
	Peterborough	—	36	55
32.	Rutland	13	15	22
33.	Shropshire	122	167	205
	Bridgenorth	5	—	—
	Ludlow	5	—	—
	Shrewsbury	24	37	52
34.	Somerset	286	354	423
	Bath	89	84	110
	Bridgewater	7	18	20
	Chard	2	—	—
35.	Staffordshire	483	718	933
	Litchfield	6	—	—
	Newcastle-under-Lyme	12	20	75
	Stoke-on-Trent	—	177	254
	Walsall	32	89	120
	Wolverhampton	69	103	170
36.	Suffolk (East)	115	176	209
	Ipswich	37	74	117
	Southwold	1	—	—
37.	Suffolk (West)	96	115	131
	Sudbury	6	—	—
38.	Surrey	123	303	536
	Goldaming	3	—	—
	Guildford	12	30	63
	Reigate	14	40	59
39.	Sussex (East)	125	220	299
	Brighton	100	202	224
	Eastbourne	—	77	113
	Hastings	29	104	114
	Hove	23	64	98
	Rye	2	—	—
40.	Sussex (West)	91	170	307
	Arundel	3	—	—
	Chichester	8	—	—
41.	Warwickshire	179	360	418
	Birmingham	400	975	1 887
	Coventry	38	100	272
	Leamington	23	41	55
	Stratford-upon-Avon	11	—	—
42.	Westmoreland	—[8]	39	62
	Kendall	11	16	23

8. Cumberland and Westmoreland forces were combined in this period.

No. on Map	Force	No. of men in 1870	No. of men in 1910	No. of men in 1939
43.	Wight, Isle of	—[9]	61	79
	Newport	7	—	—
	Ryde	11	15	—
44.	Wiltshire	201	250	351
	Salisbury	12	27	37
45.	Worcestershire	189	463	364
	Bewdley	2	—	—
	Droitwich	2	—	—
	Dudley	—	—	80
	Kidderminster	16	29	44
	Worcester	32	54	78
46.	Yorkshire, East Riding	88	138	215
	Beverley	10	16	—
	Hull	172	404	460
47.	Yorkshire, North Riding	164	272	405
	Middlesborough	53	123	196
	Richmond	2	—	—
	Scarborough	24	59	65
	York City	44	99	133
48.	Yorkshire, West Riding	743	1 289	1 681
	Barnsley	—	50	90
	Bradford	156	402	478
	Dewsbury	12	57	79
	Doncaster	18	42	94
	Halifax	57	114	149
	Huddersfield	68	122	152
	Leeds	280	654	703
	Pontefract	6	—	—
	Ripon	2	—	—
	Rotherham	—	76	89
	Sheffield	270	533	715
	Wakefield	37	61	75
49.	Anglesey, Isle of	25	32	43
50.	Breconshire	36	51	64
	Brecon	4	—	—
51.	Cardiganshire	35	41	43
52.	Carmarthenshire	50	103	148
	Carmarthen	12	12	17
53.	Carnarvonshire	60	85	124
	Pwllheli	1	—	—

9. Included with Hampshire in this period.

No. on Map	Force	No. of men in 1870	No. of men in 1910	No. of men in 1939
54.	Denbighshire	62	91	141
55.	Flintshire	41	60	118
56.	Glamorganshire	161	503	822
	Cardiff	50	289	337
	Merthyr Tydfil	—	75	87
	Neath	8	18	42
	Swansea	57	153	199
57.	Merionethshire	27	34	39
58.	Montgomeryshire	31	36	40
59.	Pembrokeshire	50	75	88
	Haverfordwest	4	—	—
	Tenby	3	—	—
60.	Radnorshire	16	20	22

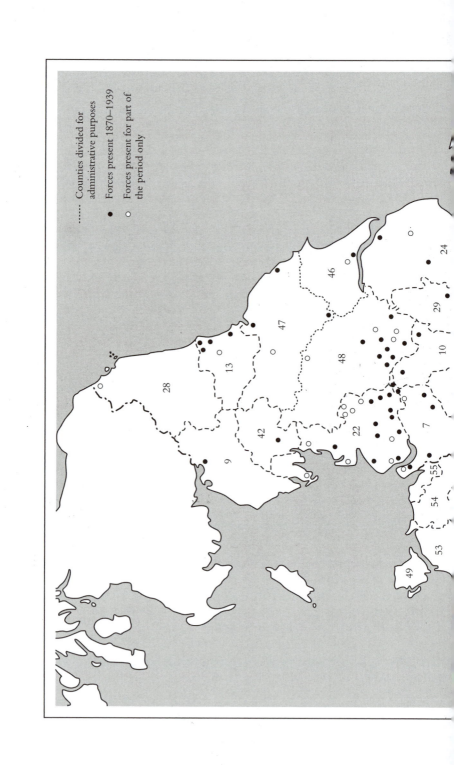

Counties divided for
administrative purposes

• Forces present 1870–1939

○ Forces present for part of
the period only

Map 1   The authorised establishment of the English and Welsh police forces in 1870, 1910 and 1939

Appendix 2: The Authorised Establishment of the English and Welsh Police Forces in 1992

Force	No. of men
Metropolitan	28 240
City of London	798
Avon and Somerset	3 087
Bedfordshire	1 178
Cambridgeshire	1 241
Cheshire	1 920
Cleveland	1 502
Cumbria	1 187
Derbyshire	1 850
Devon and Cornwall	2 928
Dorset	1 302
Durham	1 389
Essex	2 950
Gloucestershire	1 184
Greater Manchester	7 077
Hampshire	3 269
Hertfordshire	1 684
Humberside	2 034
Kent	3 096
Lancashire	3 229
Leicestershire	1 853
Lincolnshire	1 206
Merseyside	4 706
Norfolk	1 446
Northamptonshire	1 190
Northumbria	3 613
North Yorkshire	1 418
Nottinghamshire	2 344
South Yorkshire	3 031
Staffordshire	2 215

Force	No. of men
Suffolk	1 233
Surrey	1 673
Sussex	3 014
Thames Valley	3 812
Warwickshire	1 020
West Mercia	2 053
West Midlands	6 977
West Yorkshire	5 295
Wiltshire	1 181
Dyfed Powys	969
Gwent	1 010
North Wales	1 369
South Wales	3 168

Map 2   The authorised establishment of the English and Welsh police forces in 1992

Bibliographical Note

The detailed references in the notes to each chapter constitute the full bibliography to this book. This note is intended simply as an overview of the literature, pointing to some of the more useful texts and to some of the major gaps in our knowledge.

Much of the history of the English police has been written from the assumption of the Metropolitan Police model spreading from London into the provinces. While there is an element of truth in such a view, it is also probable that a dependence on national archives has accentuated it. Many of the institutional archives of the Metropolitan Police are deposited in the MEPO files of the Public Record Office at Kew, but the records of the provincial forces are scattered. Some have been handed over to county record offices, others remain in police hands and consequently under various degrees of care. Ian Bridgeman and Clive Emsley, *A Guide to the Archives of the Police Forces of England and Wales* (Cambridge: The Police History Society, Monograph No. 2, 1989), is the first survey of the surviving records; and, given the range of police tasks within society, these should be of value to social historians in general and not simply those concerned with crime and policing. Unfortunately, as yet, there is still no policy about which current documentation amassed by police forces should be preserved, and in what quantities. While what survives in the current police archives is haphazard (and whether much of it continues to survive, given the state of some of these archives, is also a moot point), the destruction policies pursued by contemporary police forces suggest that future historians will be even less well-served with documentation.

This book has been critical of the Whig historians, beginning with their reliance on Shakespeare as a source for policing before the police. Joan R. Kent, *The English Village Constable 1580–1642: A Social and Administrative Study* (Oxford: Clarendon Press, 1986), is an important re-examination of the Tudor and Stuart constables which suggests that the Bard is best left as literature. Unfortunately, there are no similar studies for the late seventeenth and the eighteenth centuries, and the subject urgently merits investigation. In spite of the criticism levelled at the Whig histories, they do contain a wealth of detail. Charles Reith's *The Police Idea* (Oxford: OUP, 1938) and *British Police and the Democratic Ideal* (Oxford: OUP, 1943), and David Ascoli's *The Queen's Peace: The Origins and Development of the Metropolitan Police 1829–1979* (London: Hamish Hamilton, 1979) are particularly useful in this respect. T.A. Critchley's *A History of Police in England and Wales*, rev. edn (London: Constable, 1978) is a thorough survey of the development of the police as an institution, and is particularly useful on the events following the Second World War with which he was intimately involved. A crop of local histories were published as forces were amalgamated in the 1960s: Dennis T. Brett, *The Police of England and Wales: A Bibliography 1829–1979*, 3rd edn (Bramshill: Police Staff College, 1979), provides a list of these as well as other important bibliographical material. Richard Cowley, *Policing Northamptonshire 1836–1986*, and Douglas J. Elliott, *Policing Shropshire* (Studley, Warks.: Brewin Books, 1986 and 1984 respectively), were too late for inclusion. So too were the histories published in 1989 and 1990 to celebrate the 150th anniversaries of several forces, such as Andrew Francis Richer, *Policing Bedfordshire 1840–1990* (Bedford: Paul Hooley, 1990), and Maureen Scollan, *Sworn to Serve: Police in Essex* (Chichester: Phillimore, 1993). However, for a critical analysis of the relations between a local police force (Liverpool), its Watch Committee, and central government, Mike Brogden, *The Police: Autonomy and Consent* (London: Academic Press, 1982), is unique.

The critical and analytical study of police history really began in the 1970s. Allan Silver, 'The demand for order in civil society: a review of some themes in the history of urban crime, police, and riot', in David J. Bordua (ed.), *The Police: Six Sociological Essays* (New York: Wiley, 1967), generated much interest, as did the essays by Robert D. Storch, ' "The plague of blue locusts": police reform and popular resistance in northern England 1840–57', *International Review of Social History* XX (1975) and 'The policeman as domestic missionary: urban discipline and popular culture in northern England, 1850–1880', *Journal of Social History* IX (1976). Since then there have been some important reappraisals of the origins of the police, notably David Philips, ' "A new engine of power and authority": the institutionalisation of law-enforcement in England 1780–1830', in V.A.C. Gatrell, Bruce Lenman, and Geoffrey Parker (eds), *Crime and the Law: The Social History of Crime in Western Europe since*

1500 (London: Europa, 1980), Ruth Paley, ' "An imperfect, inadequate and wretched system?" Policing London before Peel', *CJH* X (1989), and Elaine Reynolds, 'The night watch and police reform in London, 1720–1830', Ph.D., Cornell University, 1991. Stanley G. Palmer, *Police and Protest in England and Ireland 1789–1850* (Cambridge: CUP, 1988), is a massive and indispensible study of police development on both sides of the Irish Sea. Other comparative analyses may be found in Clive Emsley, *Policing and its Context, 1750–1870* (London: Macmillan, 1983), where the focus is mainly on England and France, and Wilbur R. Miller, *Cops and Bobbies: Police Authority in New York and London, 1830–1870* (University of Chicago Press, 1977). Phillip Thurmond Smith, *Policing Victorian London: Political Policing, Public Order, and the London Metropolitan Police* (Westport, Conn.: Greenwood Press, 1985), is also noteworthy for the additional evidence which it presents to, and its more critical approach than, Ascoli.

For a reappraisal of the origins of provincial policing, Storch again provides a starting point with 'Policing rural southern England before the police: opinion and practice, 1830–1856', in Douglas Hay and Francis Snyder (eds), *Policing and Prosecution in Britain, 1750–1850* (Oxford: Clarendon Press, 1989), and the essay co-authored with David Philips, 'Whigs and Coppers: the Grey ministry's National Police Scheme, 1832', *Historical Research* 67 (1994). This latter is the first publication of what promises to be an extremely fruitful collaboration between two of the most acute historians working in the area. Carolyn Steedman, *Policing the Victorian Community: The formation of English provincial police forces, 1856–1880* (London: Routledge and Kegan Paul, 1984), is an important introduction to its subject. It can be supplemented by some of the essays in David Jones, *Crime, Protest, Community and Police in Nineteenth-Century Britain* (London: Routledge and Kegan Paul, 1982), and Roger Swift, *Police Reform in Early Victorian York, 1835–1856* (University of York, Borthwick Paper No. 73, 1988). Two older articles by Jenifer Hart still remain of significance: 'Reform of the Borough Police 1835–1856', *EHR* LXX (1955), and 'The County and Borough Police Act, 1856', *Public Administration* XXXIV (1956).

The twentieth century is rather less well served for critical historical work on policing. For many years there was little more than the two unpublished manuscripts completed by Sir Arthur L. Dixon on his retirement from the Home Office. These are available in the Library of the Police Staff College, Bramshill: 'The Home Office and the police between the two world wars' (1966) and 'The emergency work of the police forces in the Second World War' (1963). They are essentially institutional histories which, amazingly, appear originally to have been classified documents. There are three studies of the policing of strikes: the broad overview of Roger Geary, *Policing Industrial Disputes 1890–1985* (Cambridge: CUP, 1985), and the more detailed analyses of Jane Morgan, *Conflict and Order: The Police and Labour Disputes in England and Wales 1900–1939* (Oxford: Clarendon Press, 1987), and Barbara Weinberger, *Keeping the Peace? Policing Strikes in Britain 1906–1926* (Oxford: Berg, 1991). And, since the first edition of this volume, two useful books have appeared based on interviews with former police officers: Mike Brogden, *On the Mersey Beat: Policing Liverpool Between the Wars* (Oxford: OUP, 1991), and Barbara Weinberger, *The Best Police in the World: An Oral History of English Policing from the 1930s to the 1960s* (Aldershot: Scolar Press, 1995). Joanne Marie Klein's doctoral dissertation, 'Invisible working-class men: police constables in Manchester, Birmingham and Liverpool, 1900–1939', Rice University, 1992, shows what might be done from the careful use of local police records and usefully locates the police constable as a working man.

On the subject of secrecy and political policing Bernard Porter, *The Origins of the Vigilant State: The London Metropolitan Police Special Branch before the First World War* (London: Weidenfeld & Nicolson, 1987), is sensible and thorough. Tony Bunyan, *The Political Police in Britain* (London: Julian Friedmann, 1977), is useful, but crusading, and there are some pointers in Christopher Andrew, *Secret Service: The Making of the British Intelligence Community* (London: Heinemann, 1985).

Police autobiographies can be useful but often tend to be of the 'great-cases-I-solved/great-criminals-I-caught' variety. Harry Daley, *This Small Cloud: A Personal Memoir* (Weidenfeld & Nicolson, 1987), and John Wainwright, *Wainwright's Beat* (London: Macmillan, 1987), are exceptions: the former romantic, the latter anything but. Part of the trouble is that writing about the day-to-day routine of policing can soon become uninteresting for both writer and reader. Some telling comments contrasting military and police memoirs can be found in Carolyn Steedman's introduction to *The Radical Soldier's Tale* (London: Routledge, 1988), the autobiography of the working-class radical and republican John Pearman, thirteen years a soldier and 24 years a policeman.

Index